AF372039

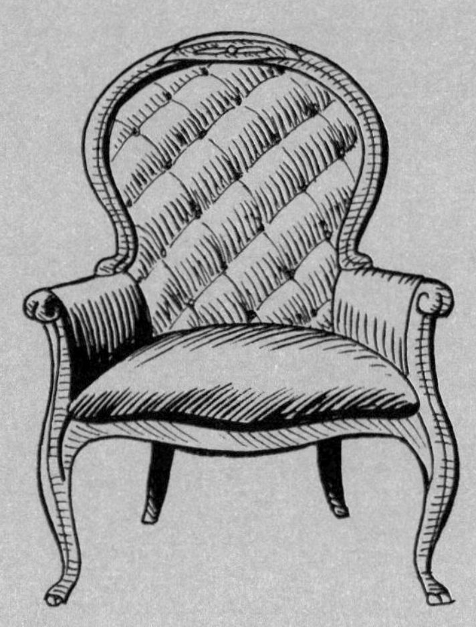

HANDMADE ILLUSTRATION
767 Vintage Drawings
767 Illustrations Vintage
767 Ilustraciones Vintage
767 Ilustraçoes Vintage

Copyright © 2013 Promopress
Promopress is a brand of:
Promotora de prensa internacional S.A.
C/ Ausiàs March 124 - 08013 Barcelona (Spain)
T + 34 93 245 14 64 - F + 34 93 265 48 93
info@promopress.es
www.promopress.es
www.promopresseditions.com
Promopress Editions @PromopressEd
facebook & **twitter**

Author: Joan Escandell
Concept & Design: Alehop
www.alewebs.com

English translation: Tom Corkett Spanish - English
French translation: Marie-Pierre Teuler Spanish - French
Spanish proofreader: Juan José Llanos Collado
Portuguese translation: Isabel Vidigal Spanish – Brazilian Portuguese

ISBN: 978-84-92810-39-0
First edition: 2013
Printed in China

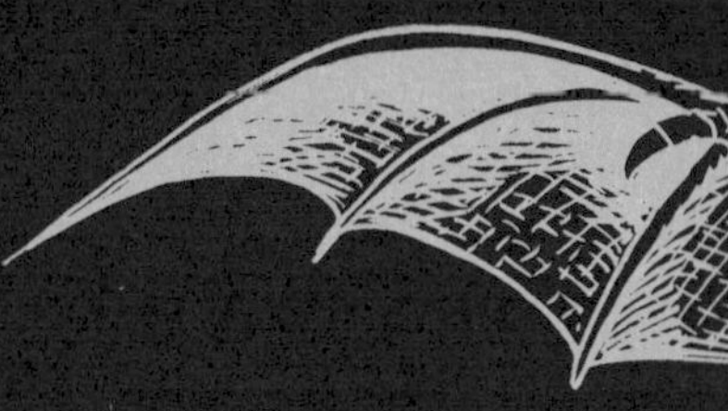

Handmade ILLUSTRATION

767

VINTAGE
DRAWINGS
ILLUSTRATIONS
VINTAGE
ILUSTRACIONES
VINTAGE
ILUSTRAÇOES
VINTAGE

By **JOAN ESCANDELL**

FREE DVD

promopress

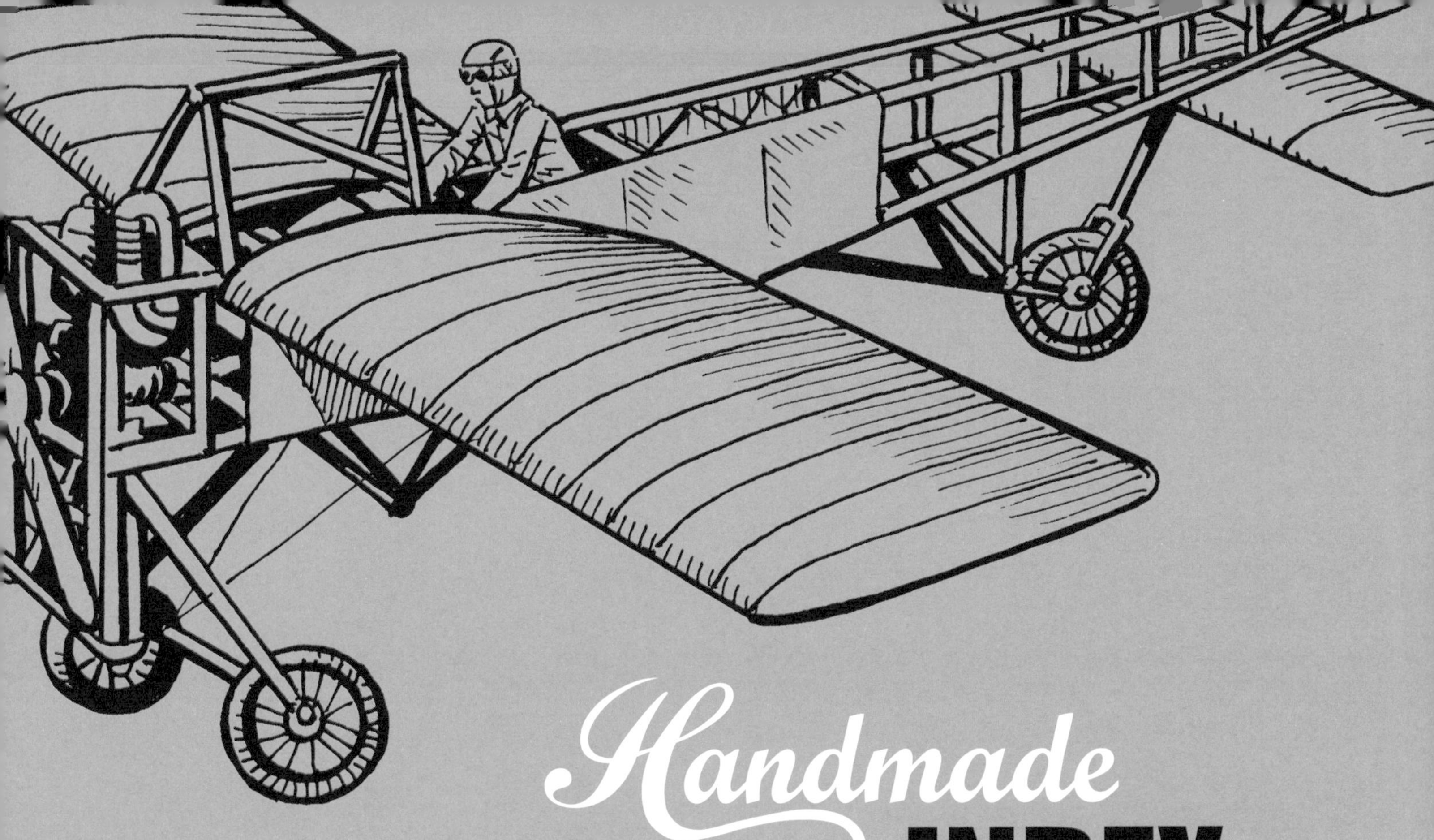

INDEX

Handmade
THE AUTHOR

L'AUTEUR
EL AUTOR
O AUTOR

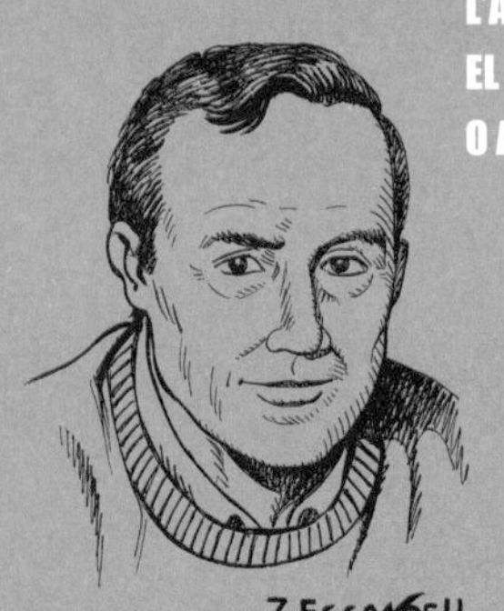

Joan Escandell is one of Spain's most internationally well-known and influential illustrators. Born in Ibiza in 1937, his career began in the 1960s at the iconic publisher Editorial Bruguera, where he contributed drawings to legendary series such as *El Capitán Trueno* and *Joyas literarias,* as well as creations of his own such as *Sargento Furia* (which was written by Cassarel) and *Astromán* (which was written by Victor Mora, creator of El Capitán Trueno).

In the late 1970s he stepped into the European market, with his career highlights from this period including his own creation *Antares*, which he drew for French audiences for fourteen years. He then worked in a range of other countries, including Italy, the USA, England and Japan, where he produced illustrations for a wide range of genres and aesthetic styles. He created comic strips for series such as *Masters of the Universe* and for Disney he drew, among many other characters, *Mickey Mouse, Cinderella, The Lion King* and *Pocahontas*.

During the final twelve years of his artistic career he worked mainly within the world of German television, developing a magazine based around the famous children's series *Bibi & Tina*.

Now Escandell brings us *Handmade Illustration*, a collection of 767 expressive illustrations produced in Indian ink and in his unmistakable style, presented across 10 highly diverse thematic categories, for you to use in your own creations and designs. This is without doubt a first-class graphical resource of indisputable quality.

Joan Miquel Morey,
director of Cómic Nostrum
International Festival, Mallorca.

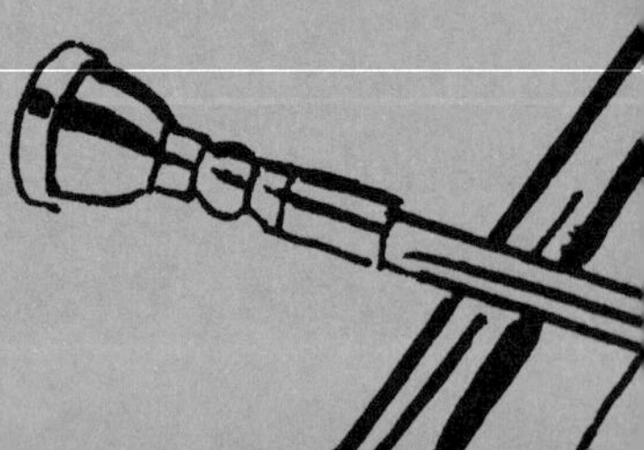

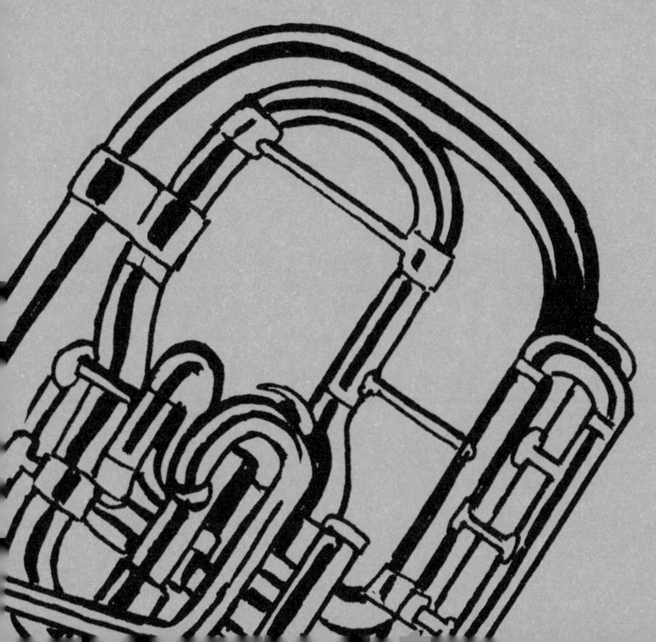

Joan Escandell (Eivissa, 1937) est un des dessinateurs espagnols les plus connus au-delà de nos frontières. Il a commencé sa carrière dans les années 1960 comme poulain de la célèbre maison d'édition Bruguera qui l'avait choisi pour illustrer des séries mythiques comme *El capitán Trueno* ou *Joyas literarias*. Il illustrera ensuite ses propres albums comme *Sargento Furia* (à partir de scénarios de Cassarel) ou *Astromán* (à partir de scénarios de Víctor Mora, le créateur du personnage El Capitán Trueno).

À la fin des années 1970, il se lance sur le marché européen avec des œuvres originales comme la série *Antares*, qu'il illustrera pendant quatorze ans pour les lecteurs français. Depuis cette époque, il travaille pour les publics de différents pays dont l'Italie, les États-Unis, l'Angleterre, le Japon, etc., passant par tous les genres et registres esthétiques. Il réalise des séries médiatiques comme *Les Maîtres de l'univers*, et dessine pour Disney de nombreux personnages dont *Mickey, Cendrillon, Le Roi Lion* et *Pocahontas*.

Au cours des douze dernières années, il s'est davantage tourné vers le monde télévisuel allemand. Il a notamment conçu un magazine entièrement consacré à la célèbre série pour enfants *Bibi & Tina*.

L'ouvrage de Joan Escandell que nous vous présentons aujourd'hui, *Handmade Illustration*, est une collection de 767 illustrations de personnages en mouvement réalisées à l'encre de chine et représentatives de son style inimitable. Elles sont regroupées selon 10 thèmes différents pour que vous puissiez facilement les utiliser dans vos propres créations. *Handmade Illustration* est une collection de graphismes d'un génie et d'une qualité indiscutables.

Joan Miquel Morey,
directeur de Cómic Nostrum,
Festival International de Mallorca.

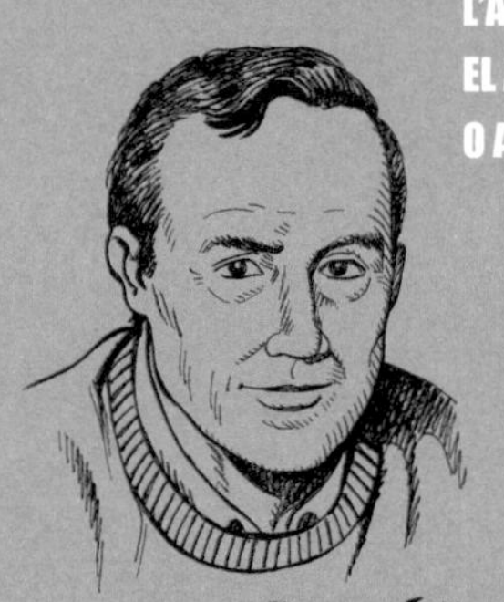

Joan Escandell (Eivissa, 1937) es uno de los dibujantes españoles con mayor proyección y recorrido fuera de nuestras fronteras. Se inicia en la década de 1960 bajo la tutela de la emblemática Editorial Bruguera, dibujando series míticas como *El capitán Trueno* o *Joyas literarias* y creaciones propias como *Sargento Furia* (con guión de Cassarel) o *Astromán* (con guión de Víctor Mora, creador de El Capitán Trueno). A finales de la década de 1970 se lanza al mercado europeo, destacando de esta época la obra *Antares*, de creación propia, que dibuja durante catorce años para el público francés.

Desde entonces trabaja para países como Italia, Estados Unidos, Inglaterra, Japón, etc., tocando todo tipo de géneros y registros estéticos. Realiza historietas de series mediáticas como *Masters of the Universe* y para Disney dibuja *Mickey, La Cenicienta, El rey León* y *Pocahontas*, entre otros muchos personajes.

Durante sus últimos doce años de trayectoria artística se dedica sobre todo al universo televisivo alemán, desarrollando toda una revista dedicada a la famosa serie infantil *Bibi & Tina*.

En esta ocasión, Escandell nos brinda *Handmade Illustration*, una colección de 767 ilustraciones gestuales realizadas con tinta china con su inconfundible estilo, englobadas en 10 categorías de temáticas muy diversas para que utilices en tus creaciones y diseños. Sin duda, un material gráfico de primera clase y una calidad indiscutible.

Joan Miquel Morey,
director de Cómic Nostrum,
Festival Internacional de Mallorca.

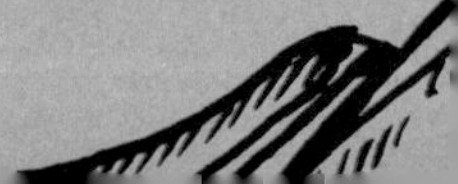

Joan Escandell (Eivissa, 1937) é um dos cartunistas espanhóis com maior projeção e mais forte atuação fora de nossas fronteiras. Ele iniciou sua trajetória na década de 1960, sob a tutela da emblemática Editorial Bruguera, desenhando séries míticas como *El capitán Trueno* ou *Joyas literarias*, além de criações próprias, como *Sargento Furia* (com texto de Cassarel) ou *Astromán* (com texto de Victor Mora, criador de El Capitán Trueno).

Ao final da década de 70, ele se lança no mercado europeu e, dessa época, destaca-se a obra *Antares*, de criação própria, que ele desenhou durante quatorze anos para o público francês.

Desde então, ele tem trabalhado para países como Itália, Estados Unidos, Inglaterra, Japão, etc., abrangendo todos os tipos de gêneros e registros estéticos. Ele criou histórias em quadrinhos de séries mediáticas, como *Master of the Universe* e, para a Disney, desenhou *Mickey, Cinderela, O Rei Leão* e *Pocahontas*, entre muitos outros personagens.

Nos últimos doze anos de sua trajetória artística, dedicou-se, sobretudo, ao universo televisivo alemão, desenvolvendo uma revista inteira dedicada à famosa série infantil *Bibi & Tina*.

Nesta ocasião, Escandell nos oferece *Handmade Illustration*, uma coleção de 767 ilustrações gestuais realizadas com tinta nanquim com seu estilo inconfundível, englobadas em 10 categorias de temáticas bem distintas e que podem ser utilizadas em suas criações e desenhos. Definitivamente, um material gráfico de primeira classe e de uma qualidade inquestionável.

Joan Miquel Morey,
diretor do Cómic Nostrum,
Festival Internacional de Mallorca.

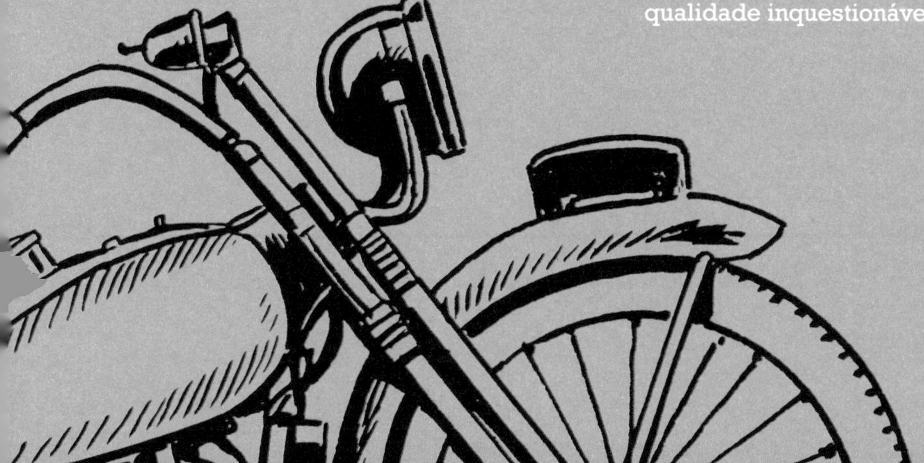

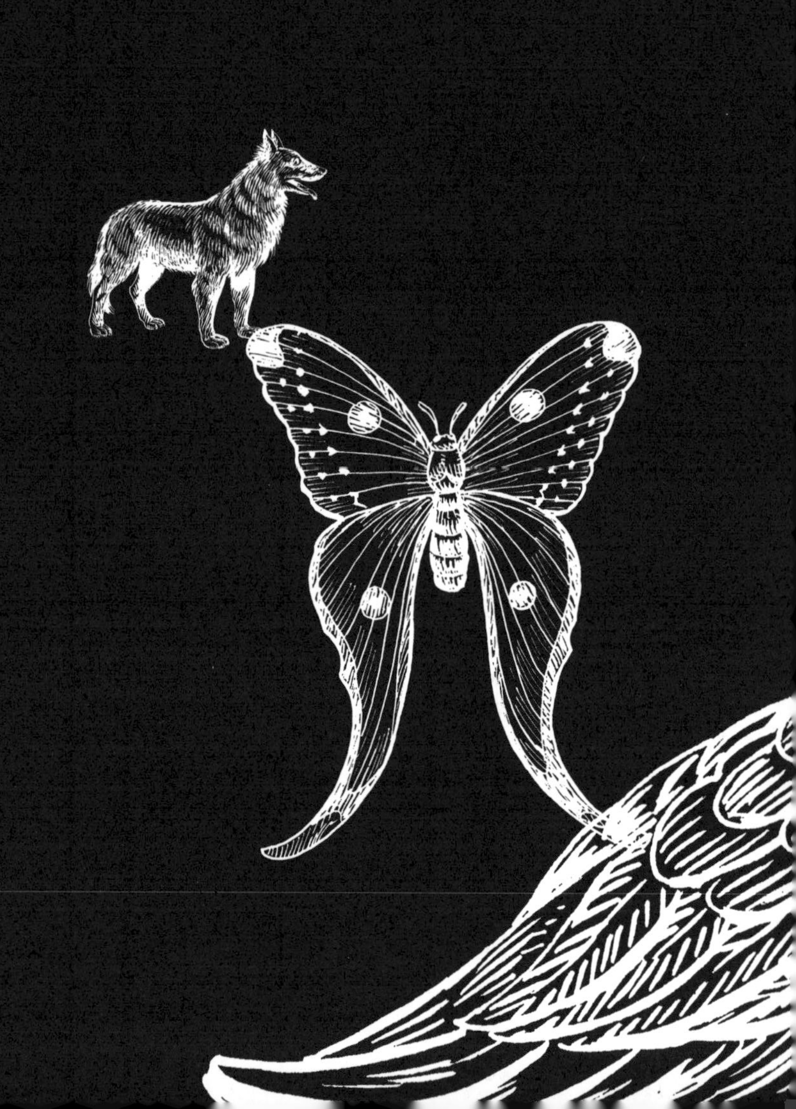

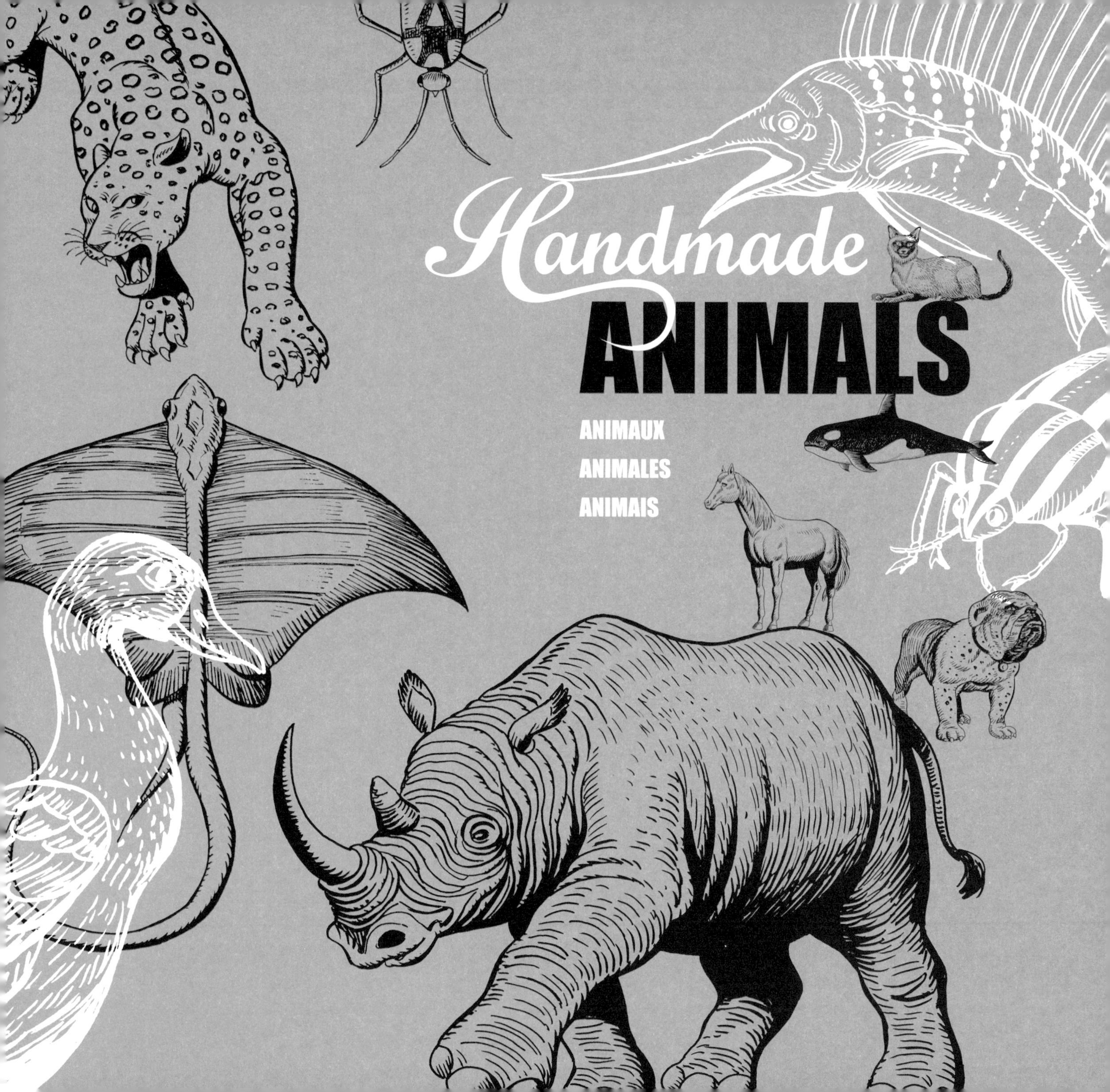
Handmade
ANIMALS
ANIMAUX
ANIMALES
ANIMAIS

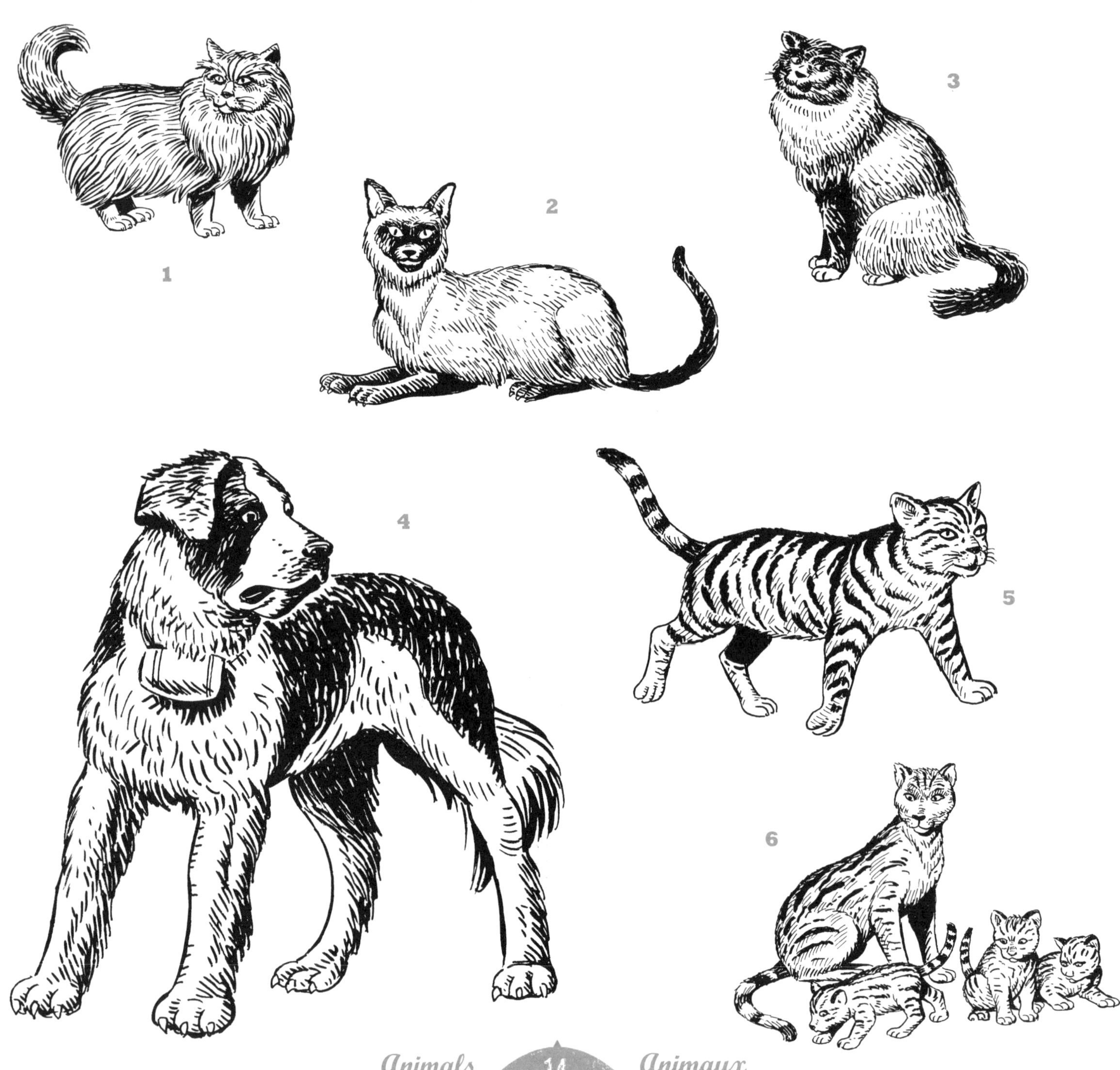

1
2
3
4
5
6

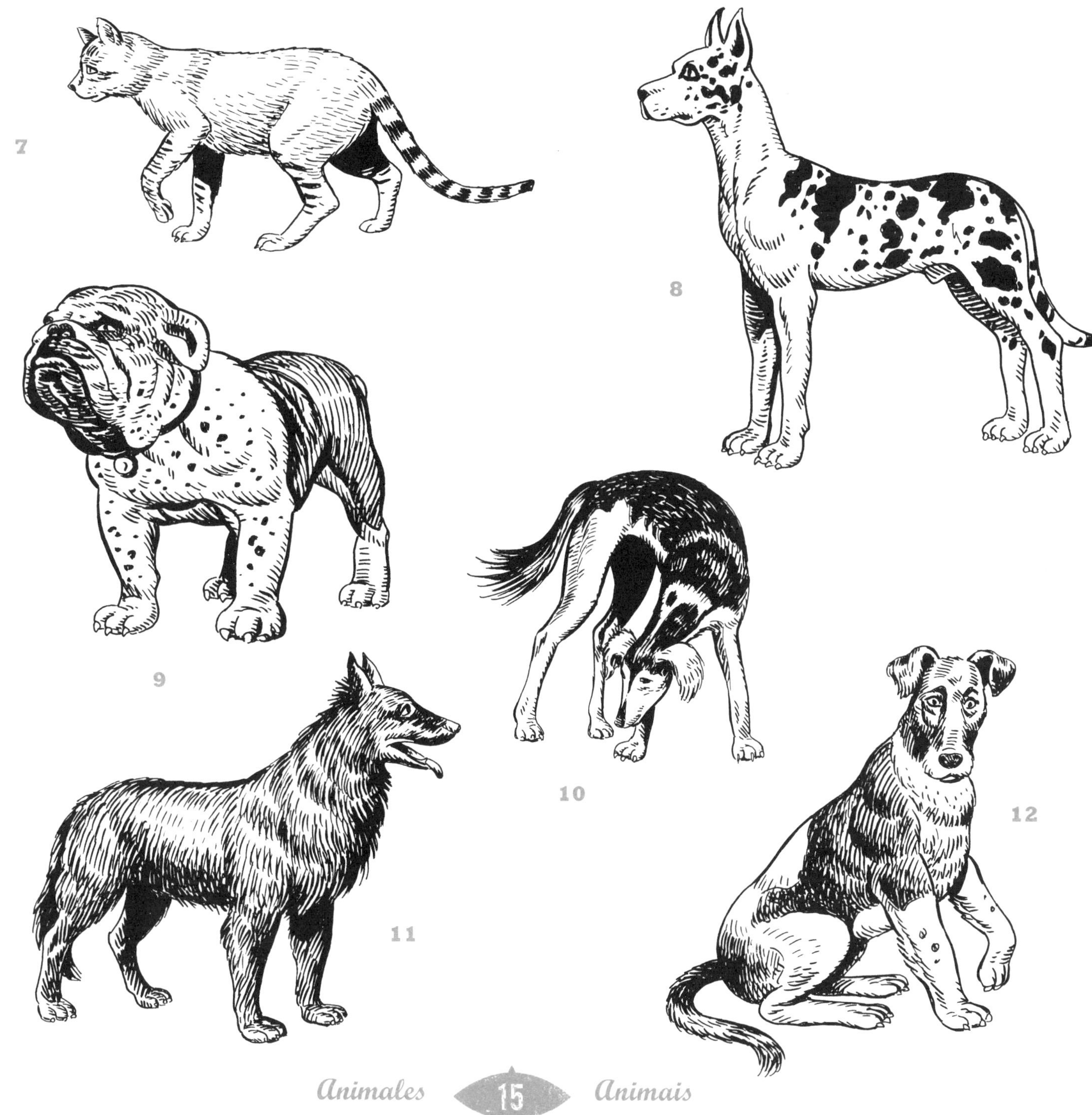

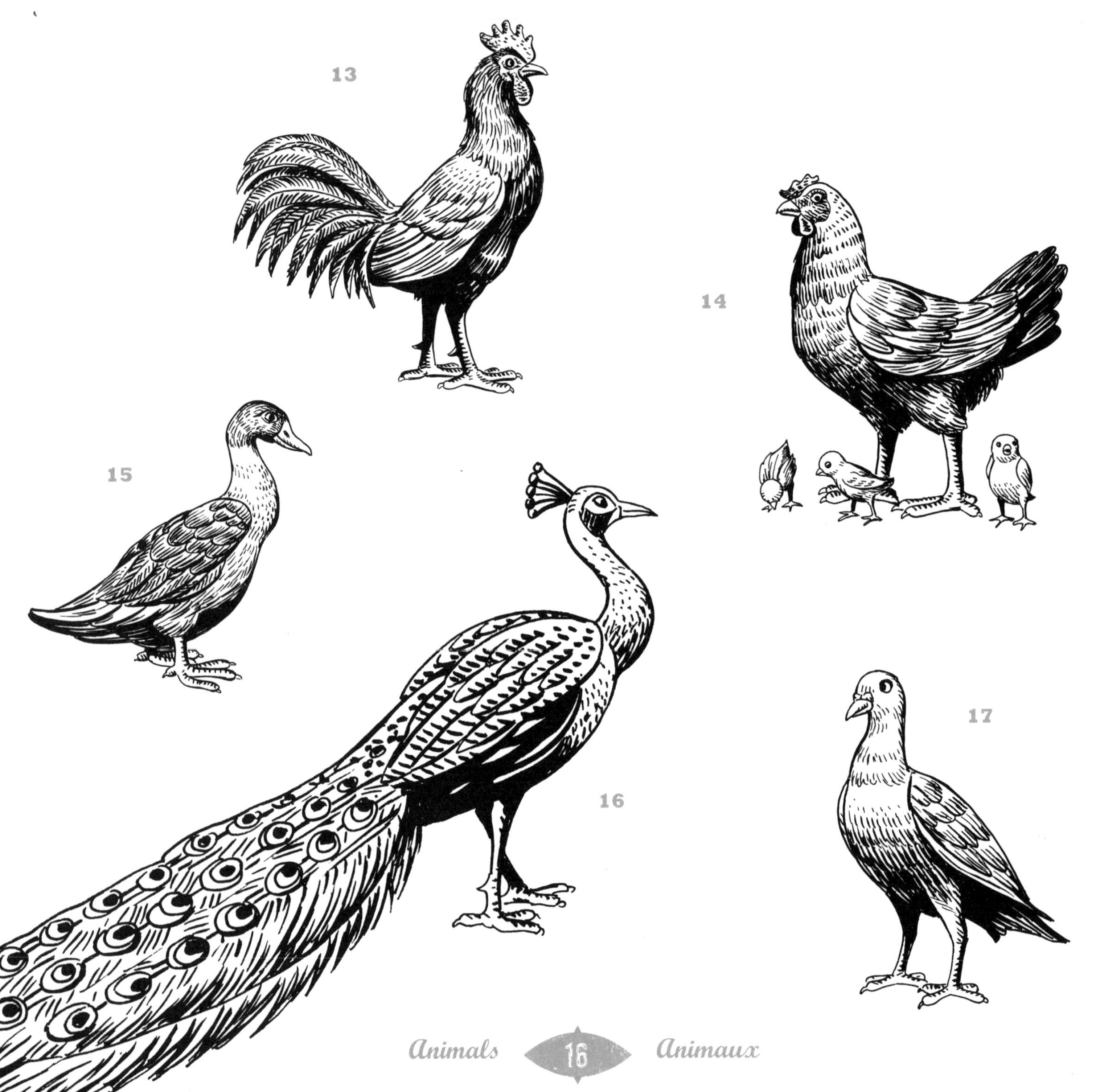

13
14
15
16
17

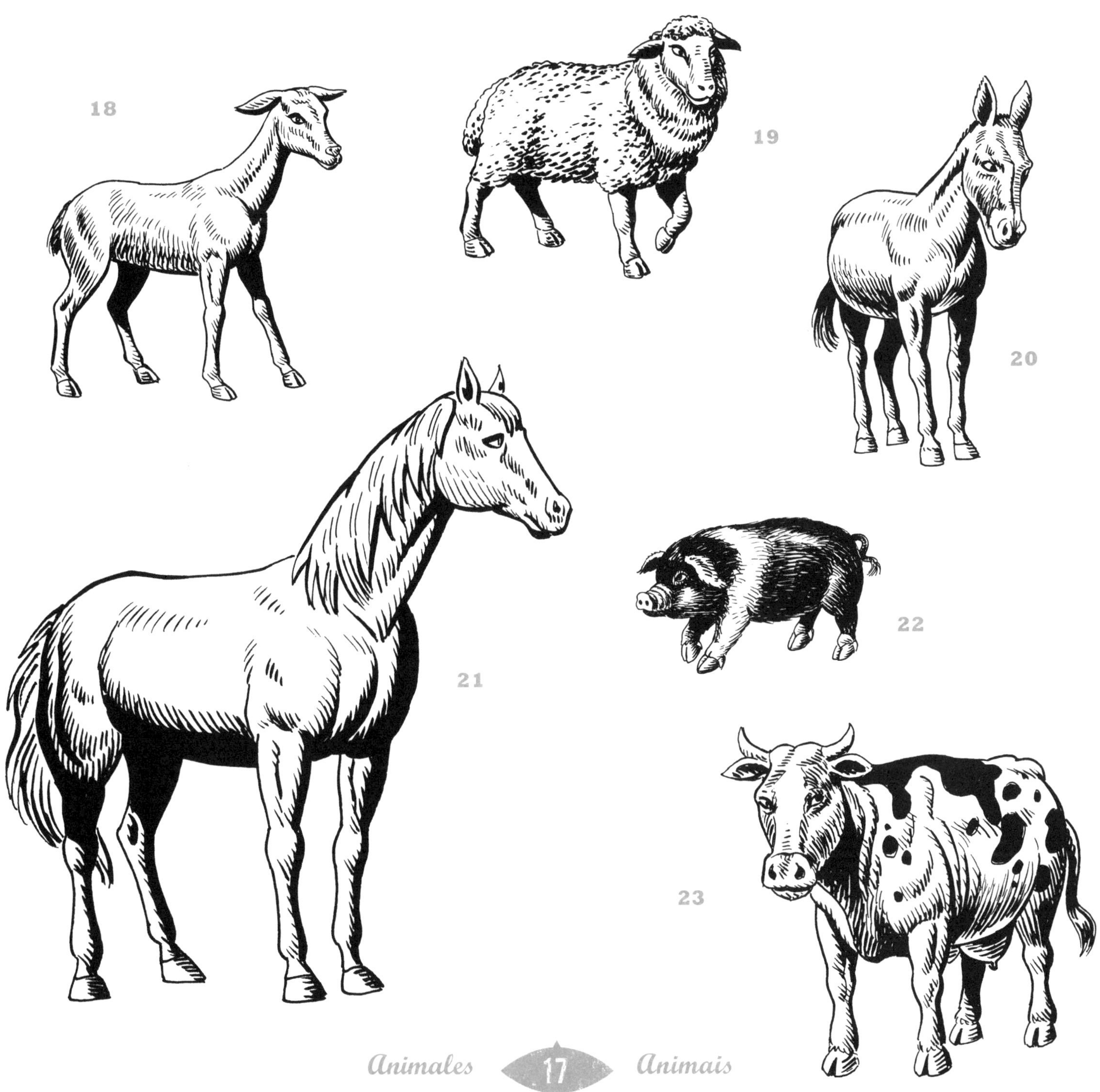

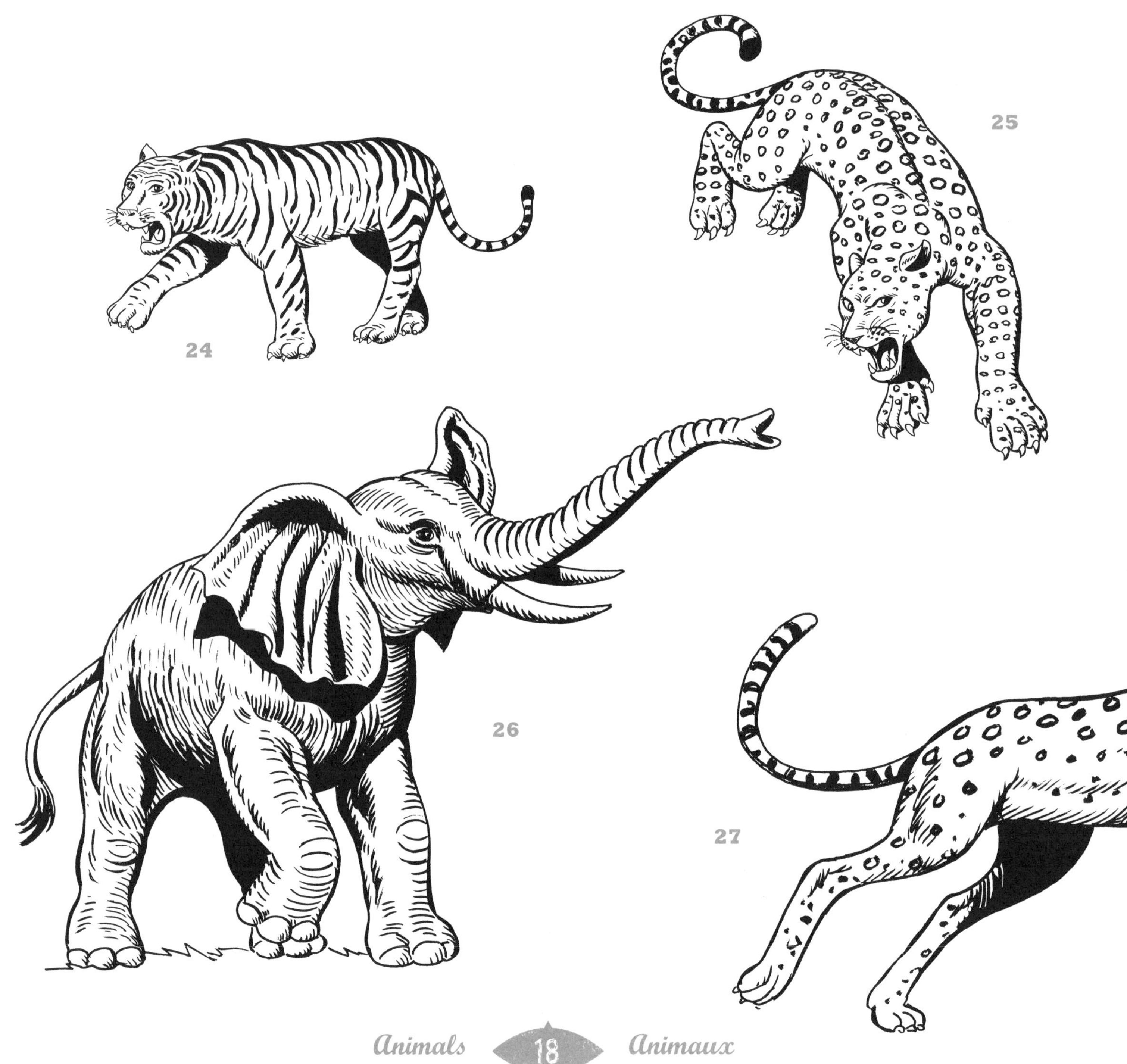

24
25
26
27

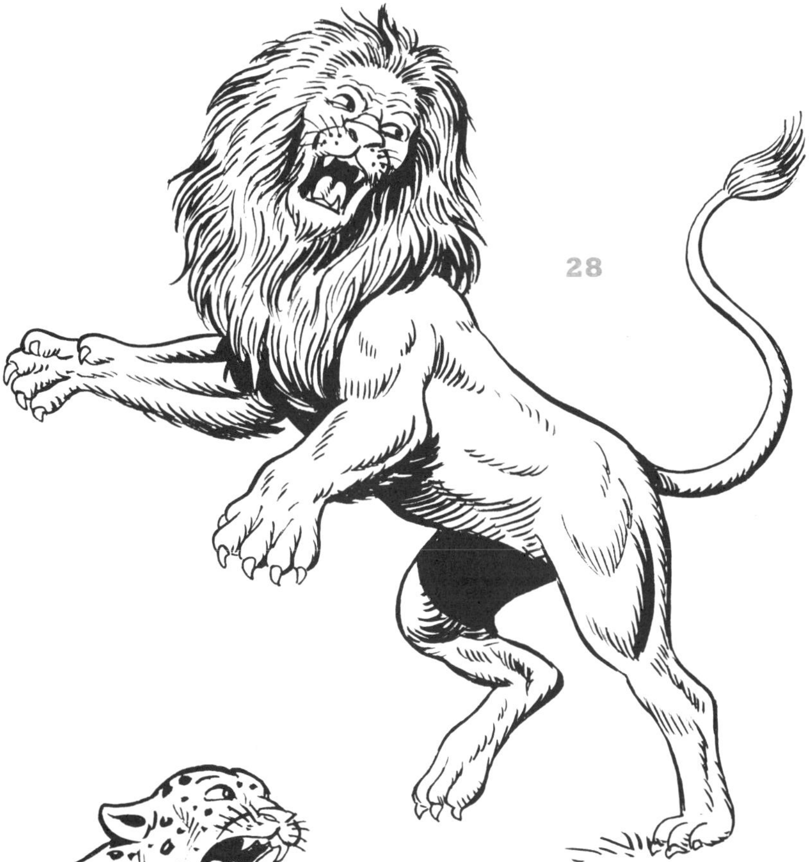

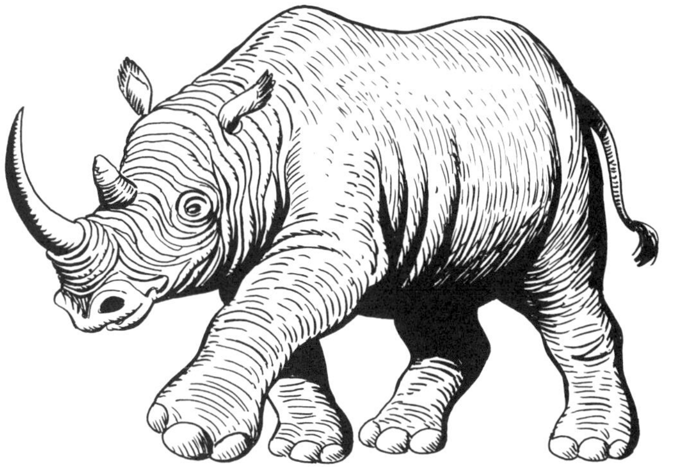

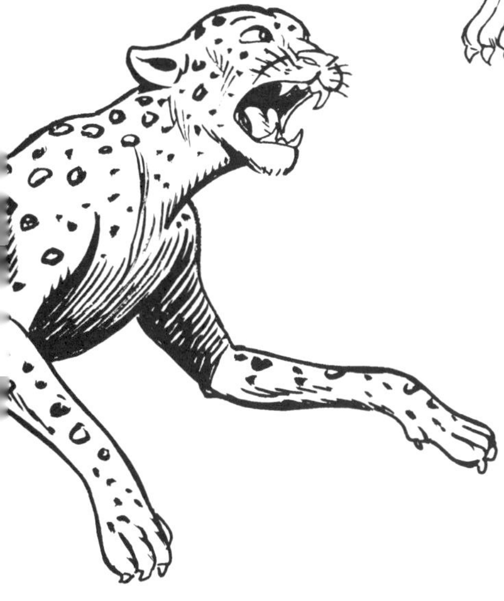

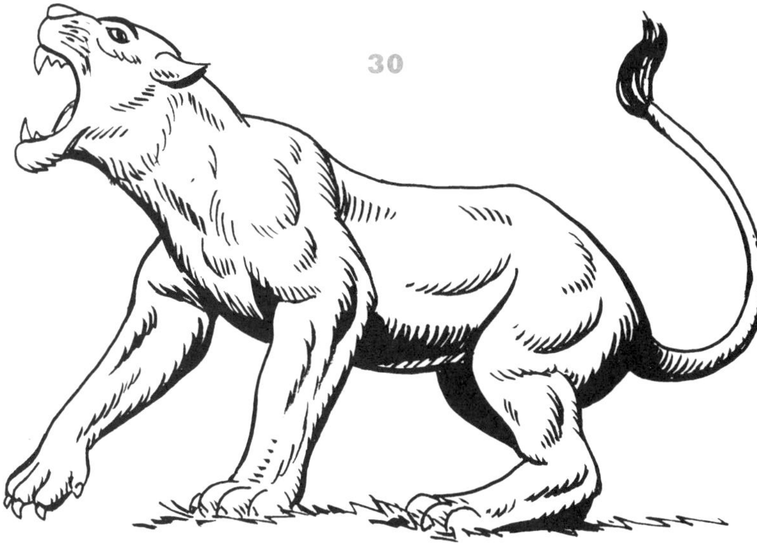

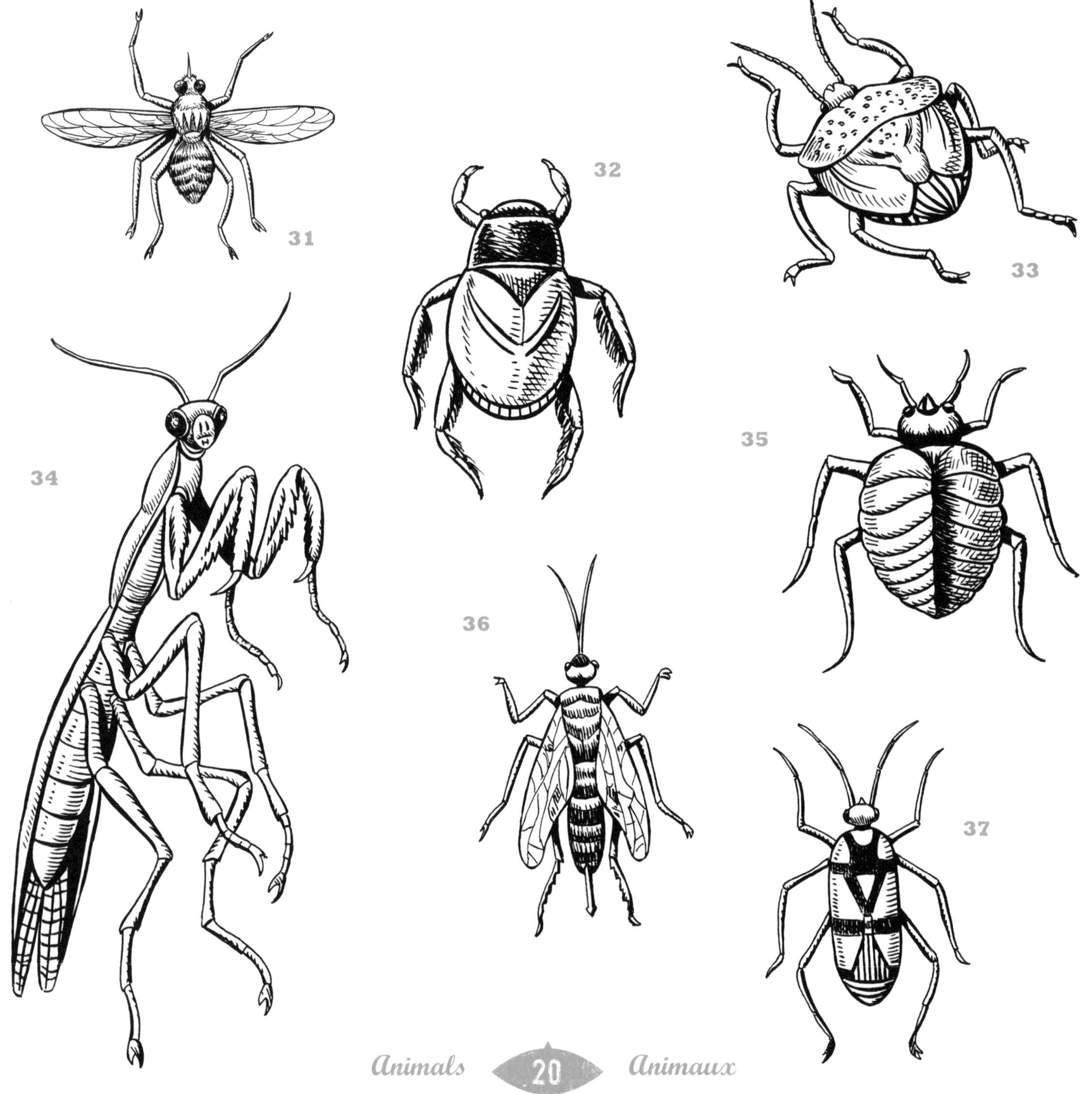
31
32
33
34
35
36
37

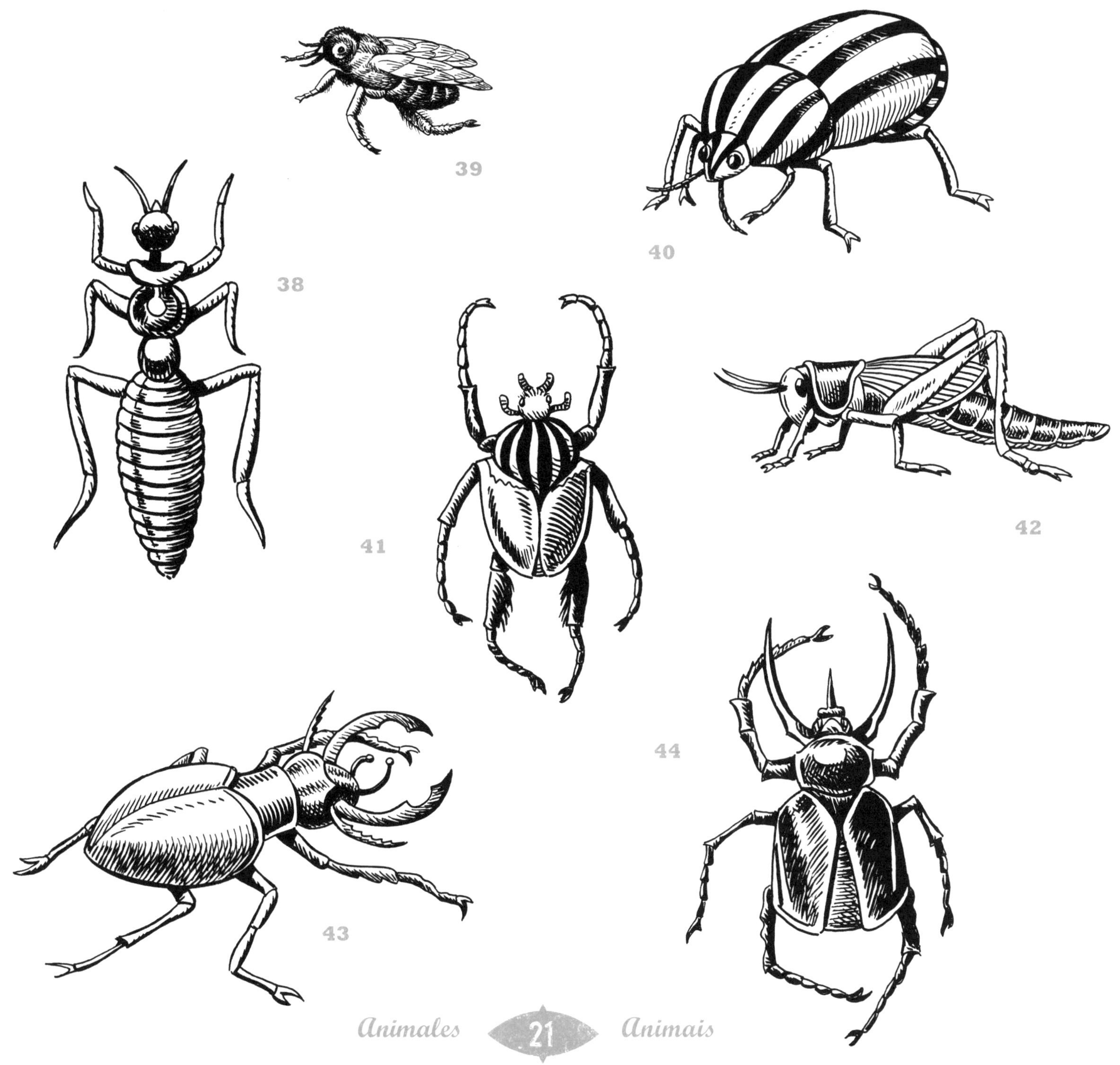

39
40
38
41
42
43
44

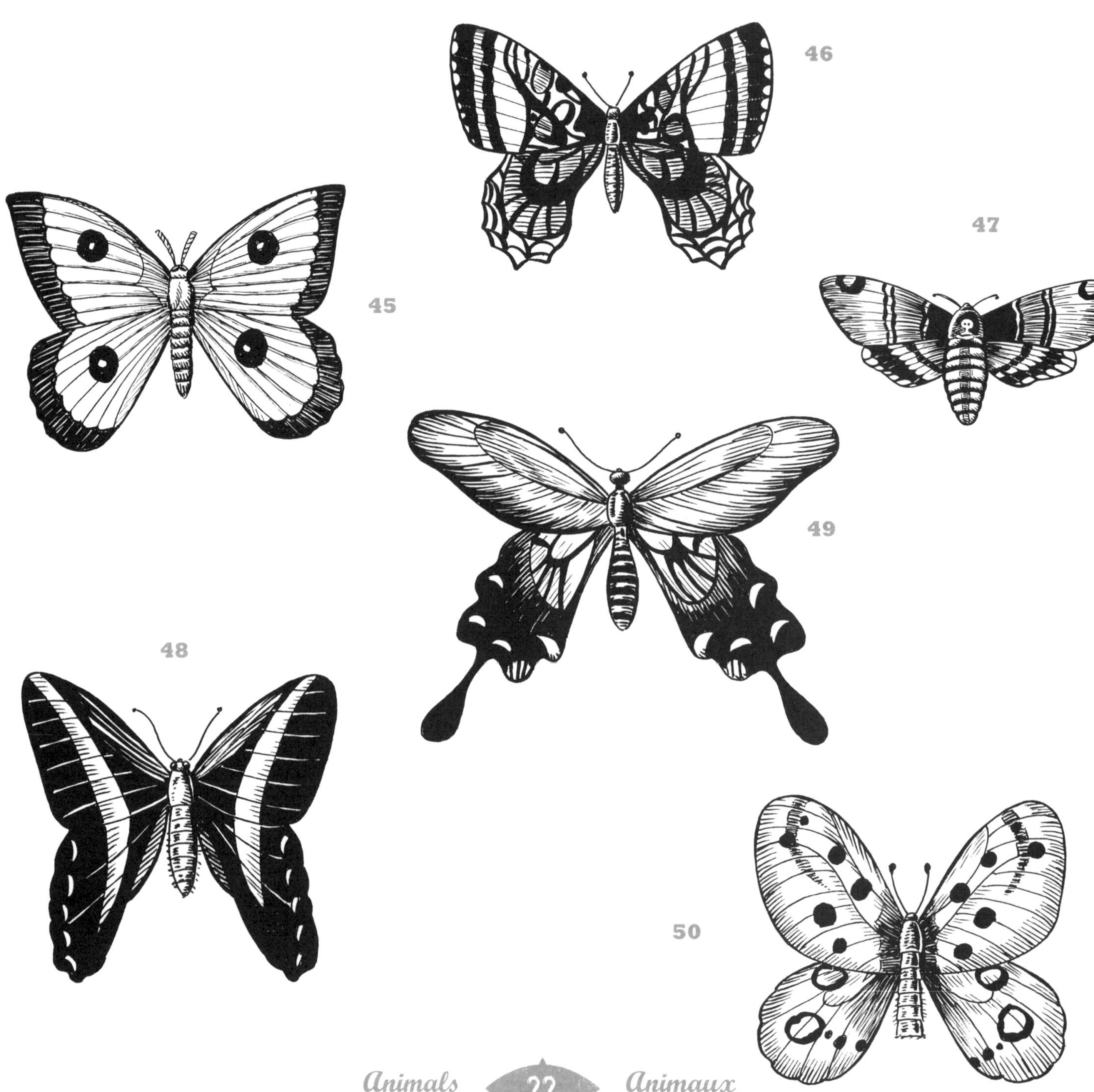

46
47
45
49
48
50

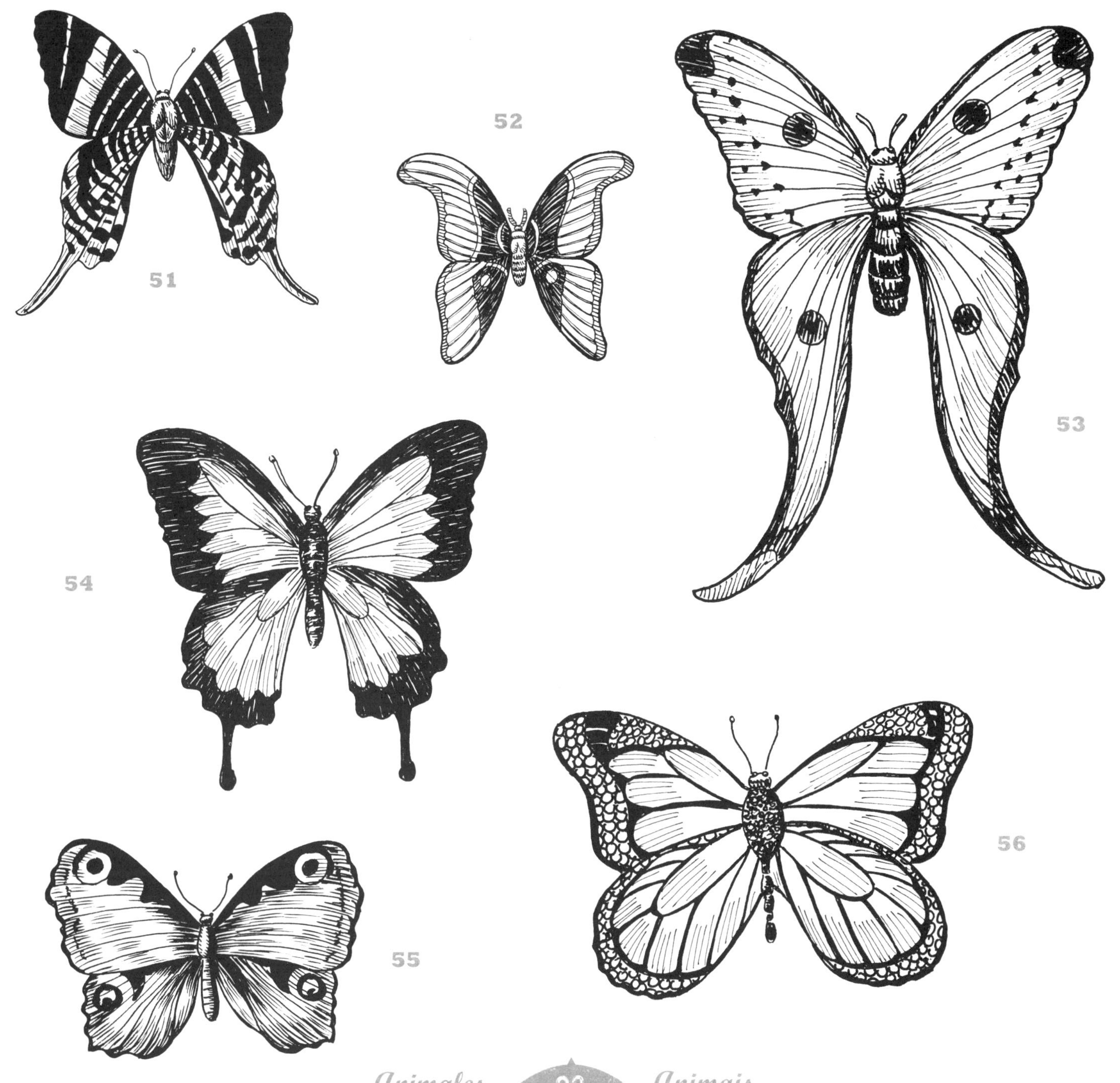

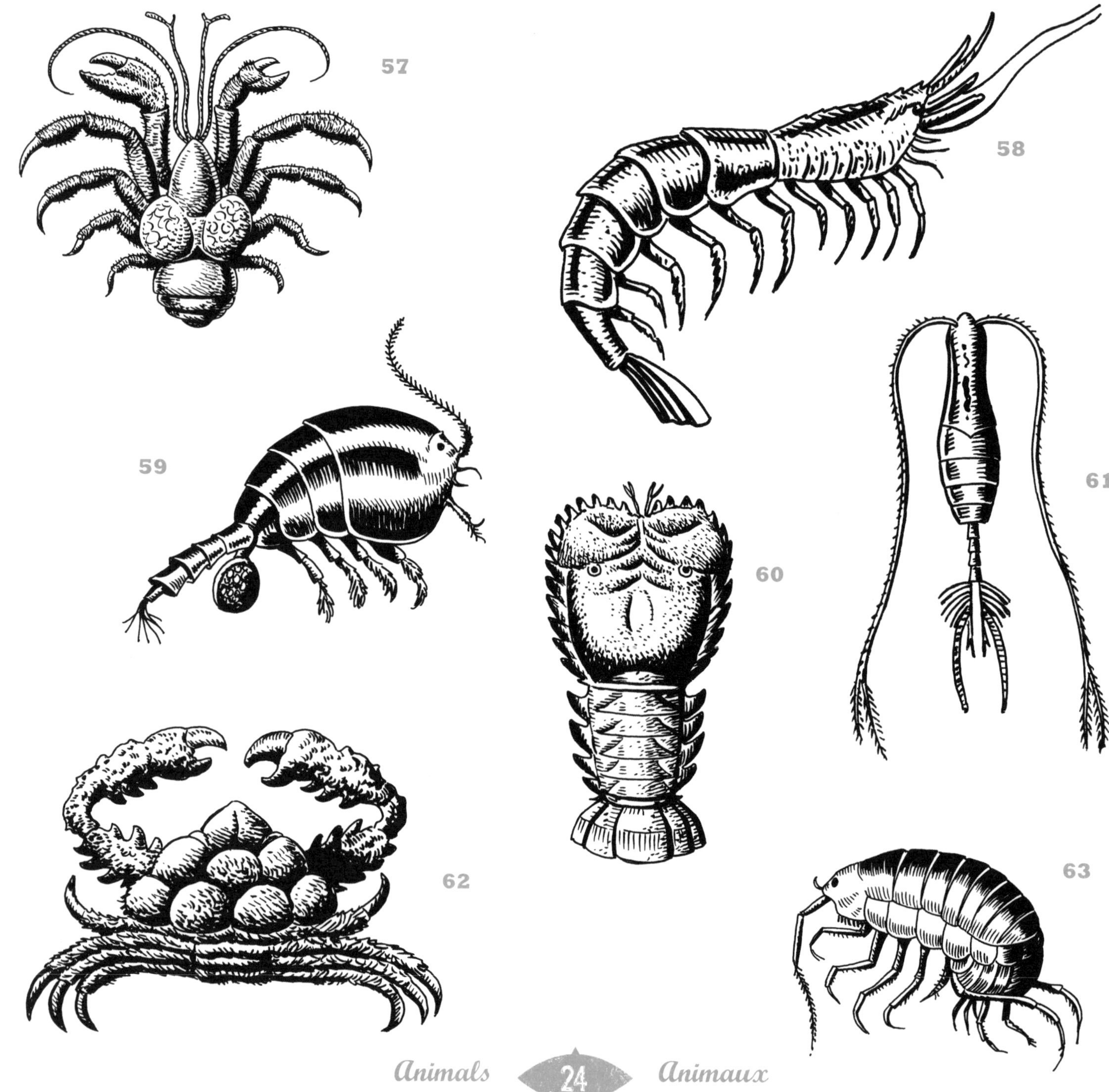

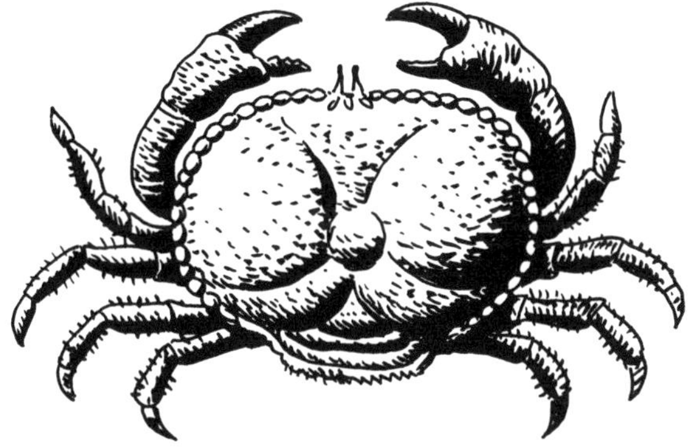

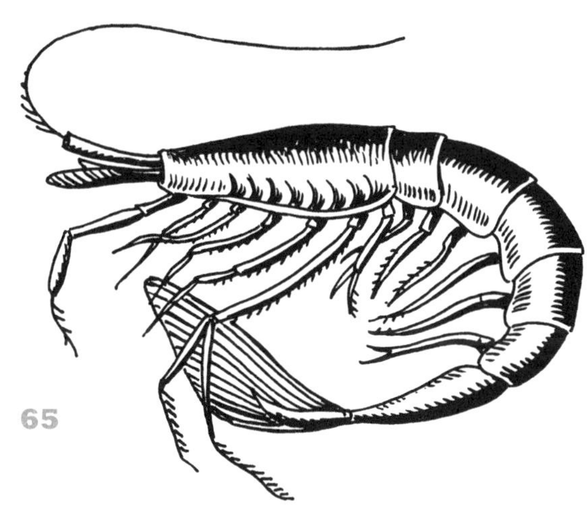

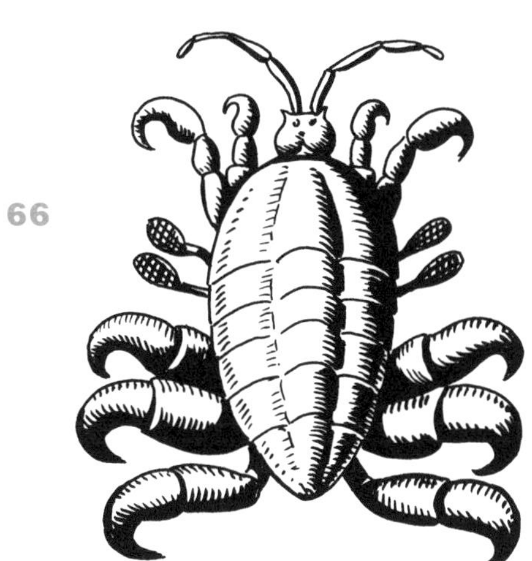

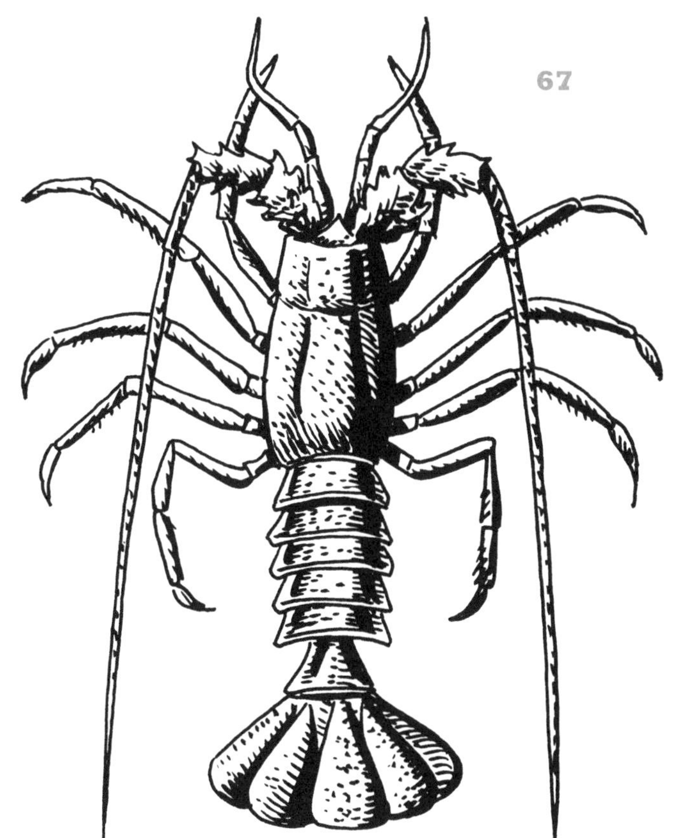

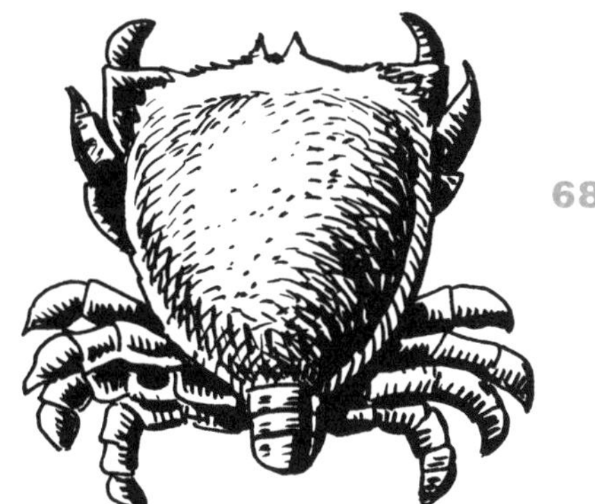

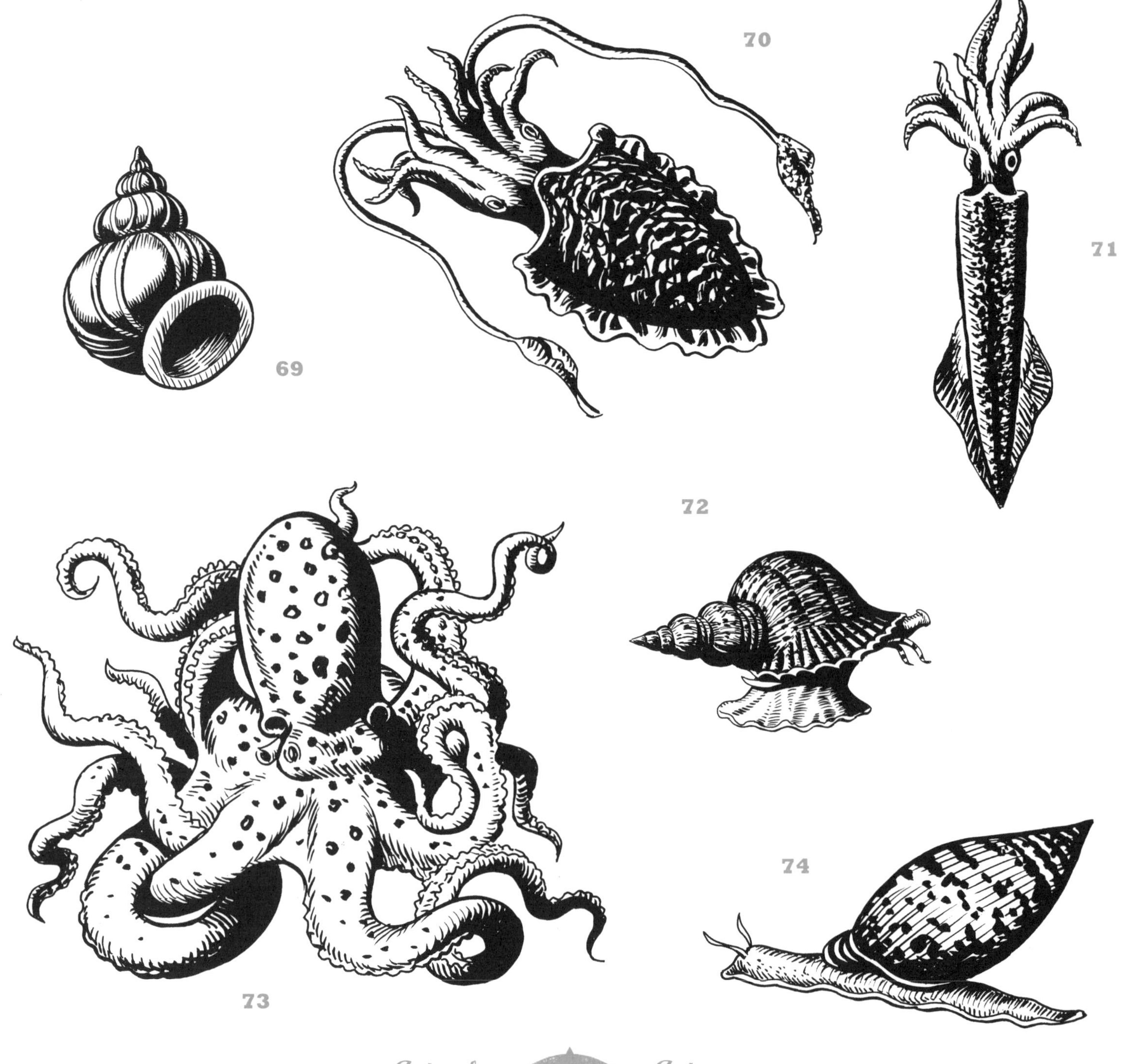
69
70
71
72
73
74

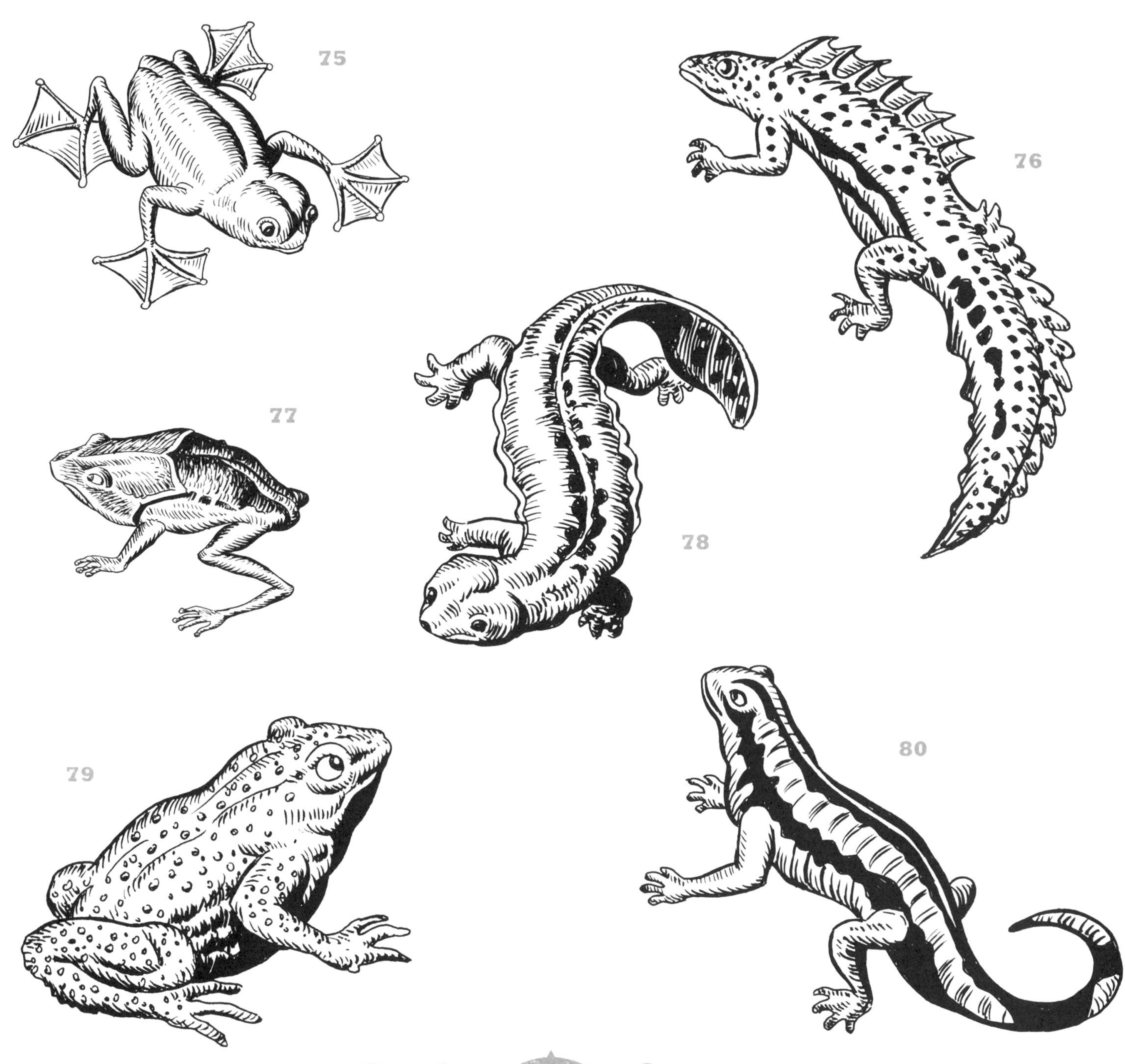

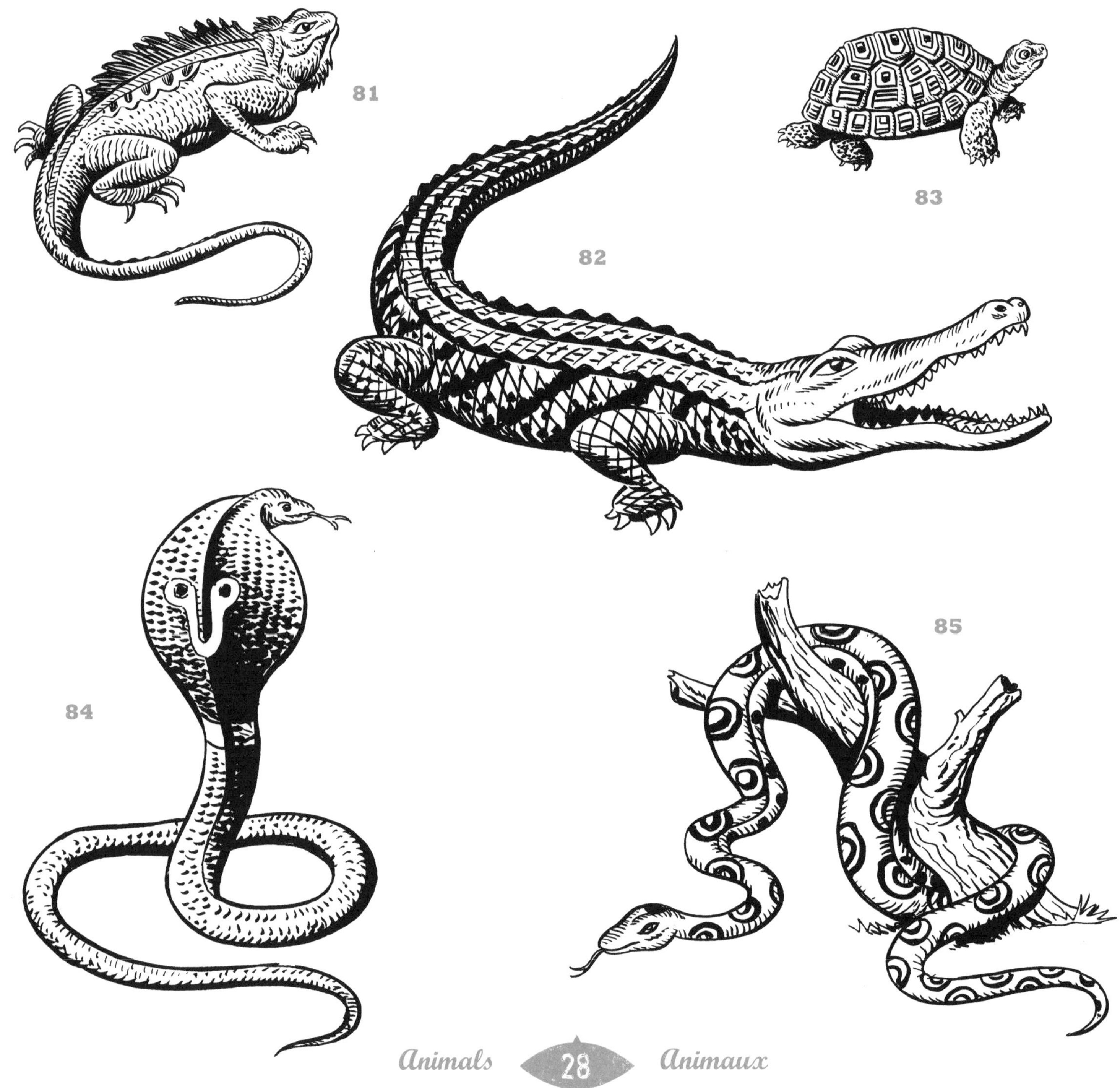

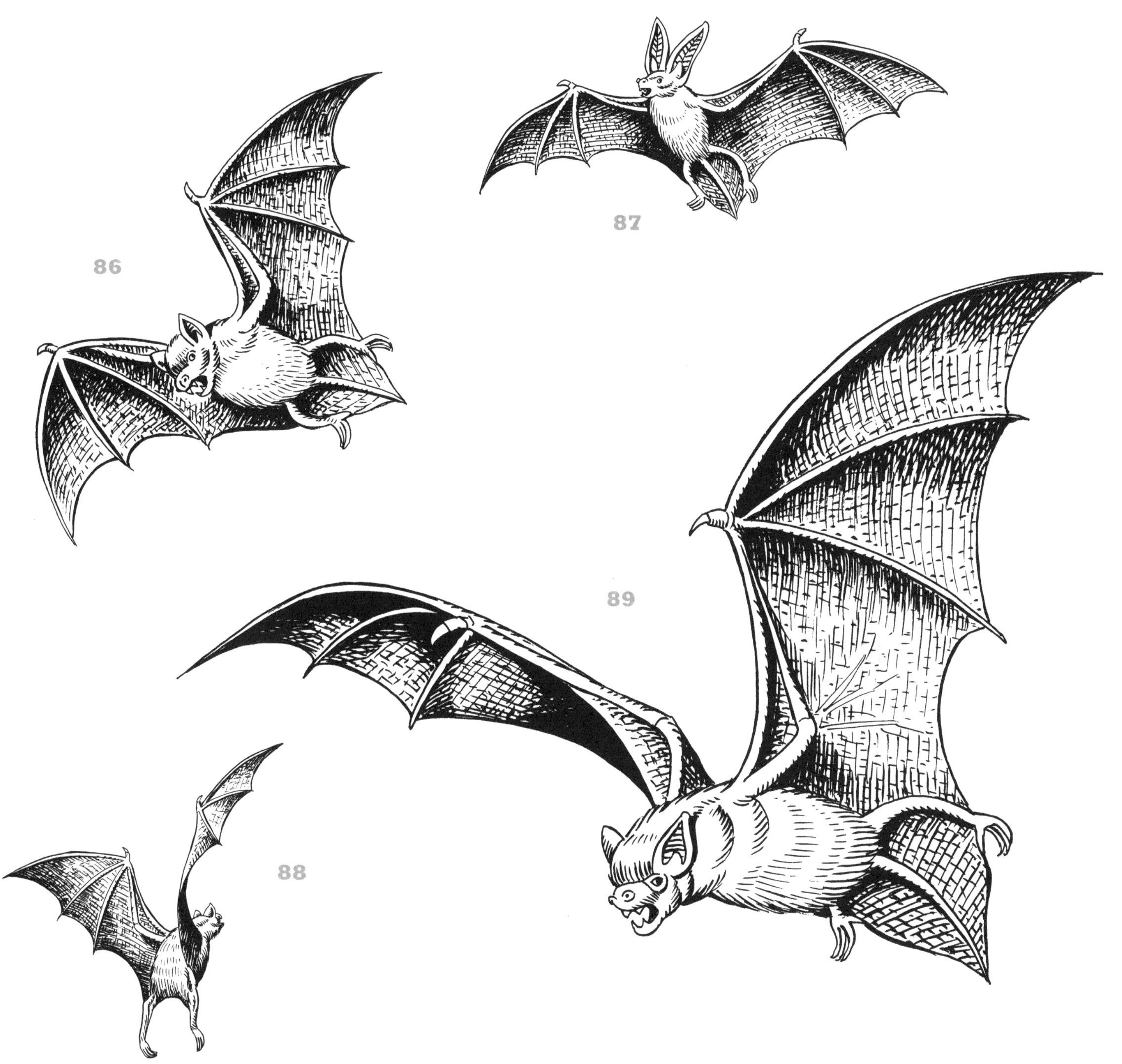
86
87
88
89

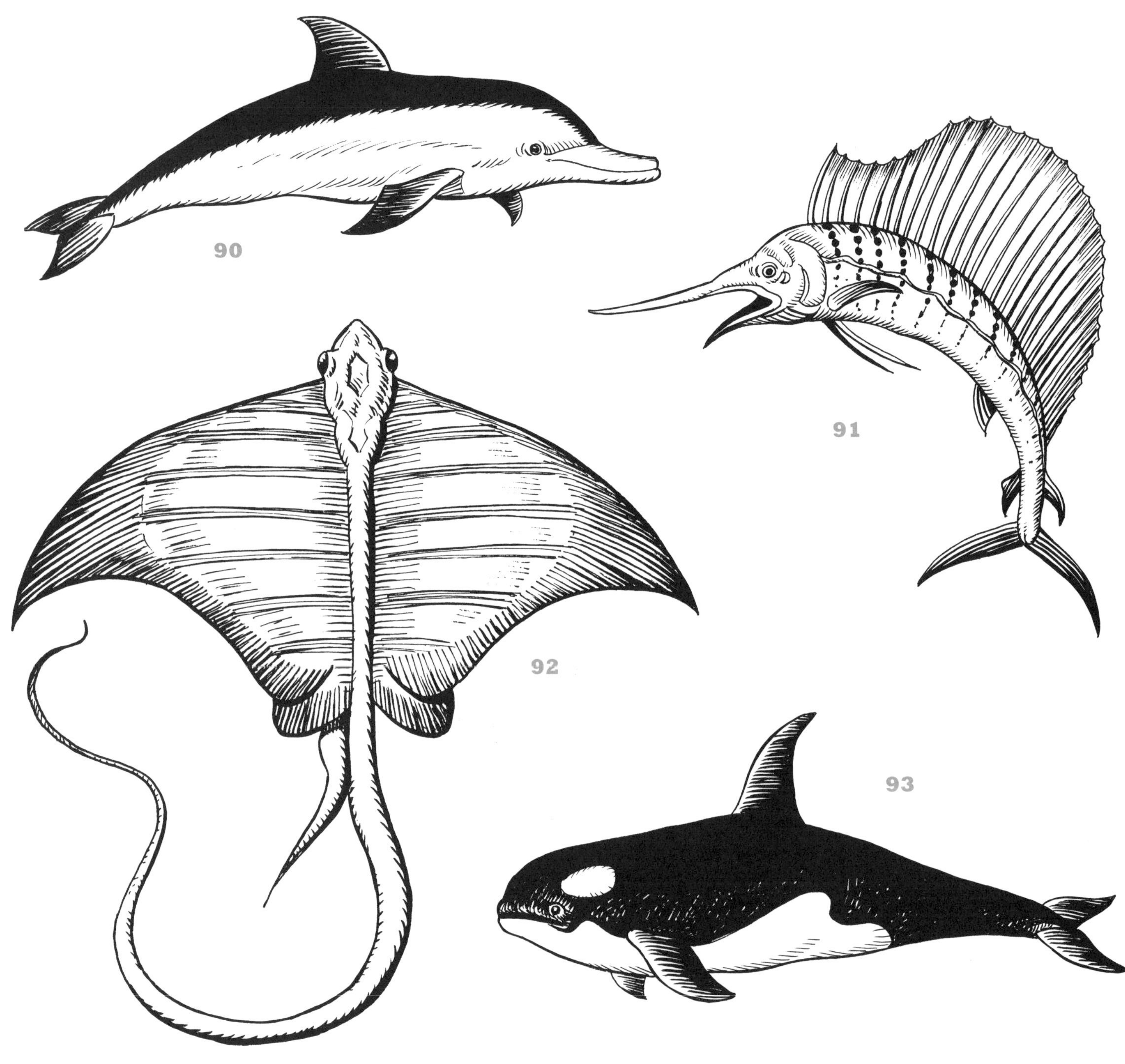
90
91
92
93

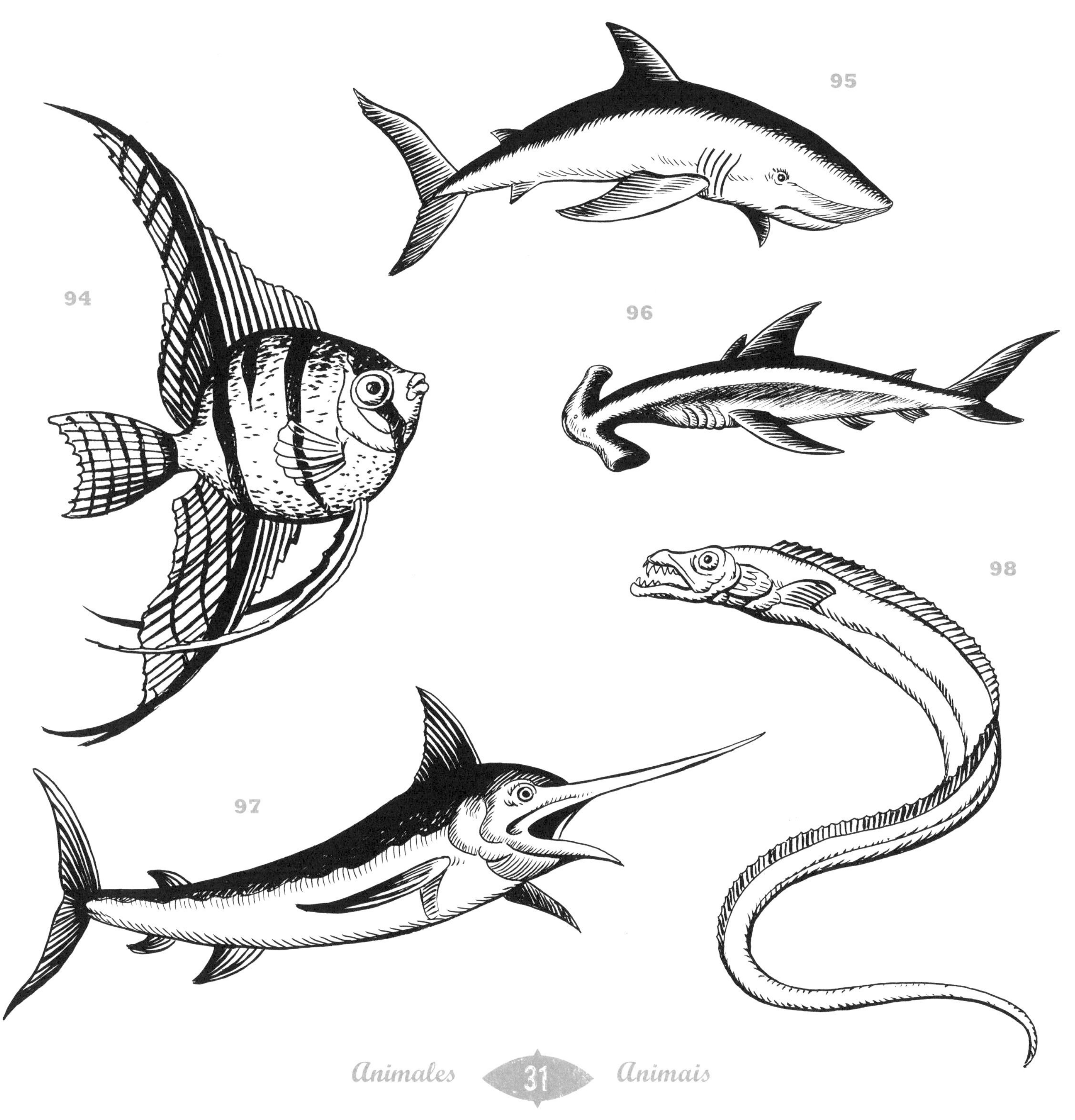

95
94
96
98
97

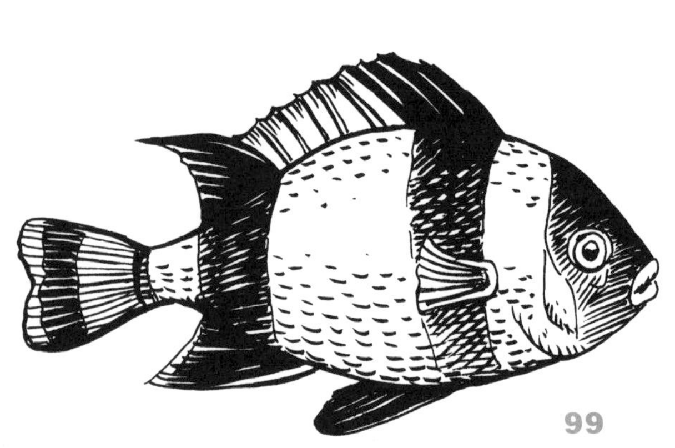

99

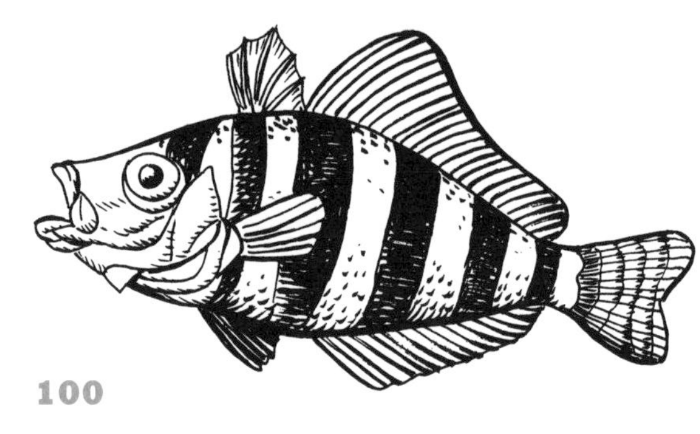

100

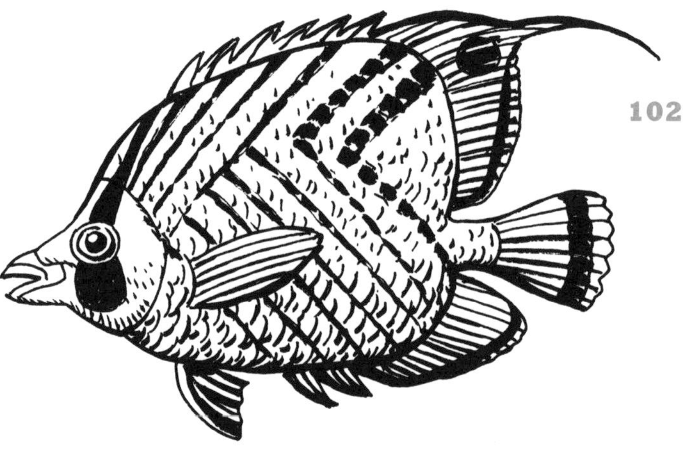

102

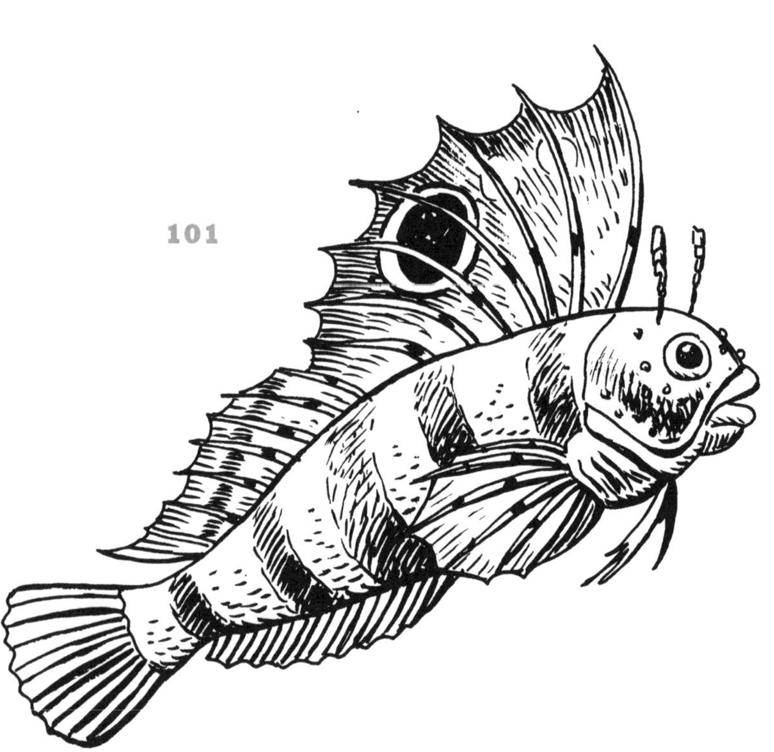

101

103

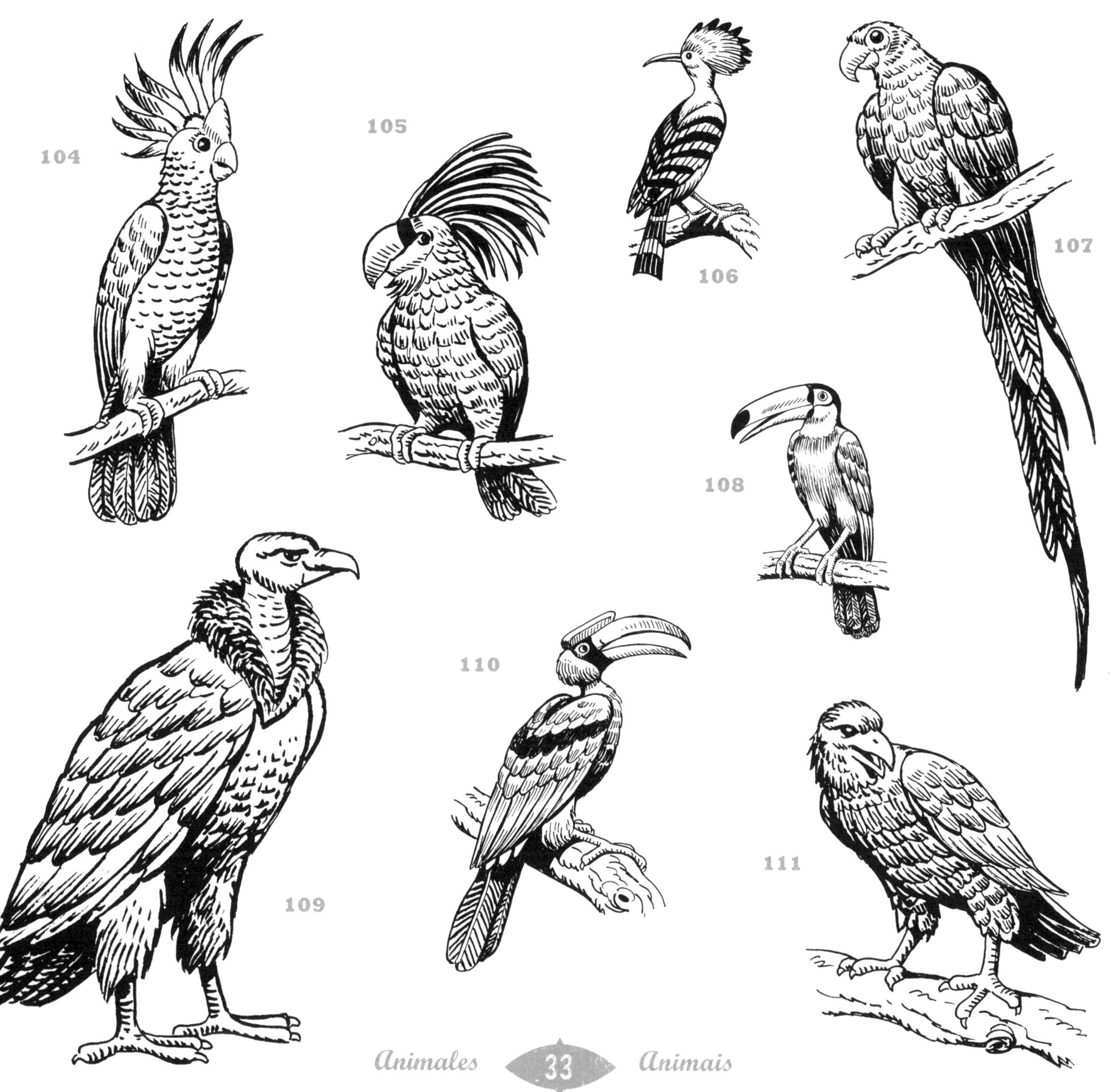

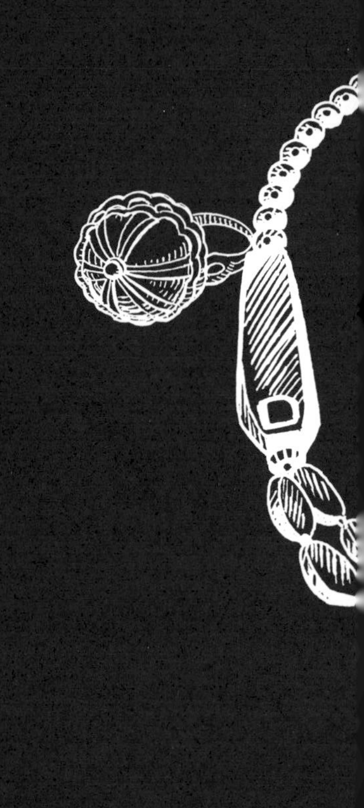

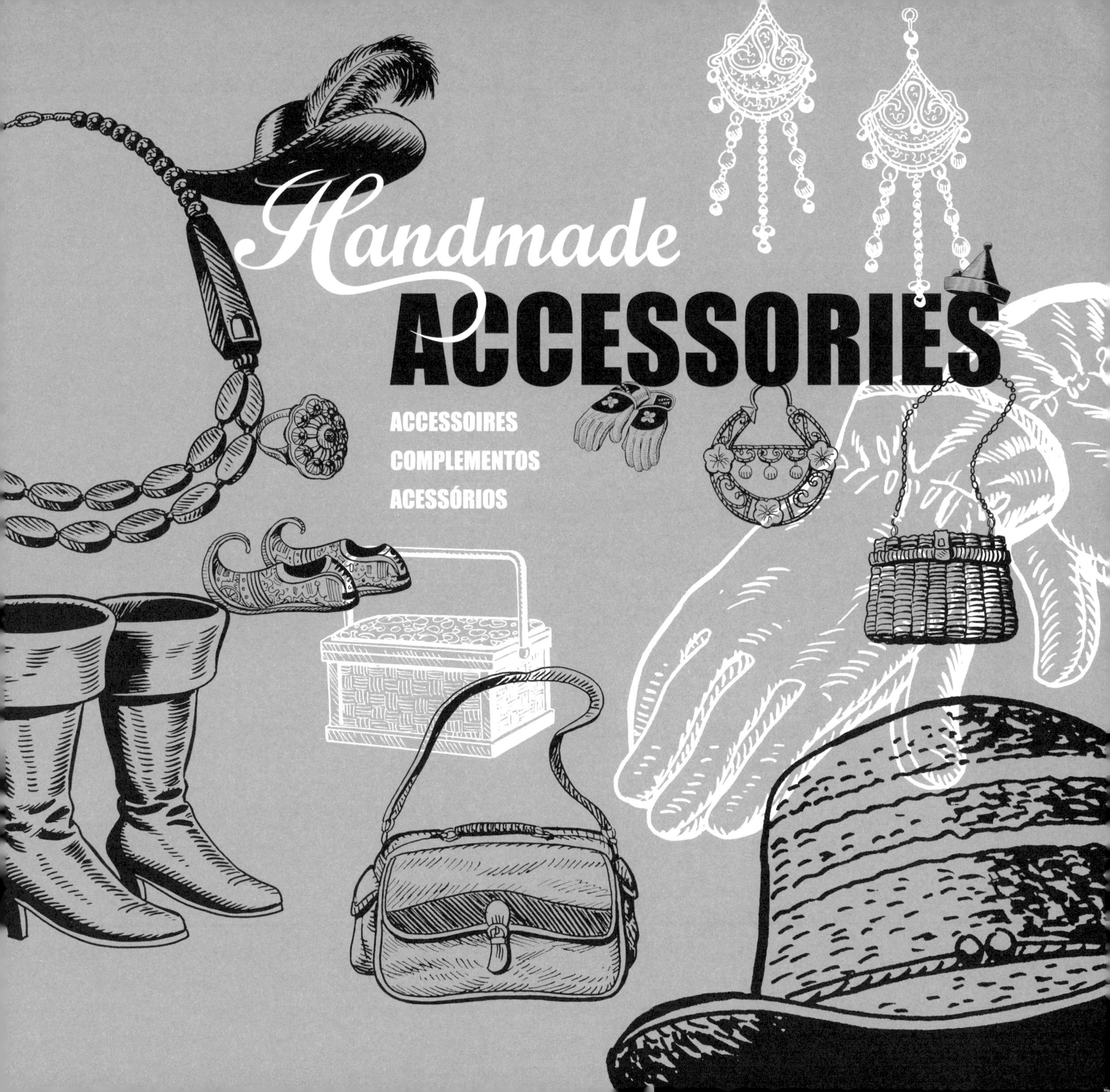
Handmade
ACCESSORIES
ACCESSOIRES
COMPLEMENTOS
ACESSÓRIOS

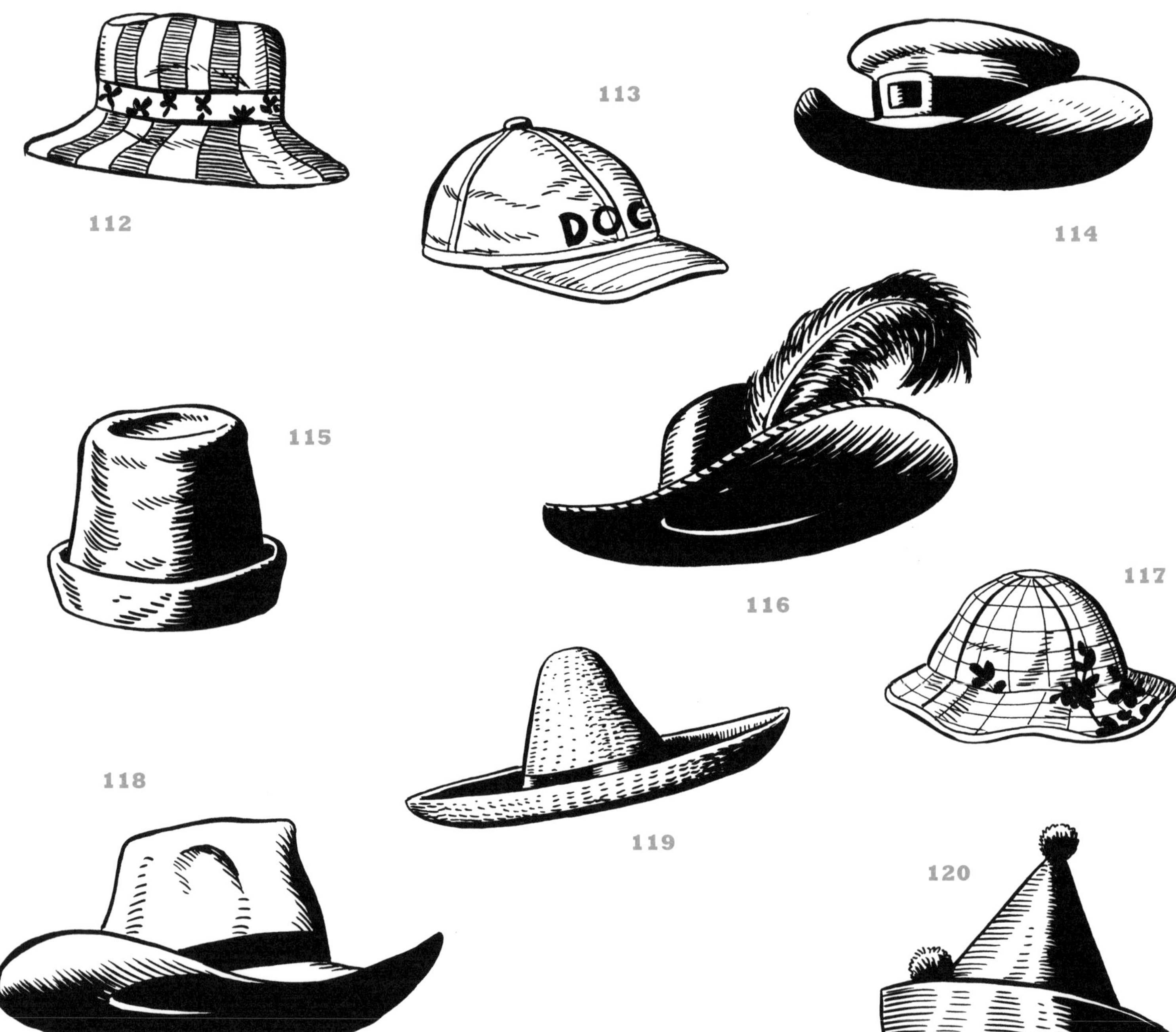
112
113
114
115
116
117
118
119
120
DOG

122

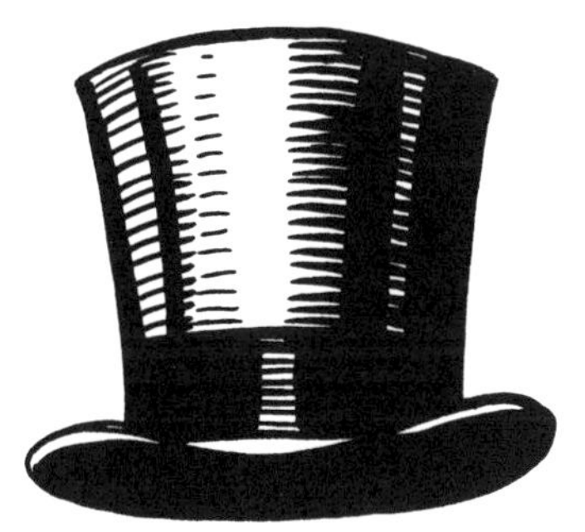

121

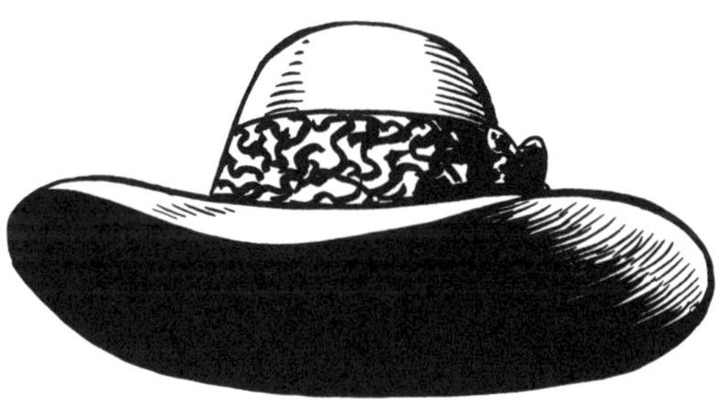

123

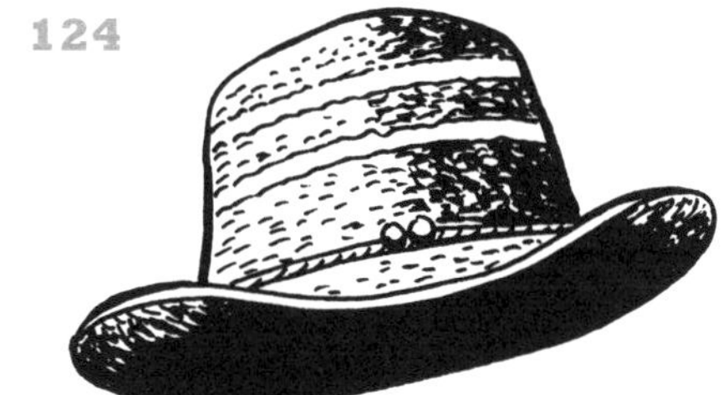

124

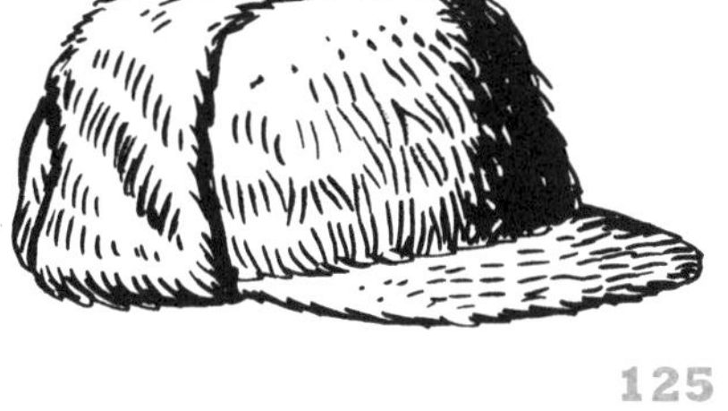

125

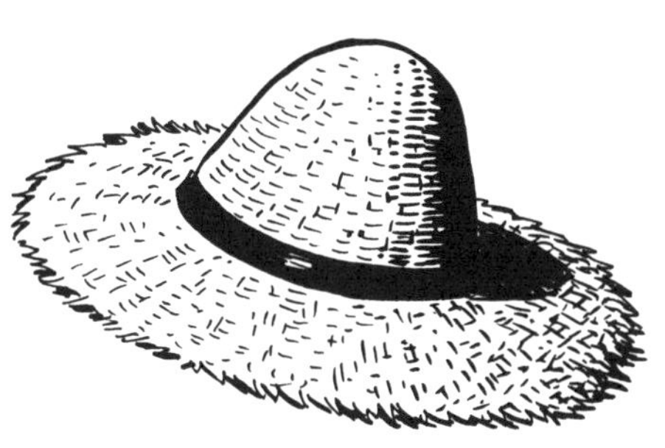

128

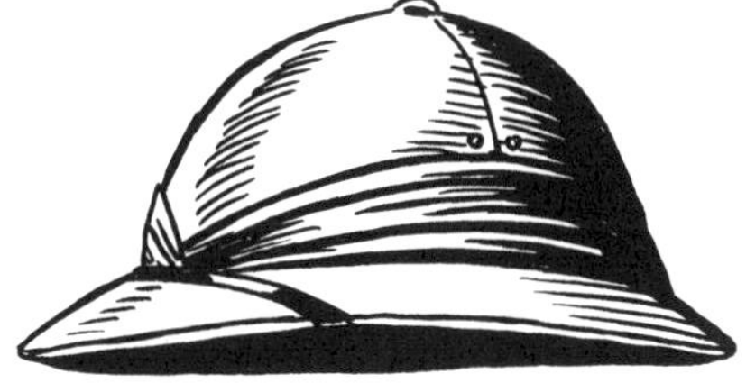

127

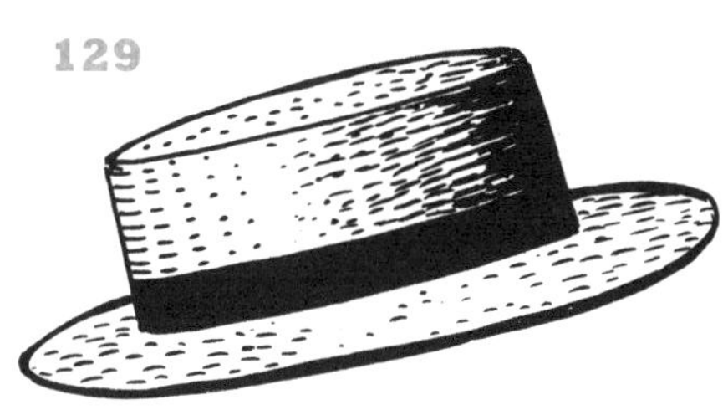

126

129

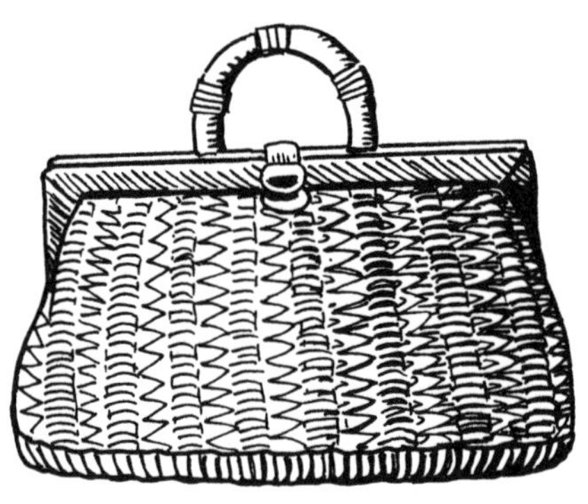

130

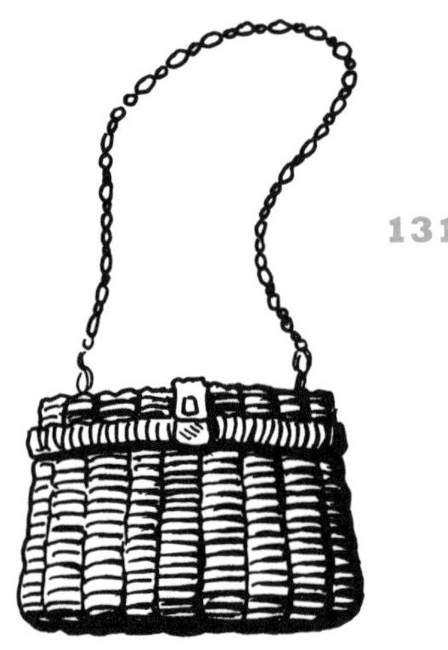

131

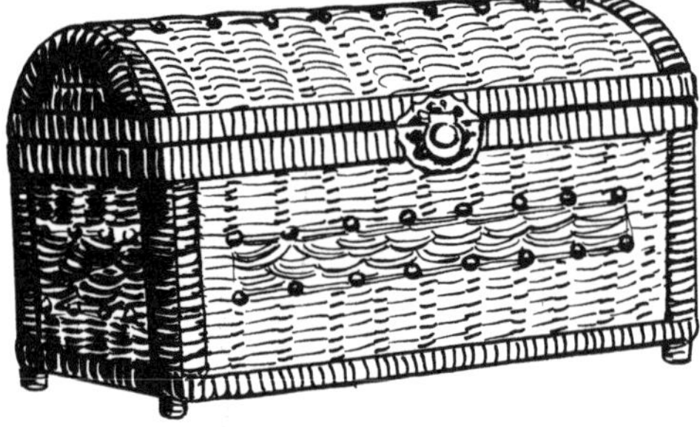

133

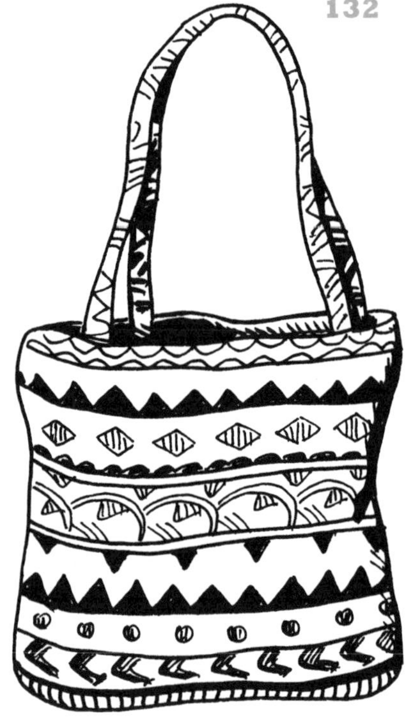

132

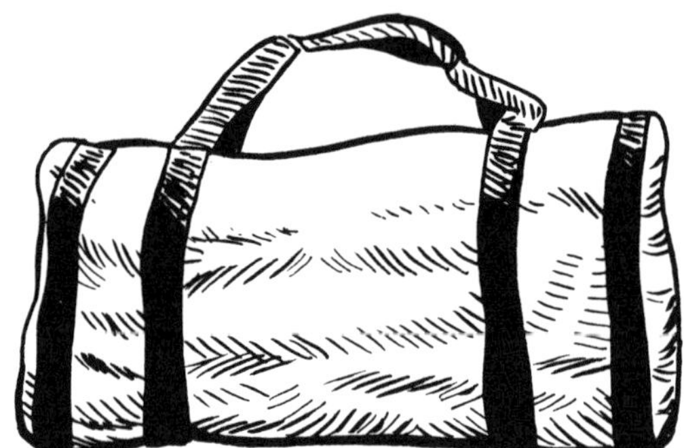

134

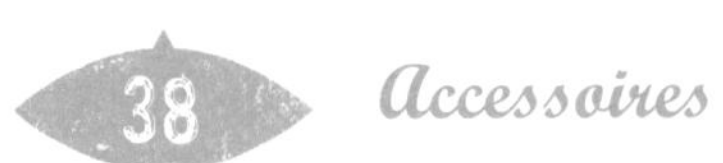

135

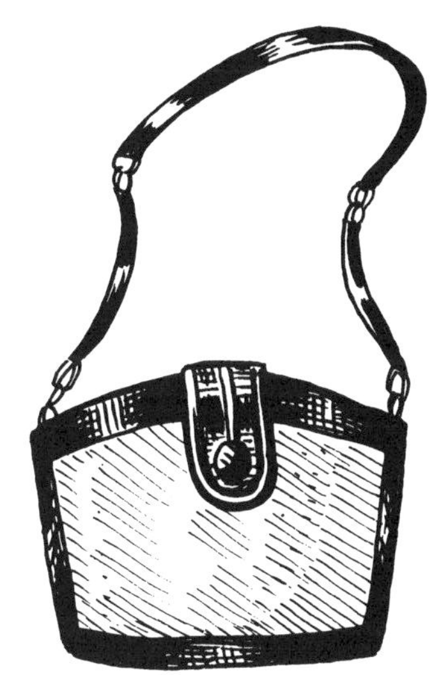 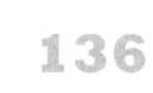

136

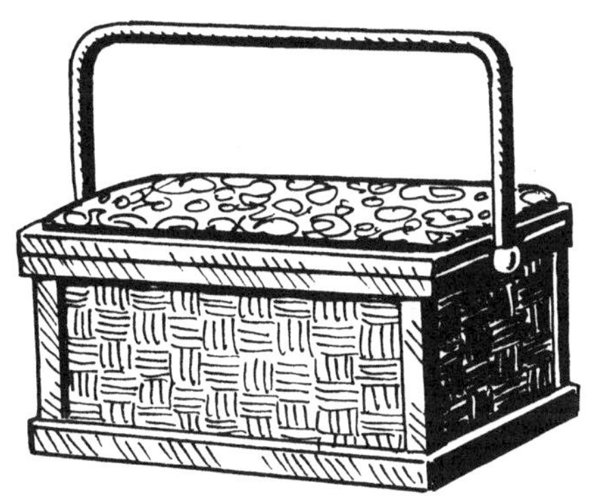

137

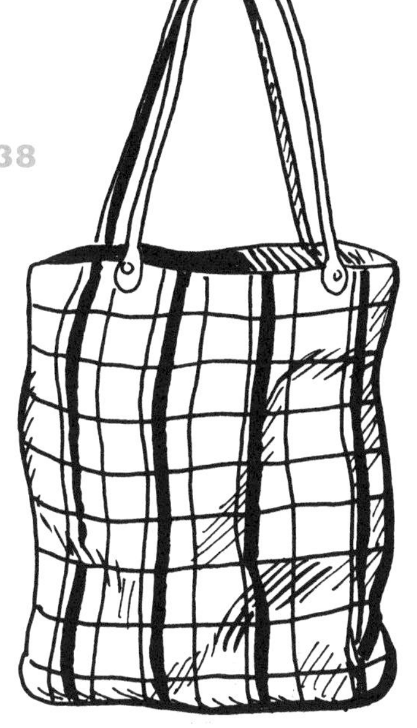

138

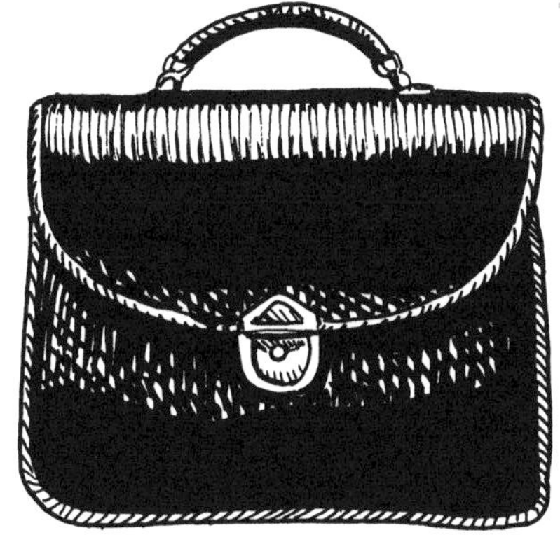

139

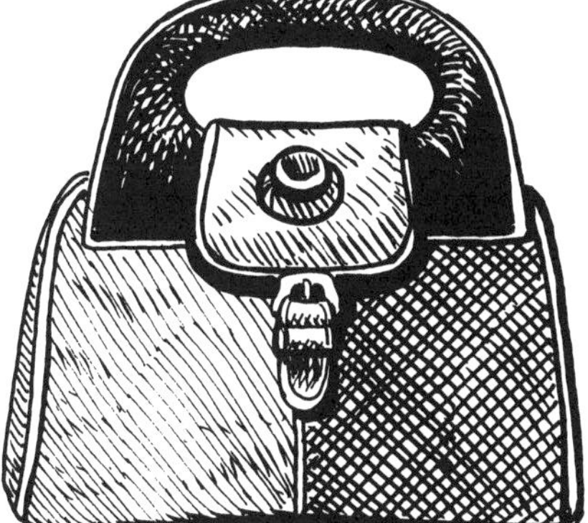

140

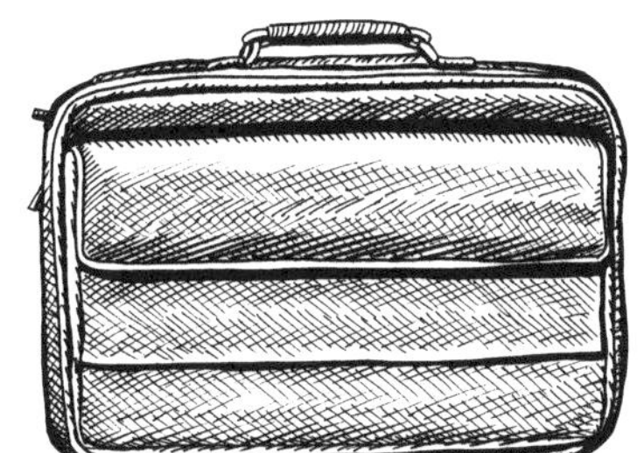

141

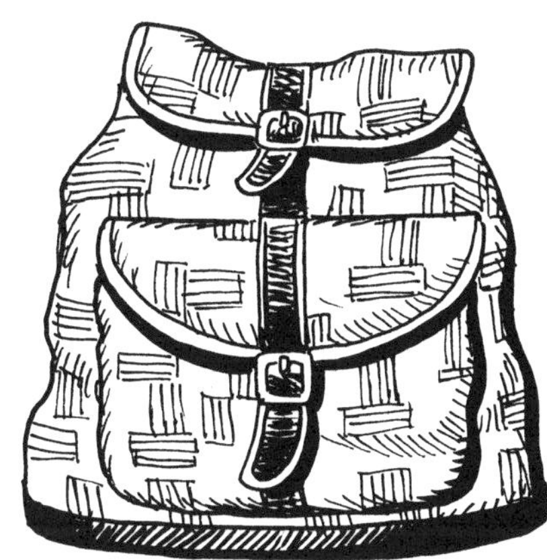

142

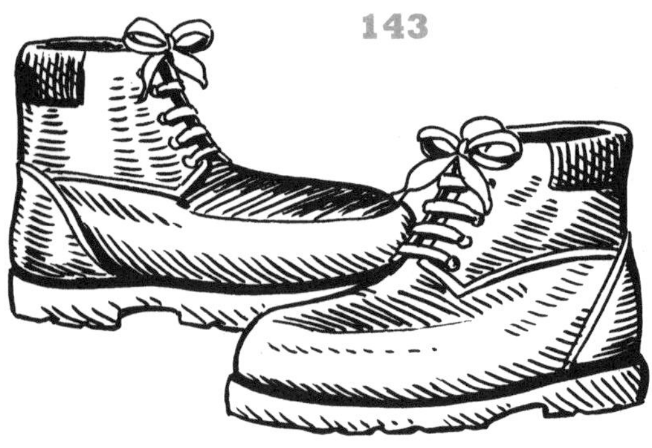

143

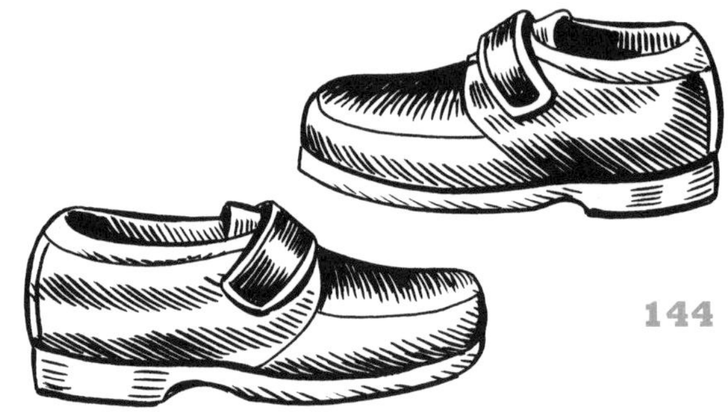

144

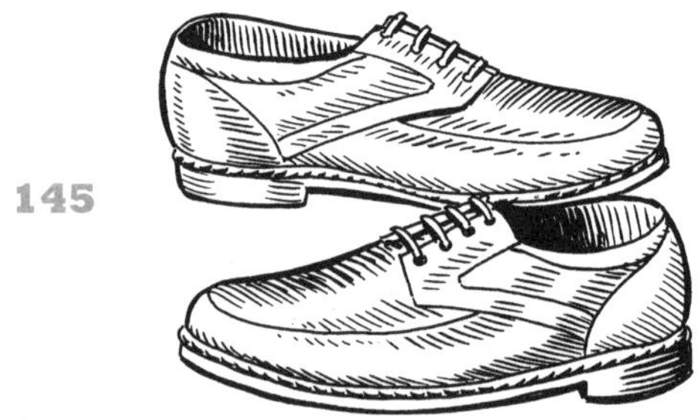

145

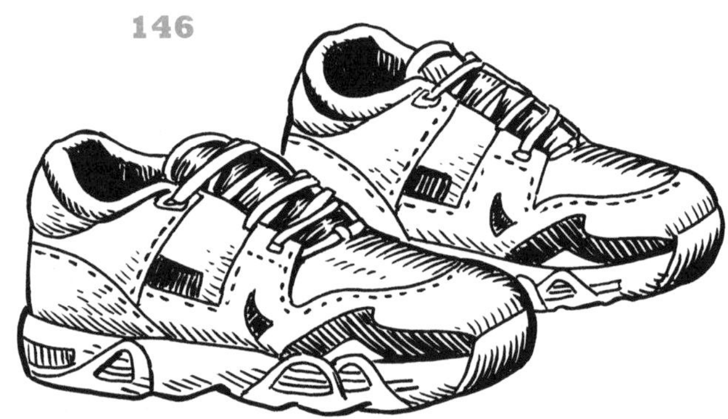

146

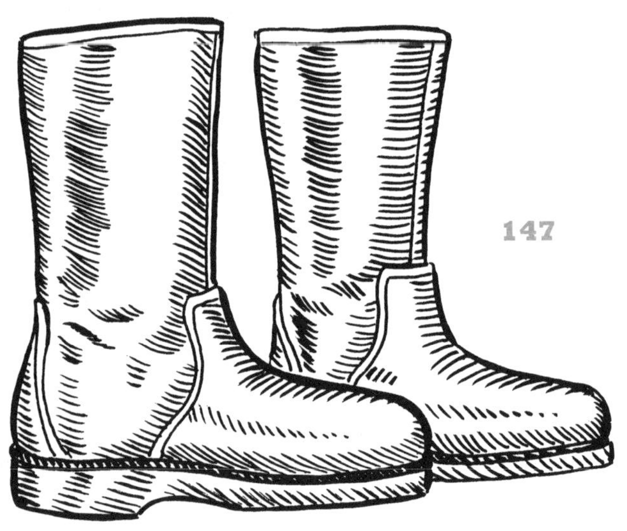

147

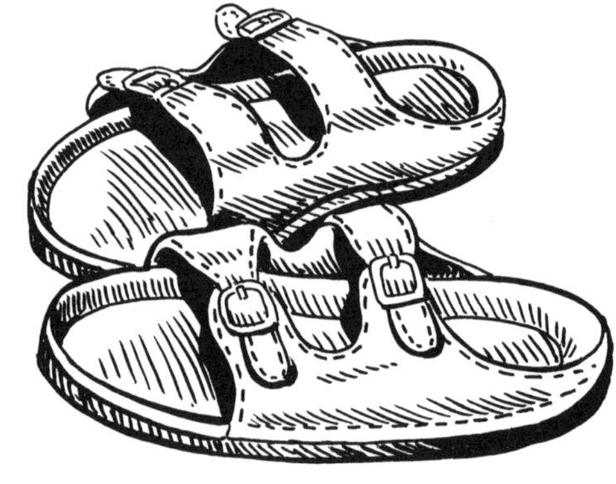

148

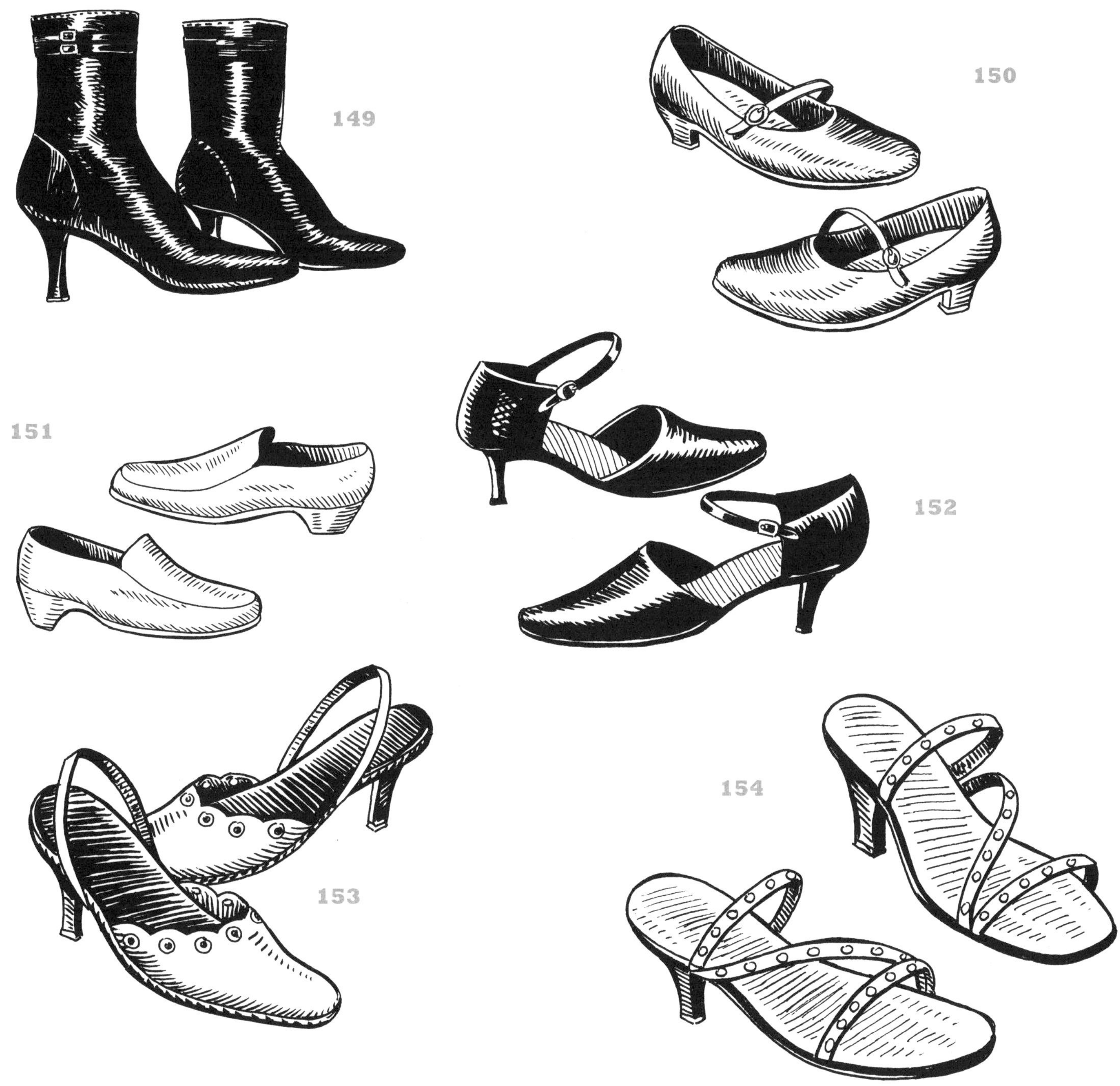

149
150
151
152
153
154

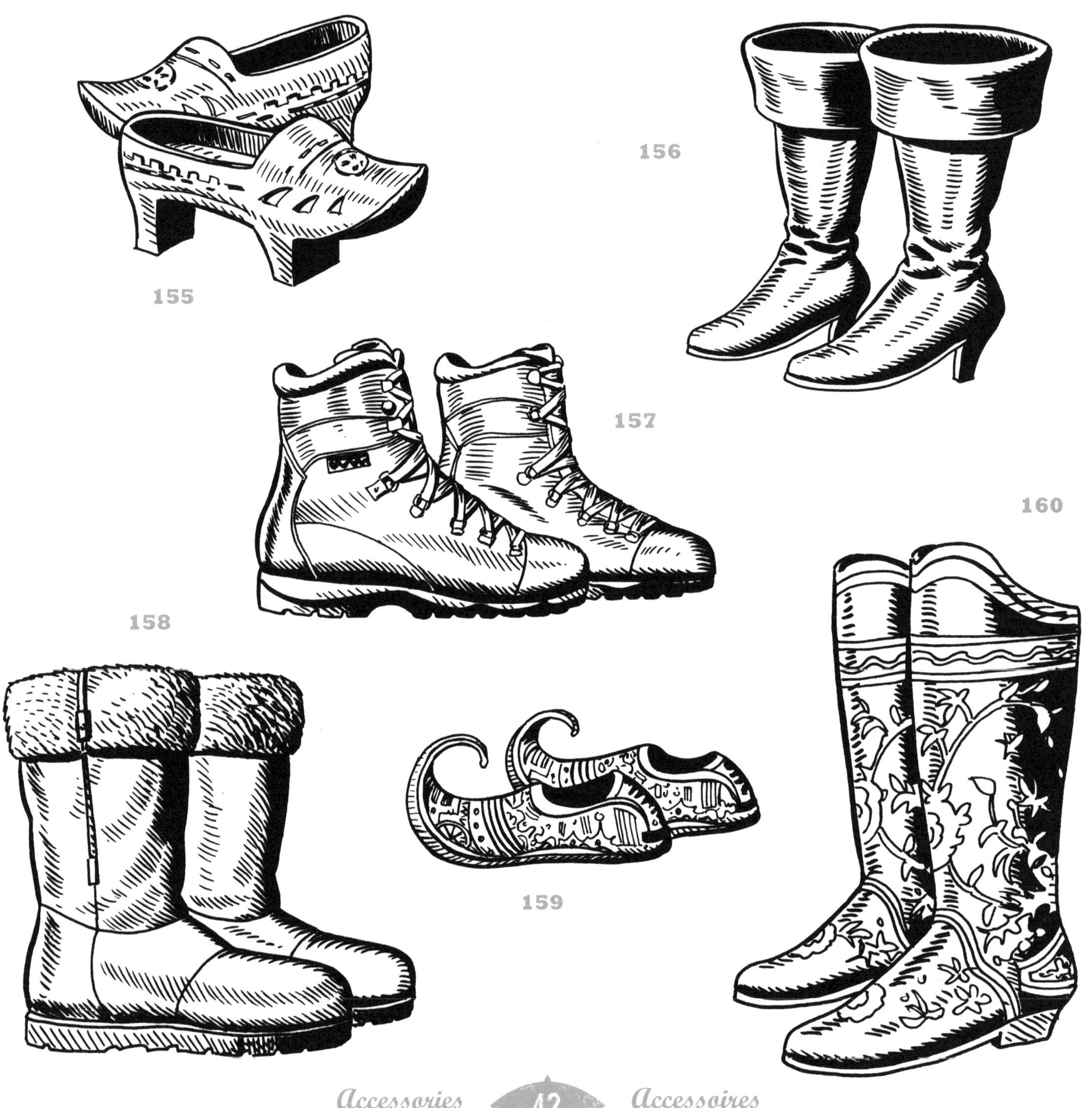

155
156
157
158
159
160

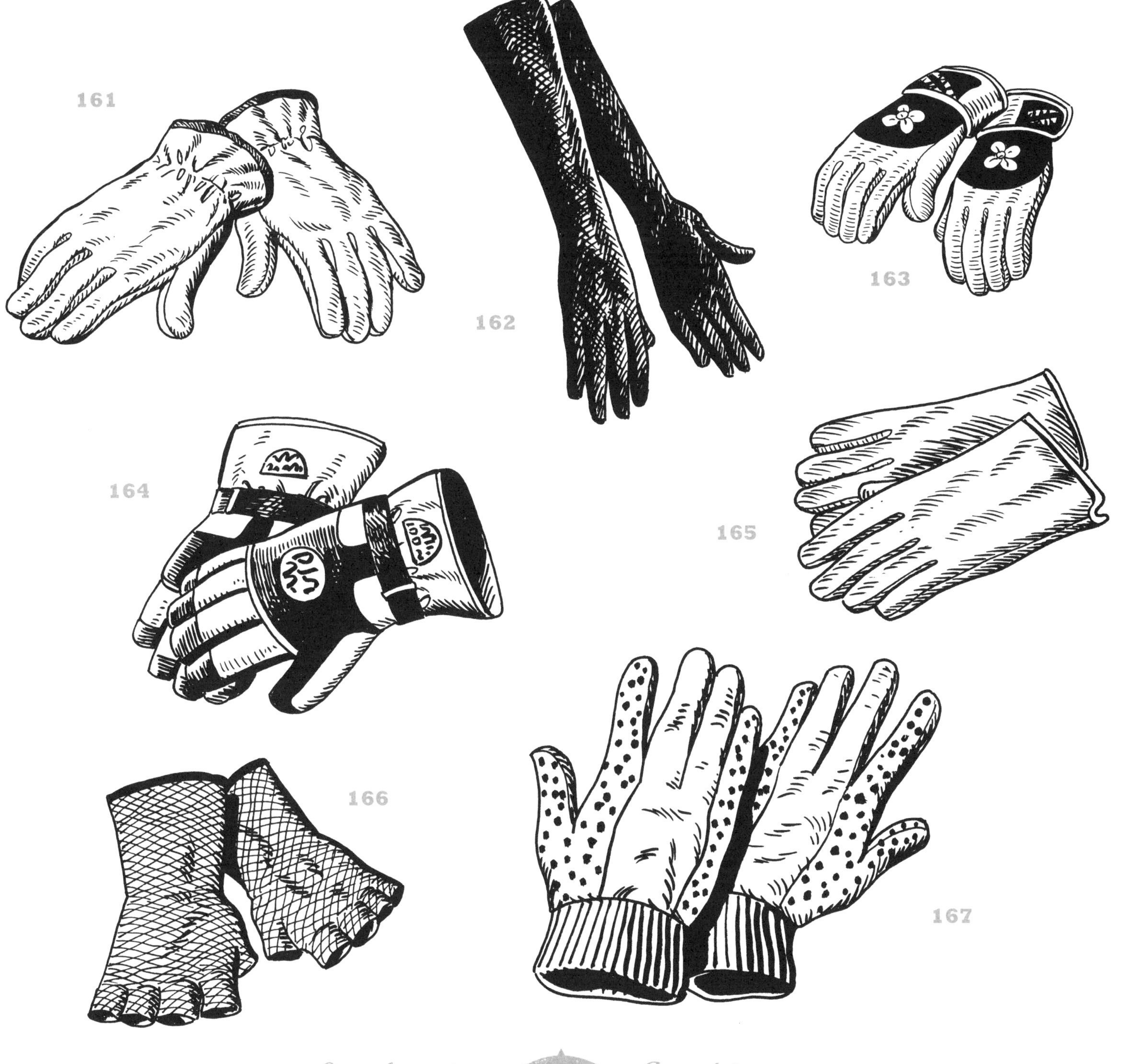

161
162
163
164
165
166
167

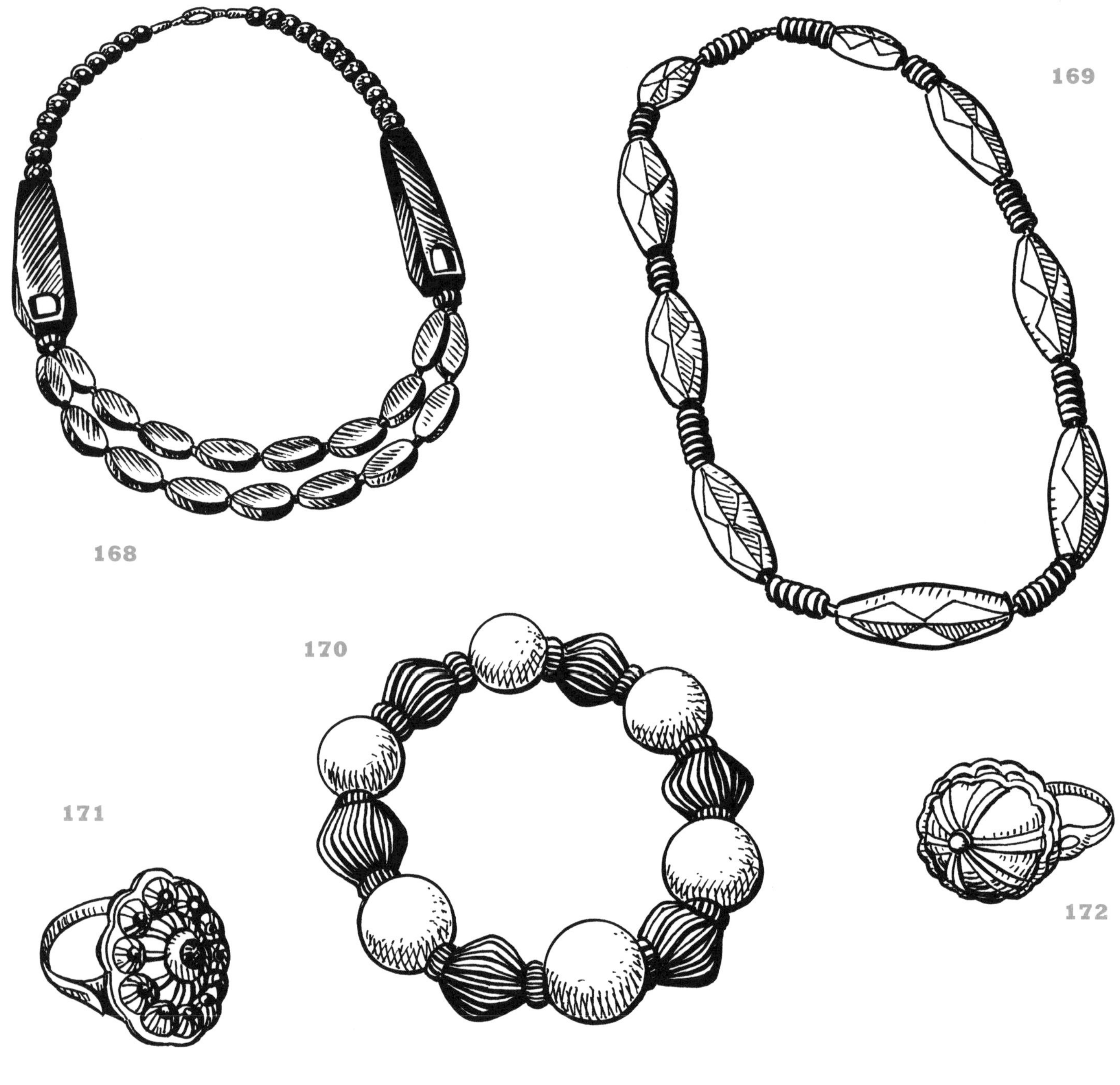

168
169
170
171
172

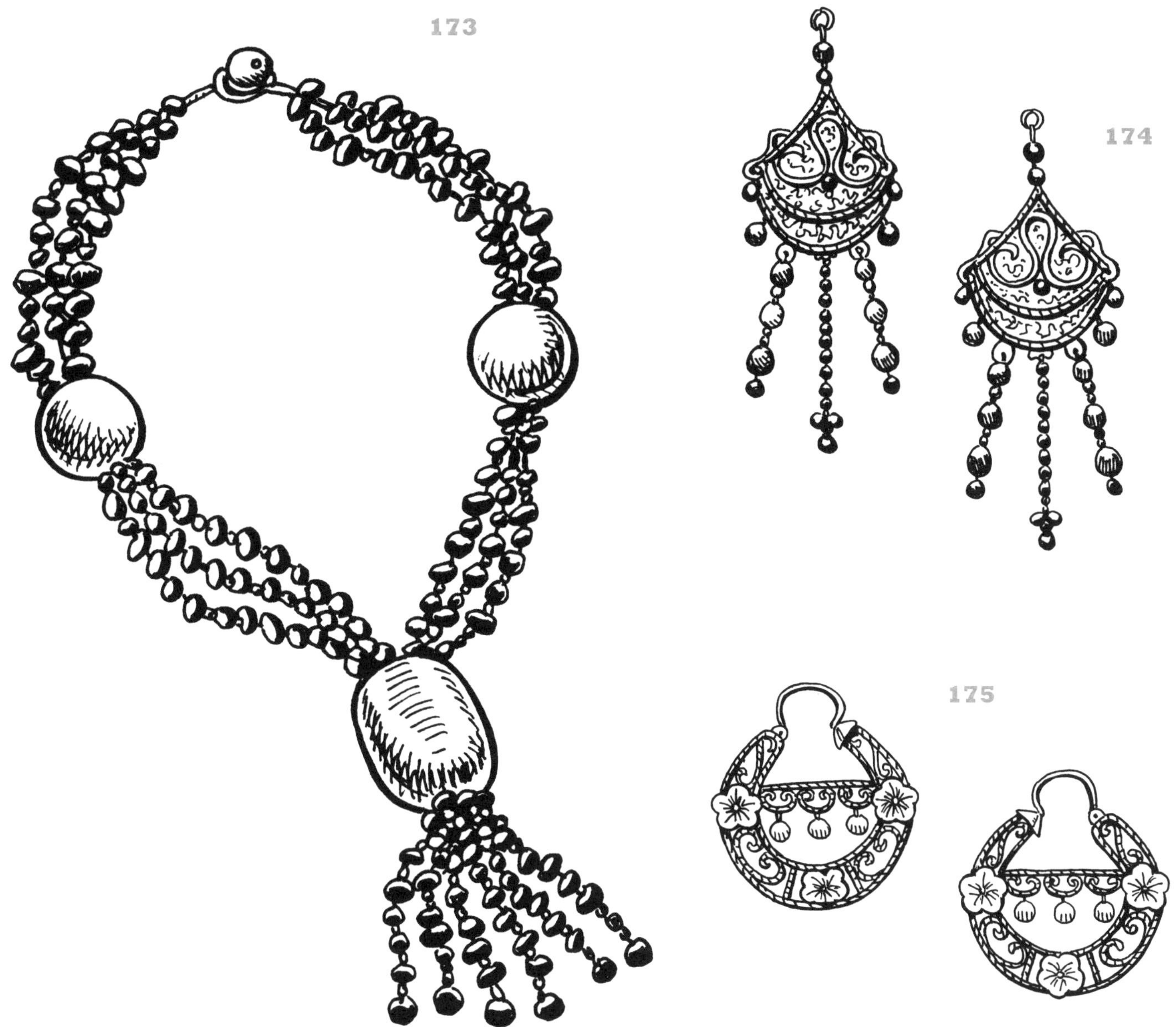

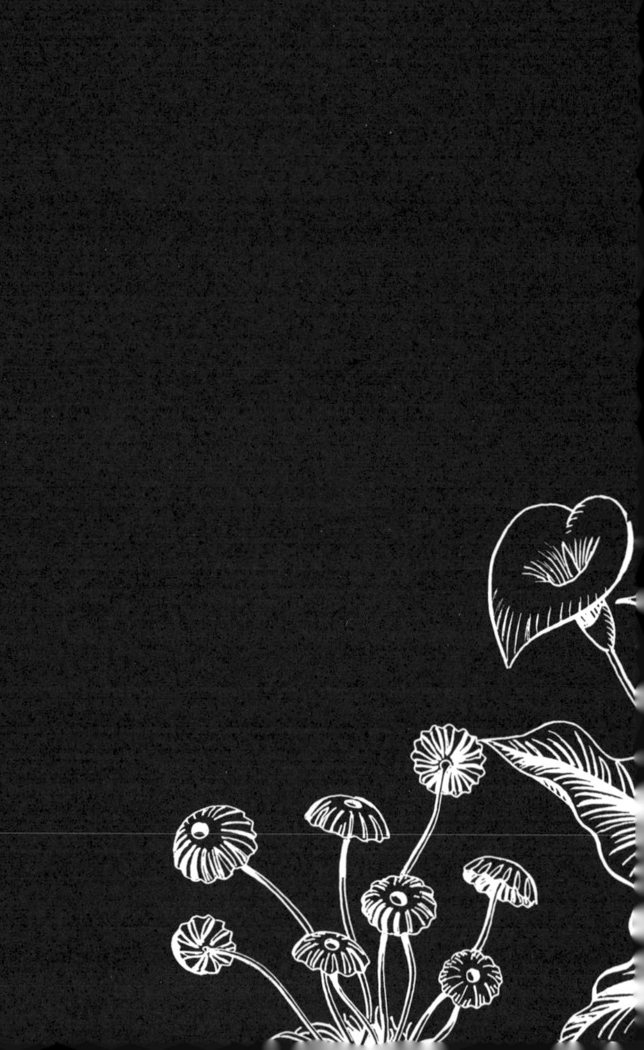

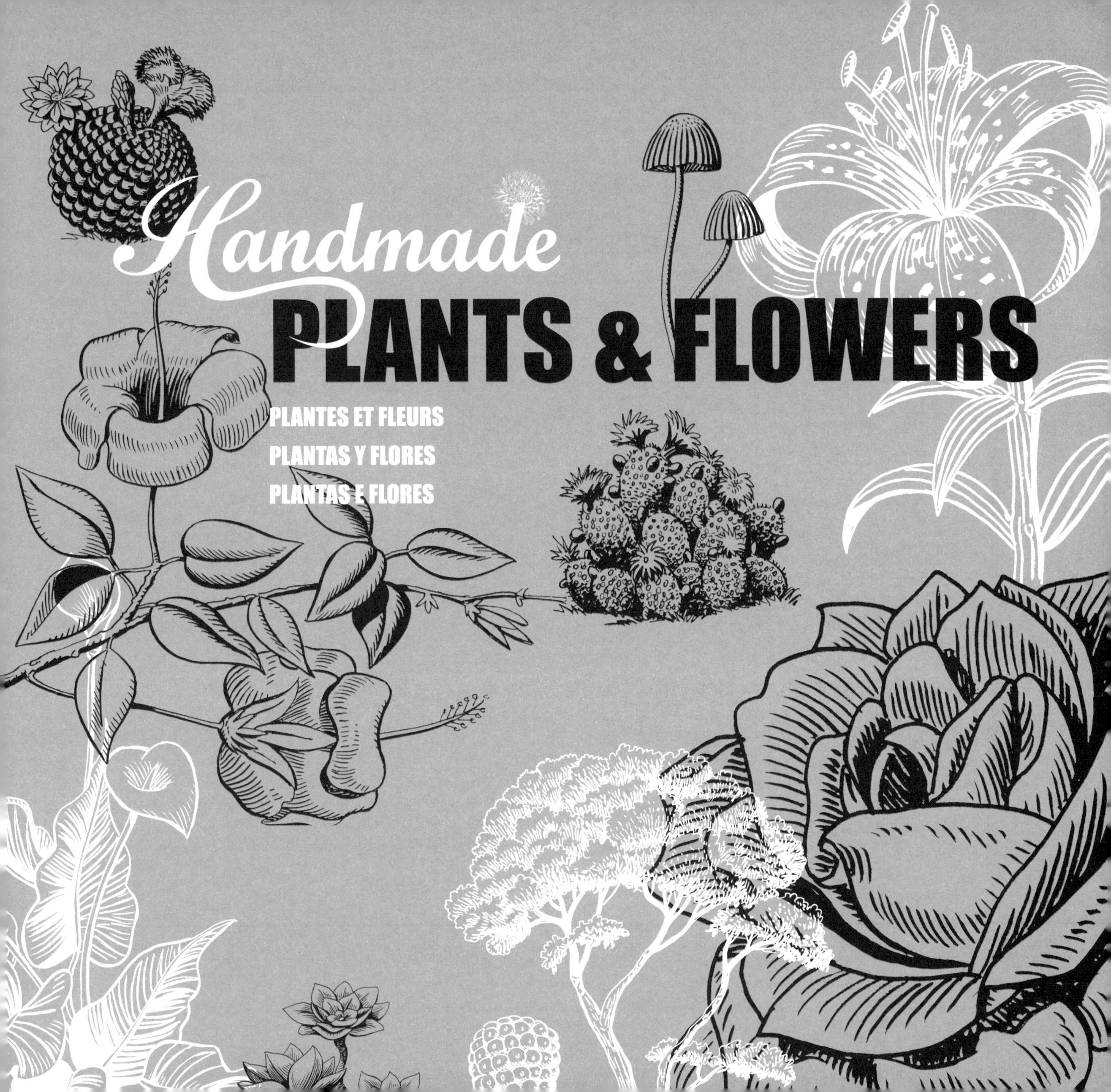

Handmade PLANTS & FLOWERS

PLANTES ET FLEURS
PLANTAS Y FLORES
PLANTAS E FLORES

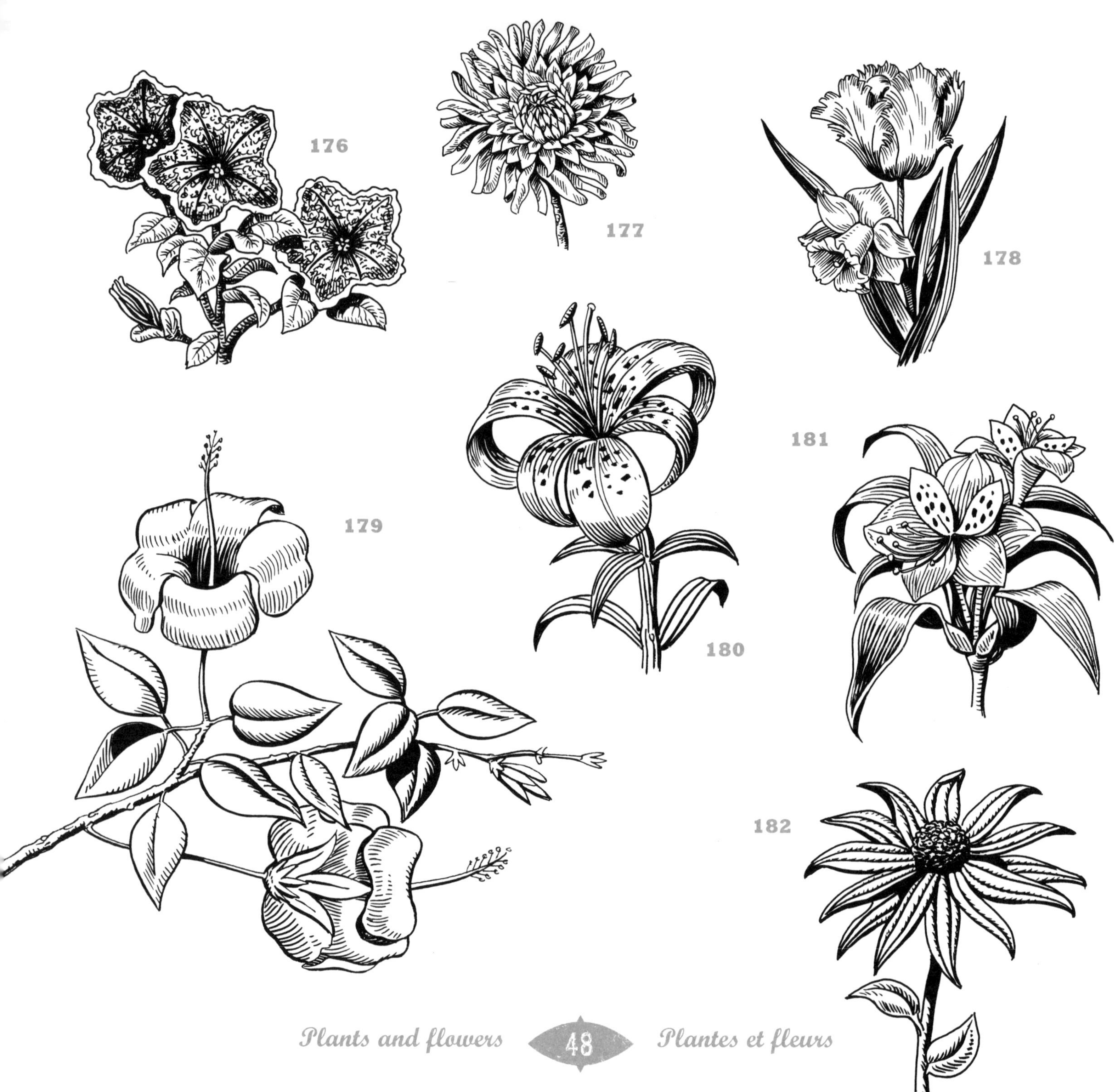

176
177
178
179
180
181
182

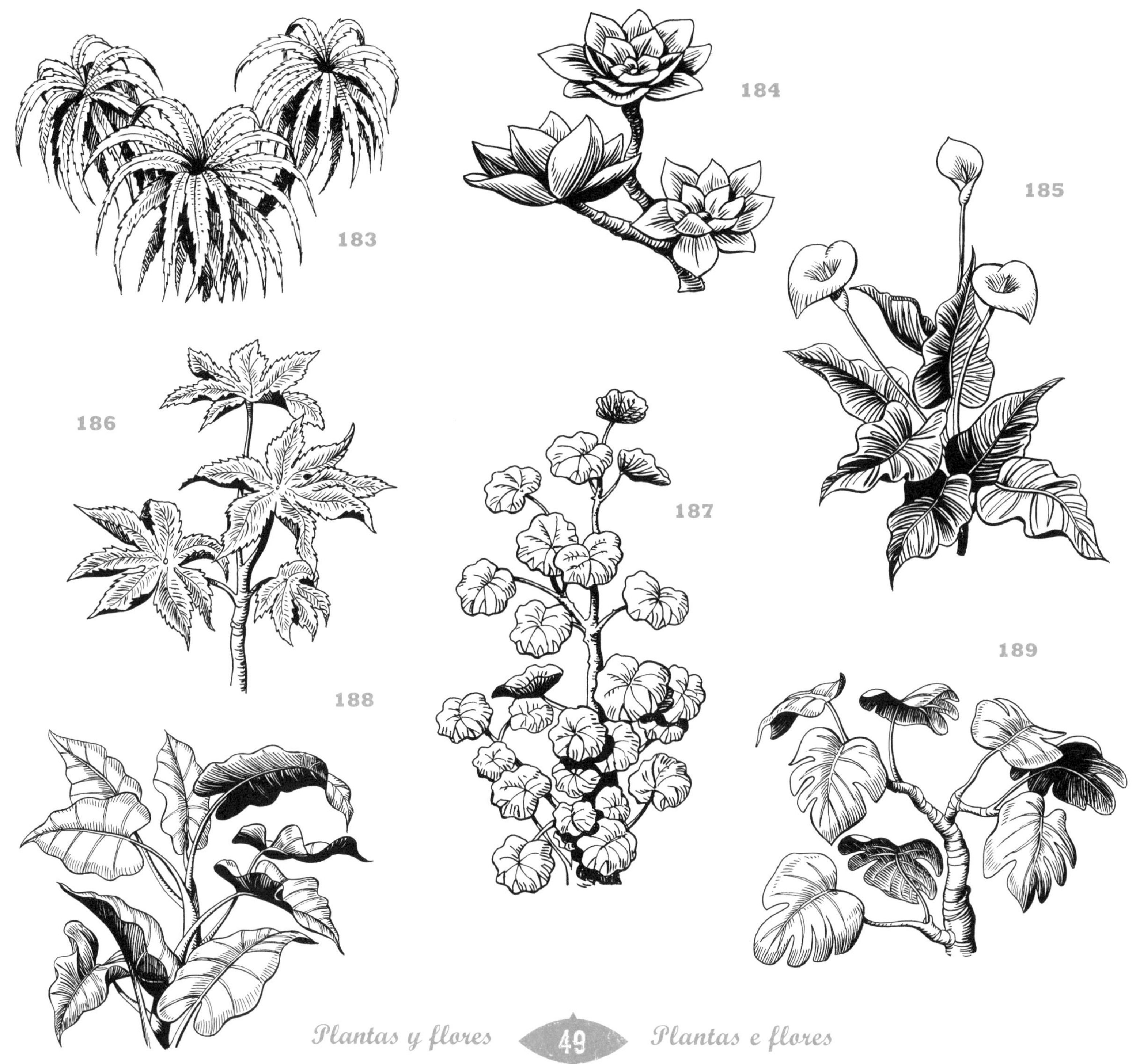

183
184
185
186
187
188
189

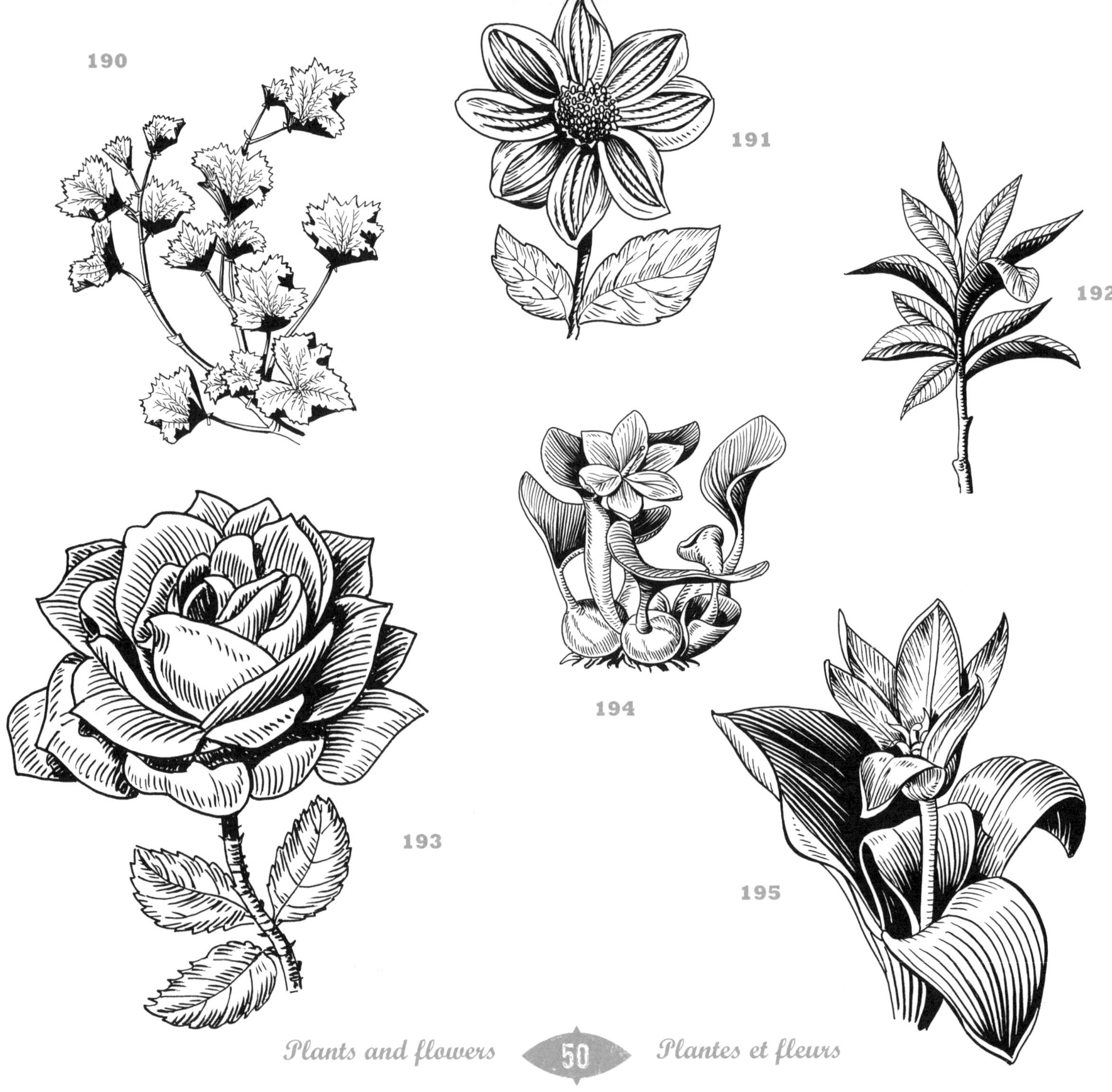
190
191
192
193
194
195

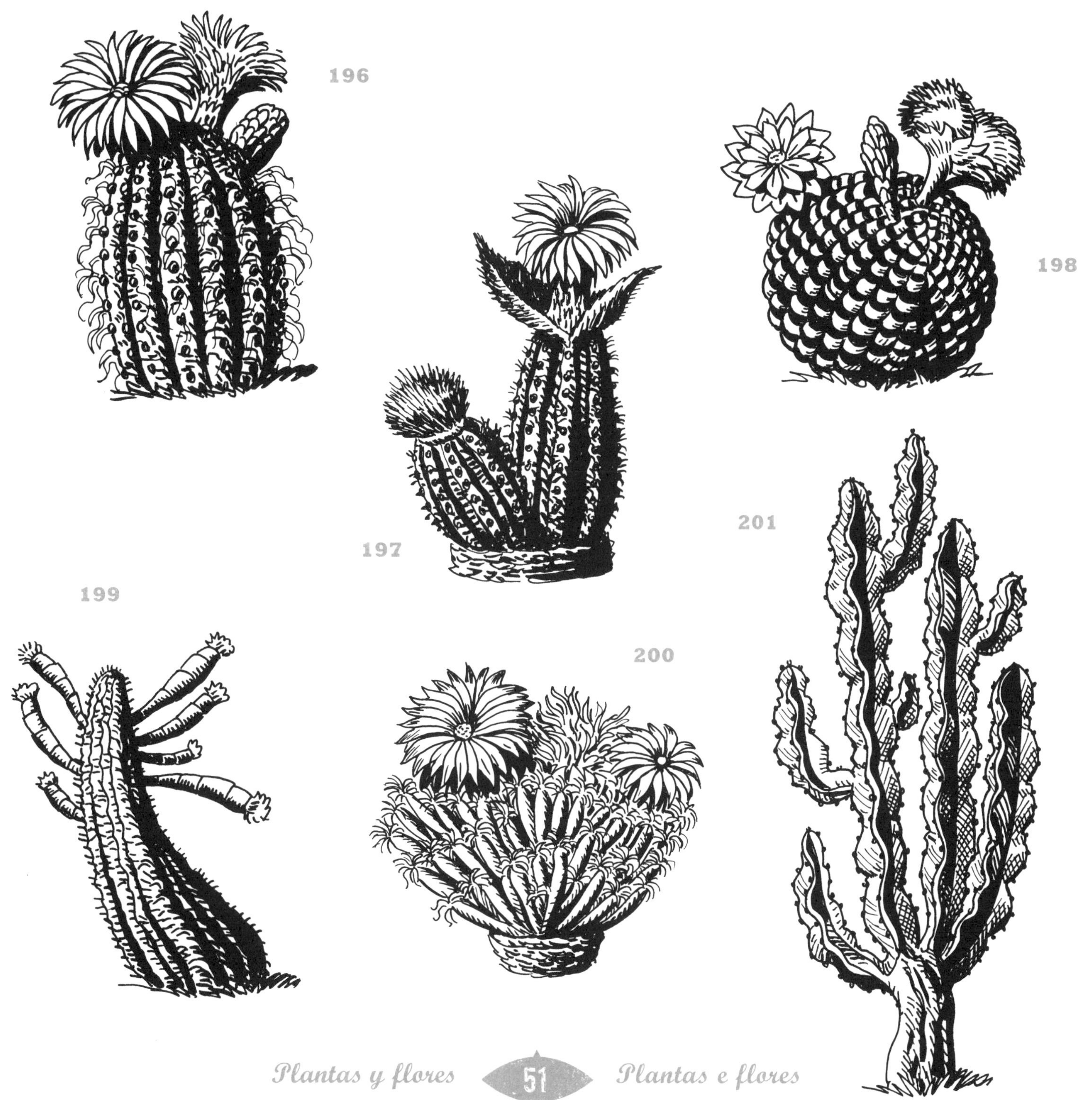
196
197
198
199
200
201

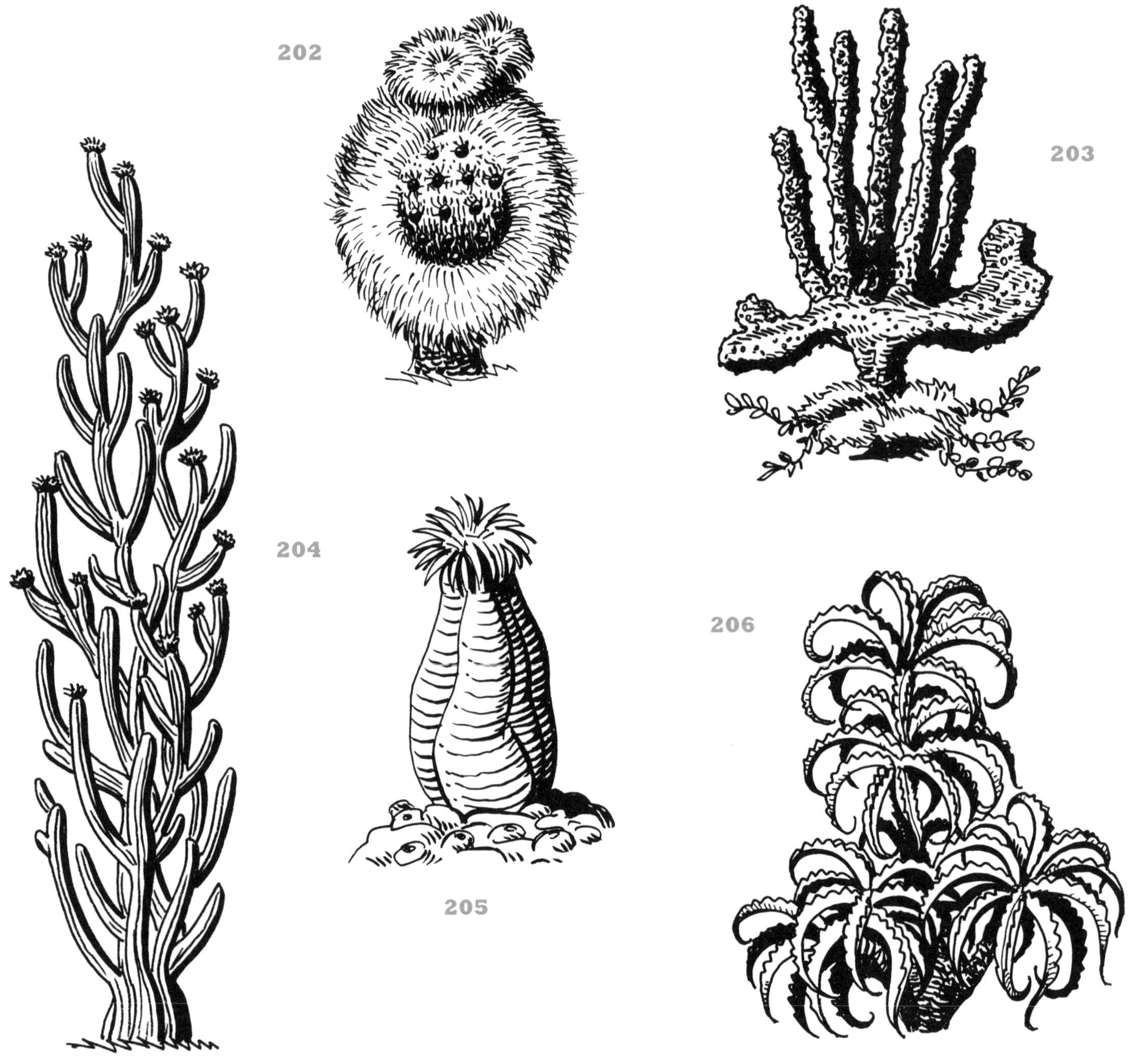

202
203
204
205
206

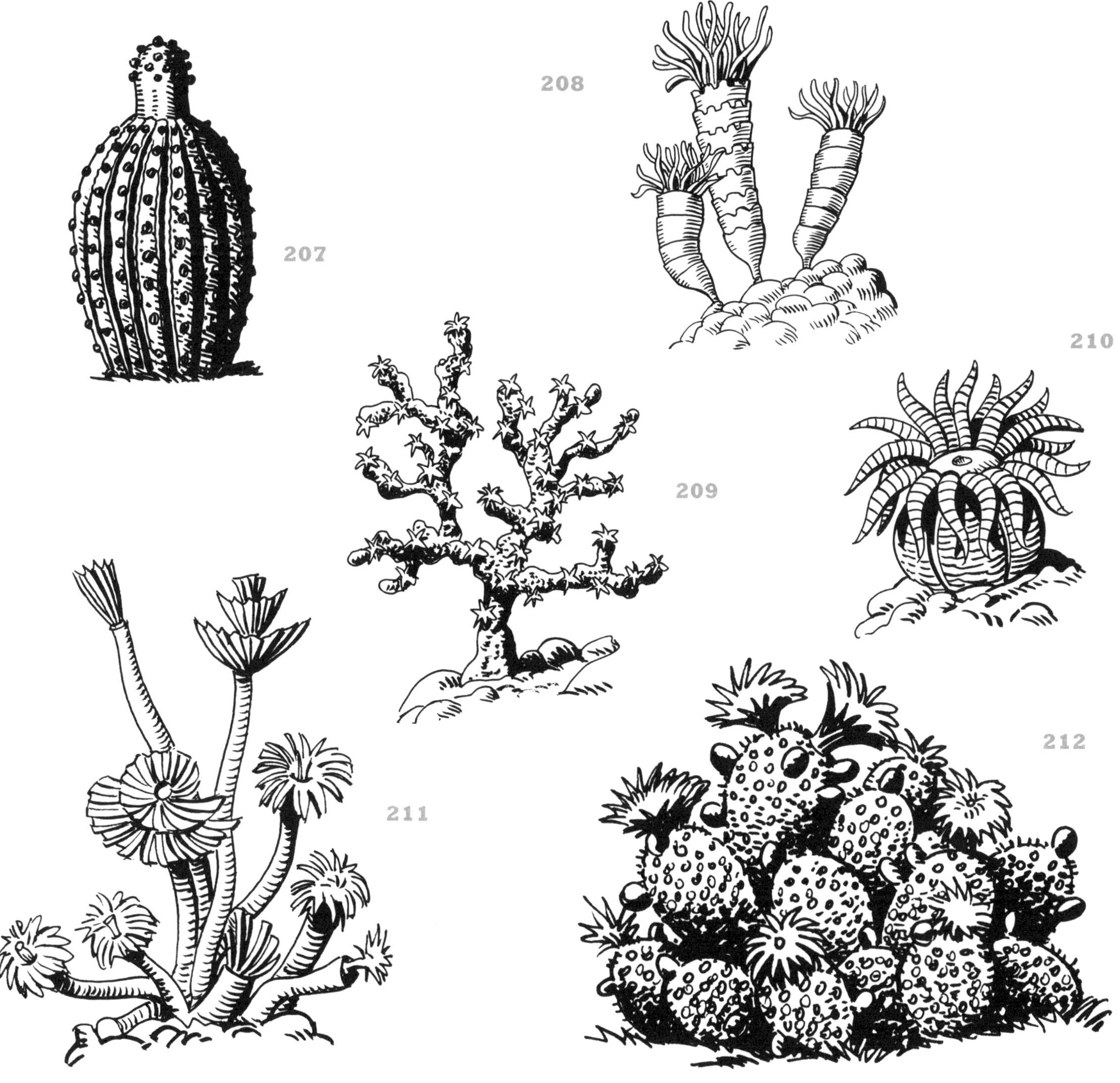

207
208
209
210
211
212

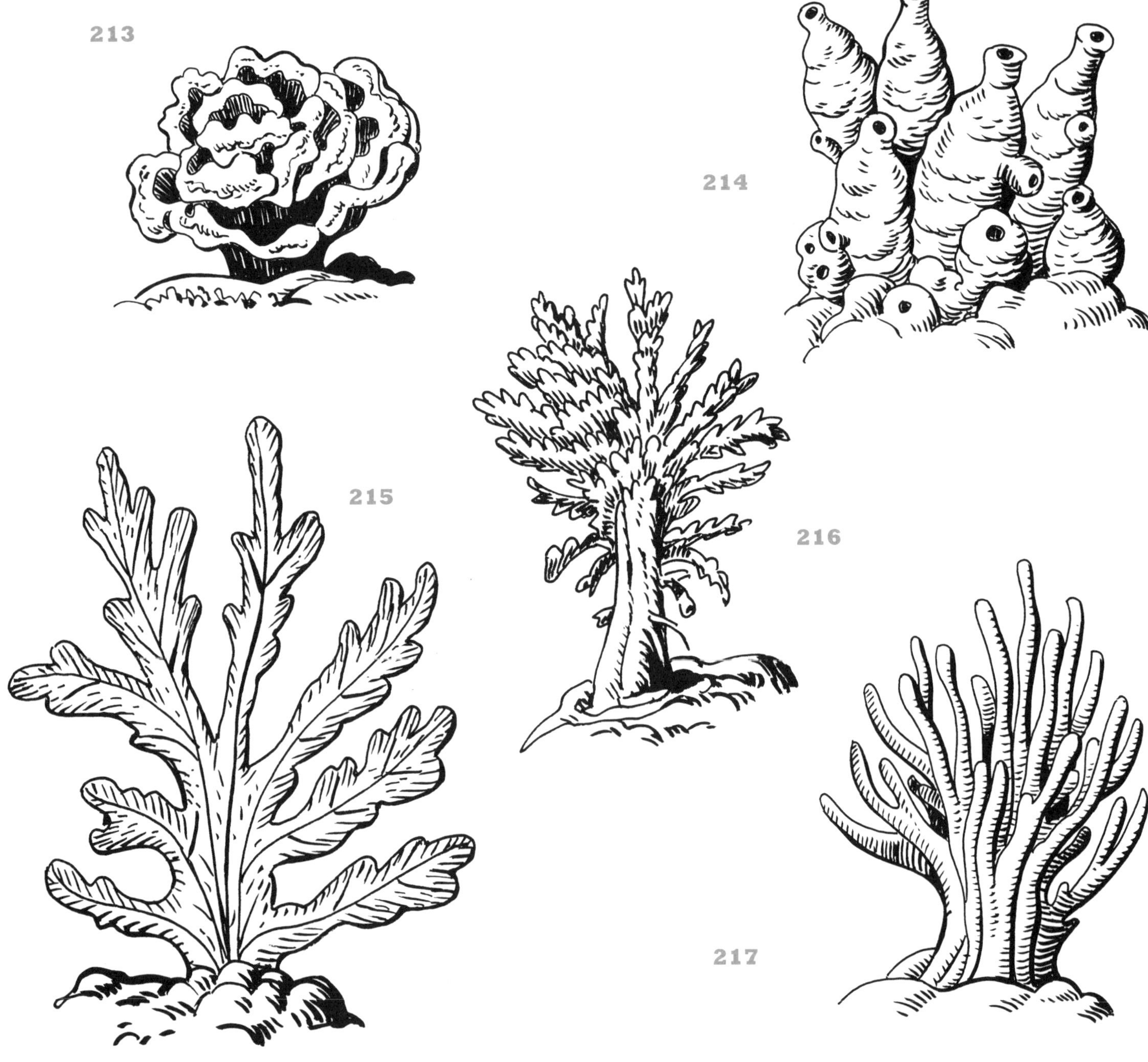
213
214
215
216
217

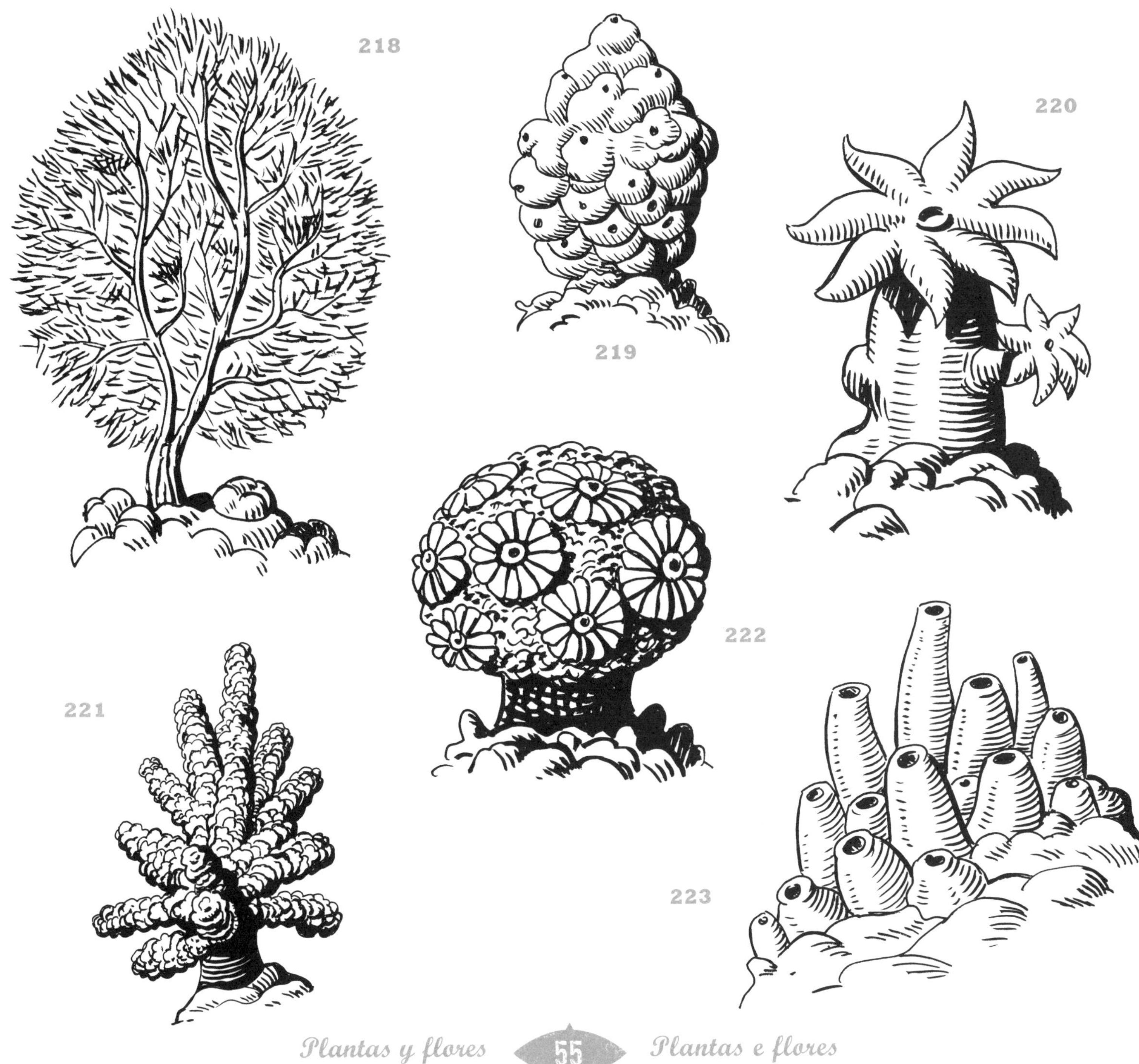
218
219
220
221
222
223

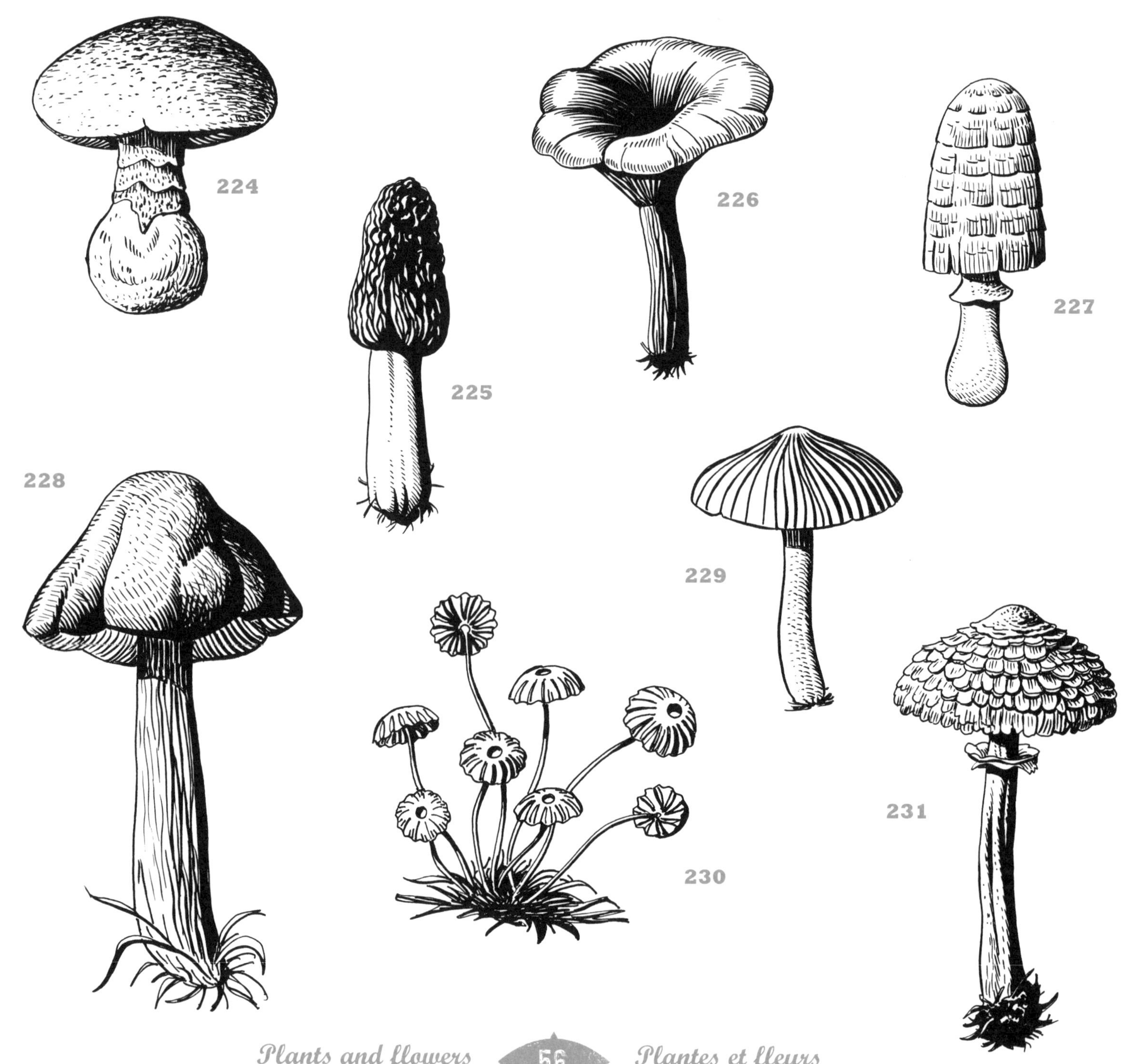
224
225
226
227
228
229
230
231

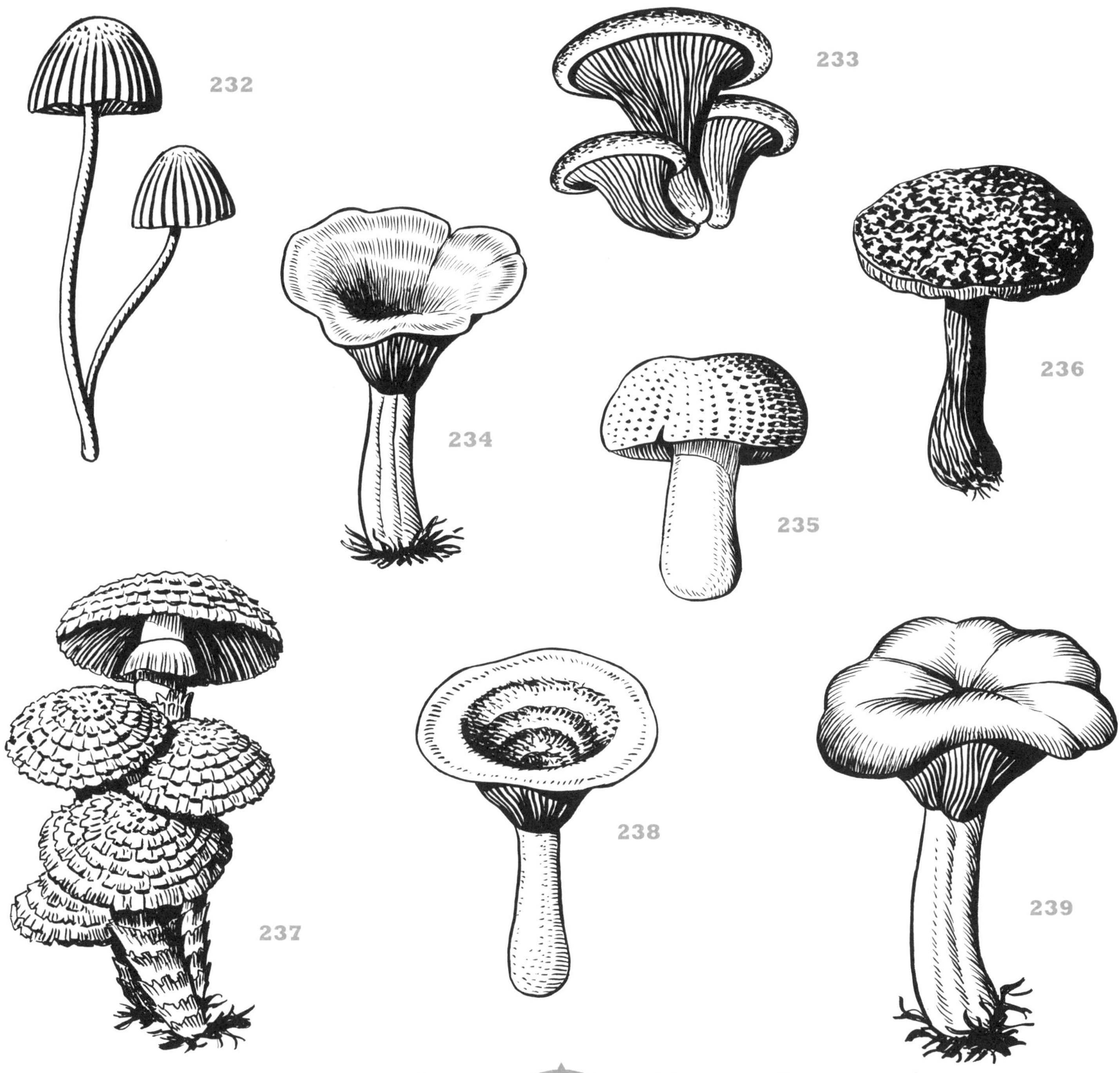

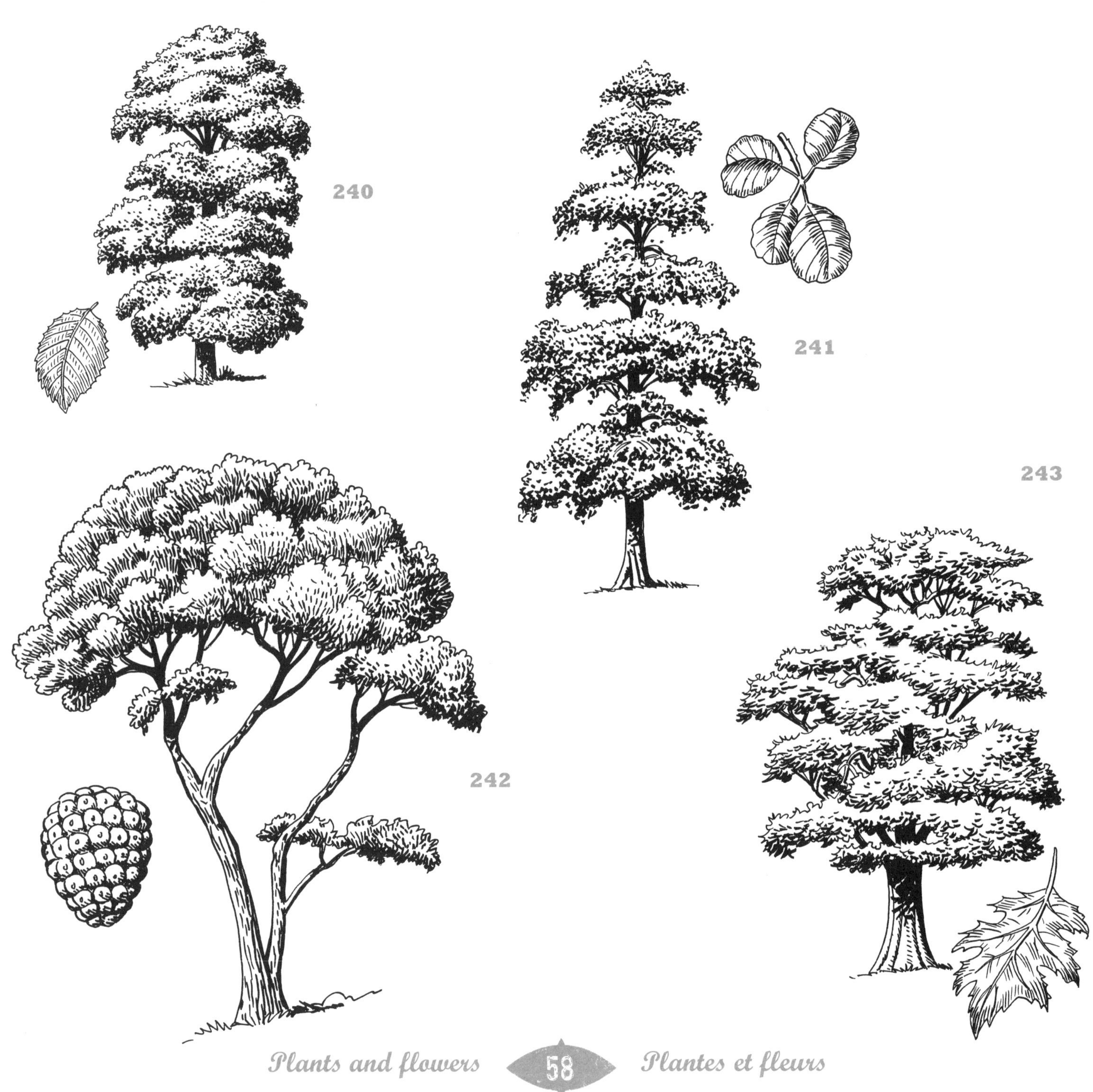
240
241
242
243

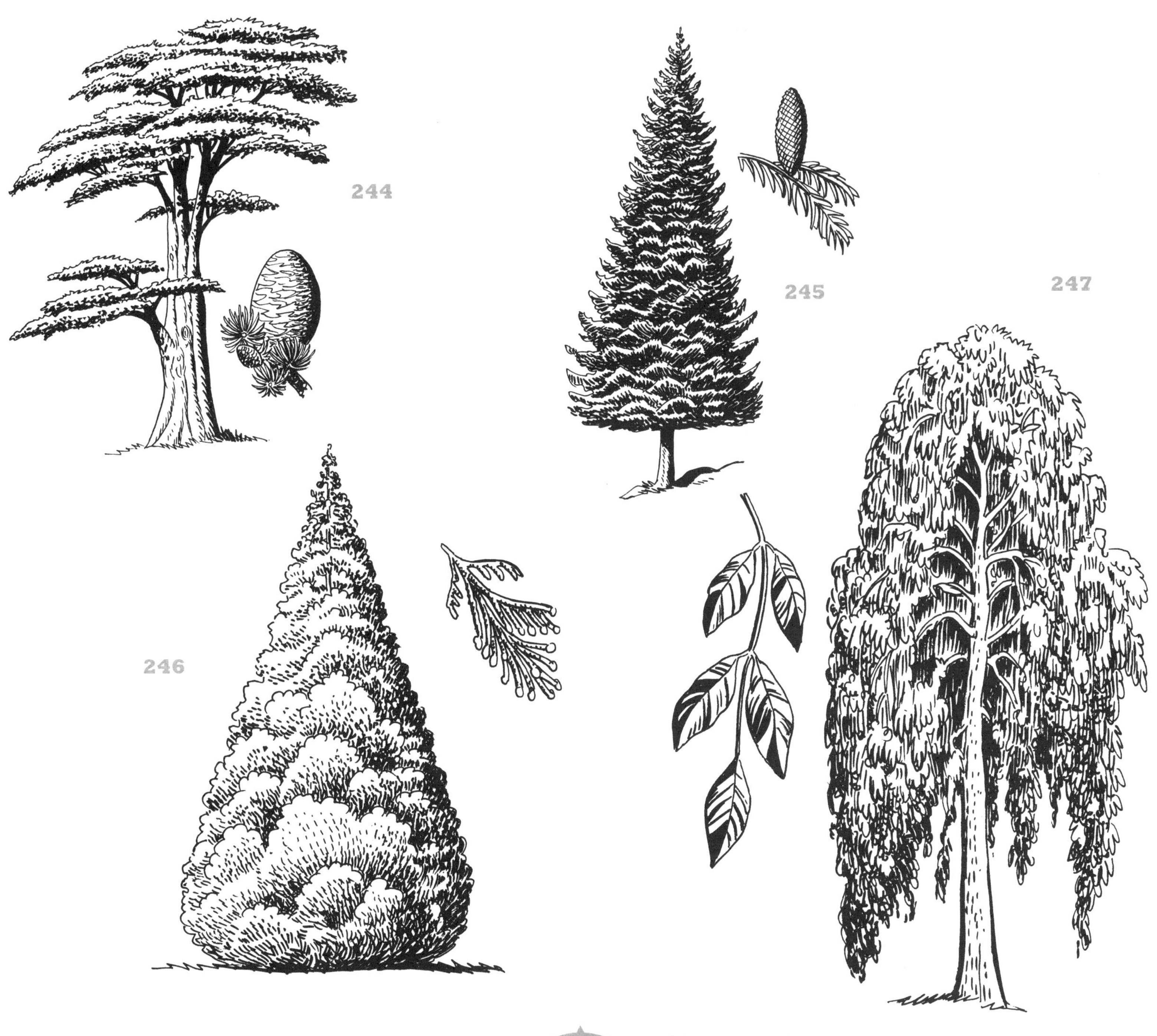

244
245
246
247

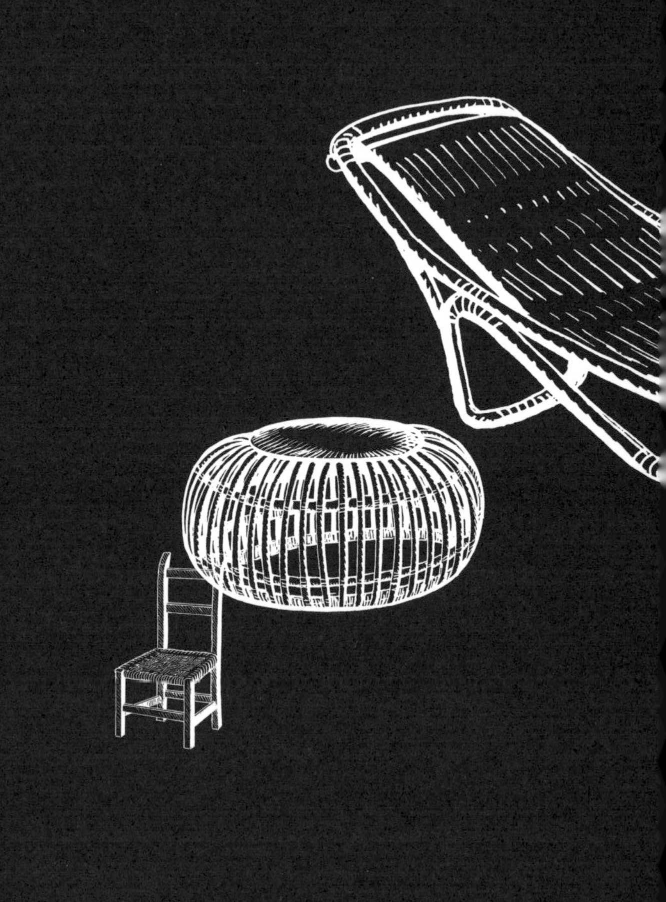

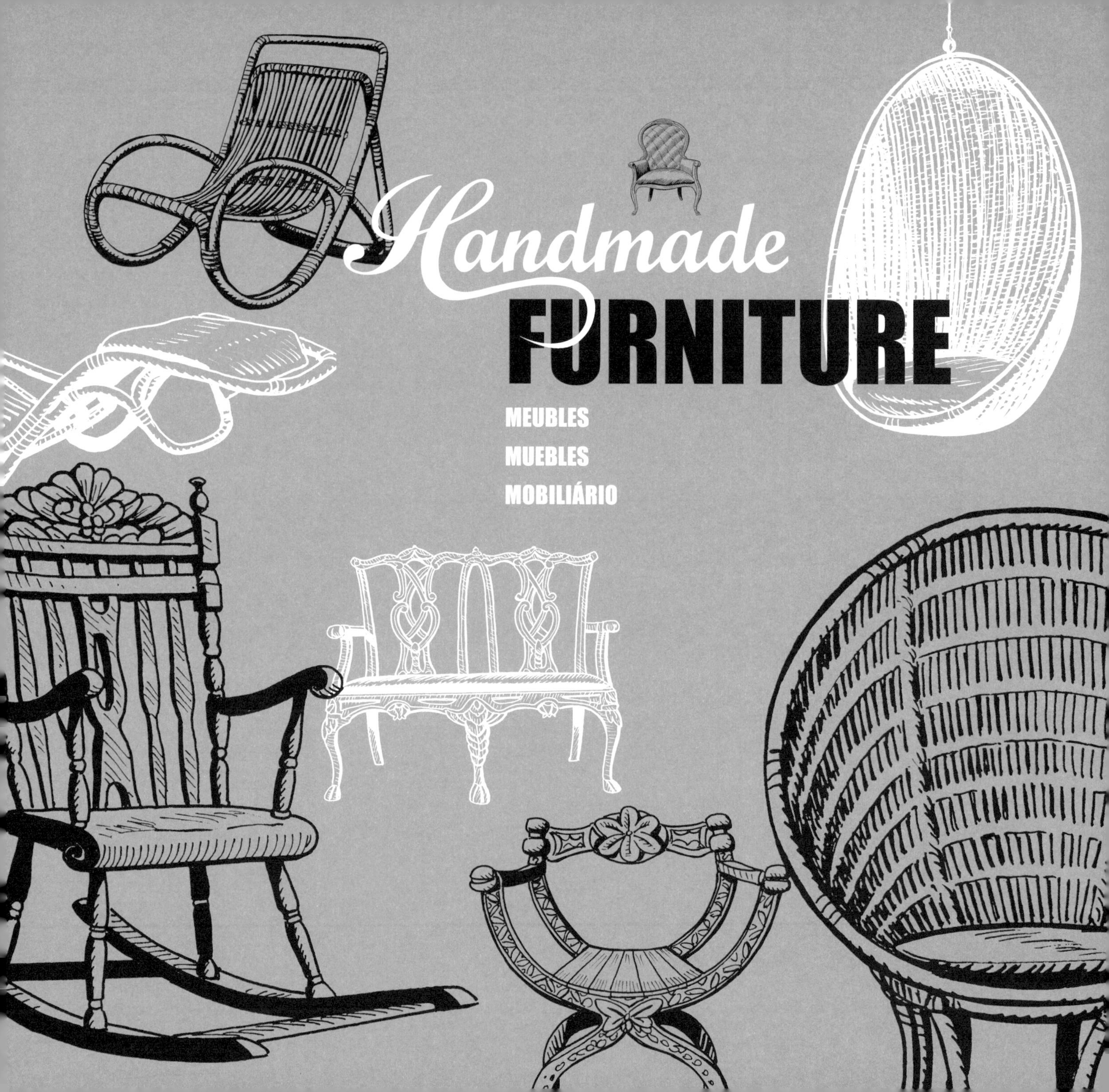

Handmade
FURNITURE
MEUBLES
MUEBLES
MOBILIÁRIO

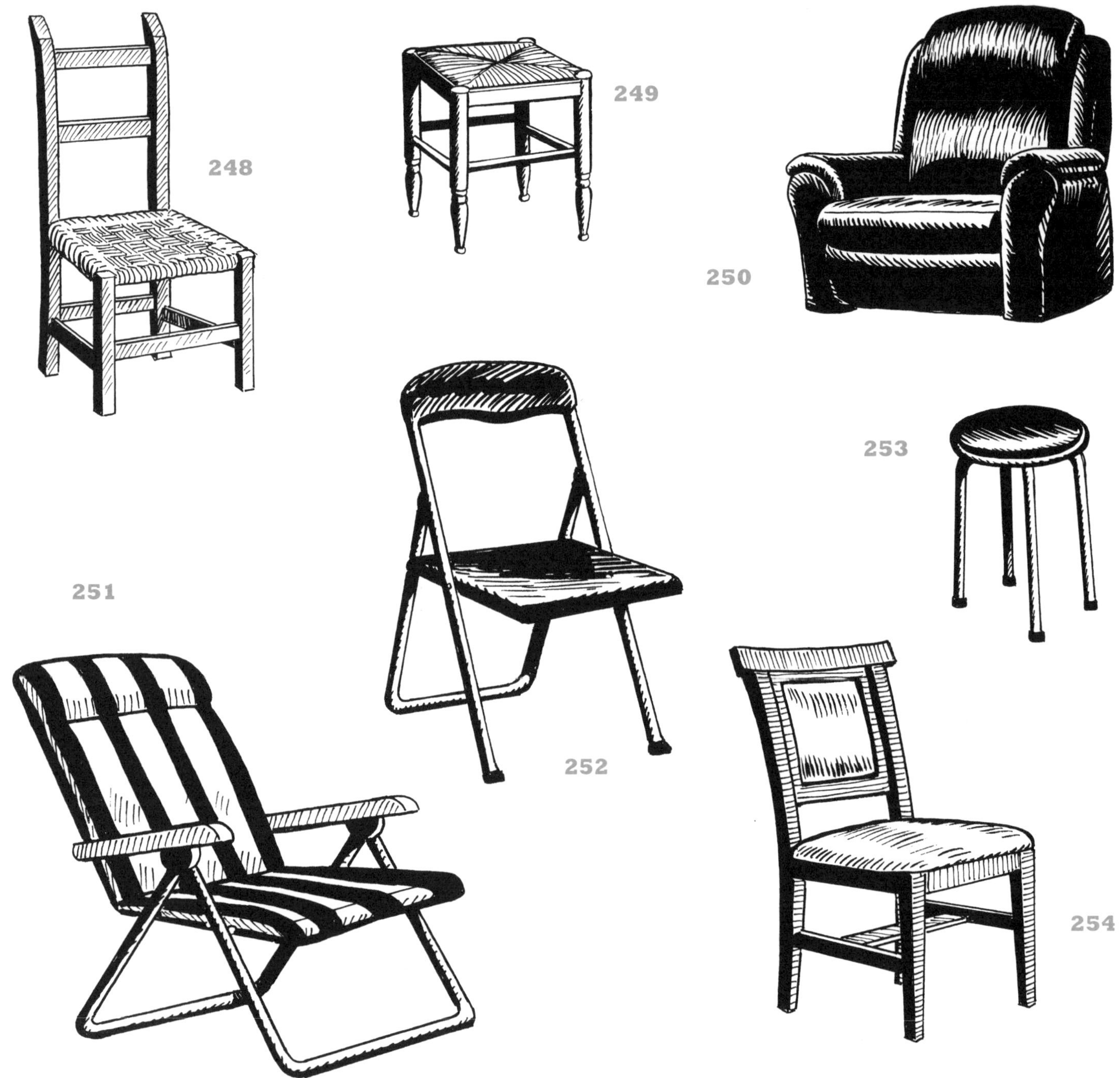

248
249
250
251
252
253
254

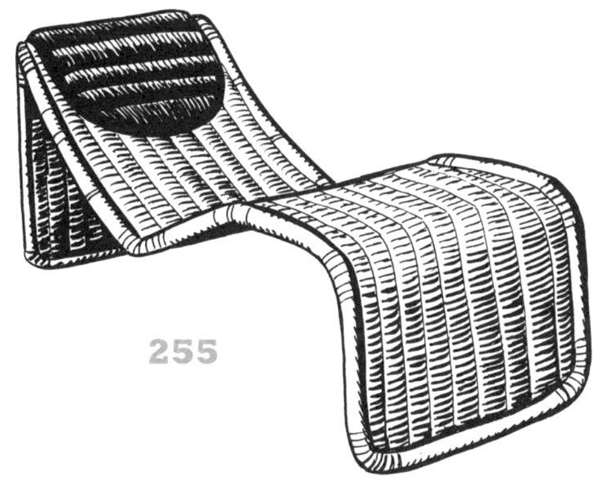

255

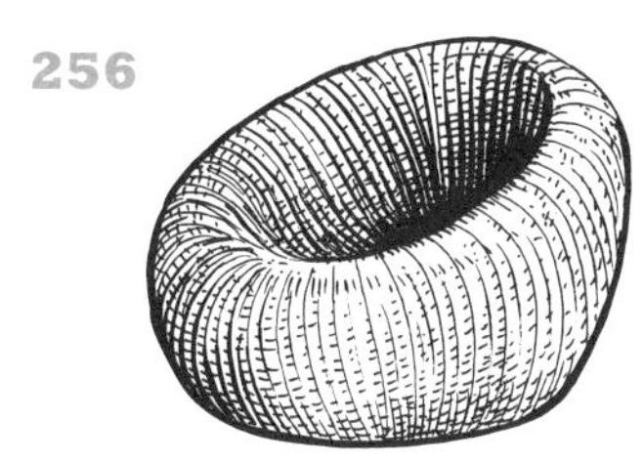

256

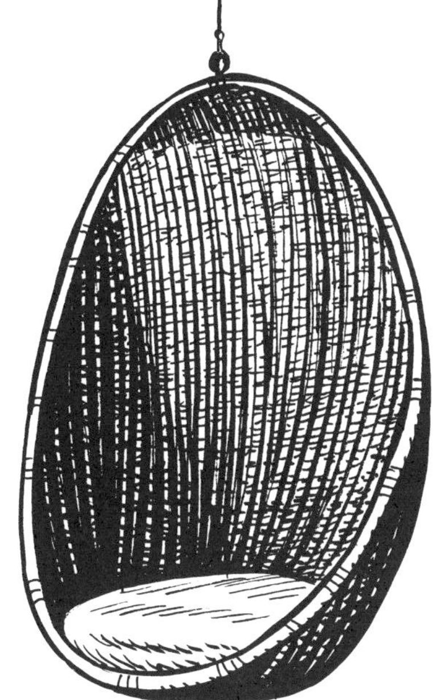

257

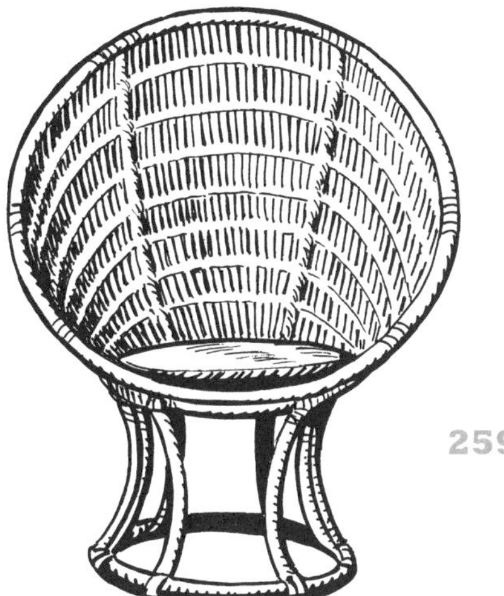

259

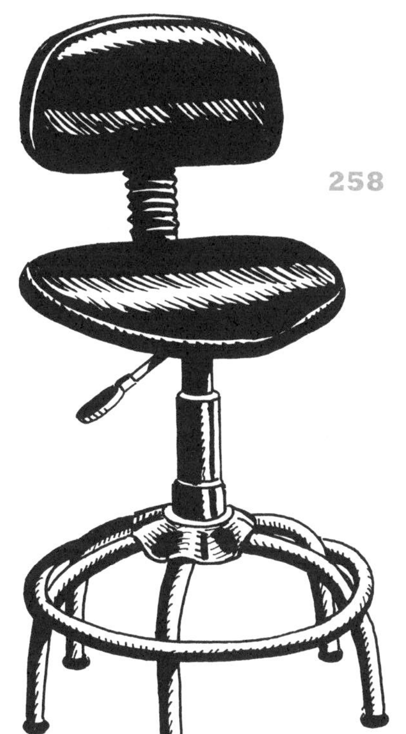

258

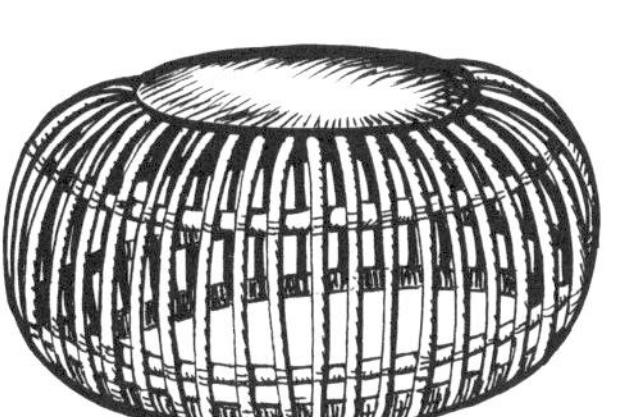

260

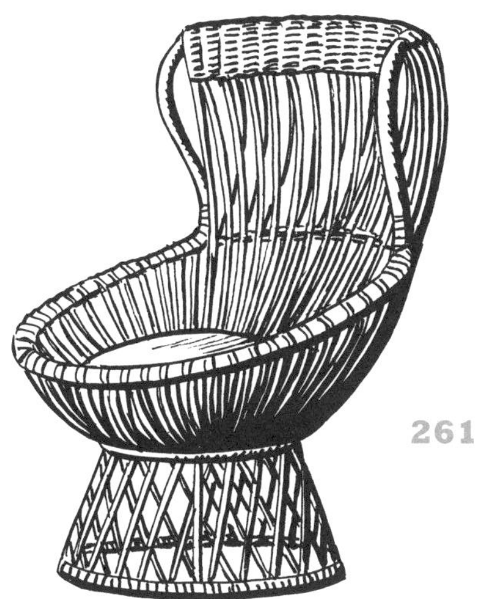

261

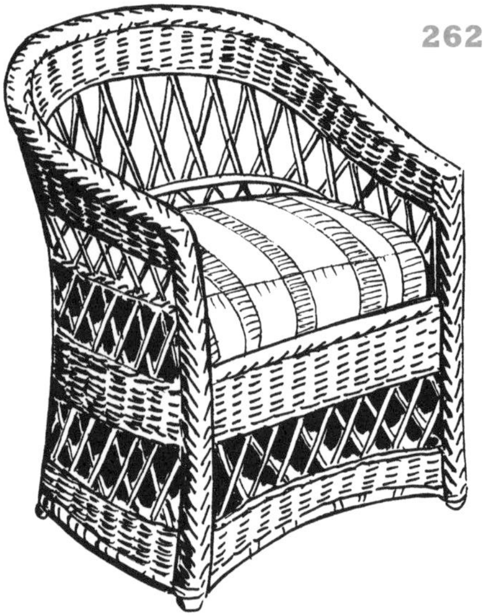

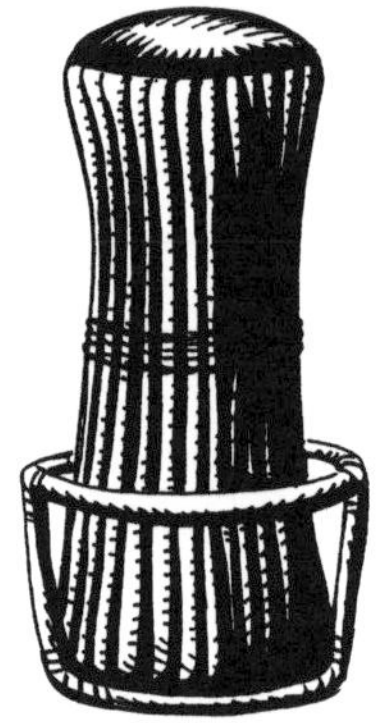

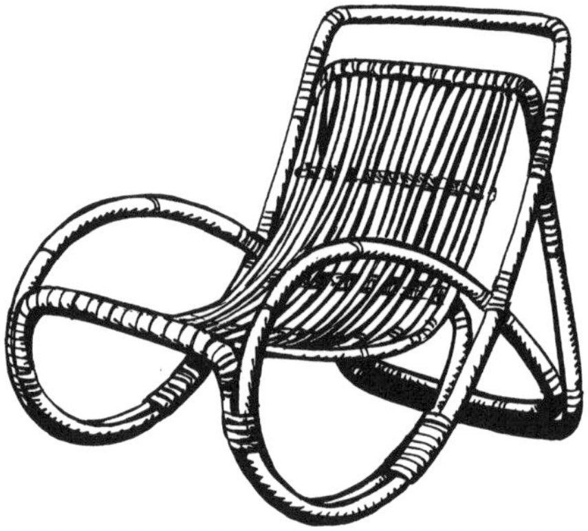

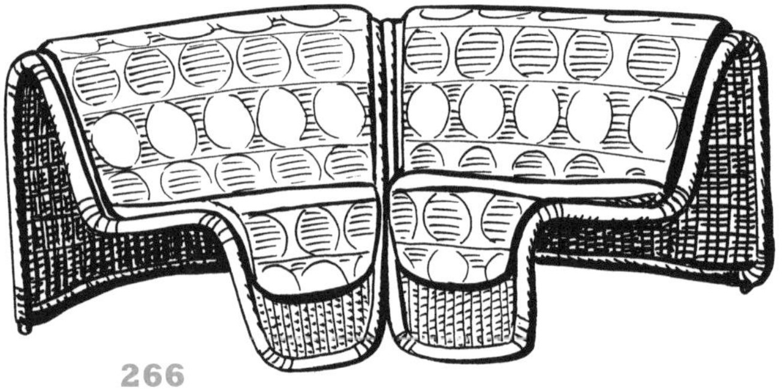

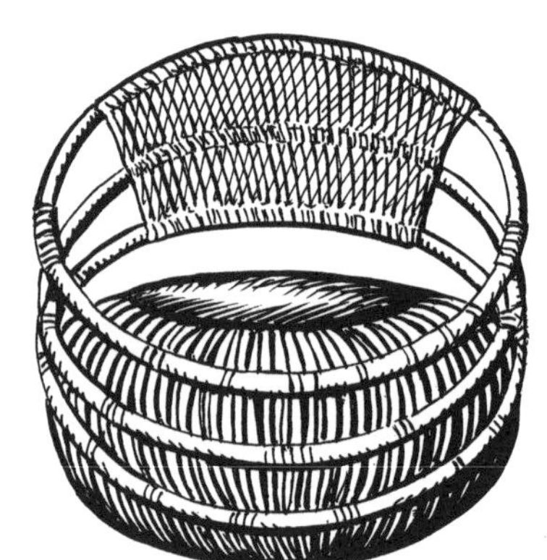

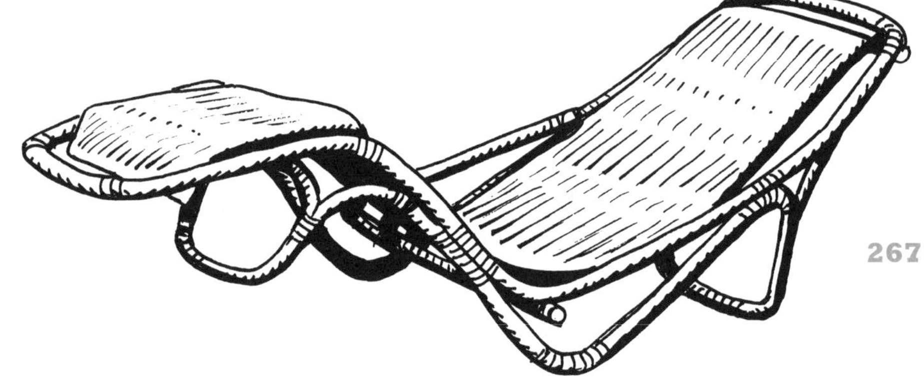

268

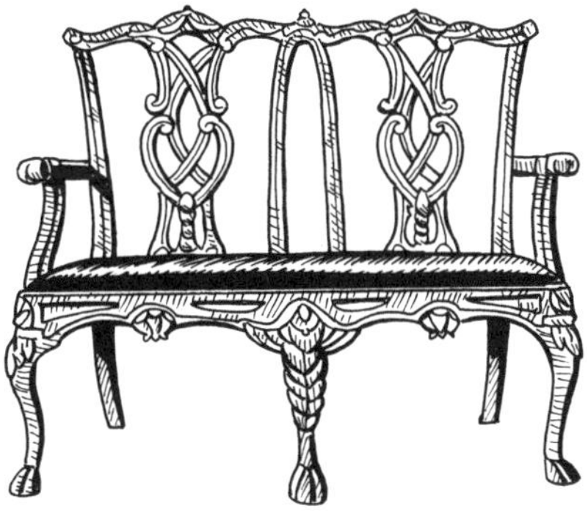

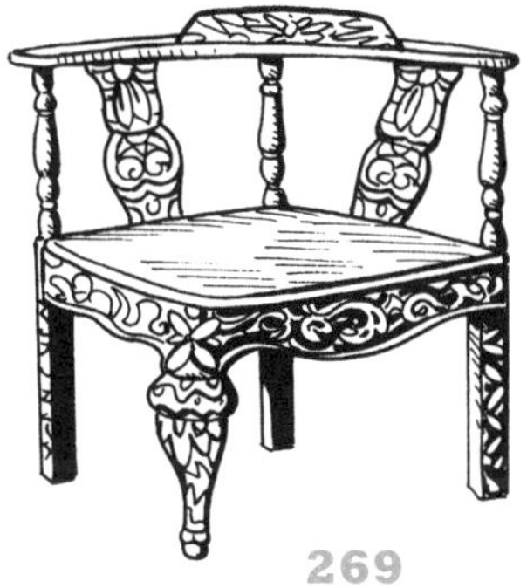

269

270

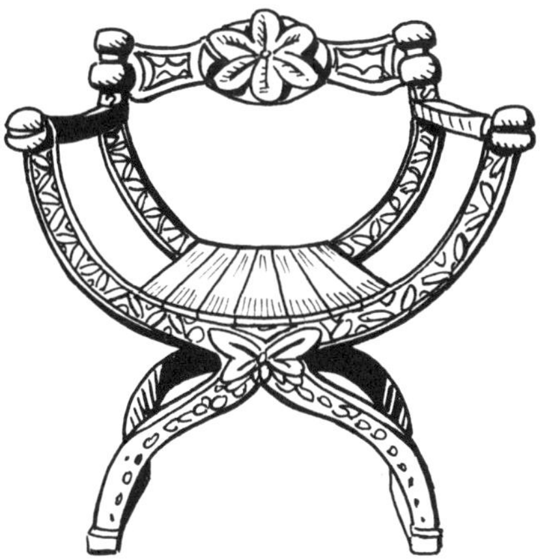

271

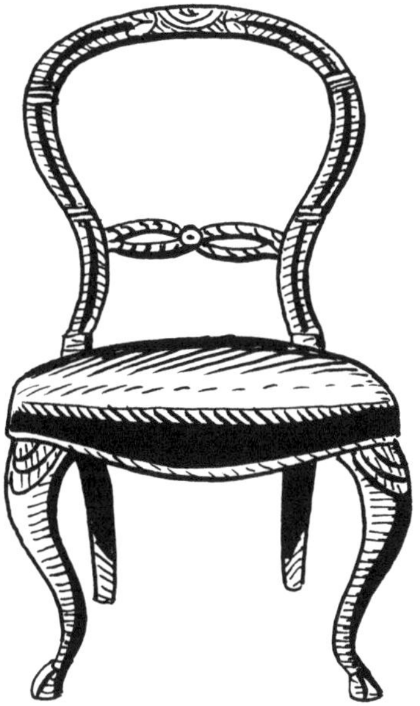

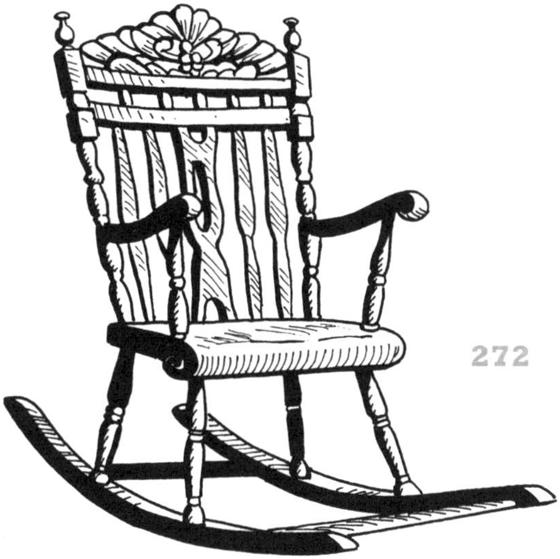

272

273

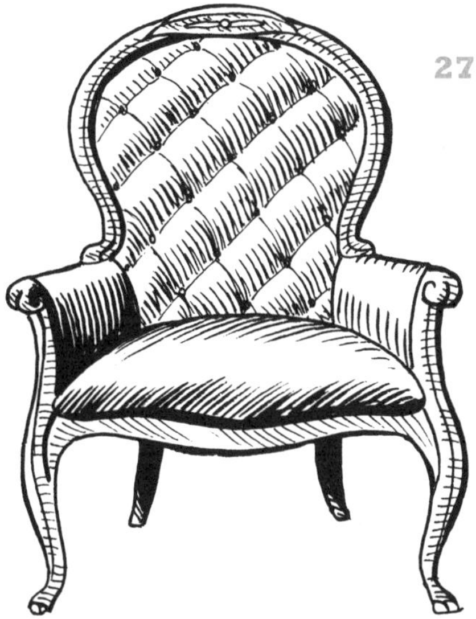

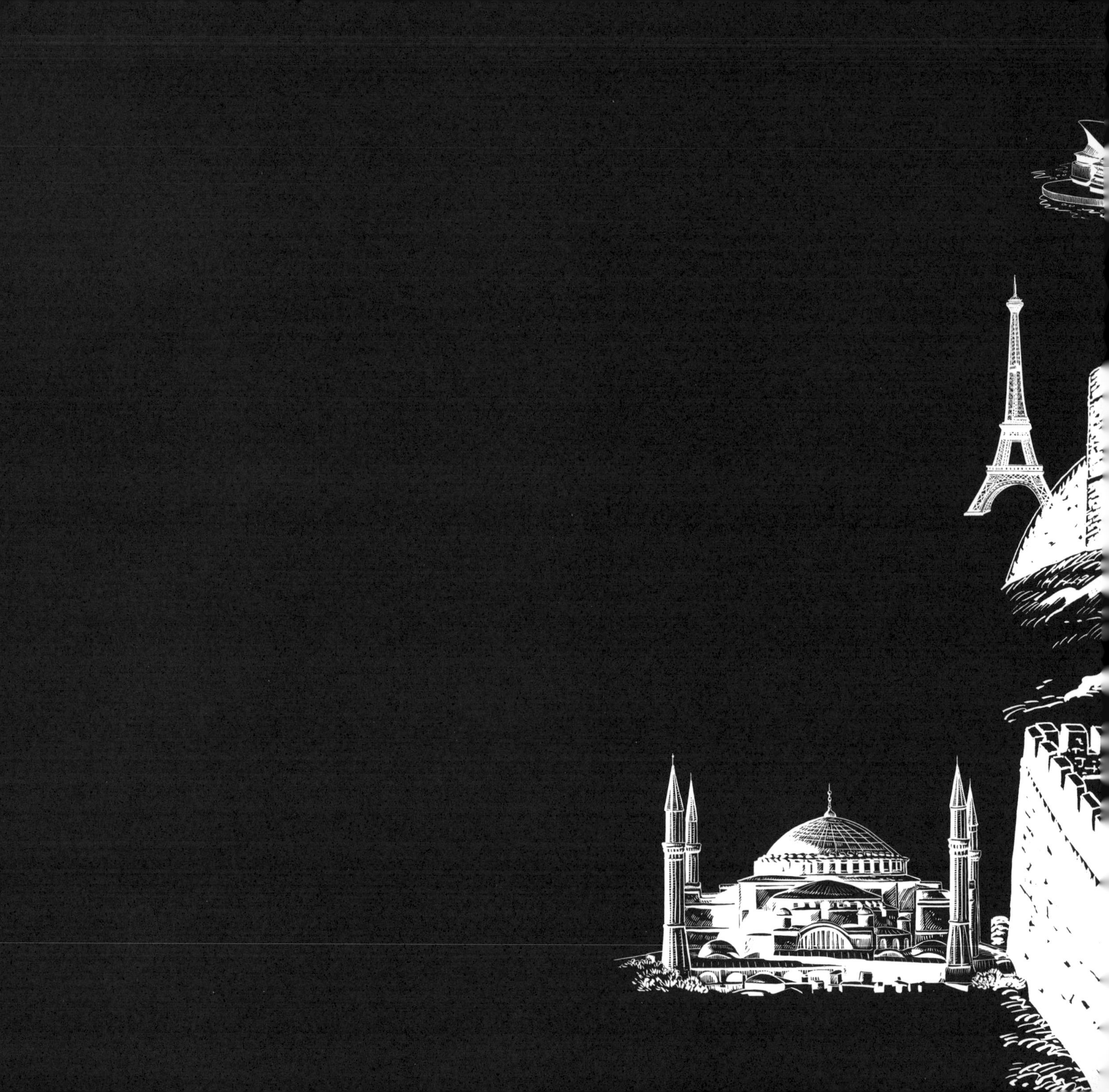

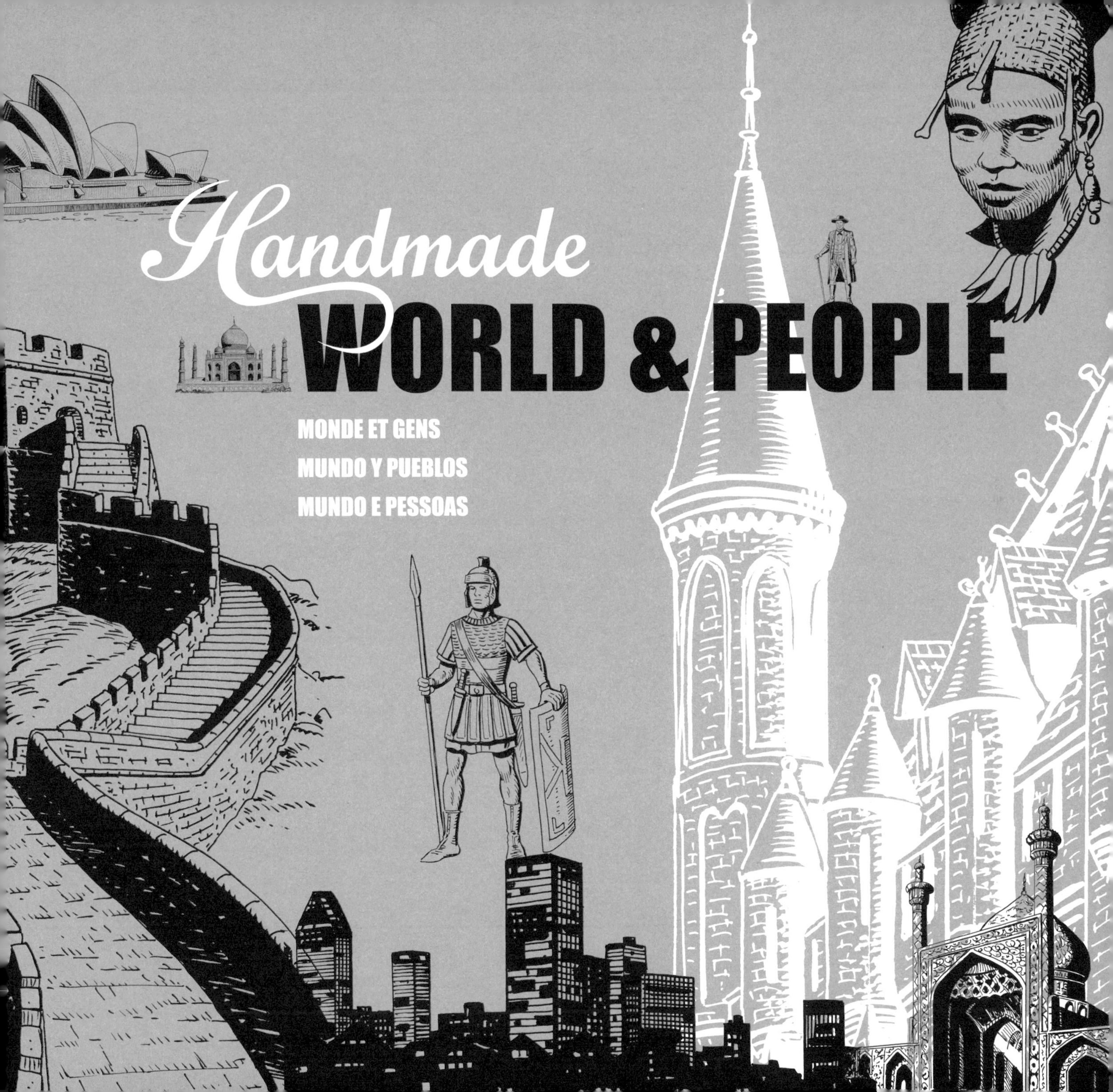
Handmade
WORLD & PEOPLE
MONDE ET GENS
MUNDO Y PUEBLOS
MUNDO E PESSOAS

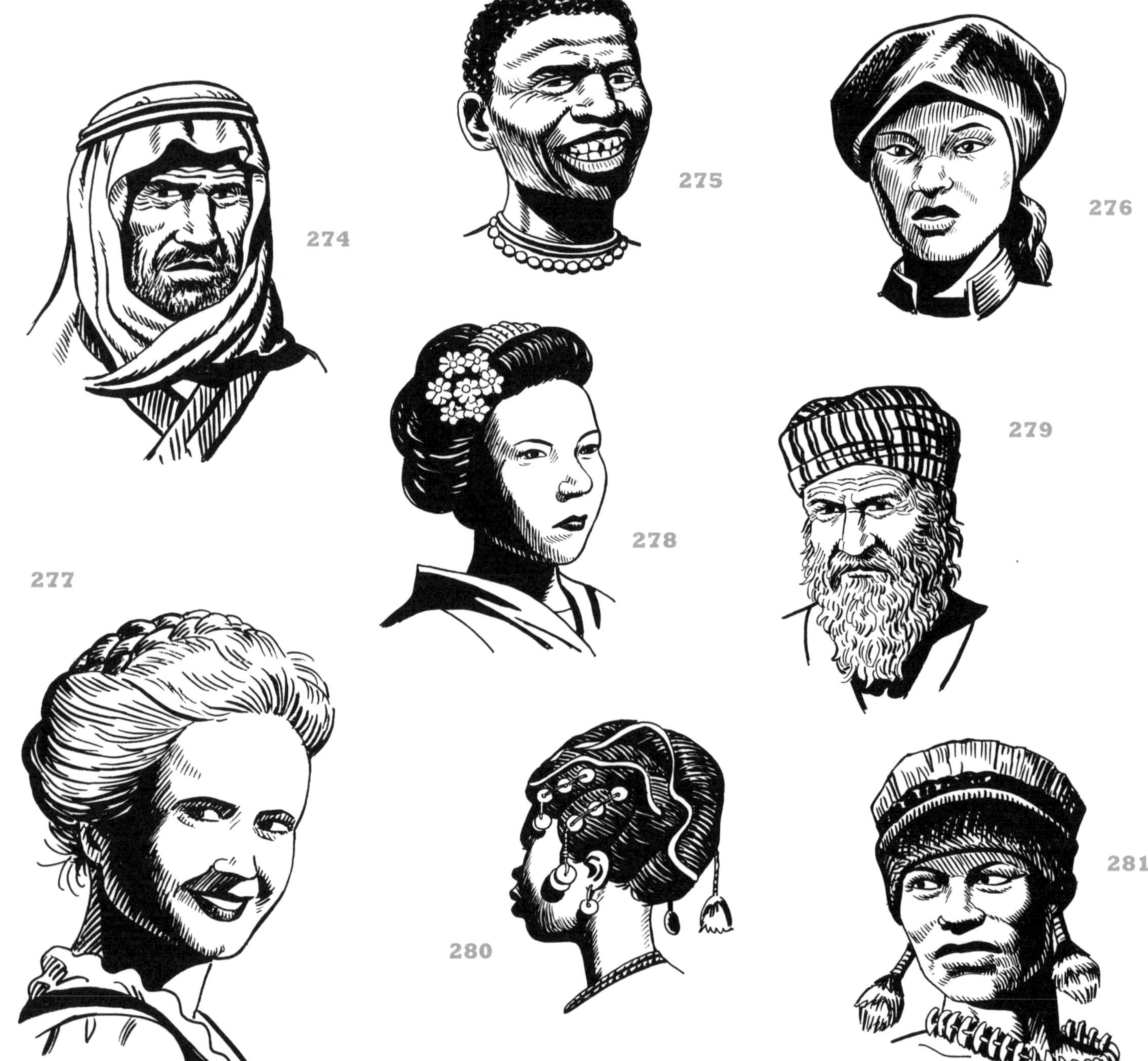

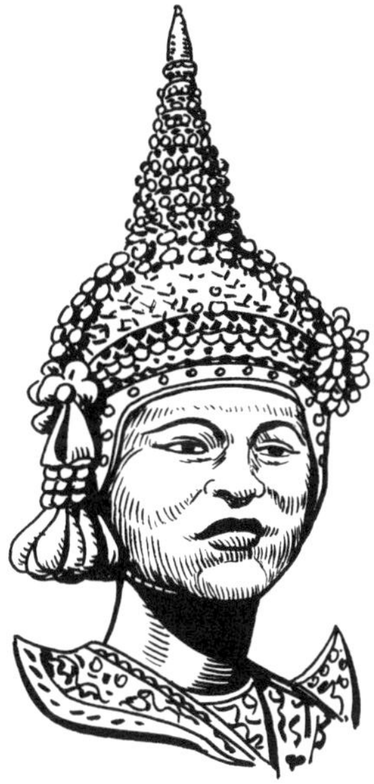

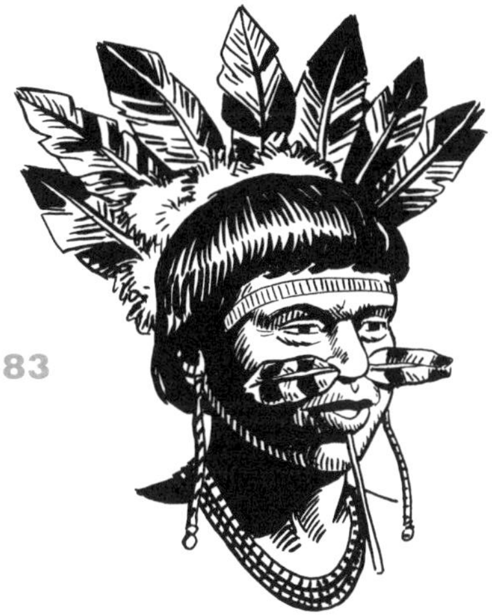

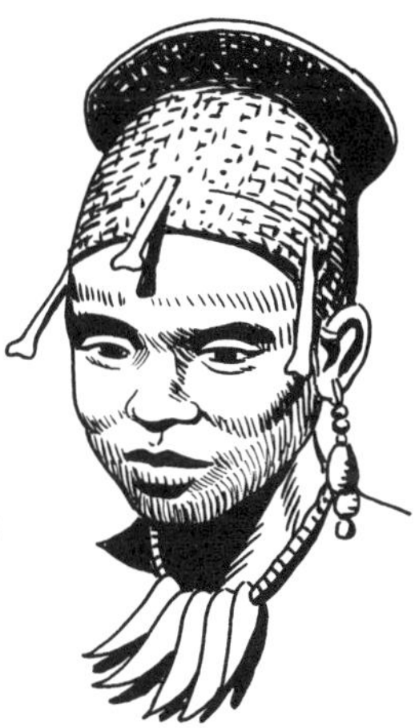

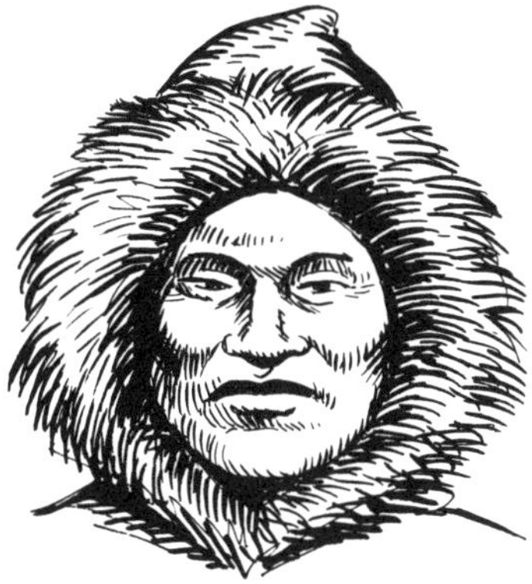

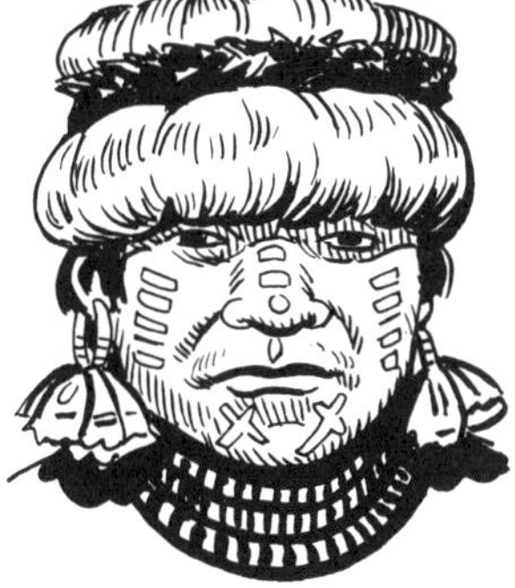

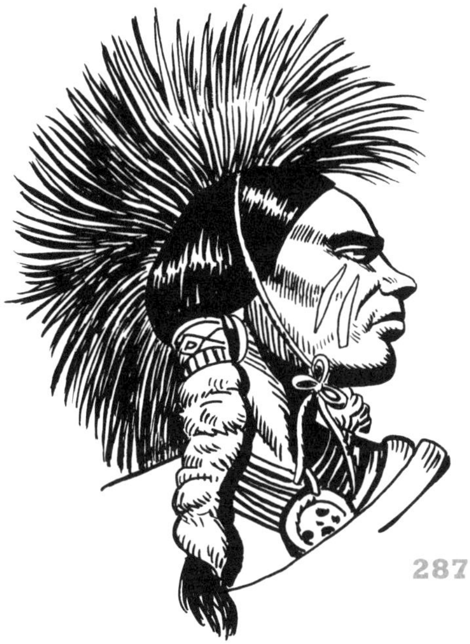

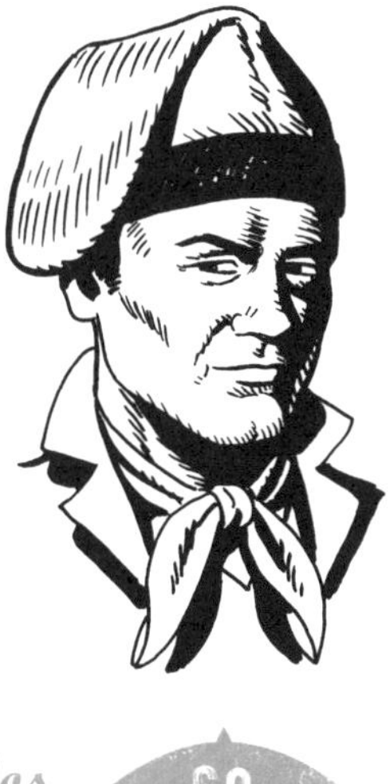

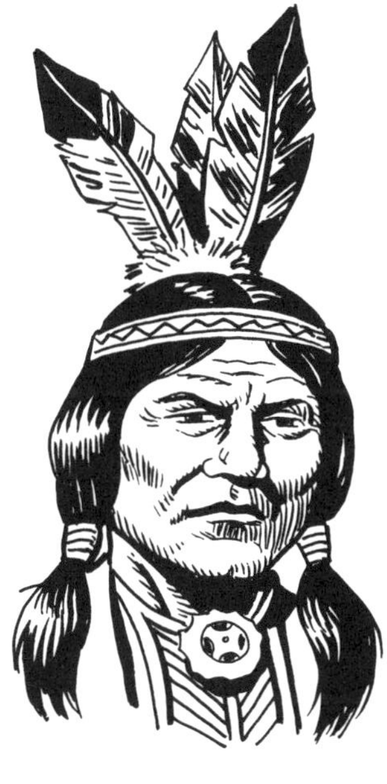

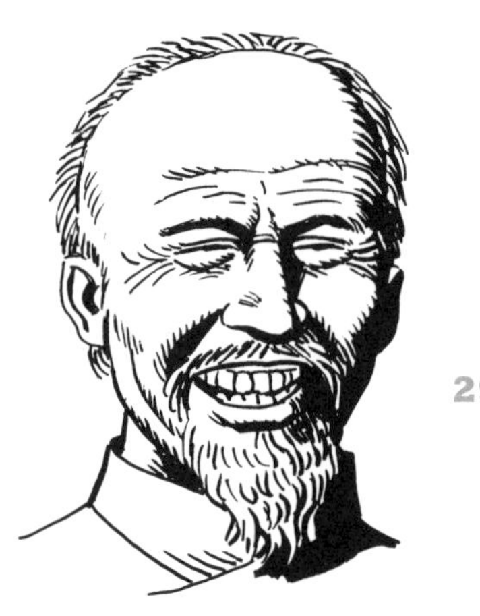

290

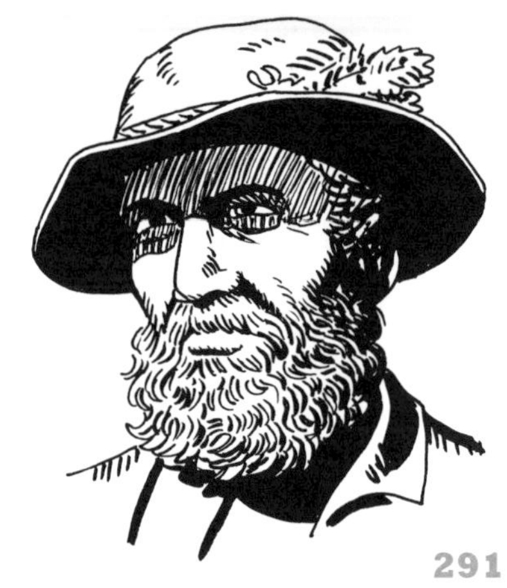

291

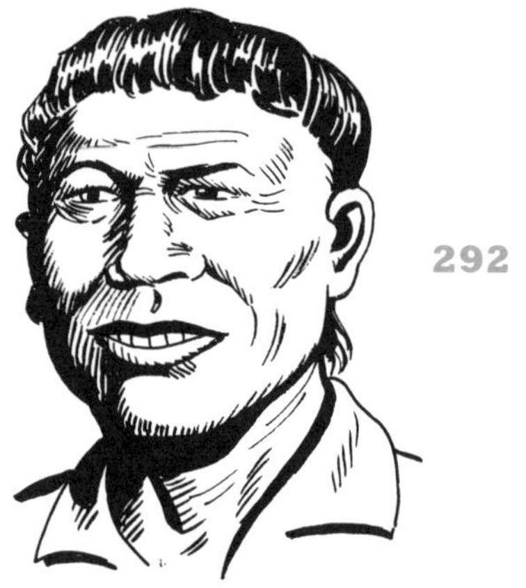

292

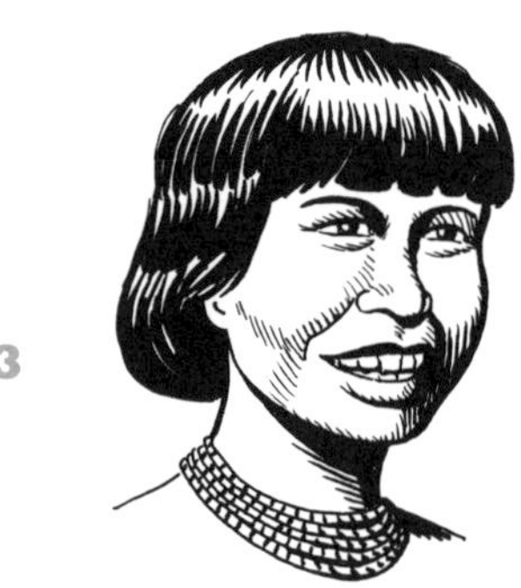

293

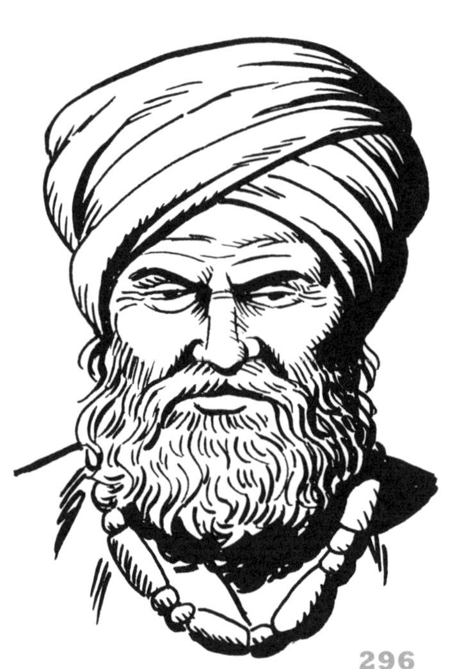

296

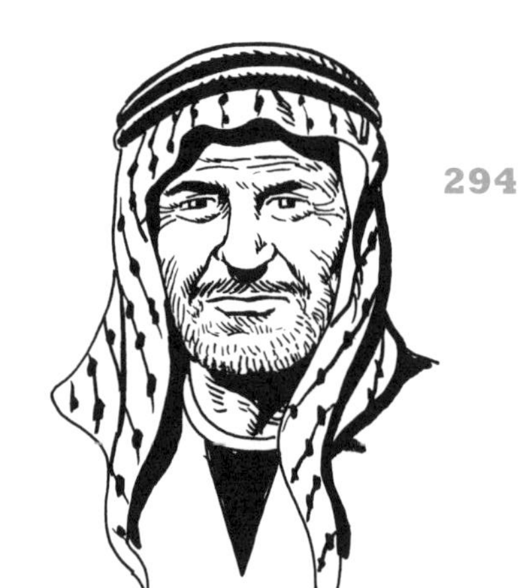

294

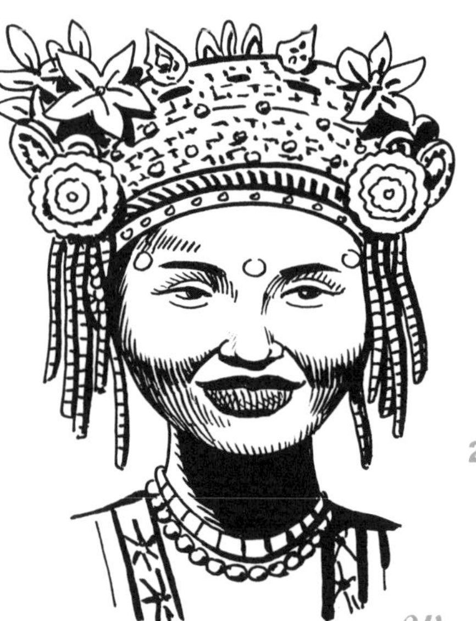

295

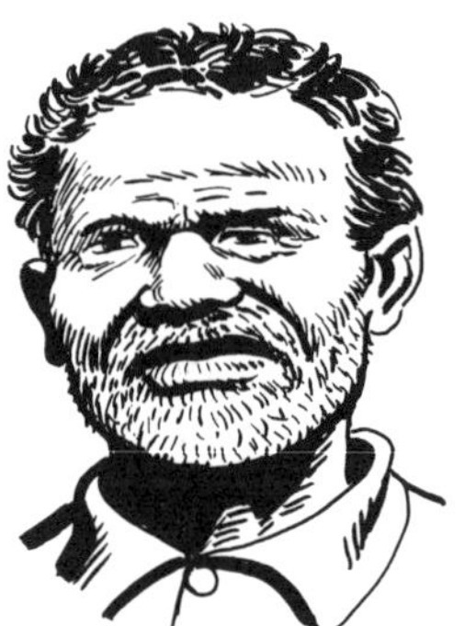

297

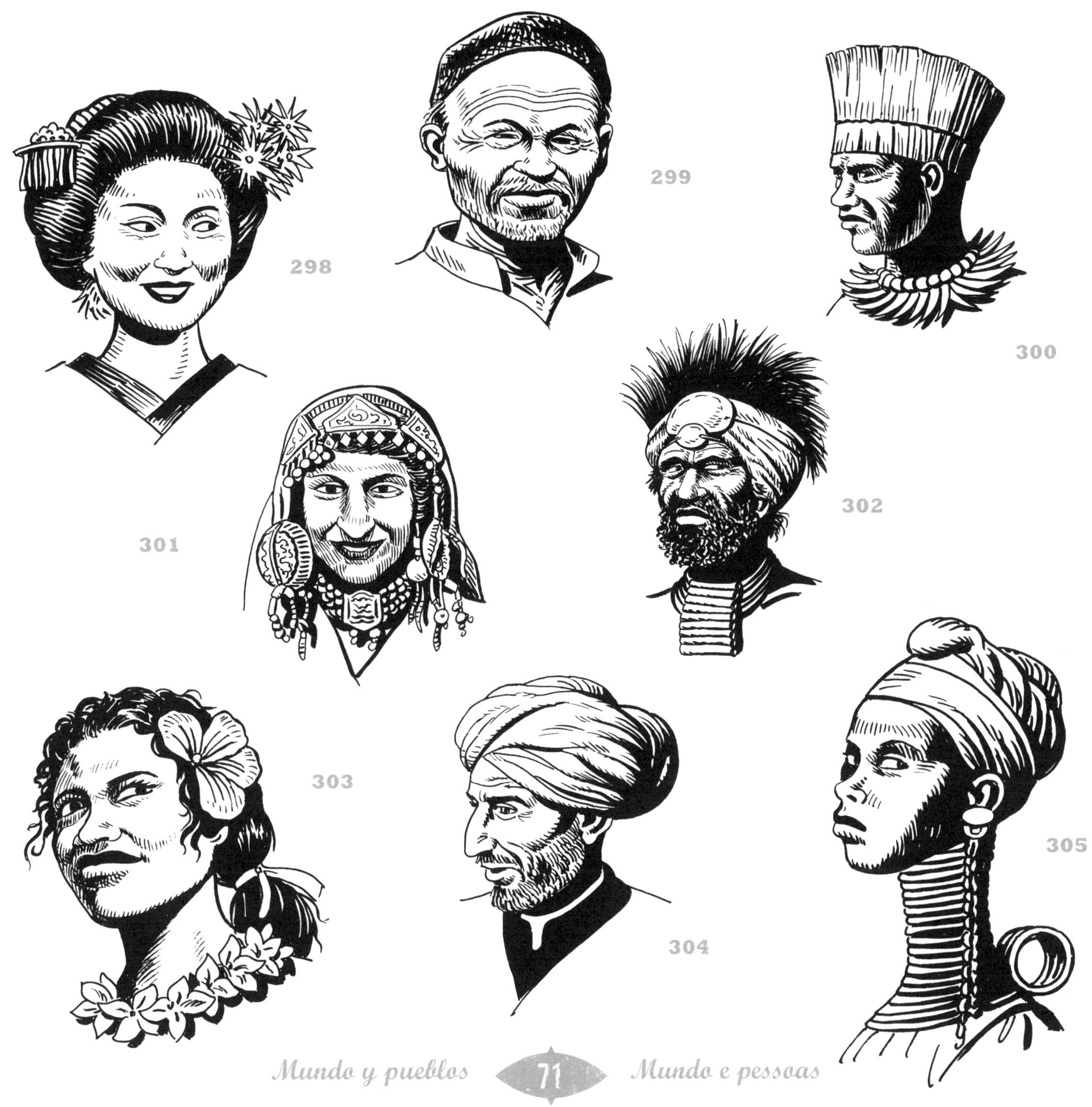

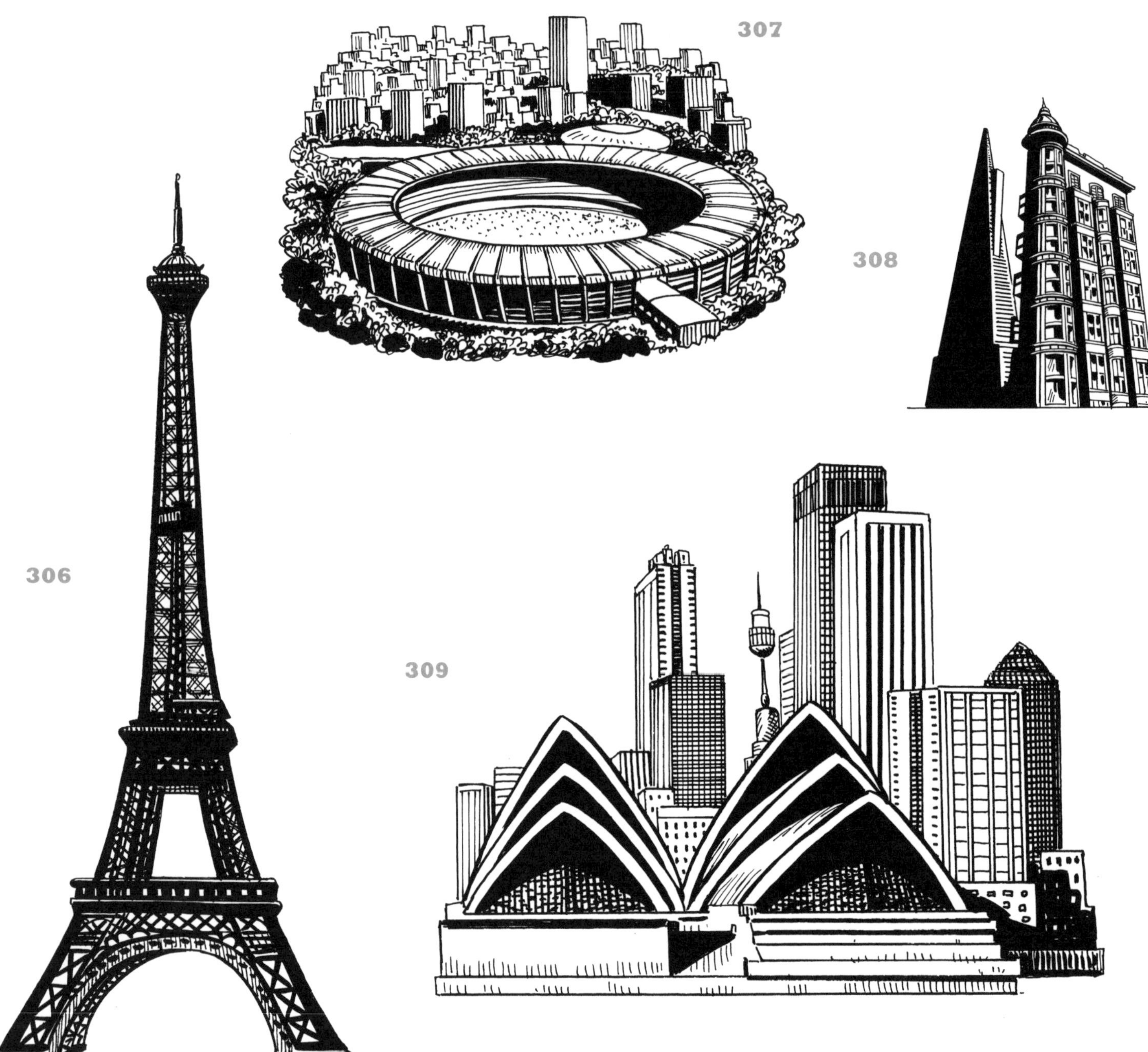

307
308
306
309

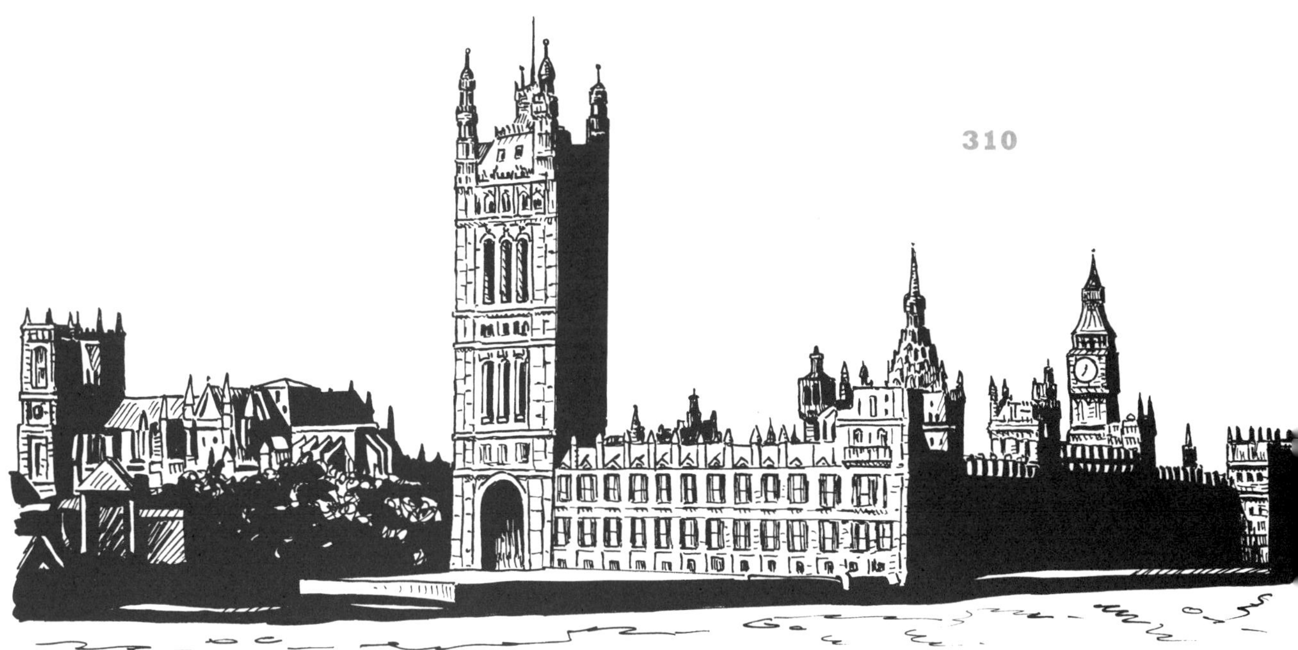

310

311

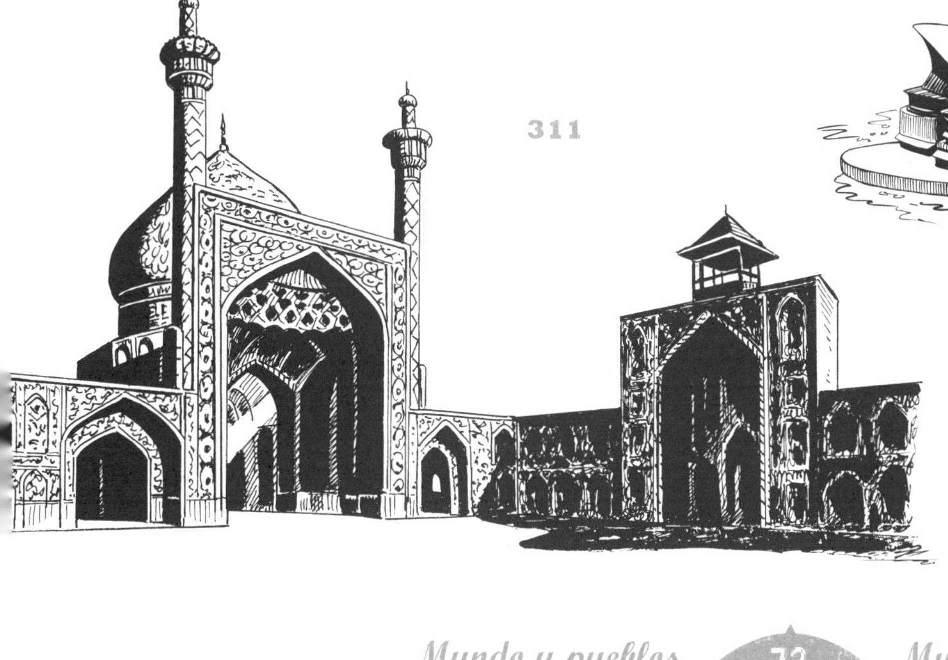

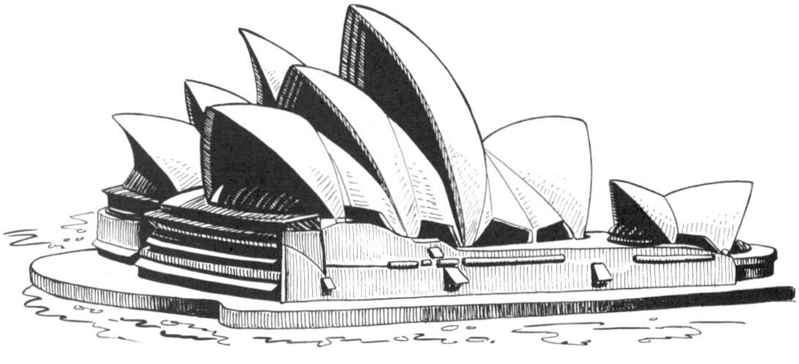

312

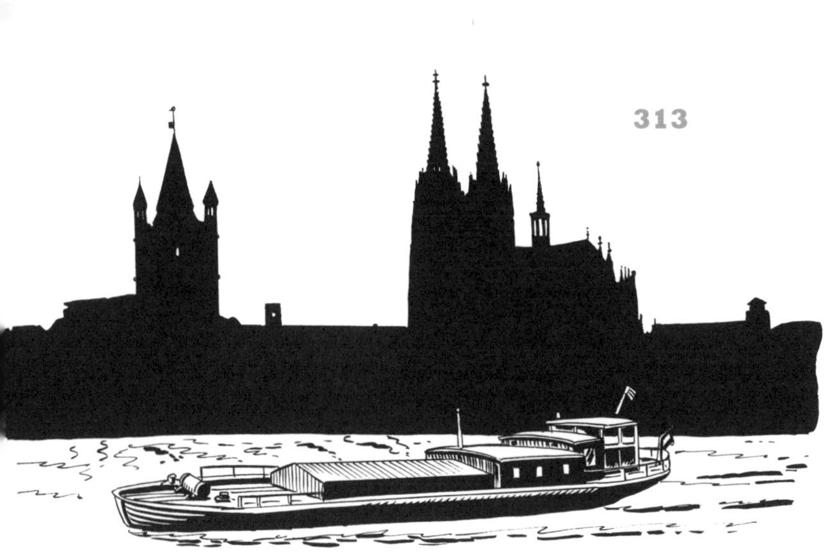

313

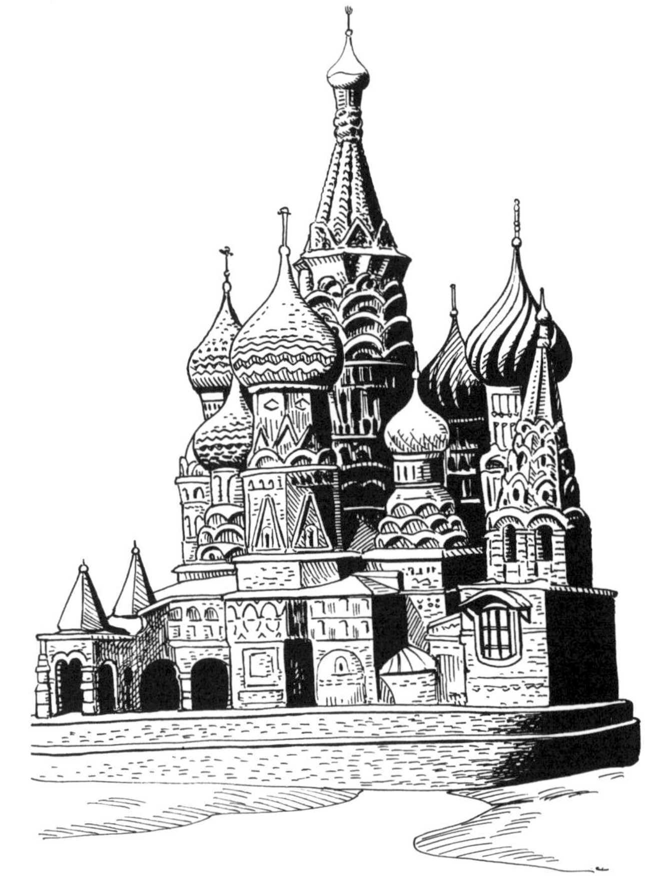

314

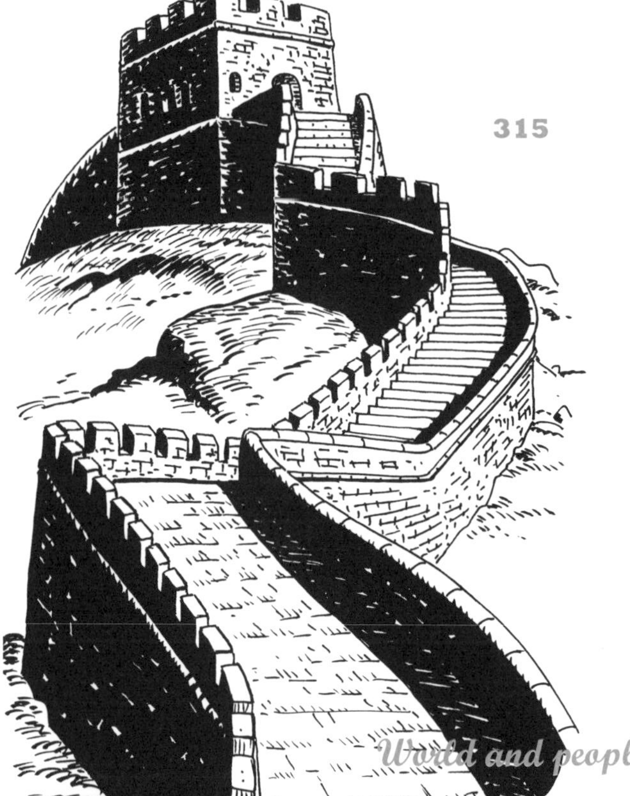

315

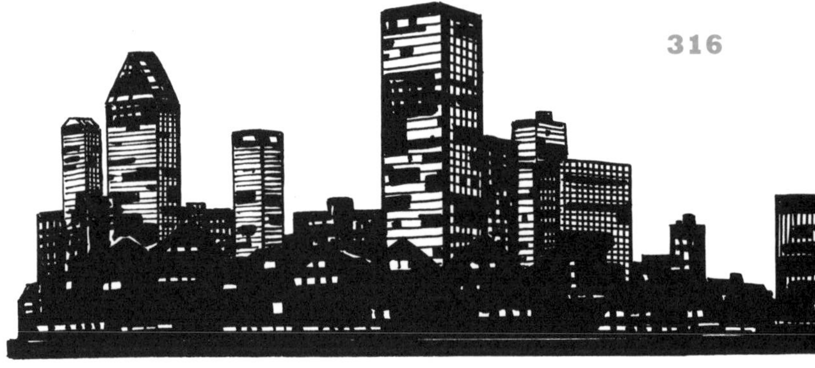

316

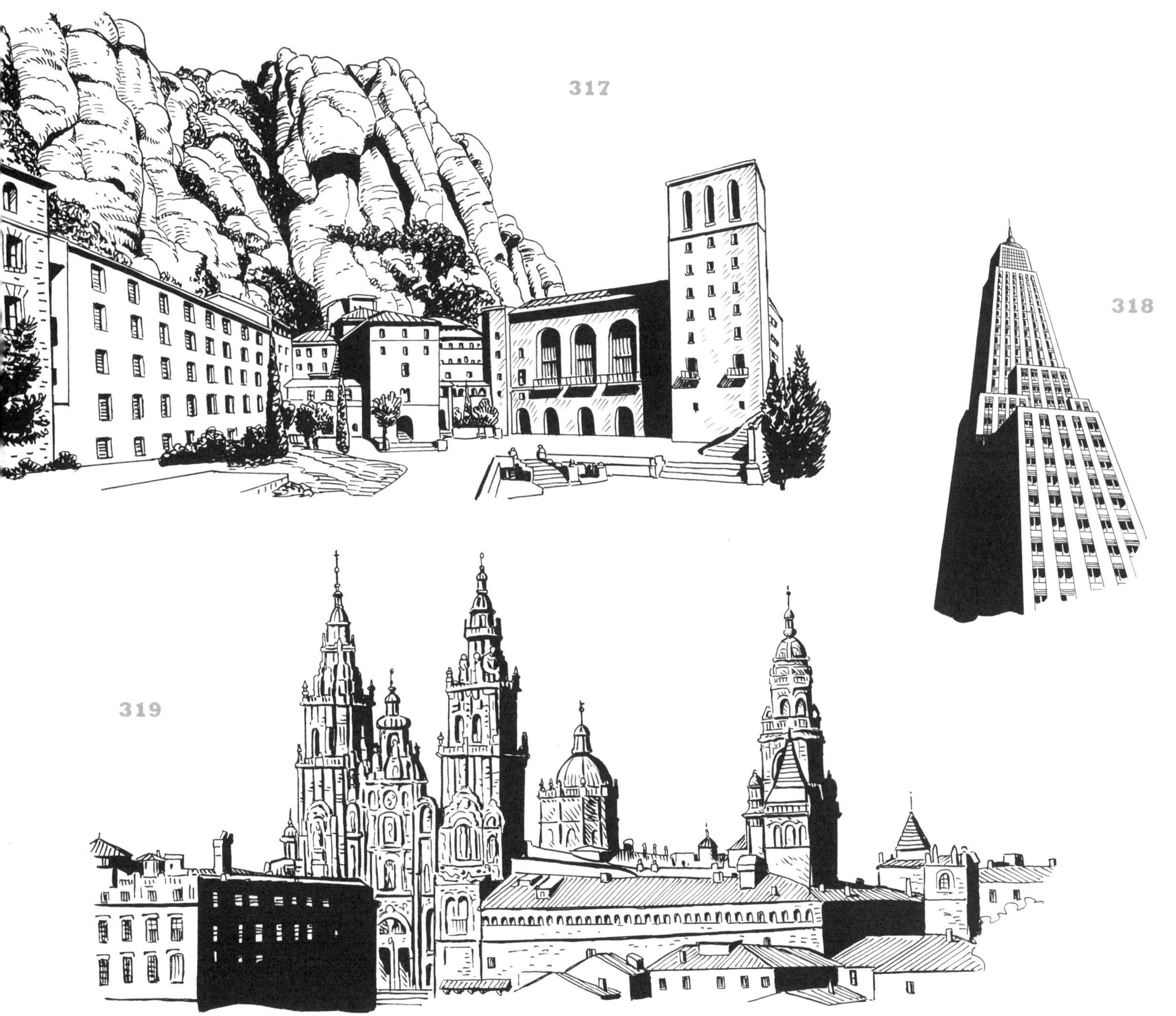

317
318
319

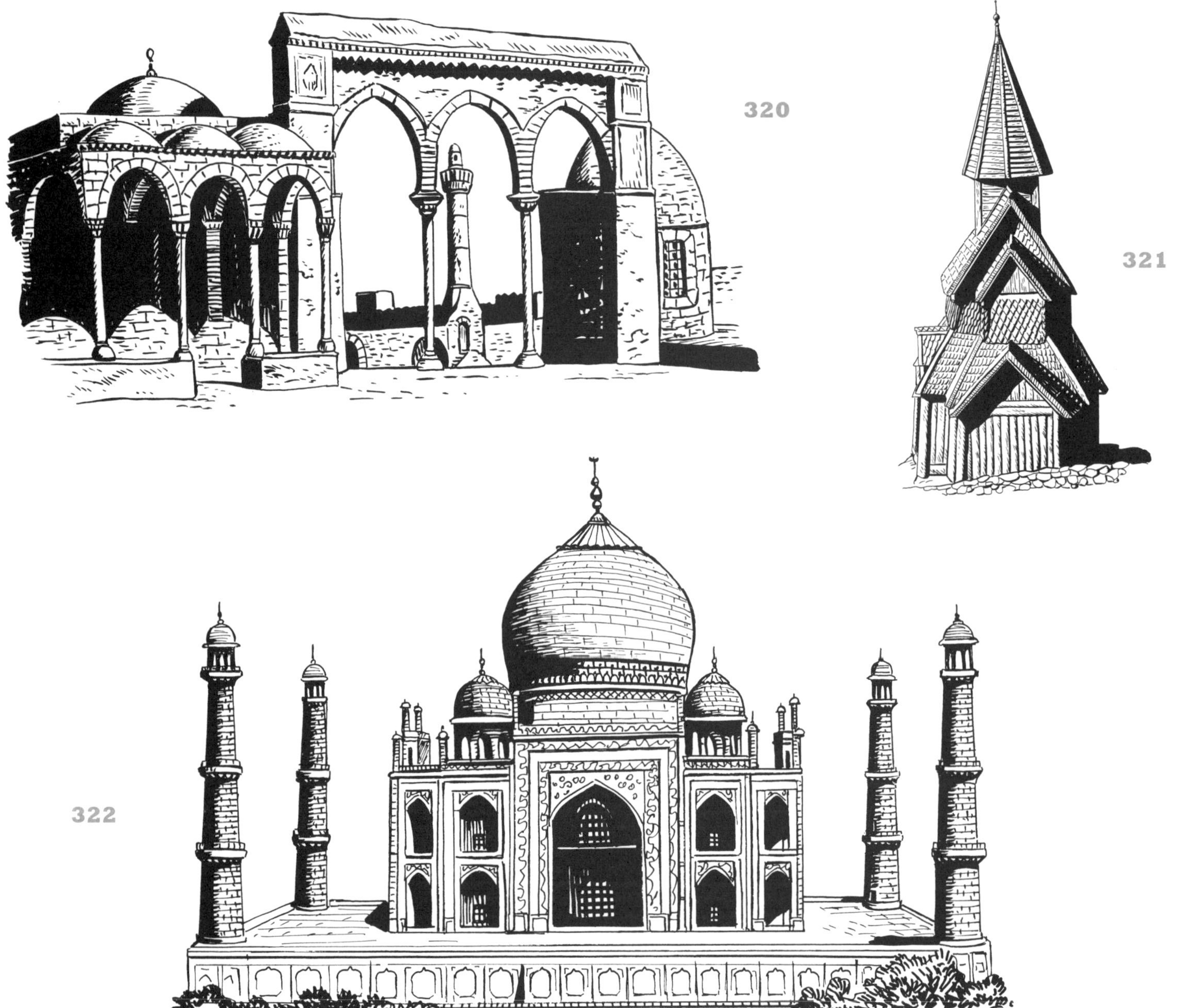

320
321
322

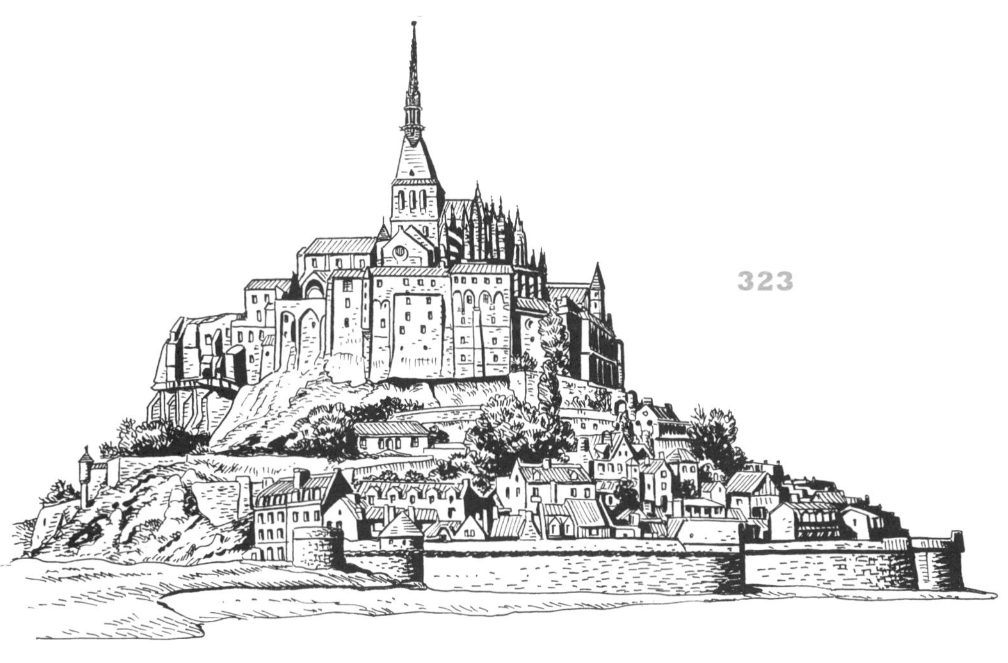

323

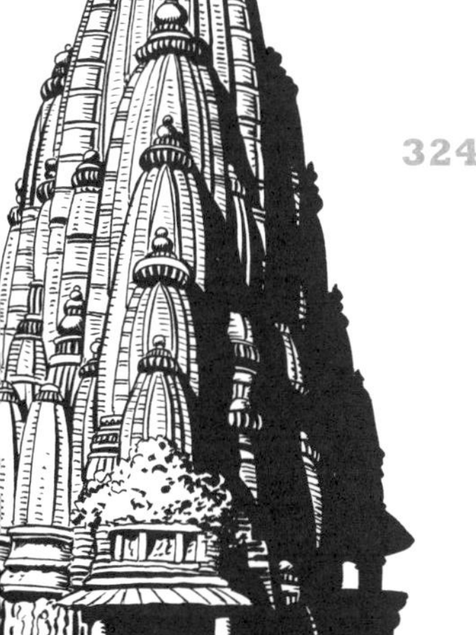

324

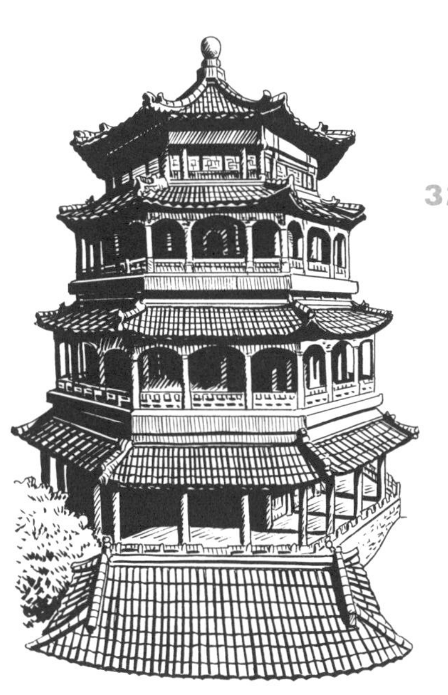

325

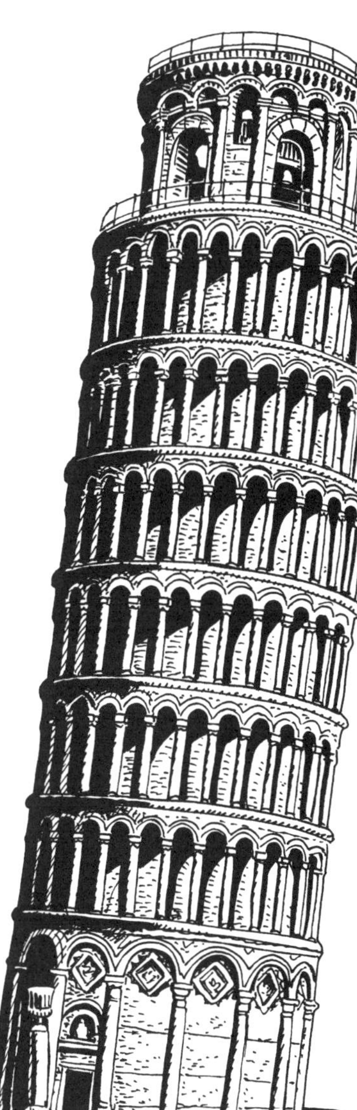

326

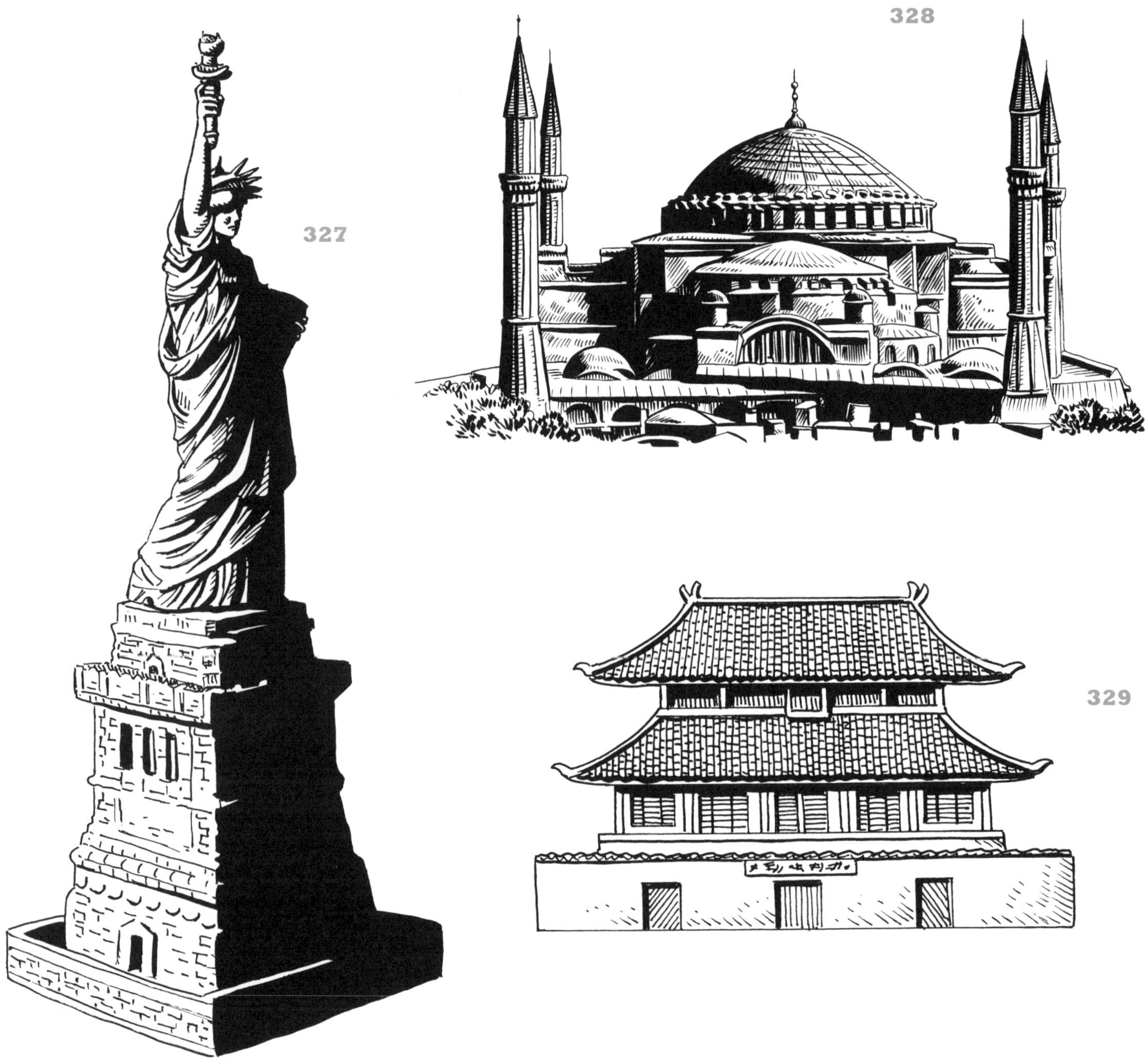

327
328
329

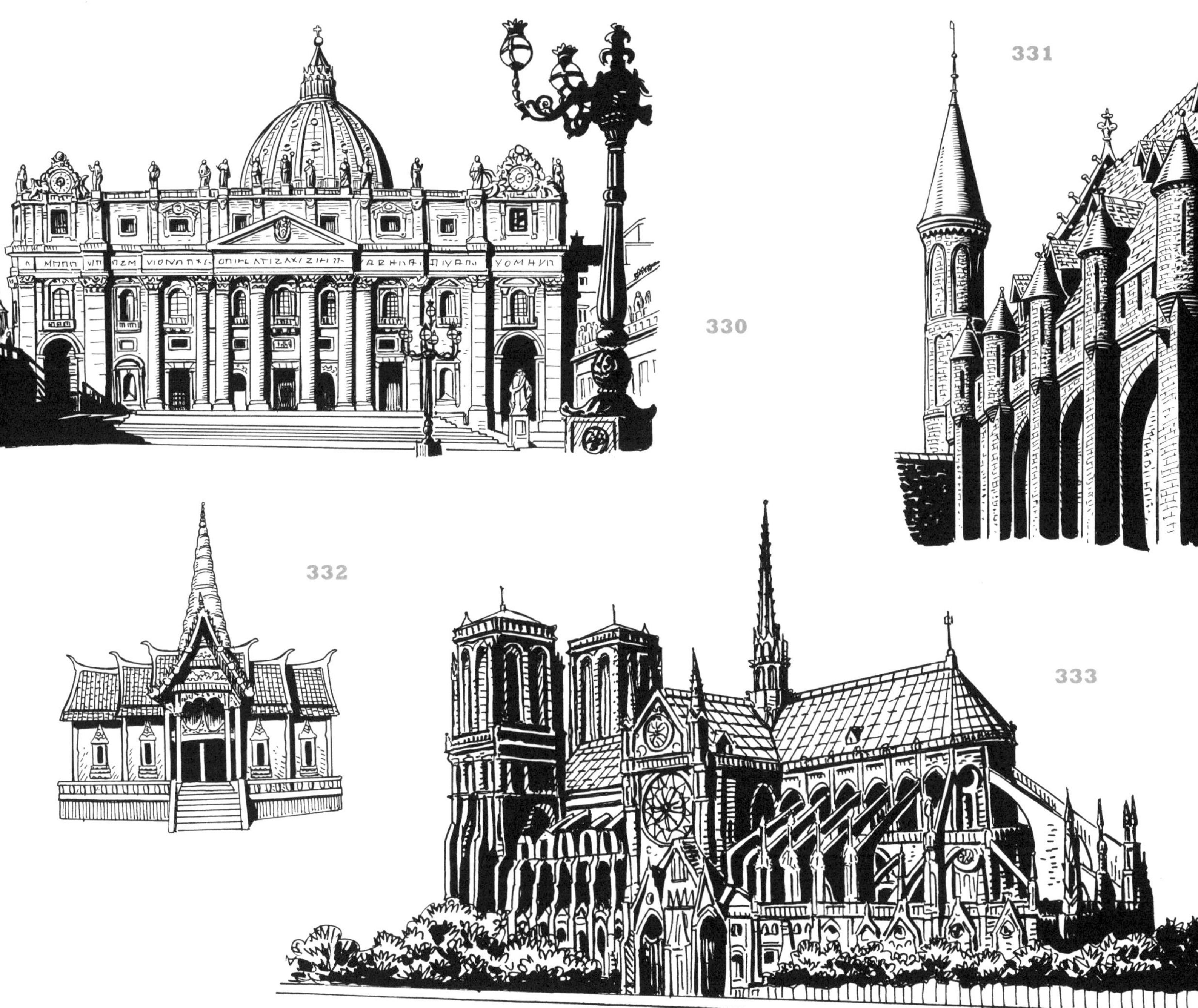

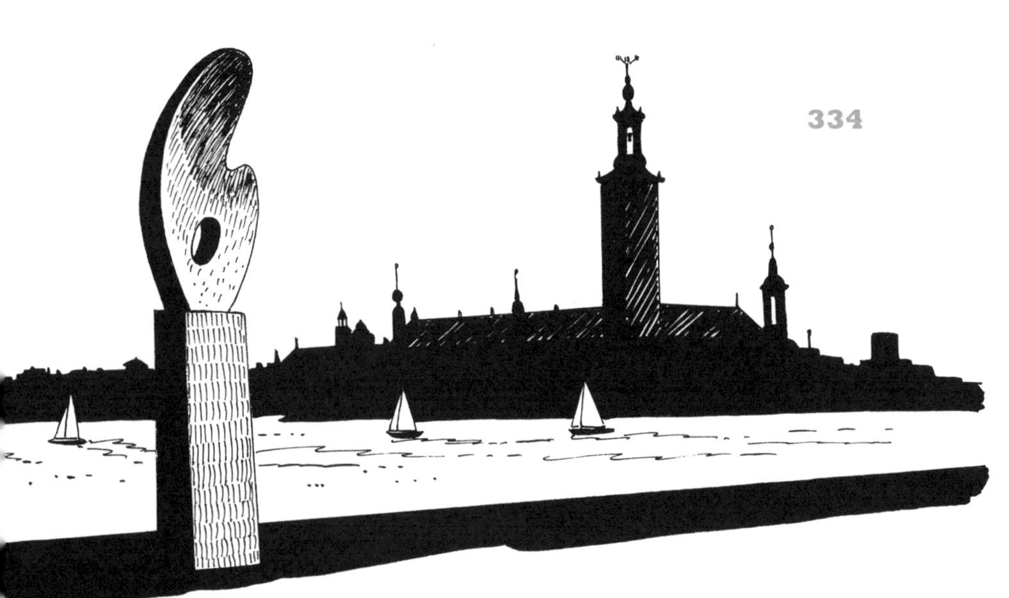

334

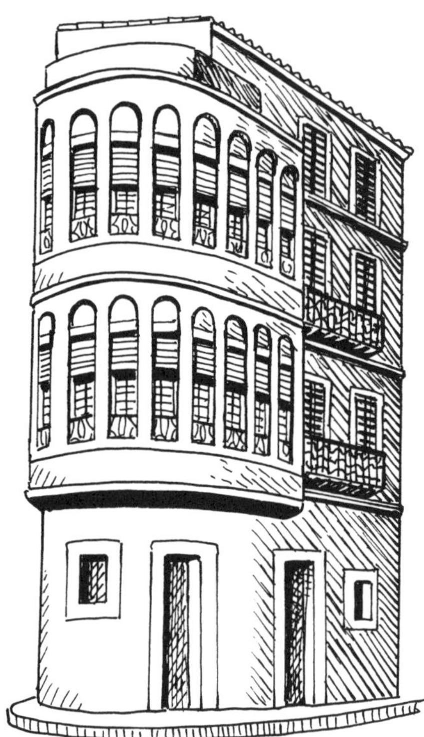

336

335

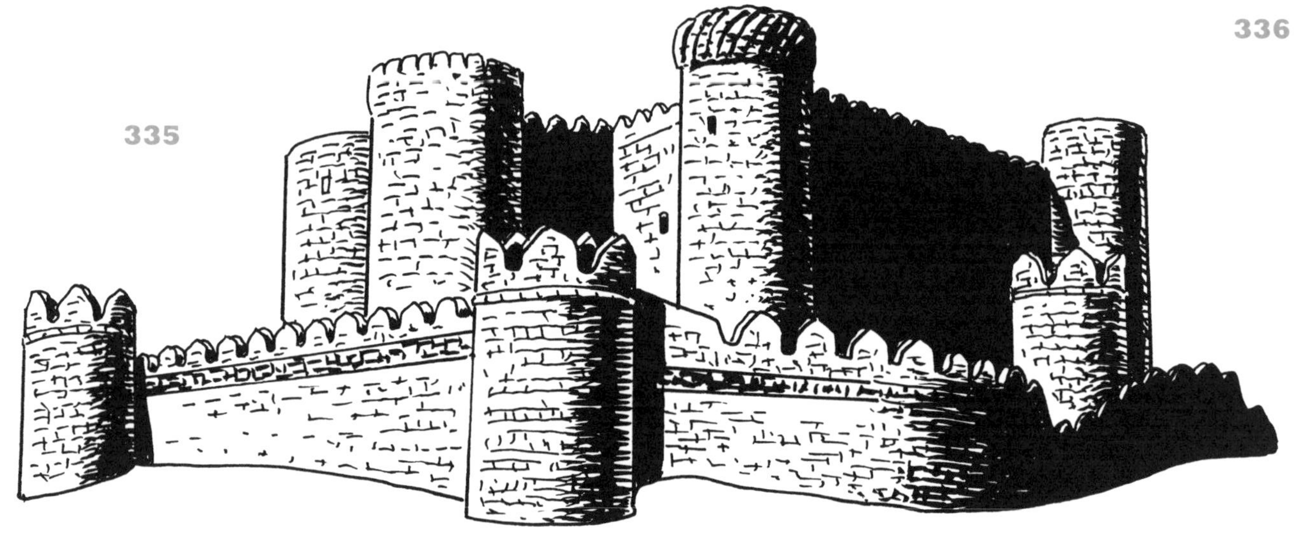

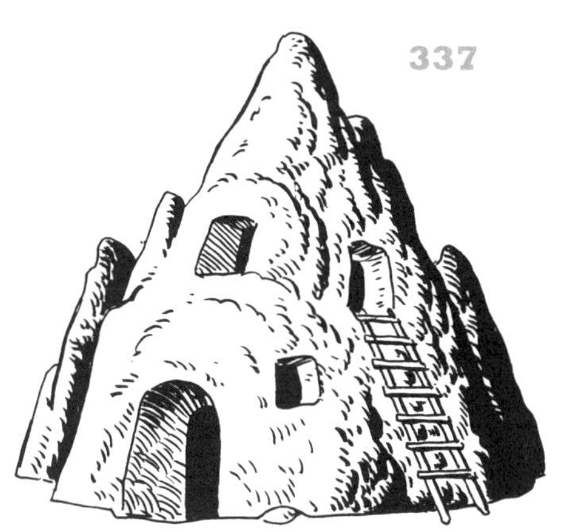

337

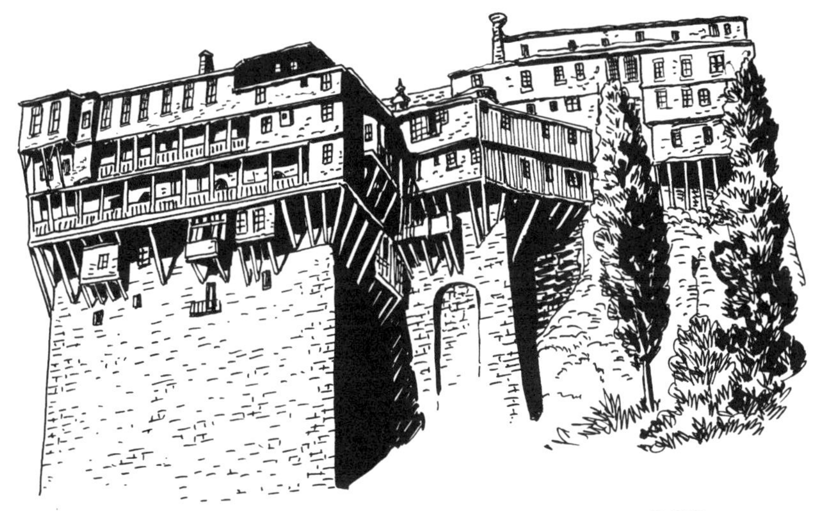

338

339

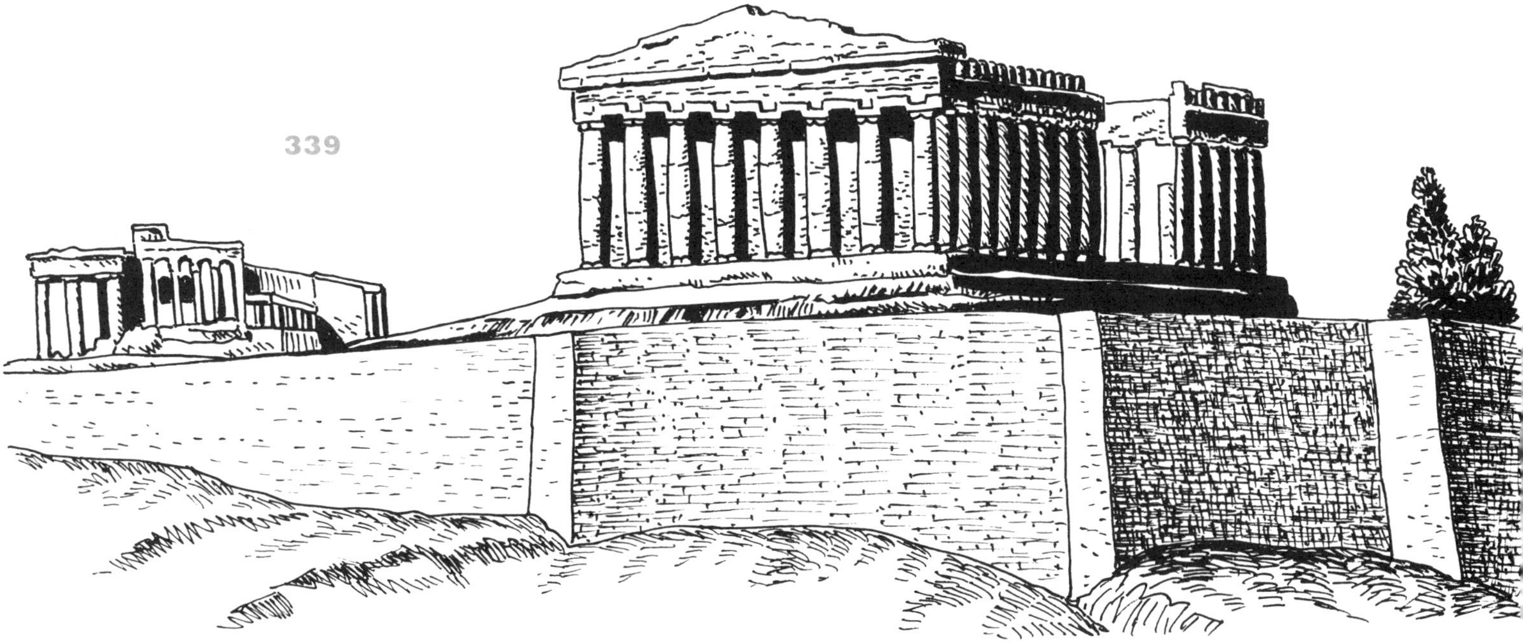

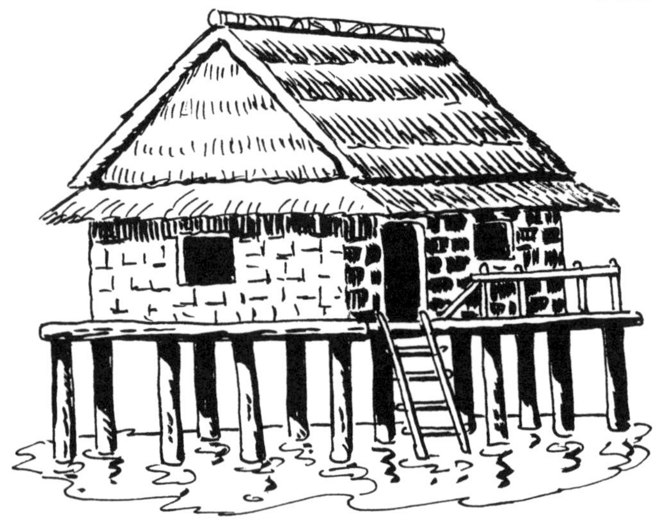

340

341

342

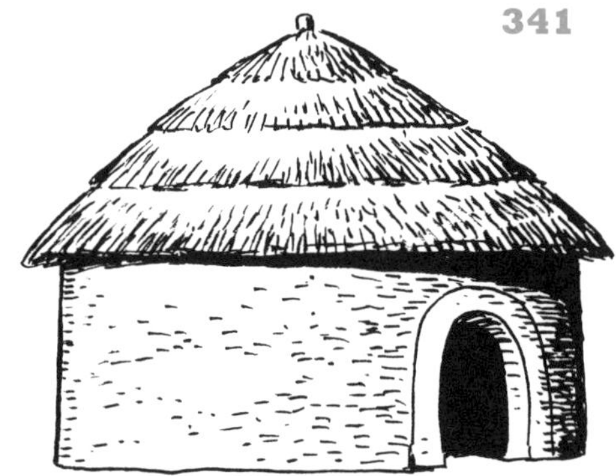

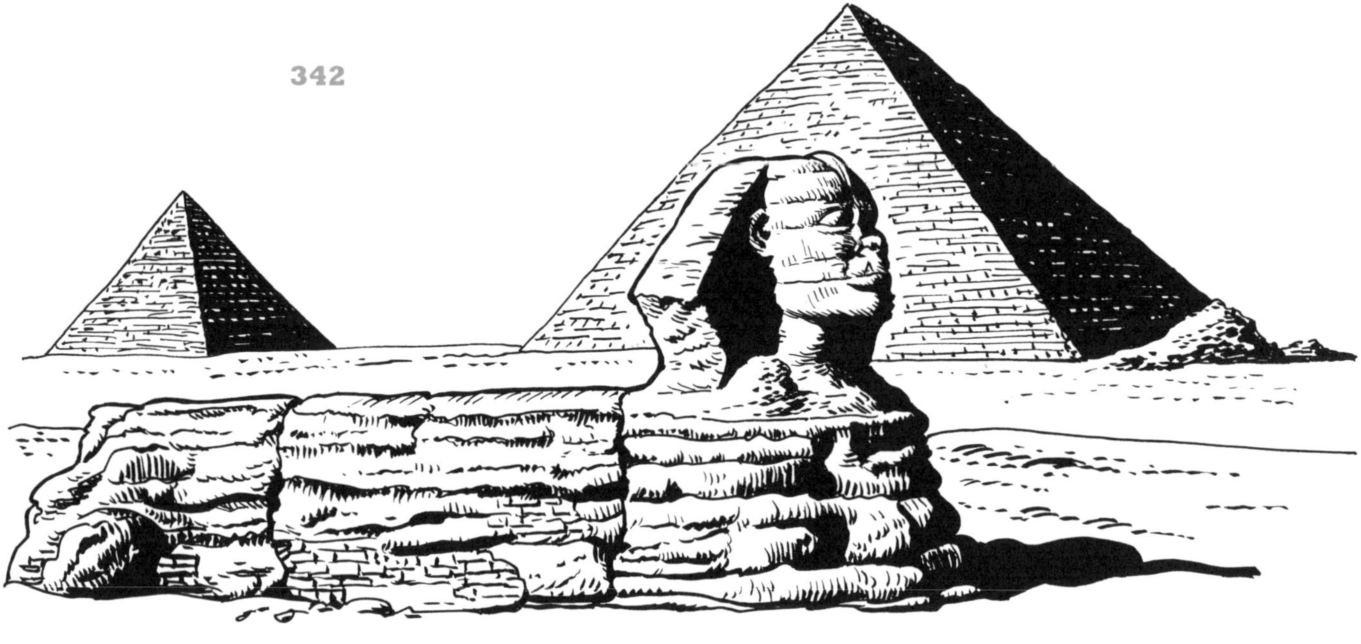

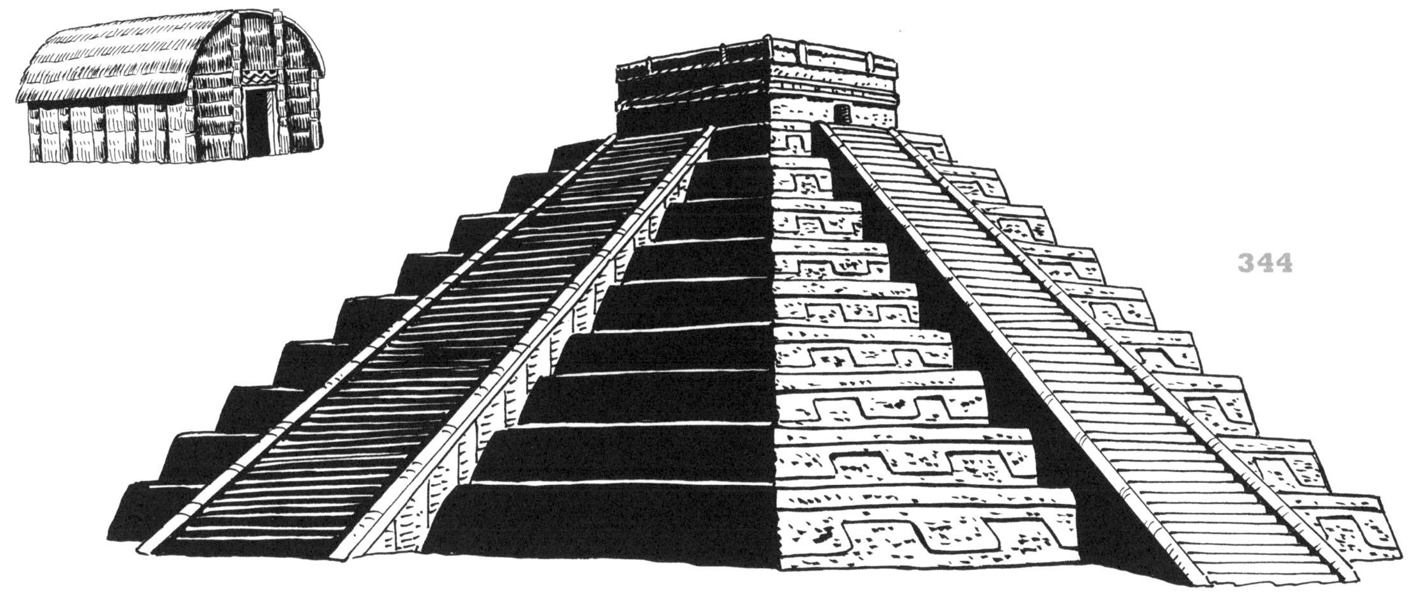

343

344

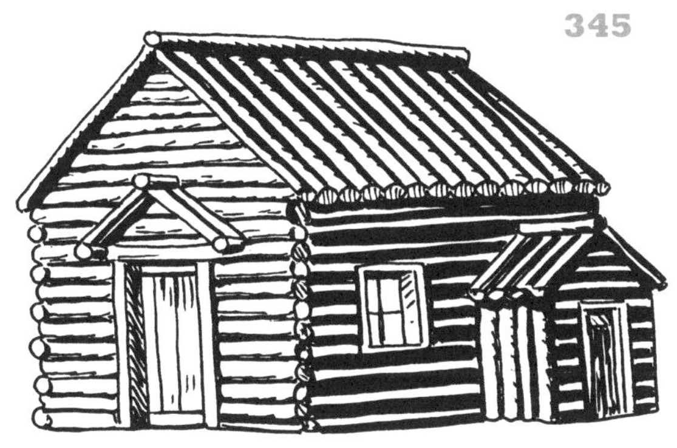

345

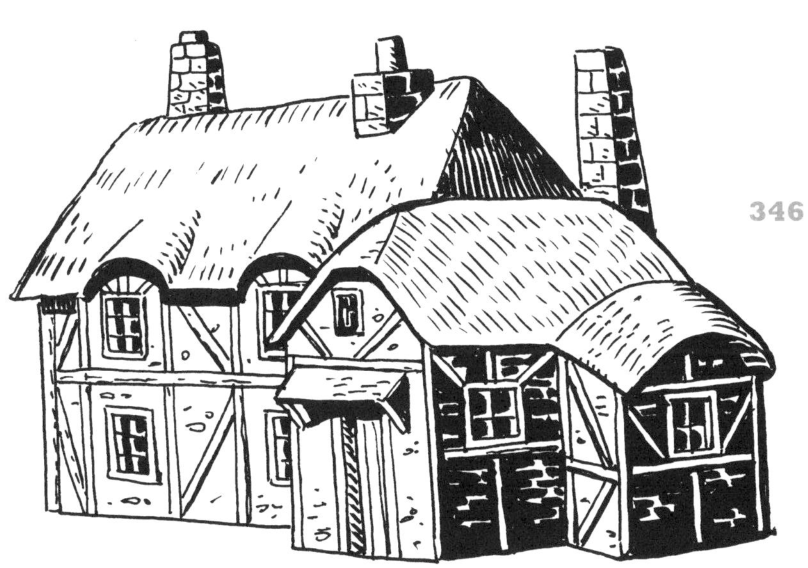

346

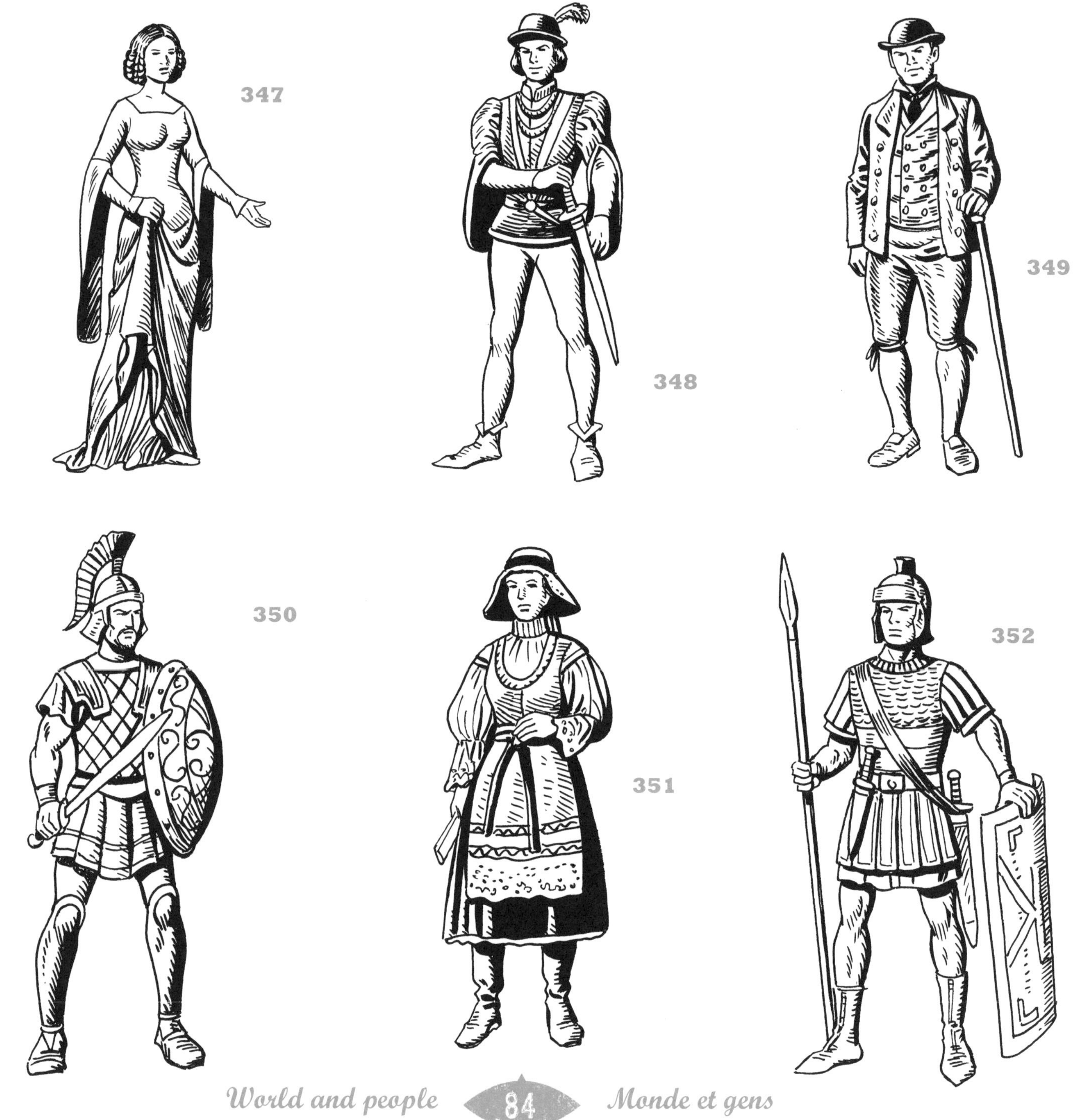

347
348
349
350
351
352

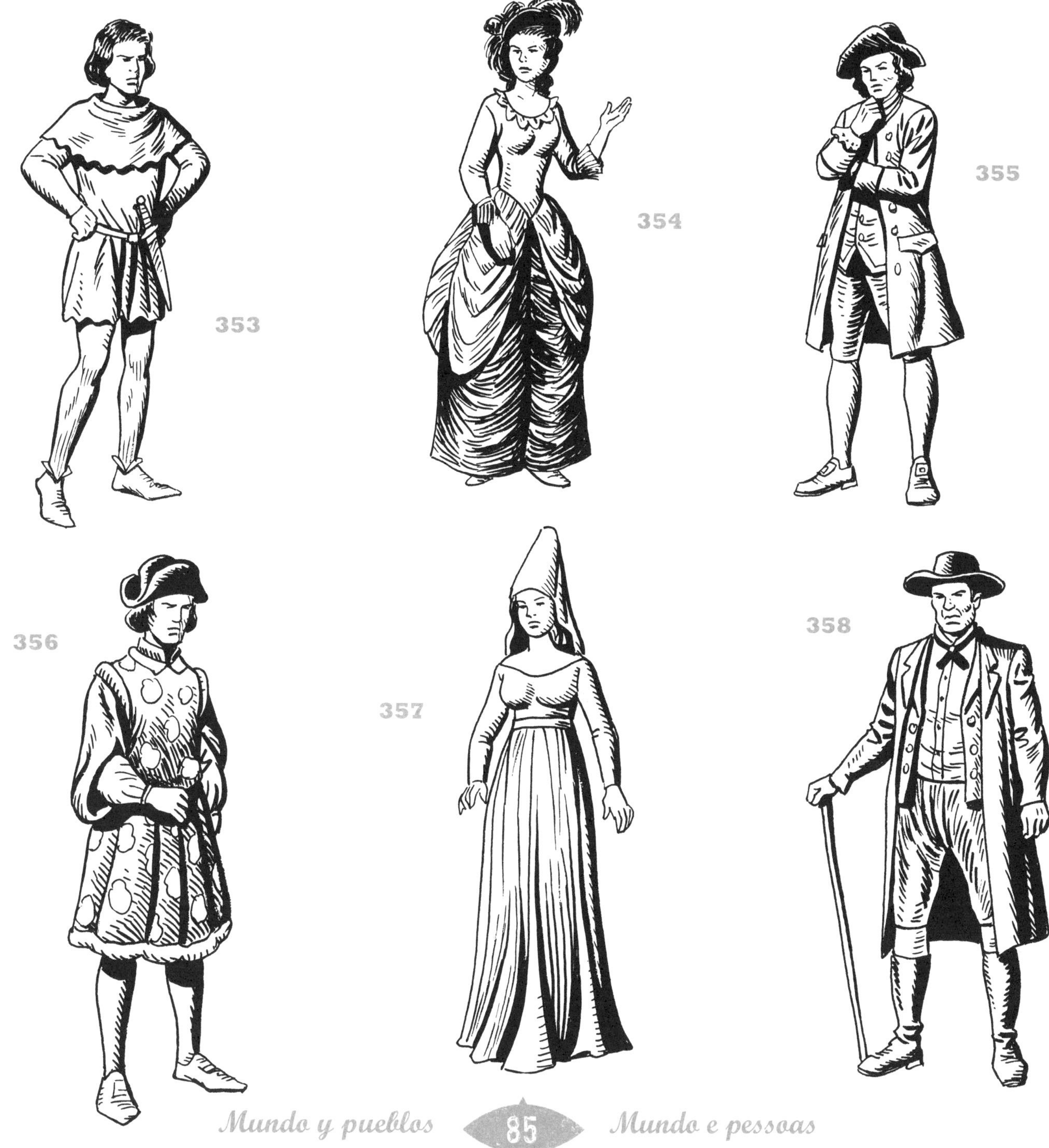

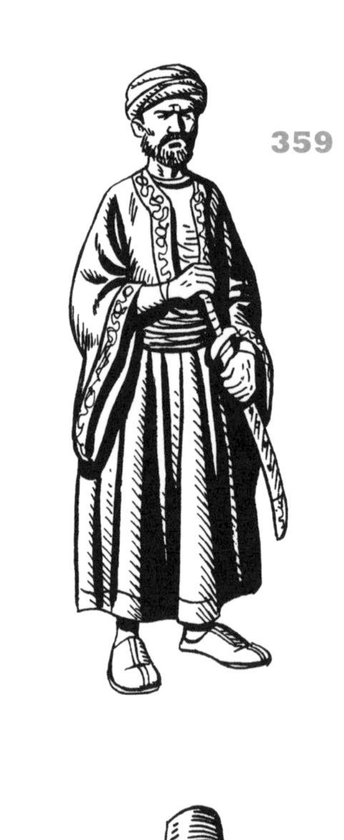

359

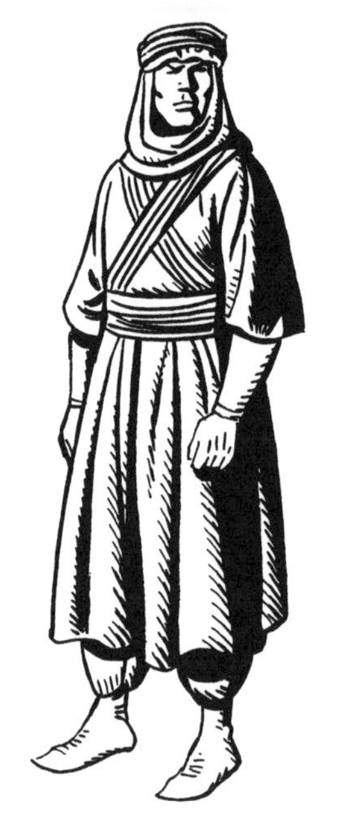

360

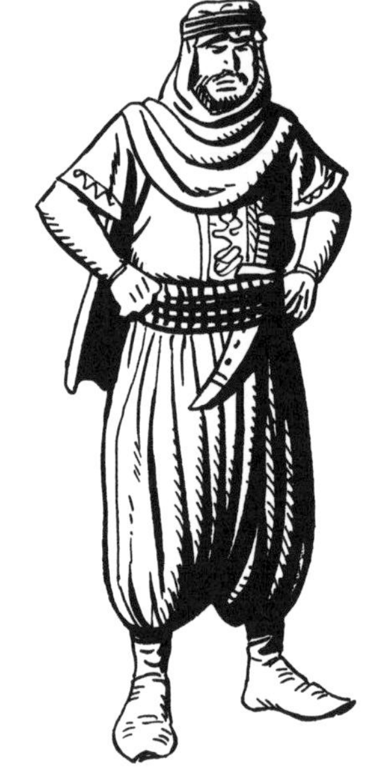

361

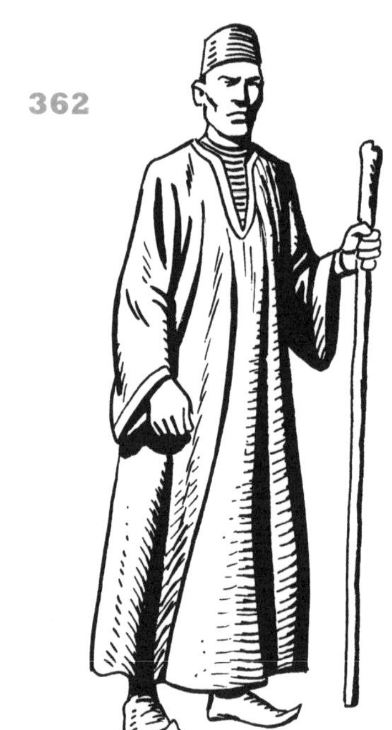

362

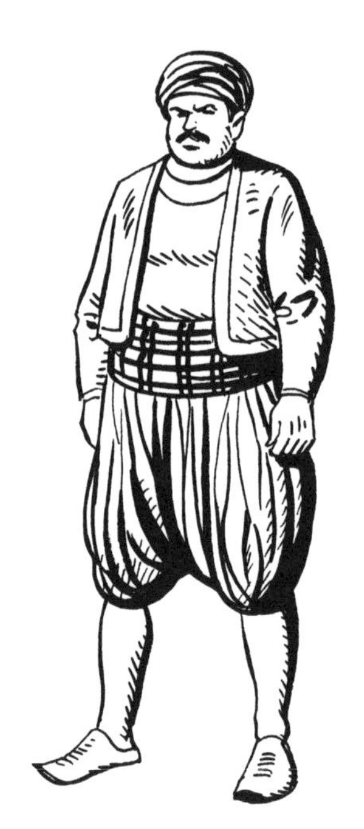

363

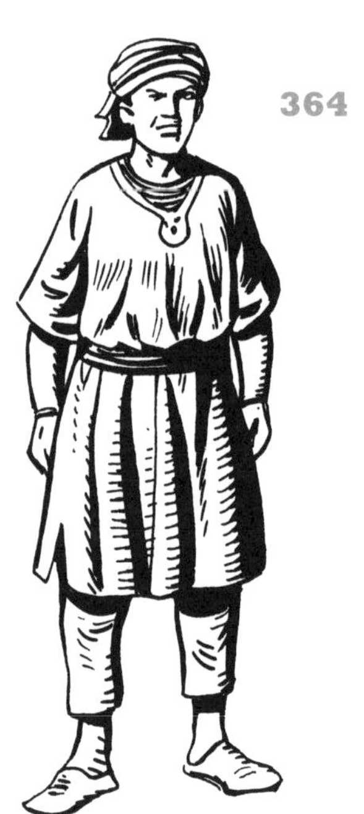

364

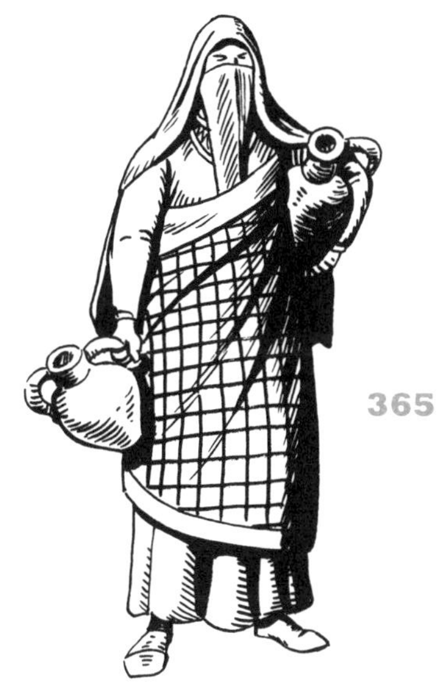

365

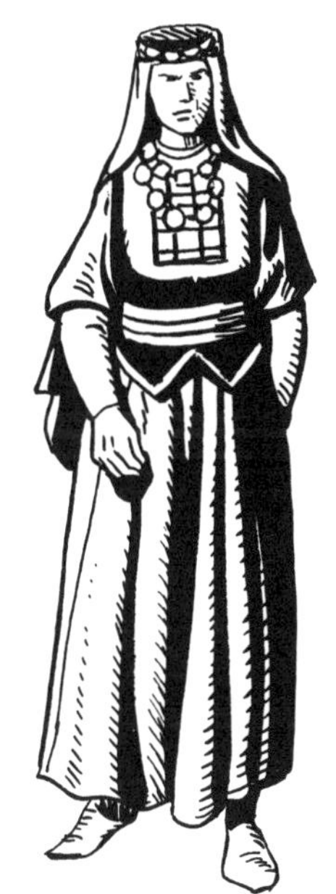

366

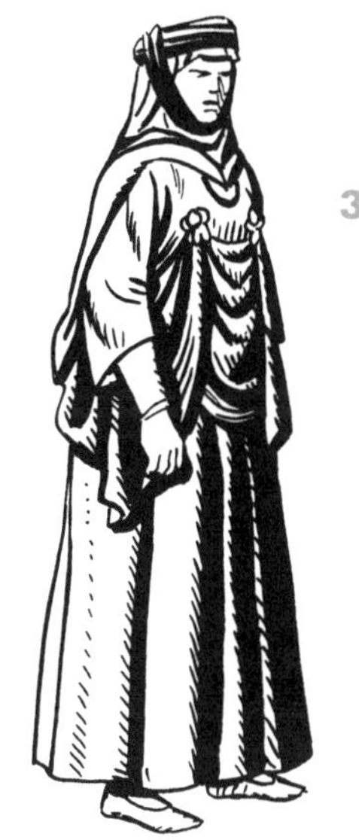

367

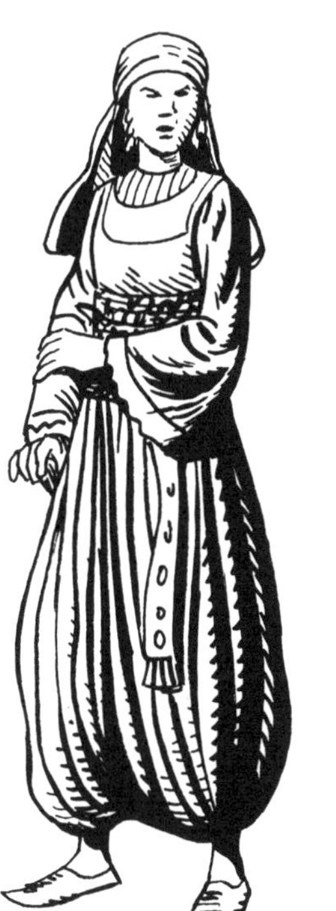

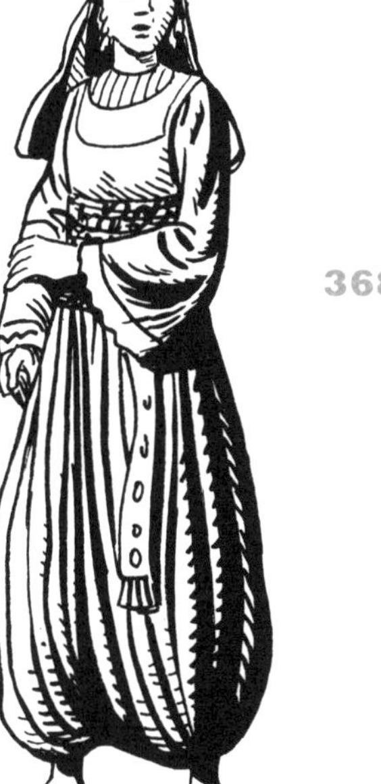

368

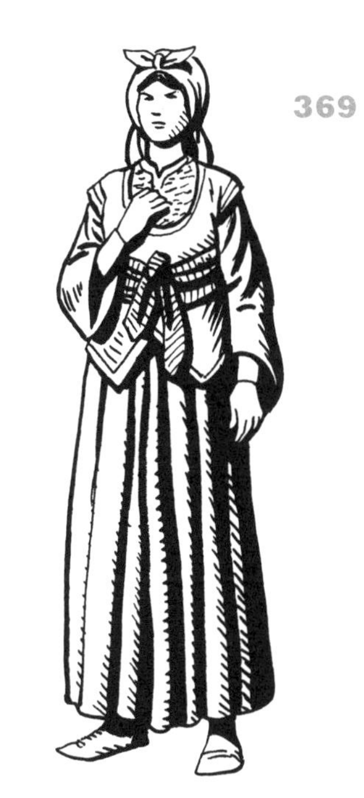

369

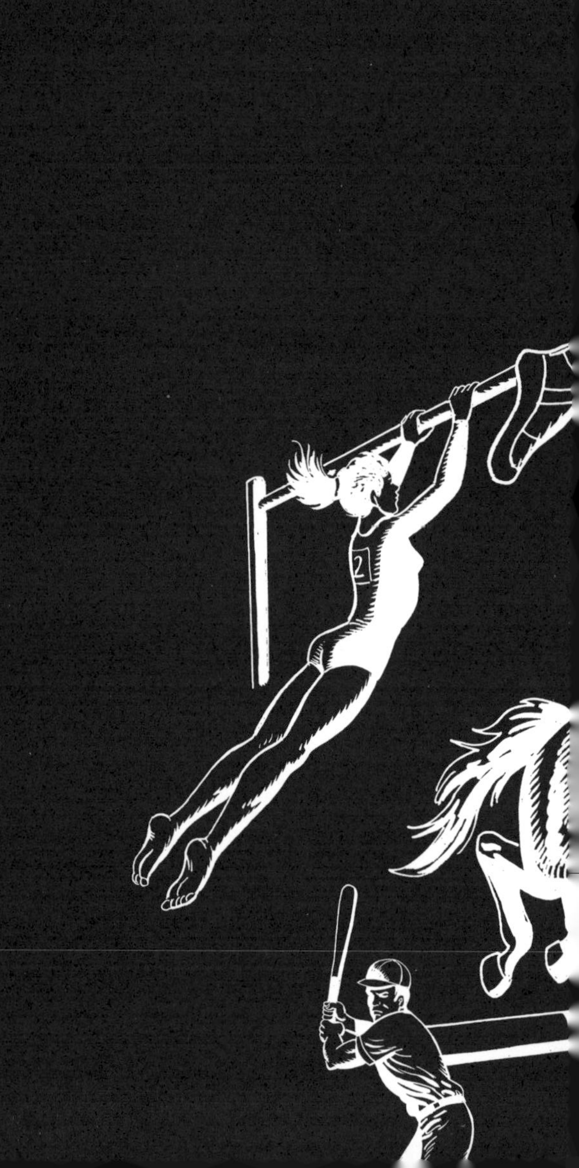

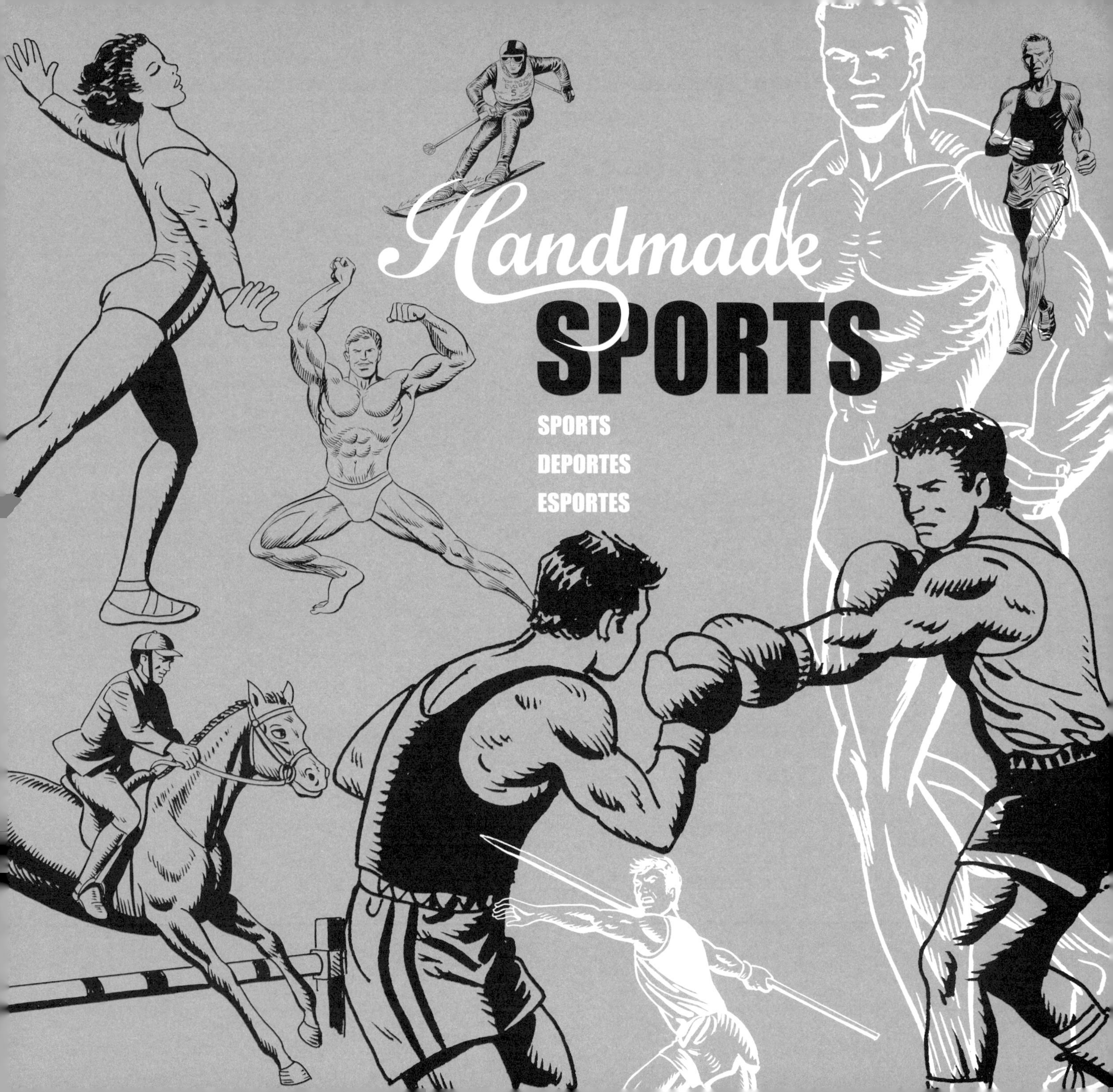

Handmade
SPORTS
SPORTS
DEPORTES
ESPORTES

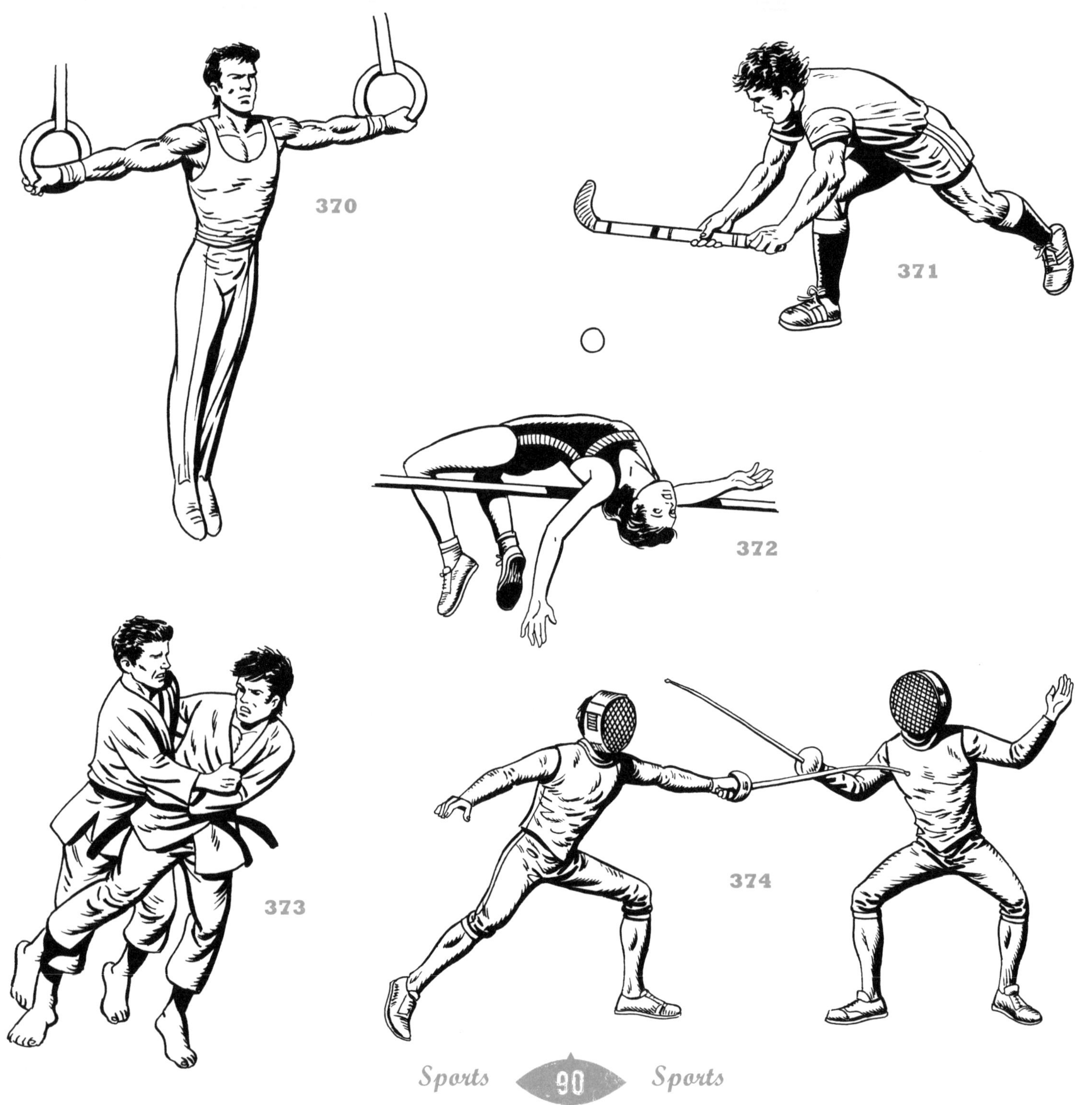

370
371
372
373
374

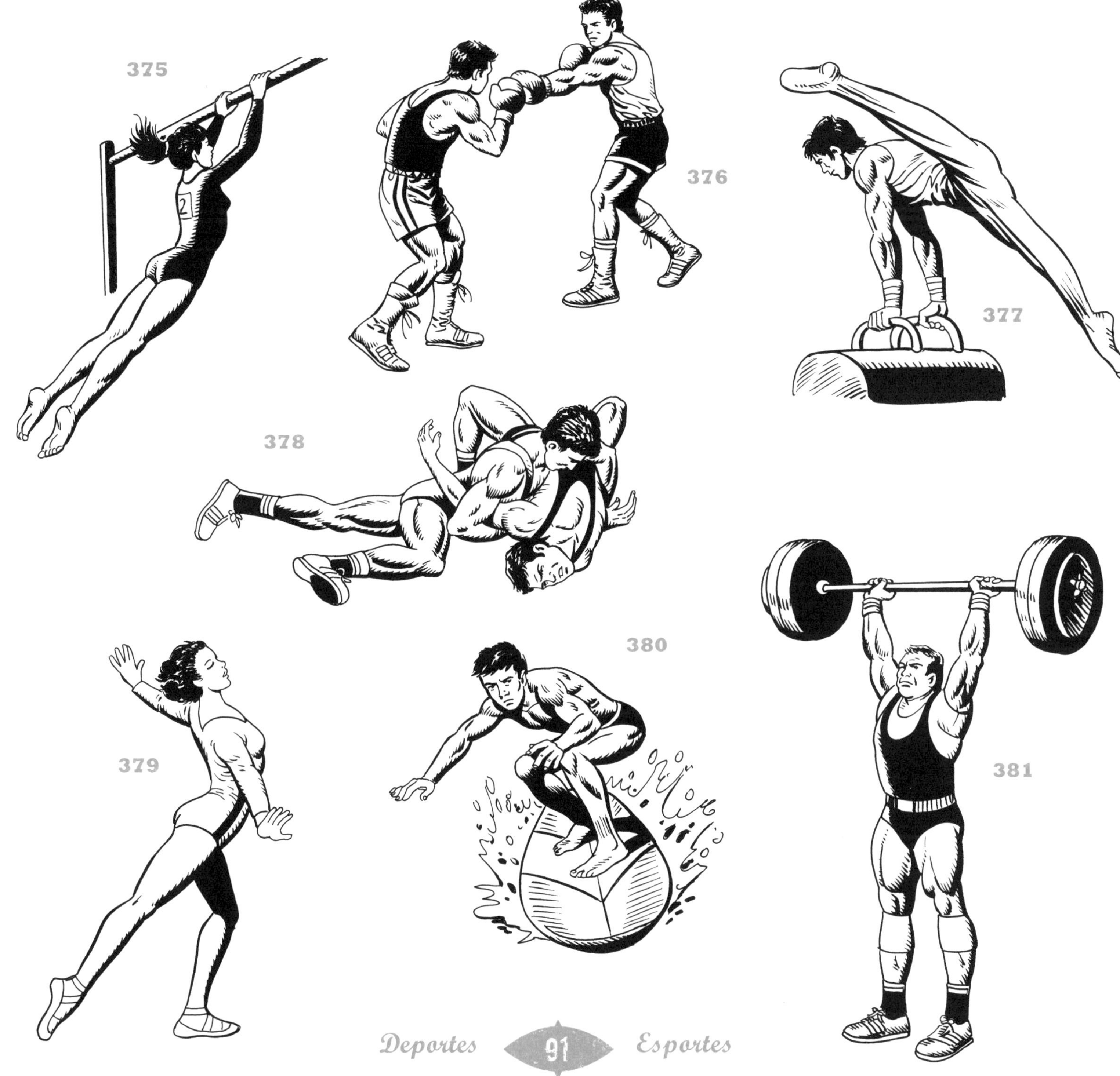

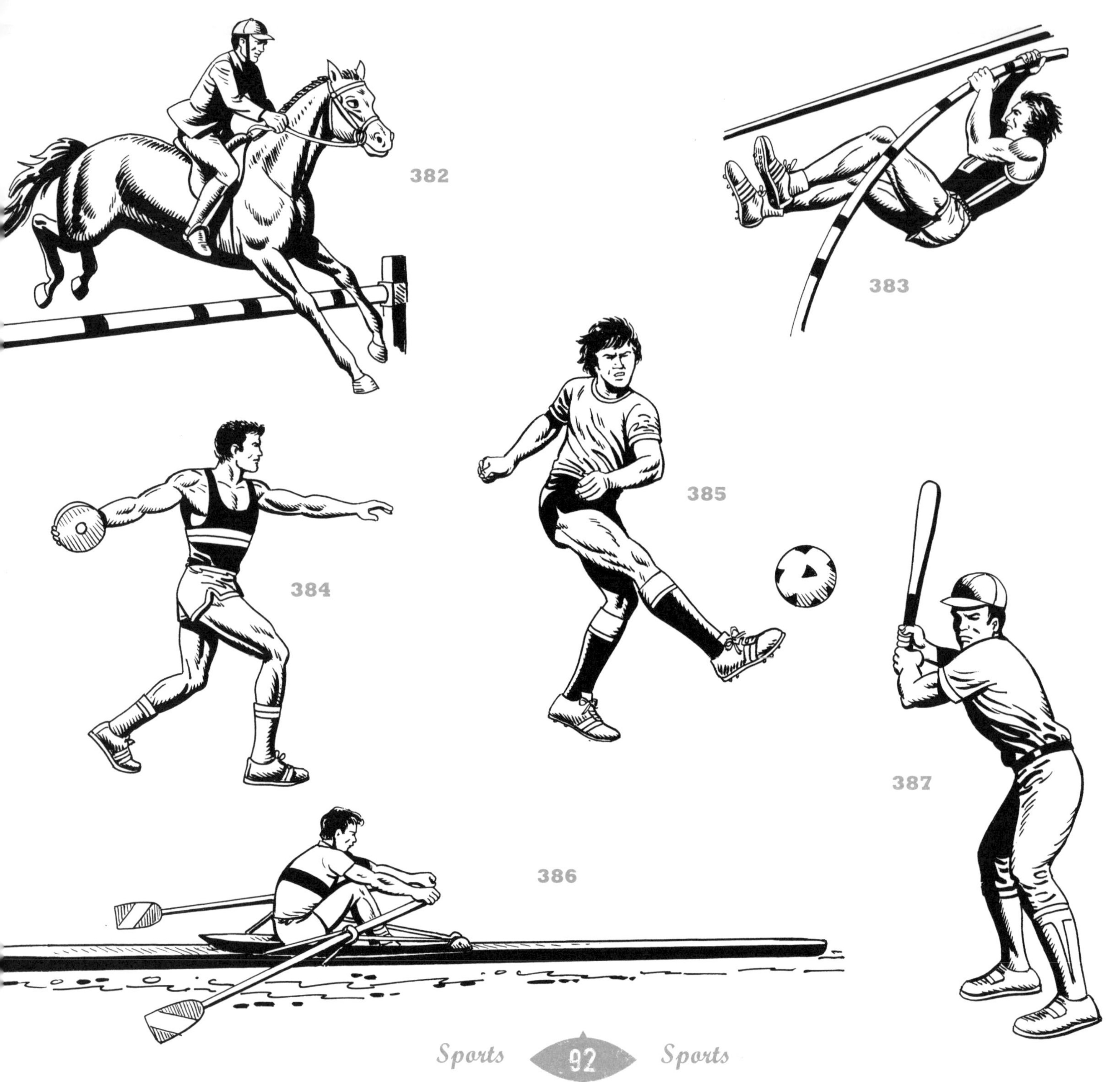

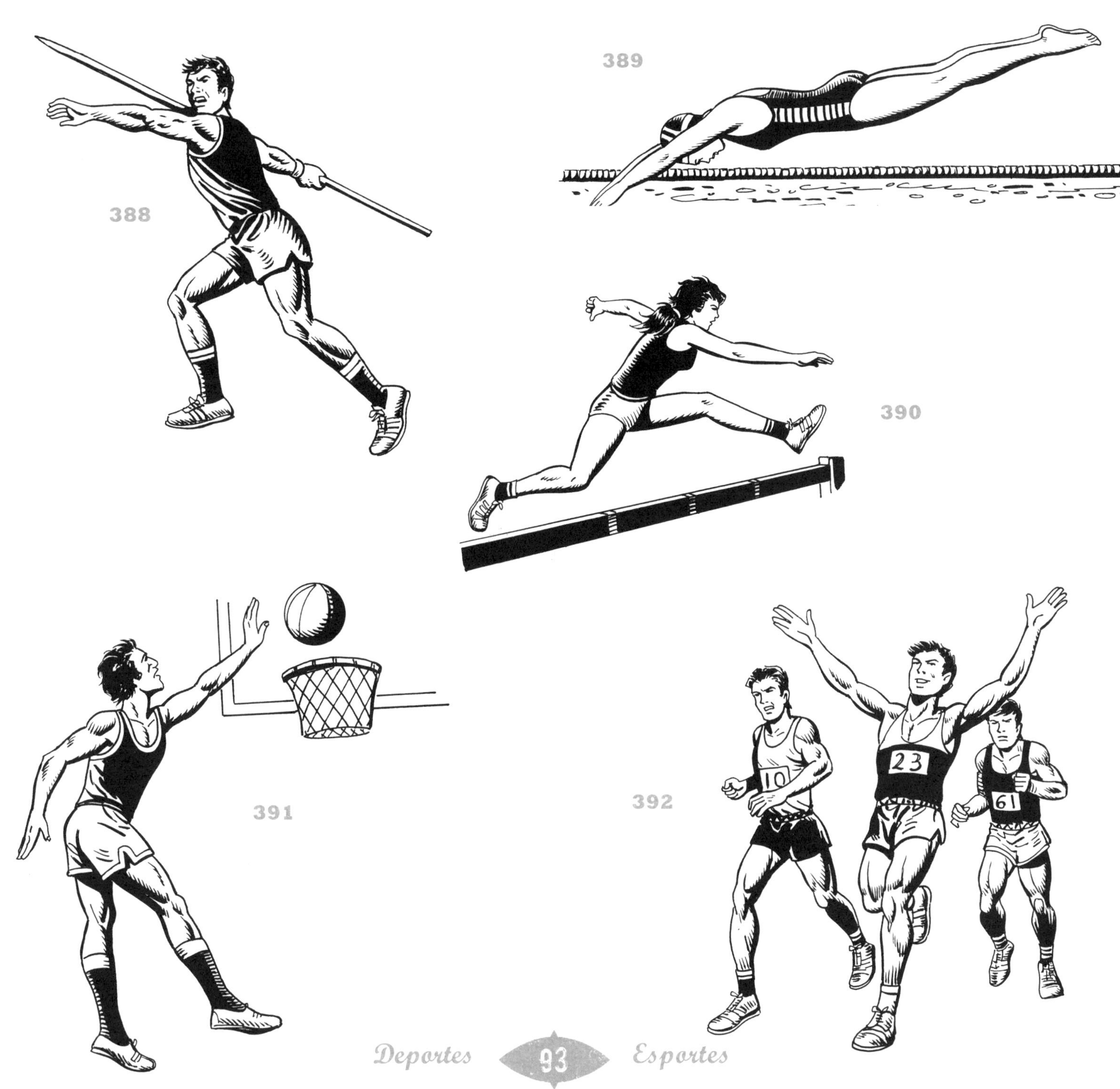
388
389
390
391
392

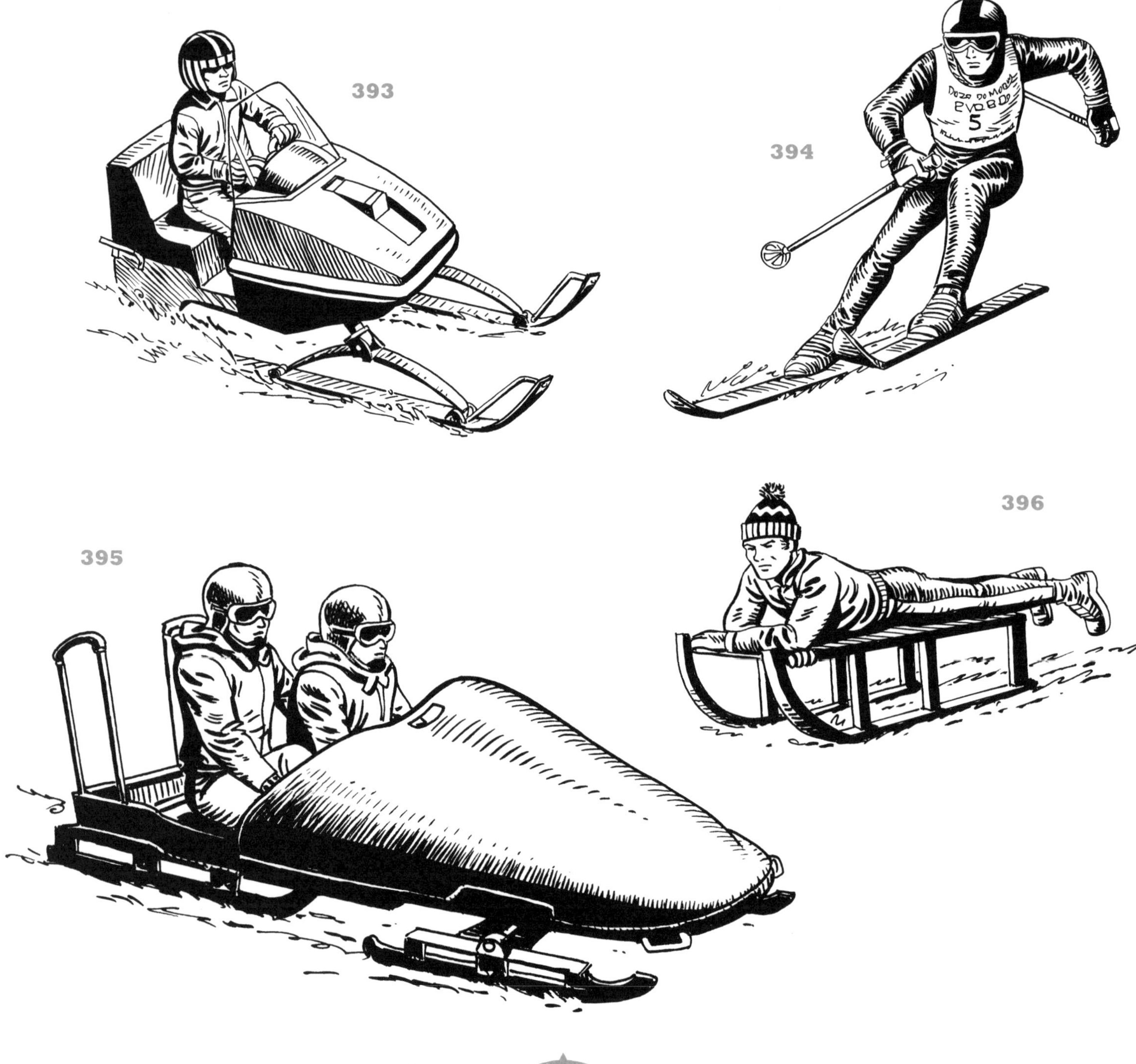

393

394

395

396

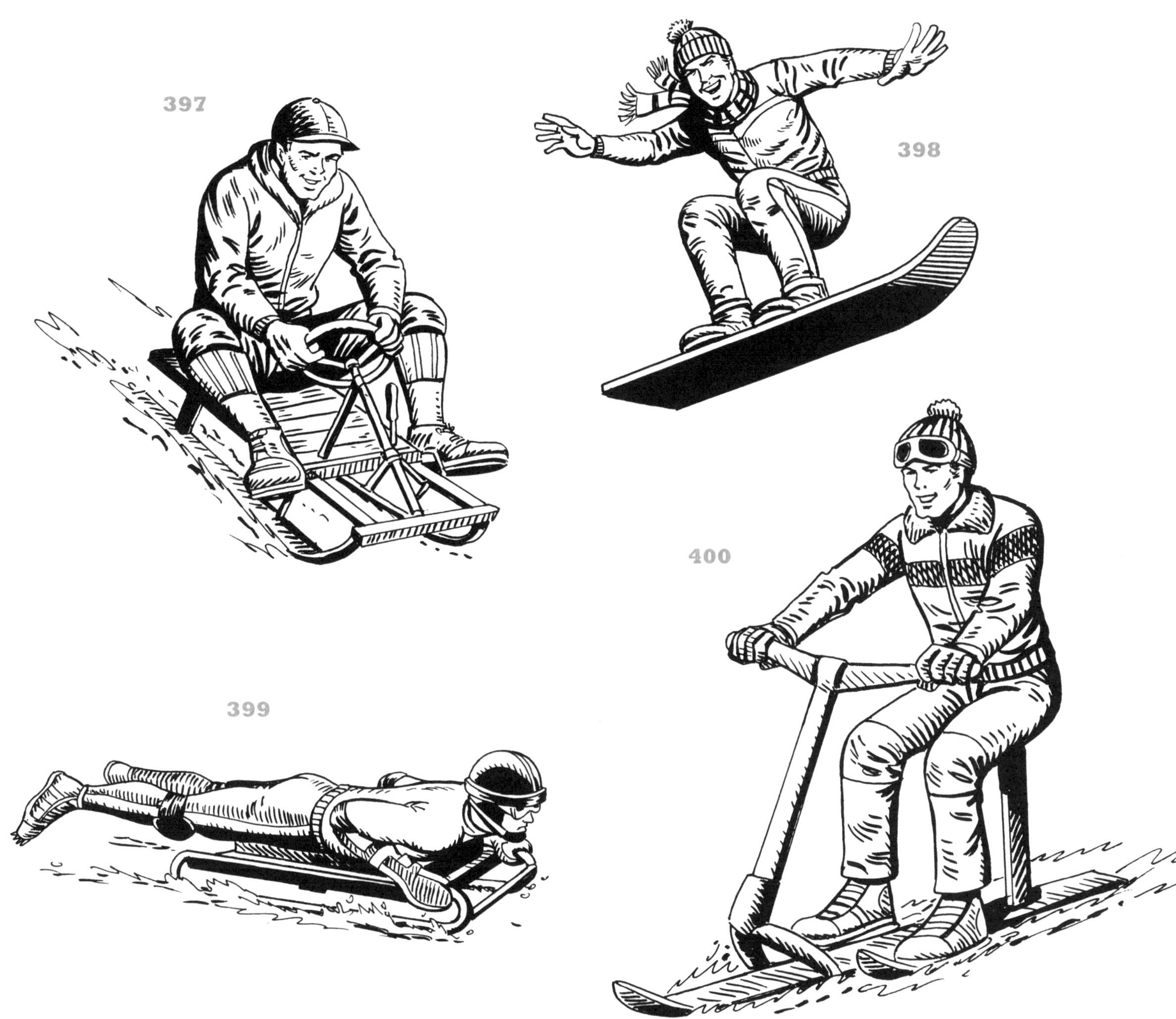

397
398
399
400

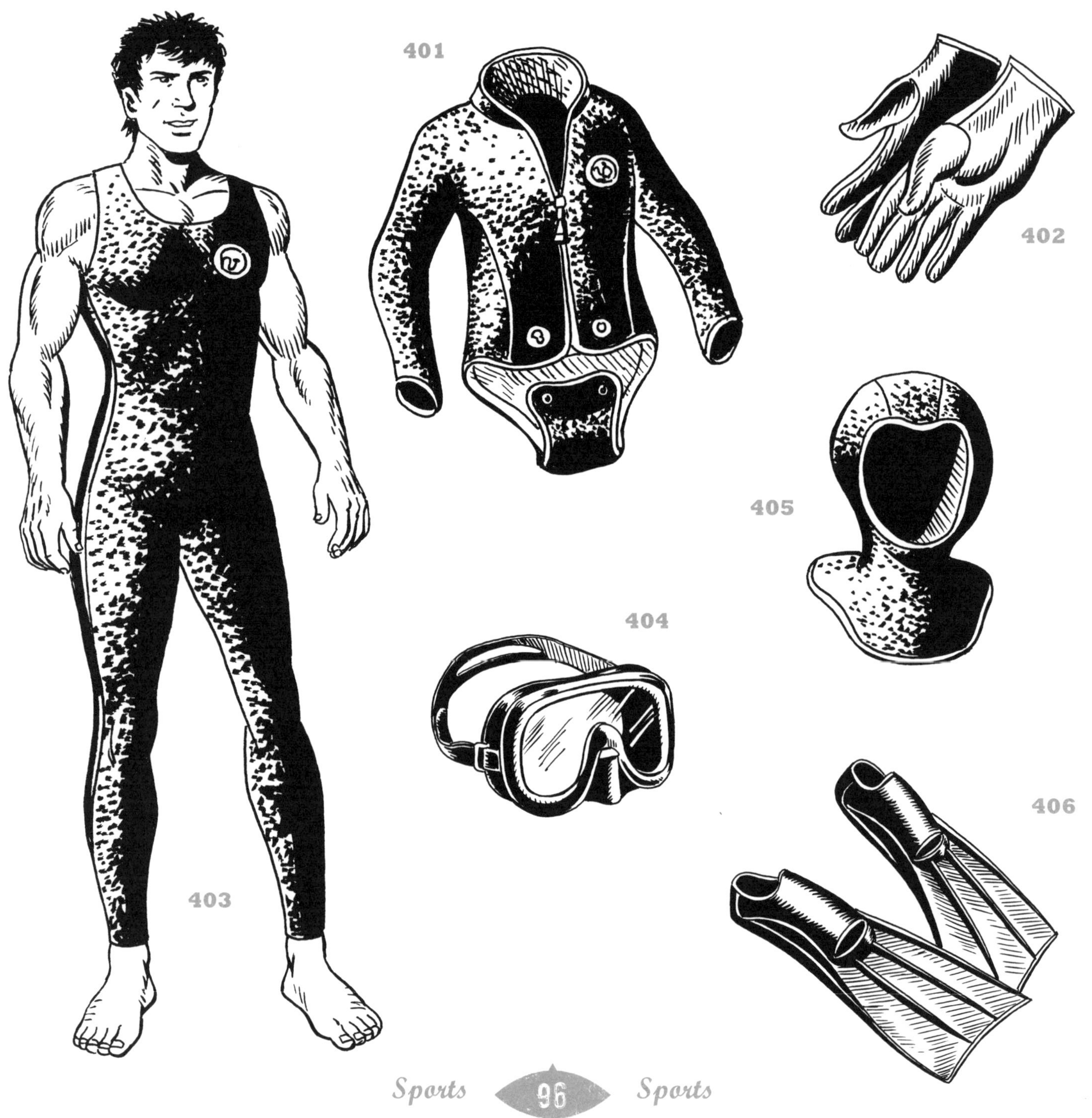

401
402
405
404
403
406

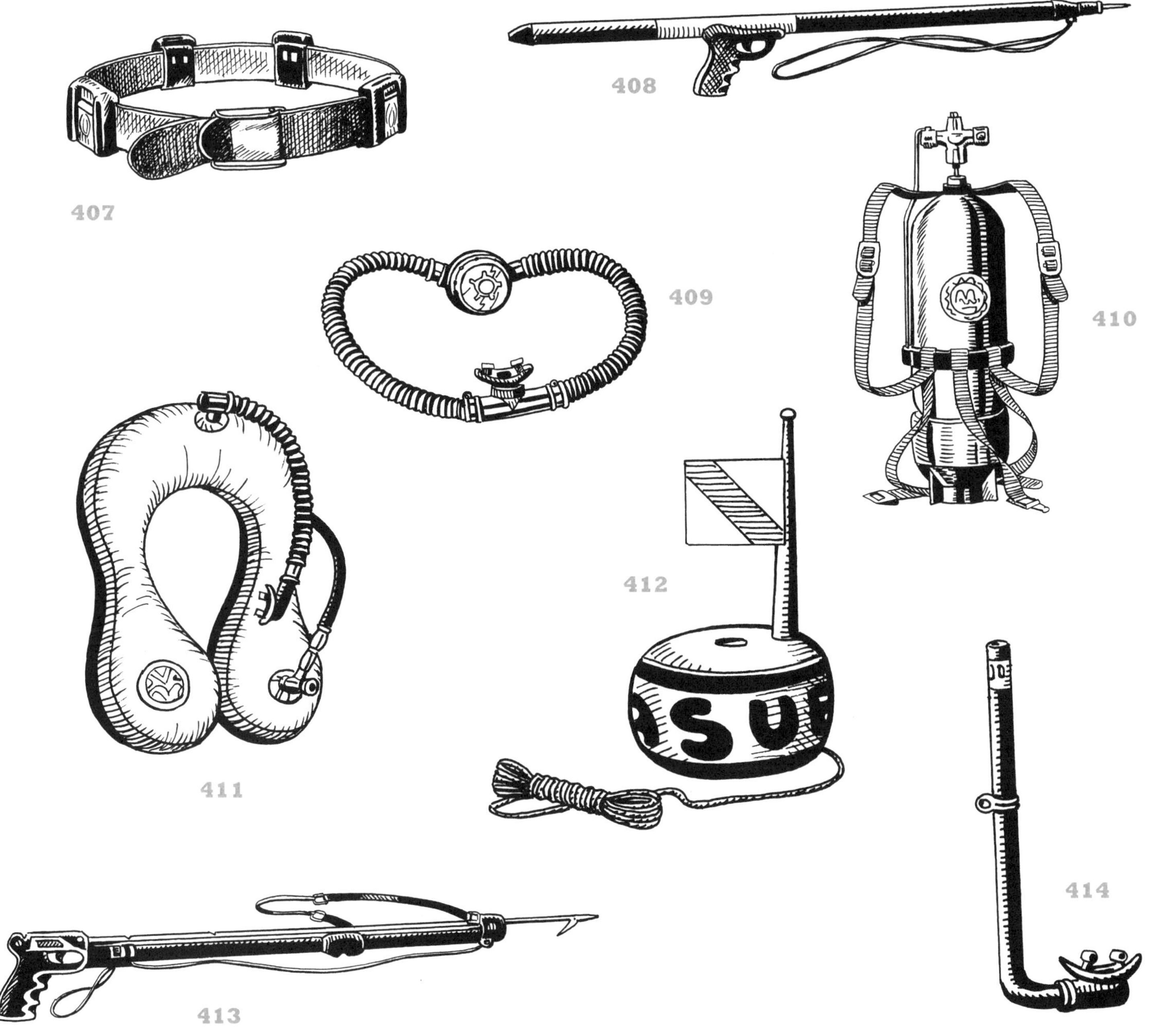

407
408
409
410
411
412
413
414

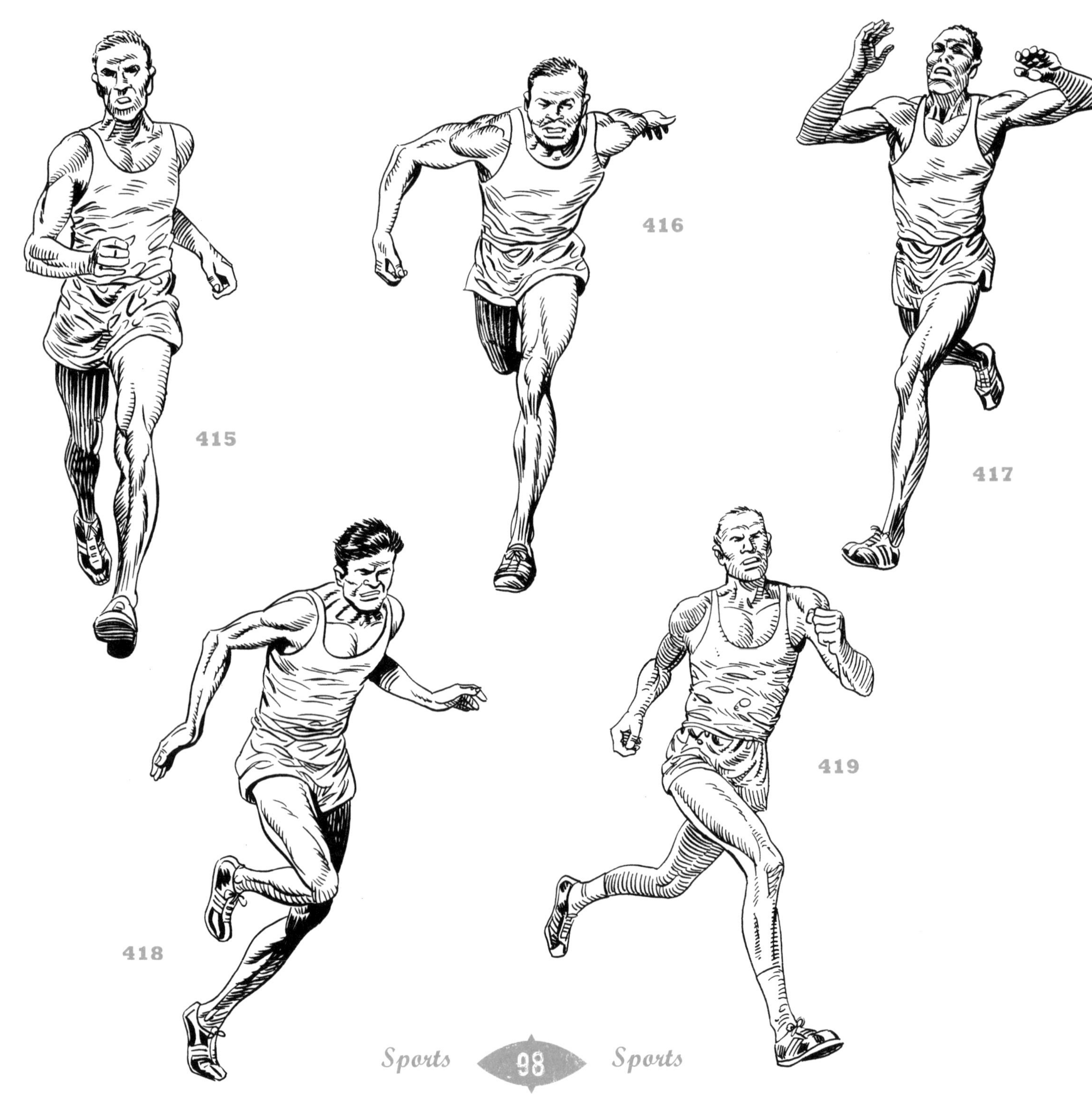

415
416
417
418
419

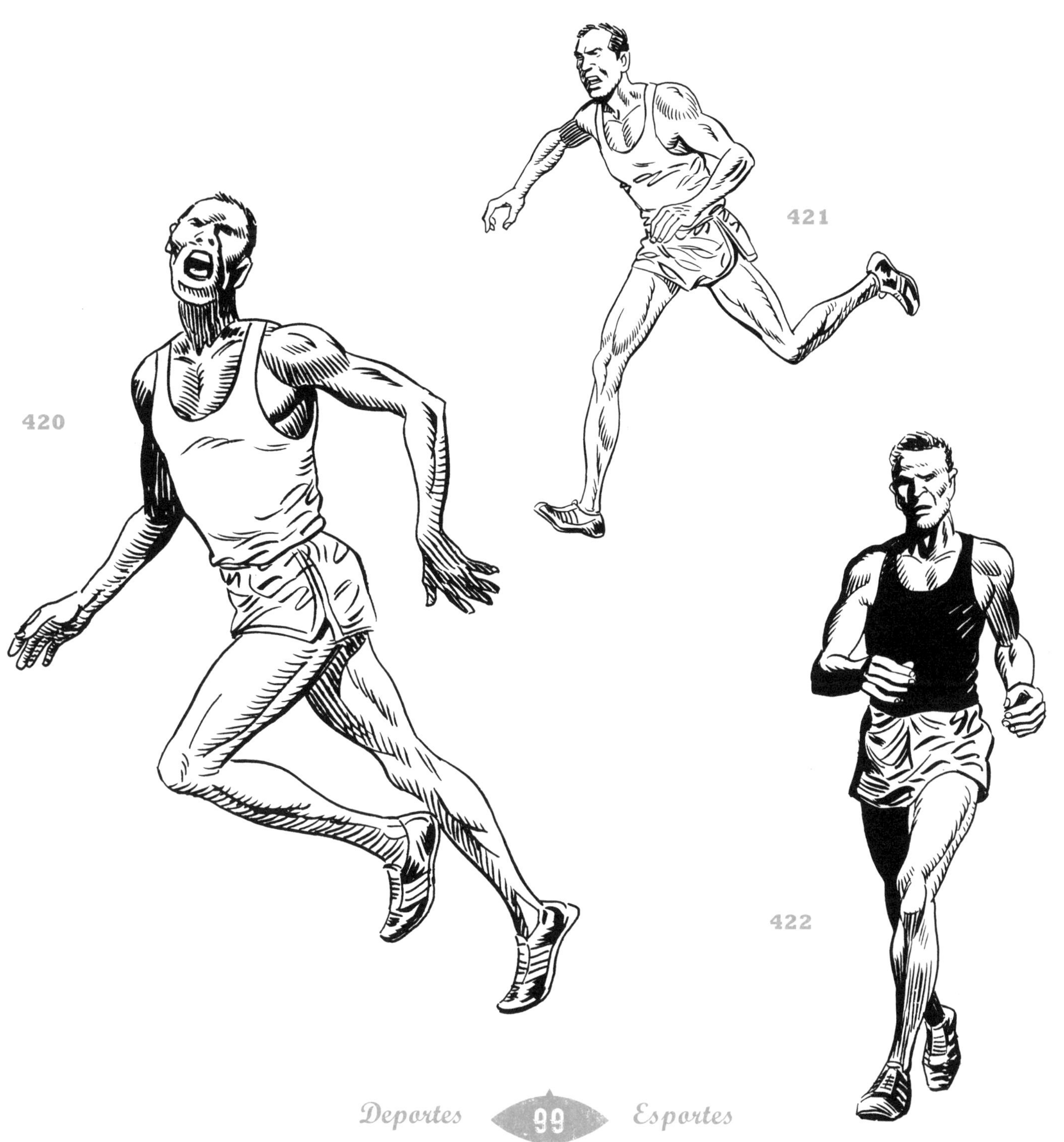

420
421
422

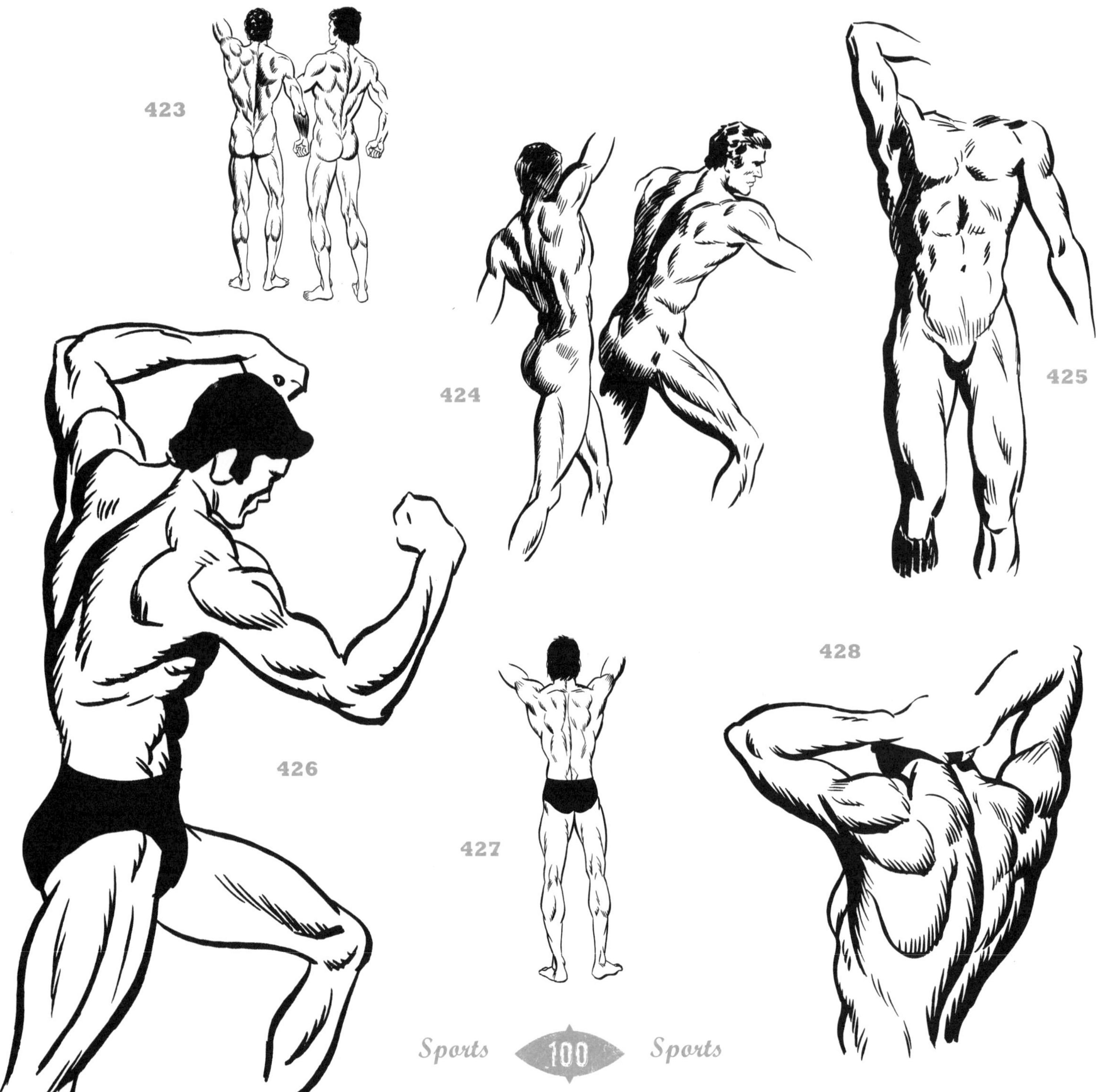

423
424
425
426
427
428

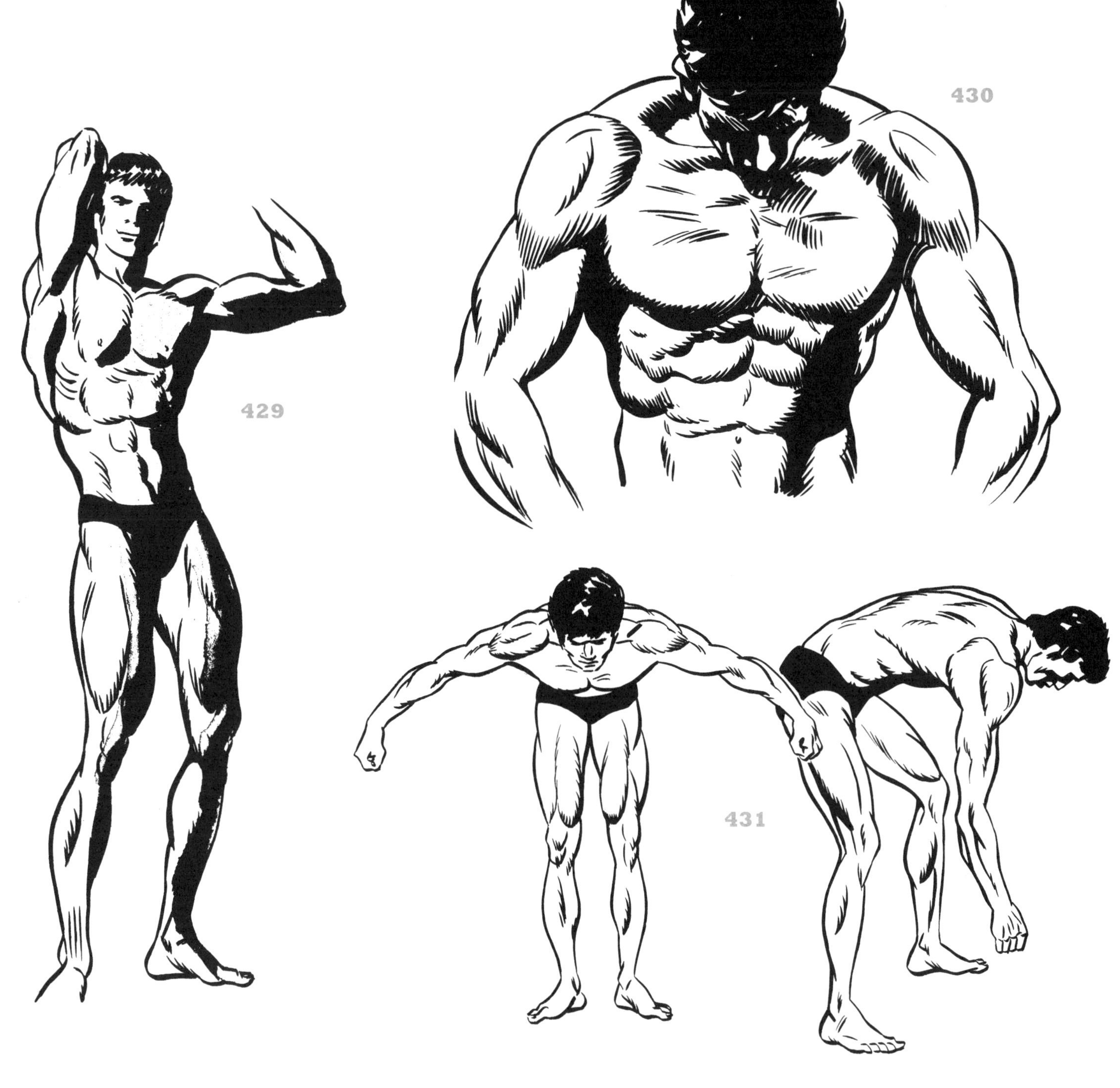

429
430
431

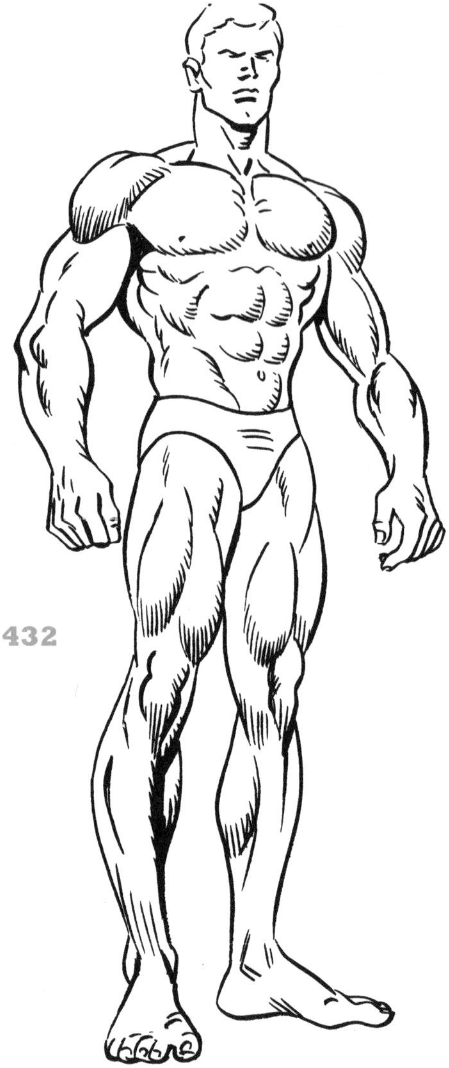

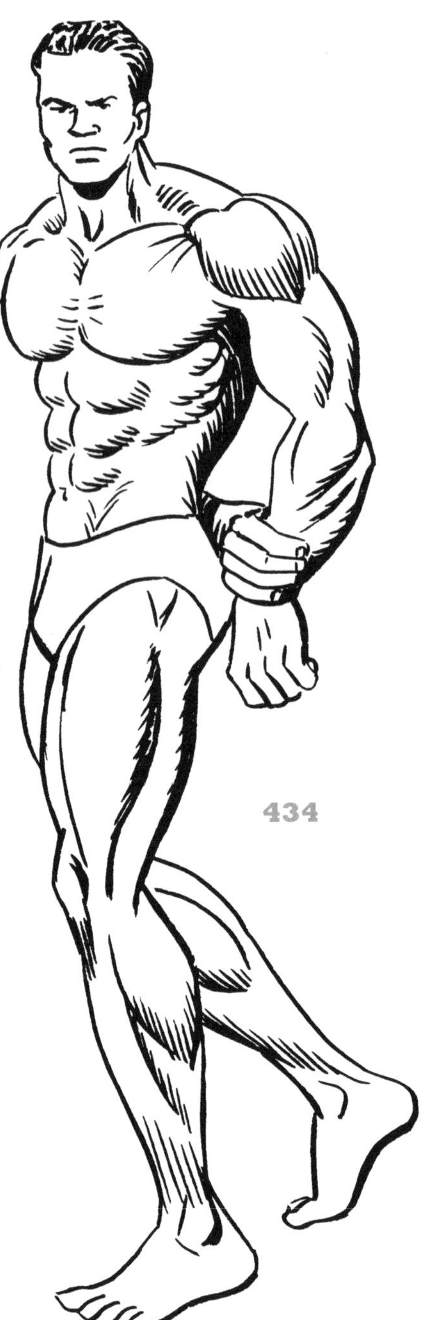

432

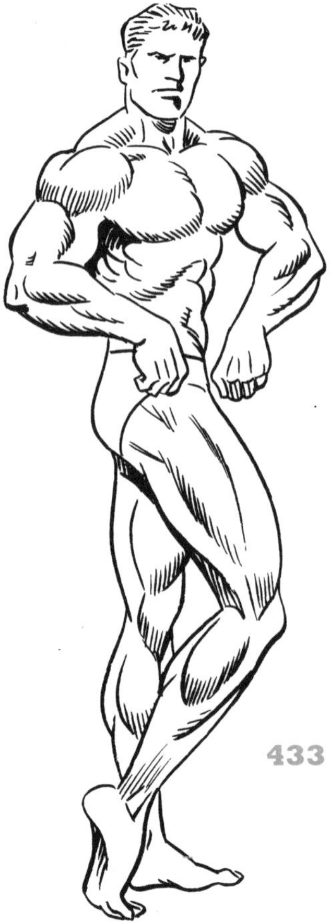

433

434

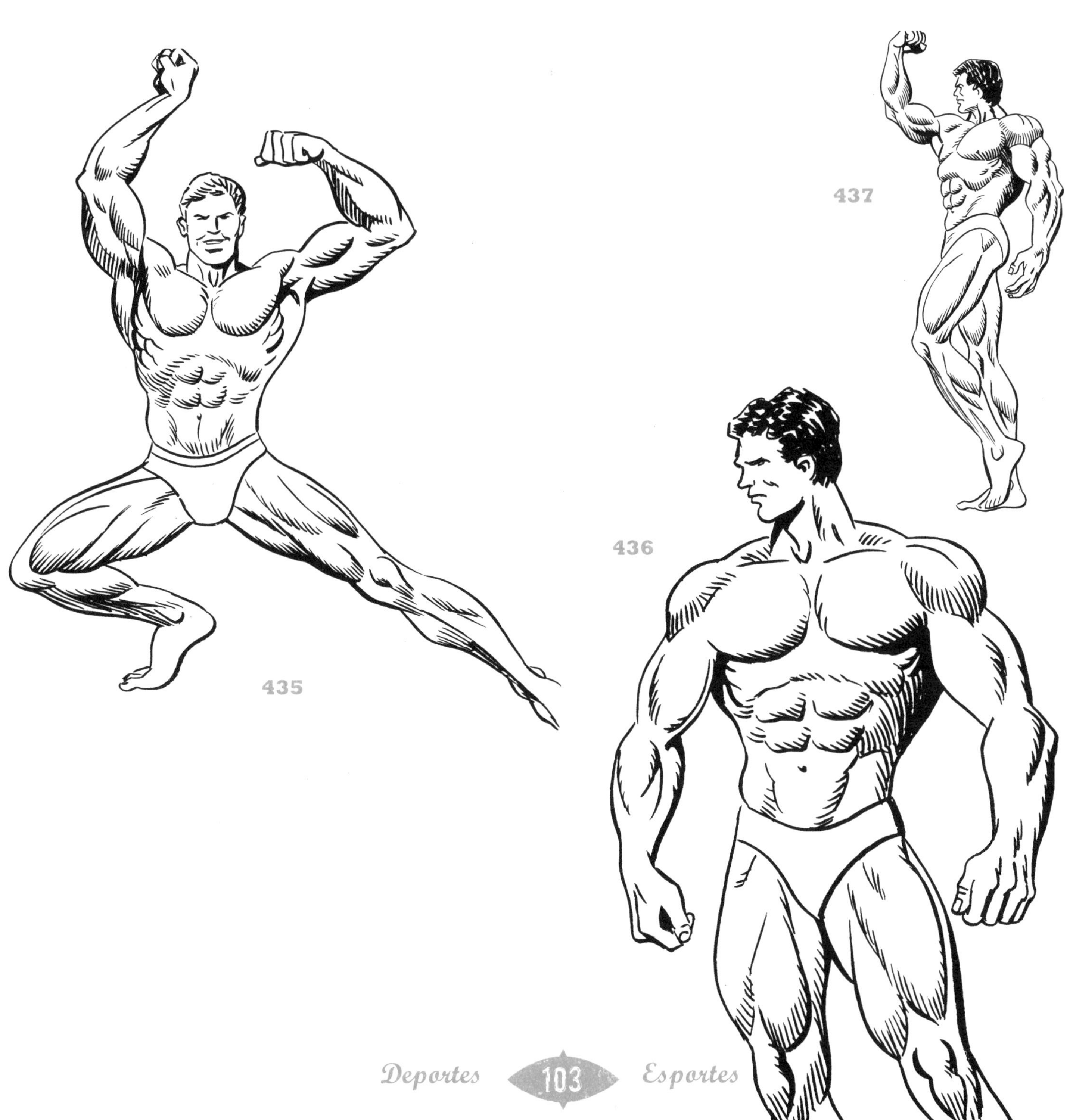

437
436
435

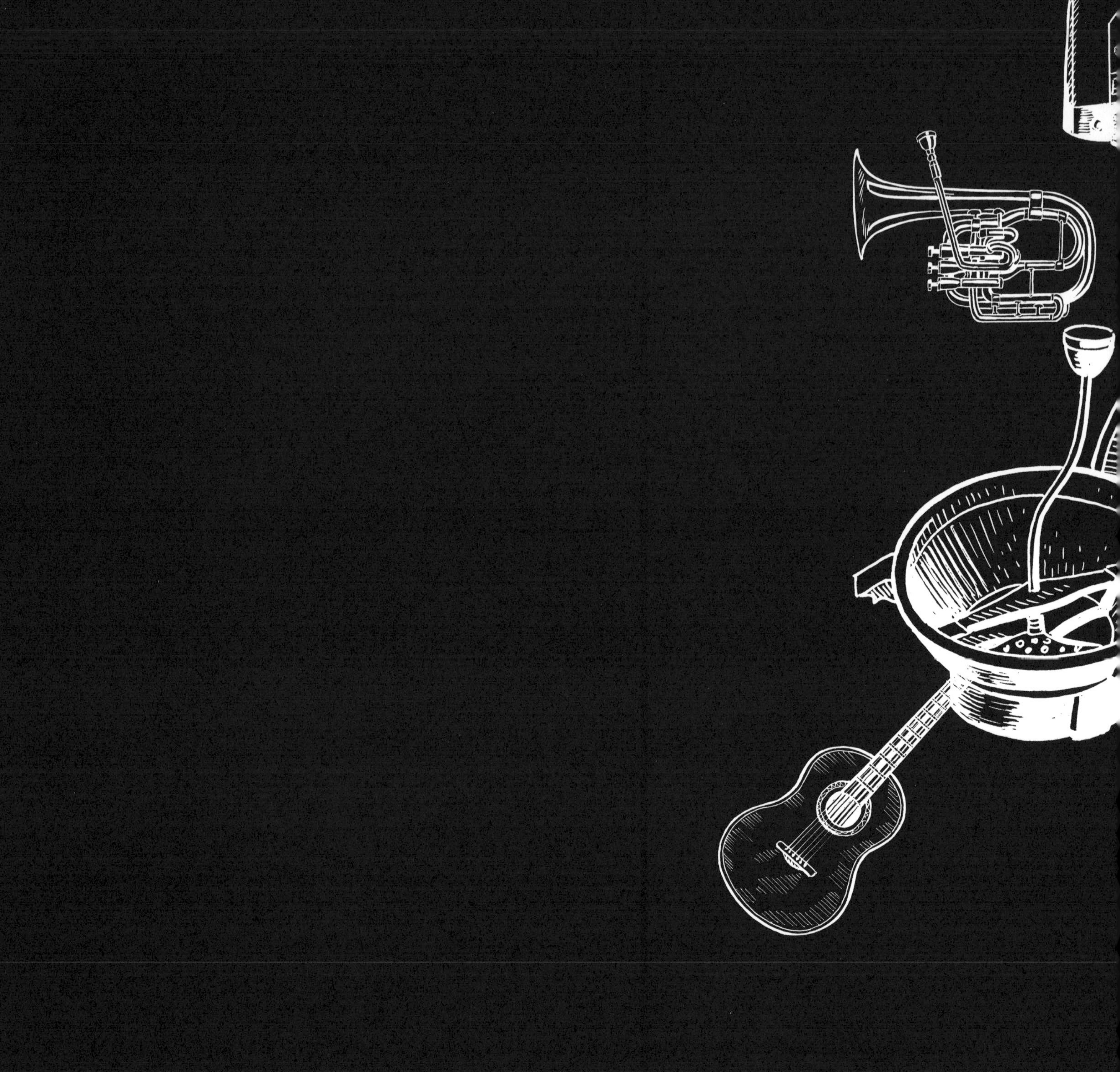

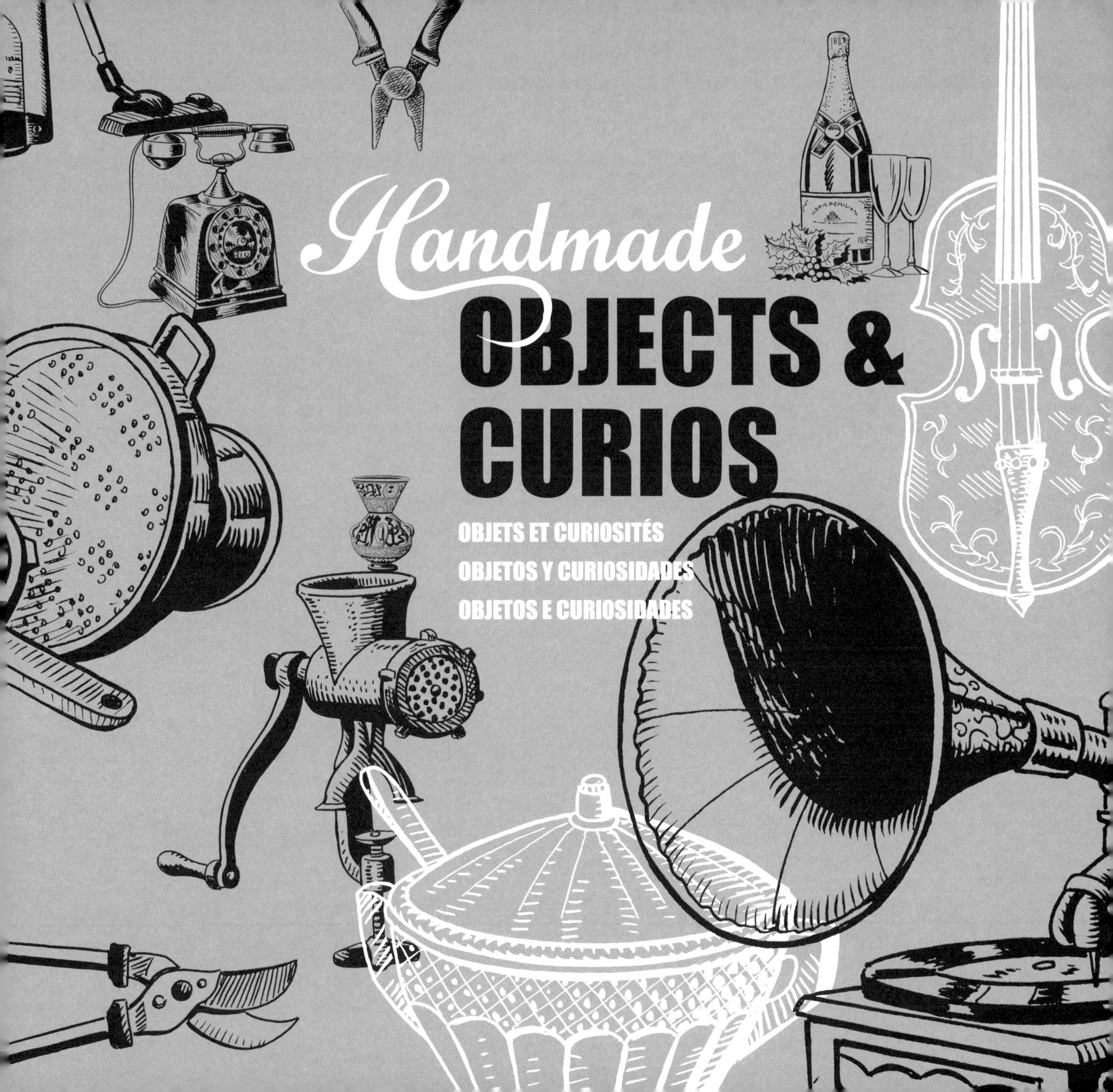

Handmade
OBJECTS &
CURIOS
OBJETS ET CURIOSITÉS
OBJETOS Y CURIOSIDADES
OBJETOS E CURIOSIDADES

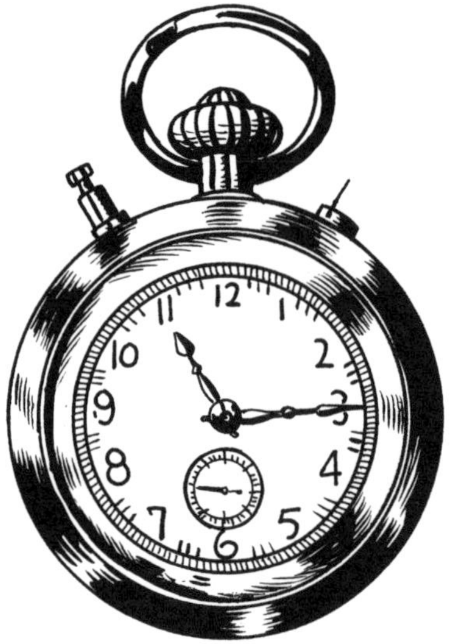

438

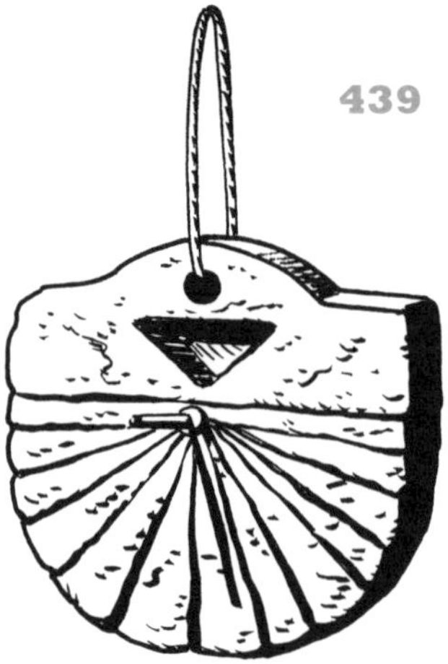

439

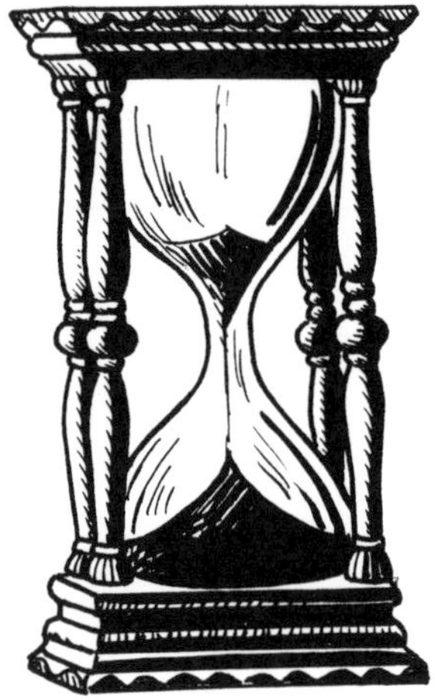

440

441

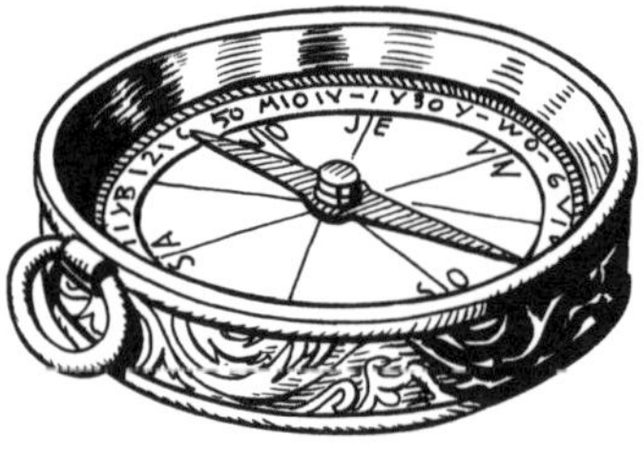

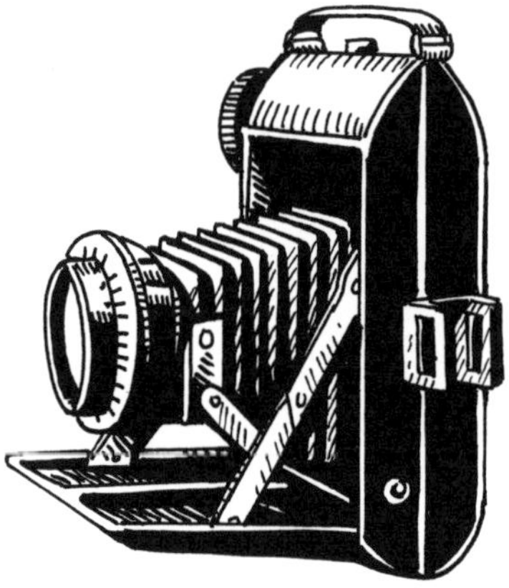

442

443

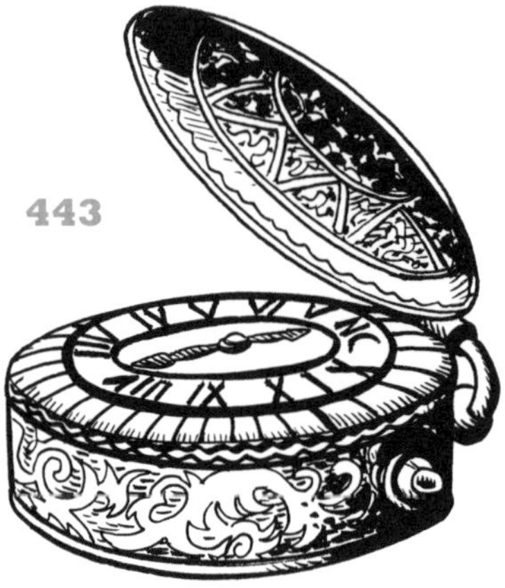

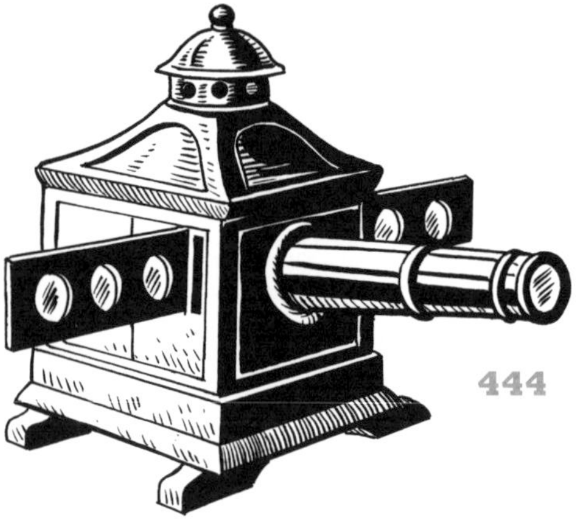

444

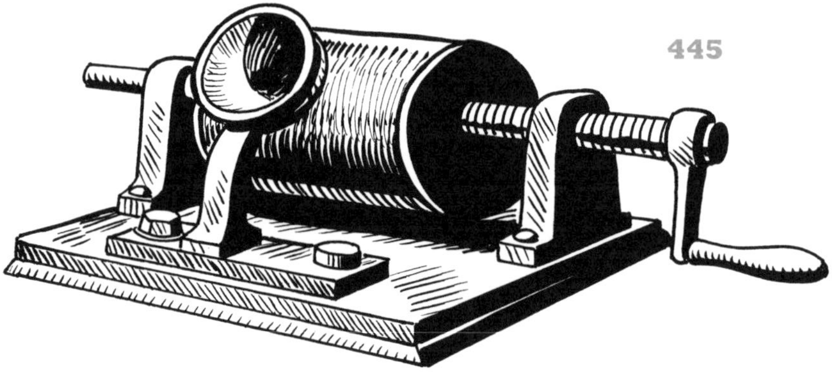

445

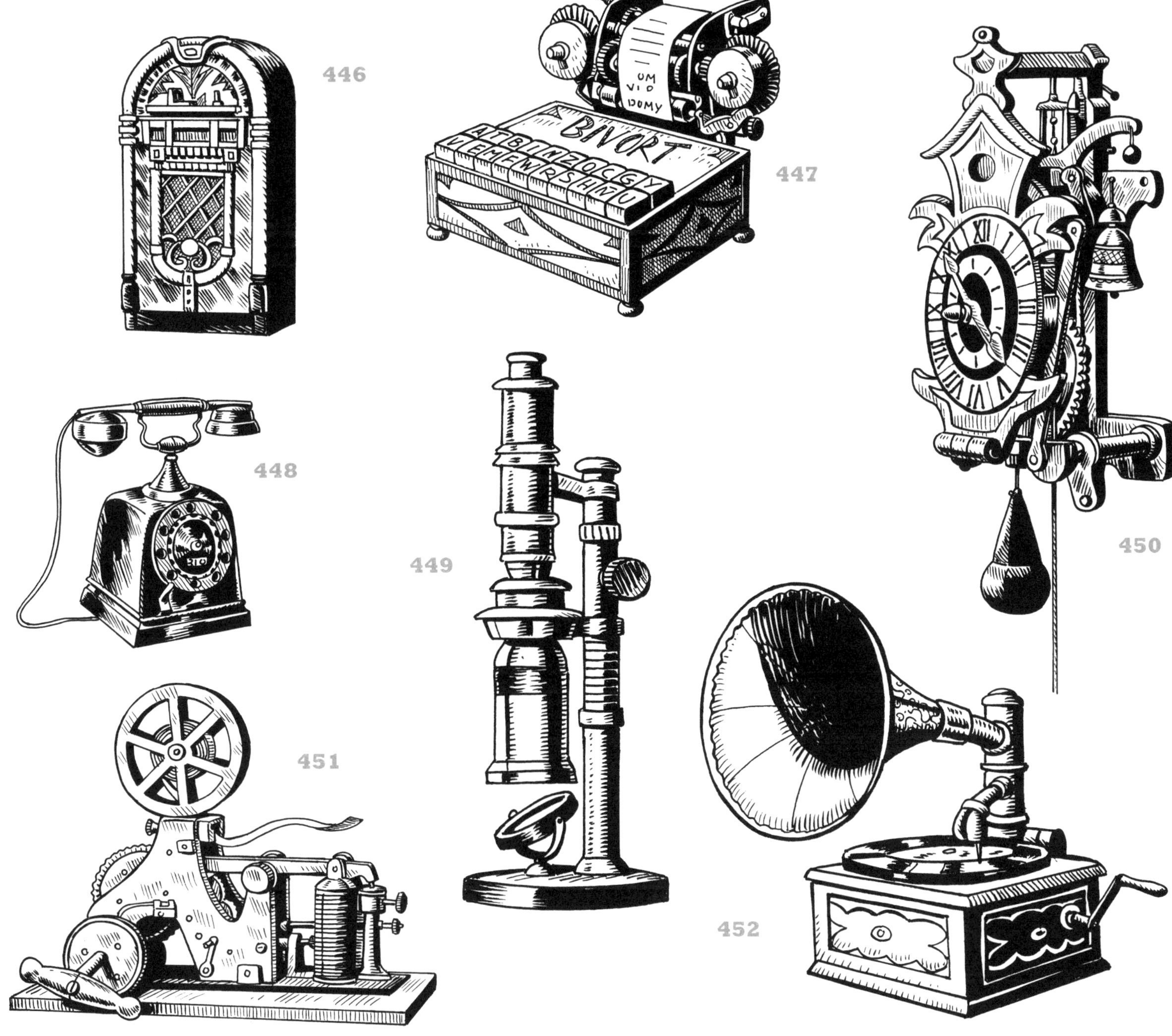

446
447
BIVORT
448
449
450
451
452

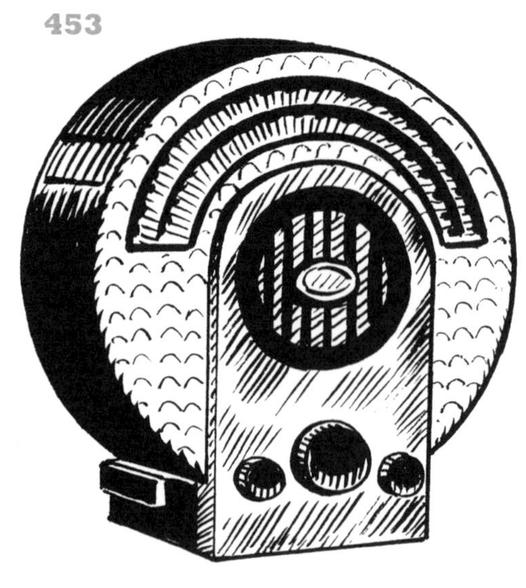

453

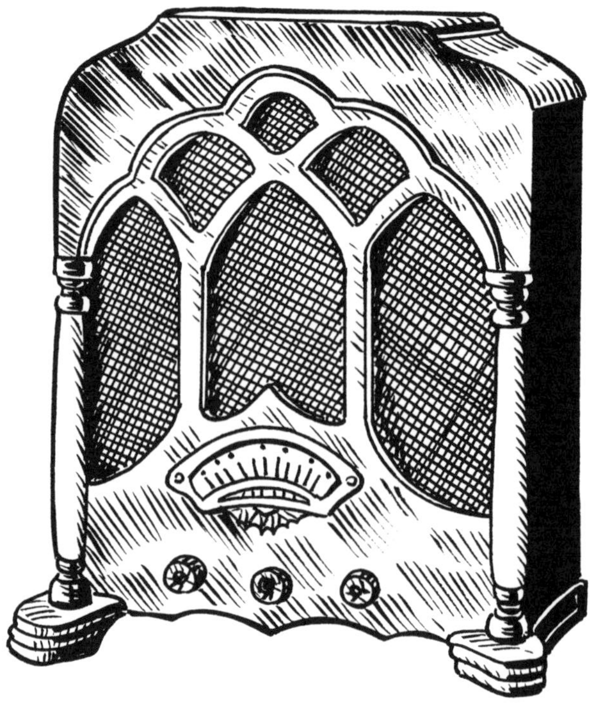

454

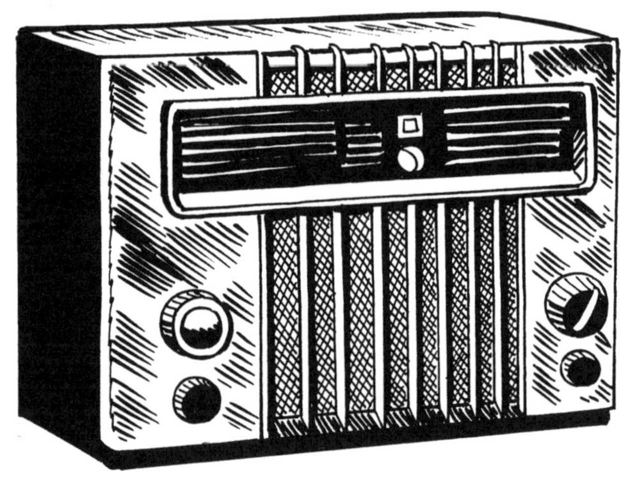

455

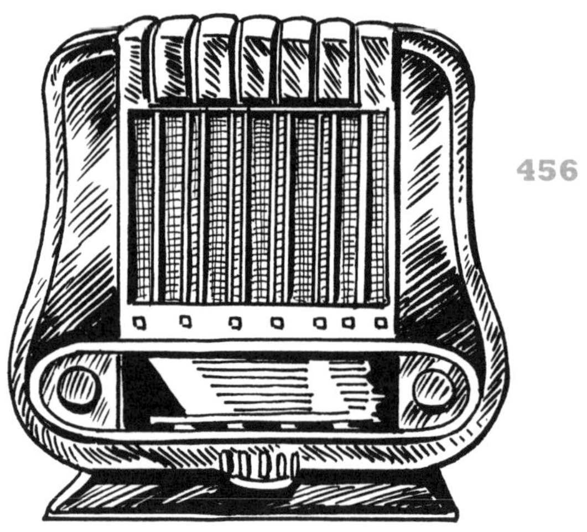

456

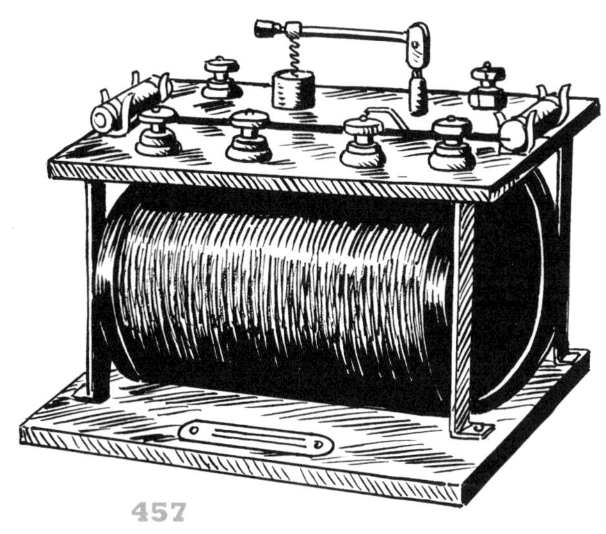

457

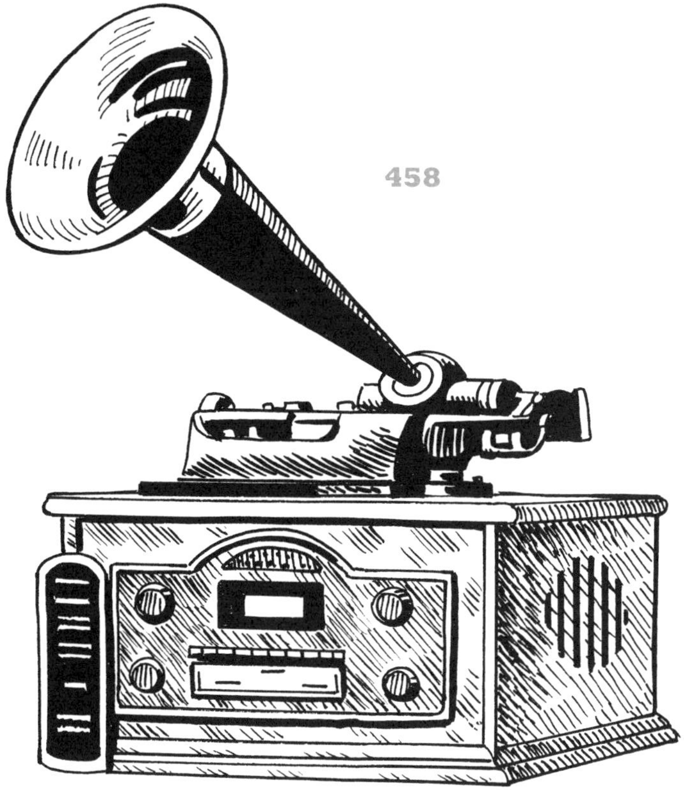

458

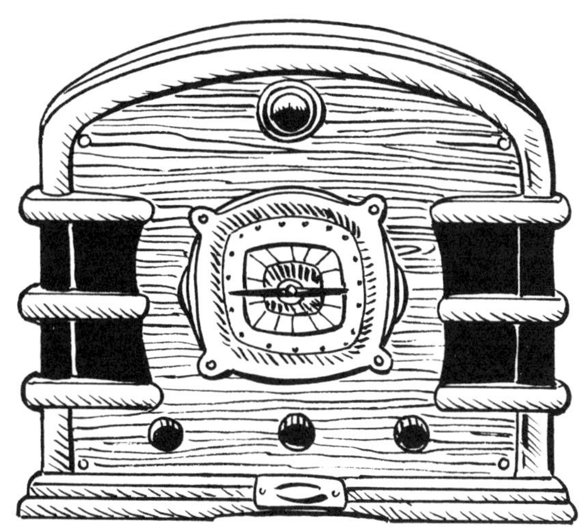

459

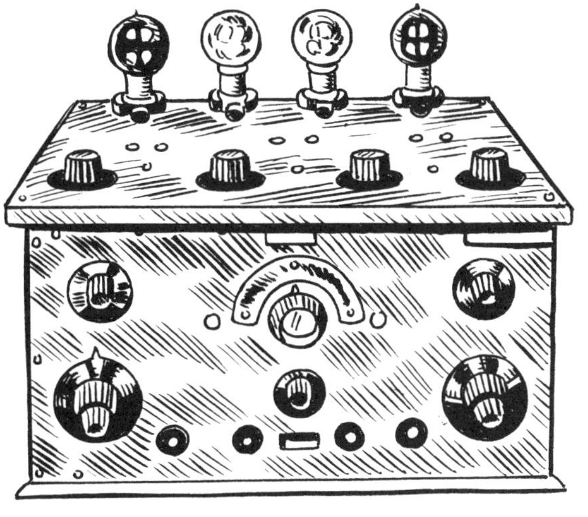

460

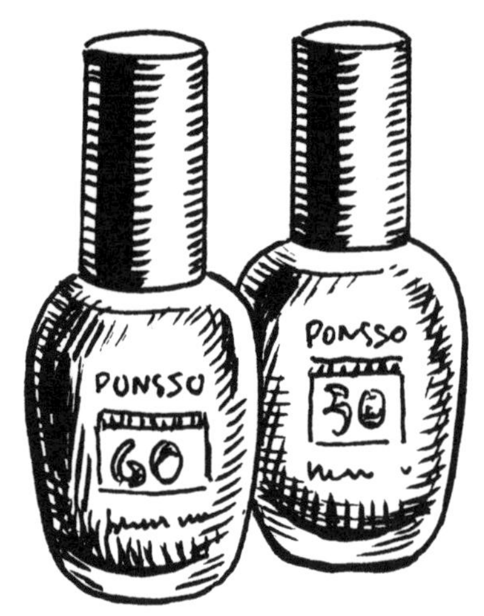

461

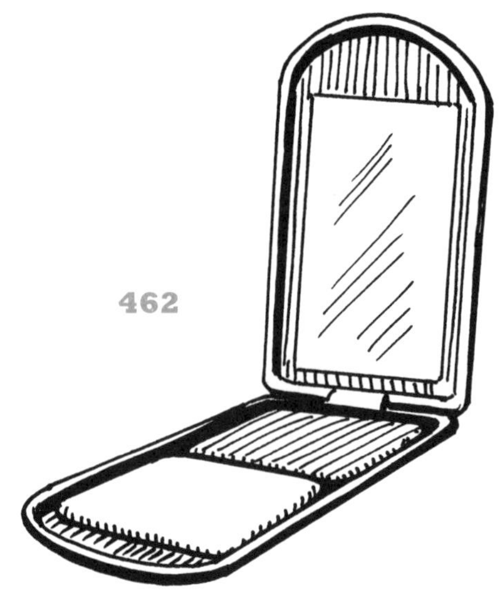

462

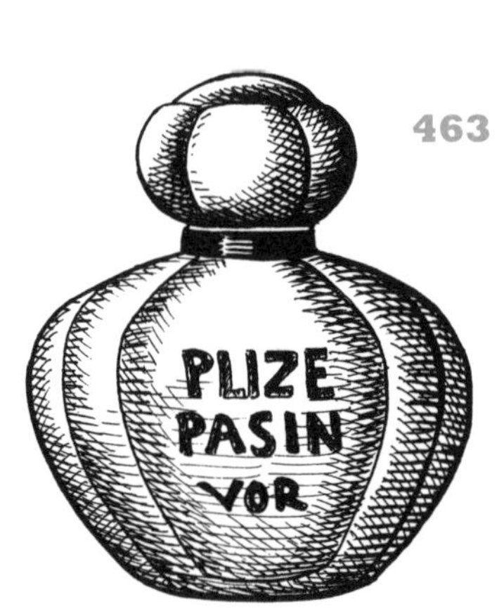

463

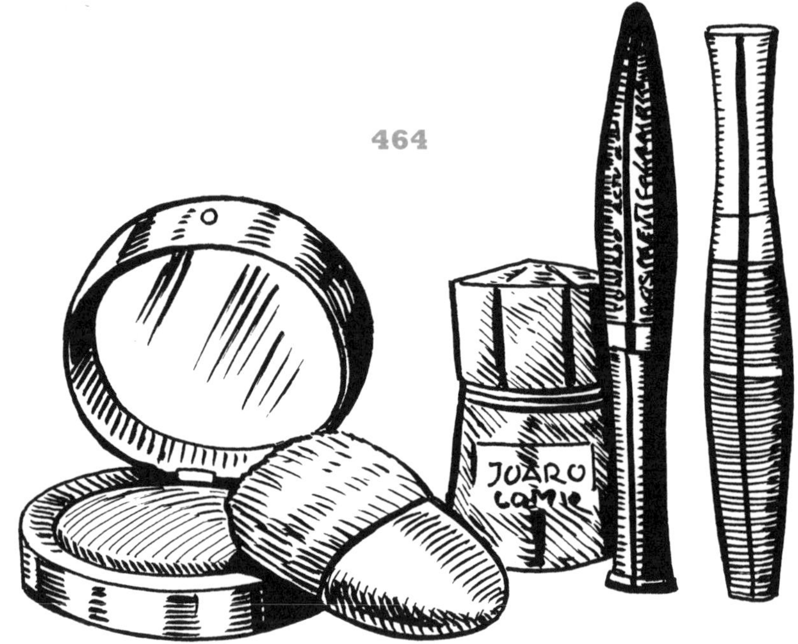

464

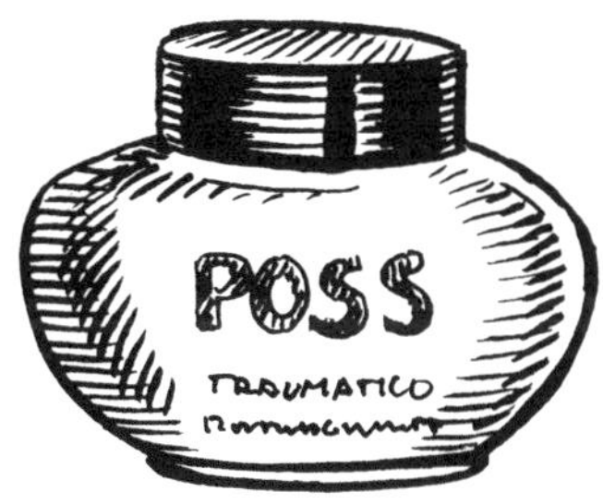

465

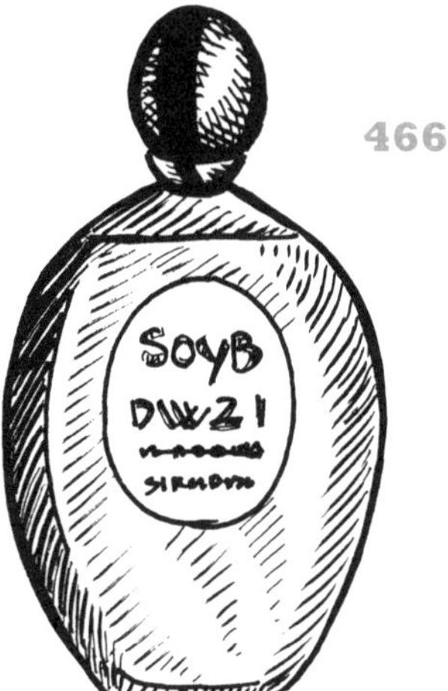

466

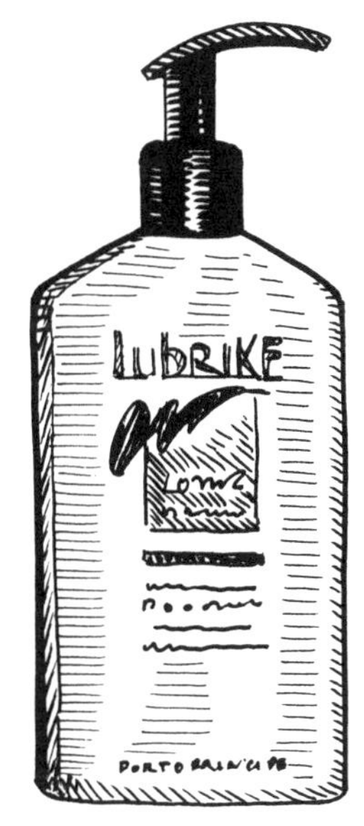

467

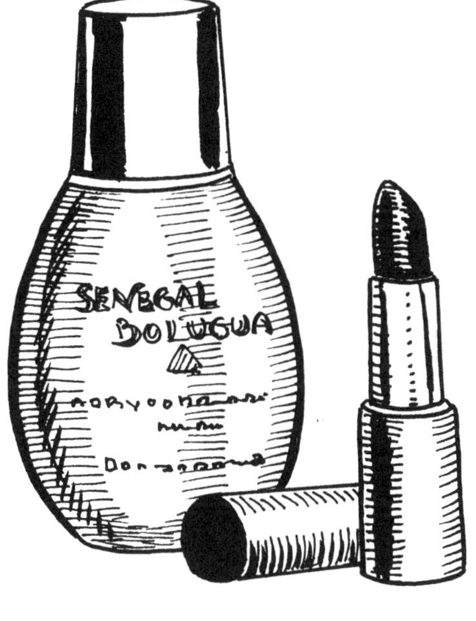

468

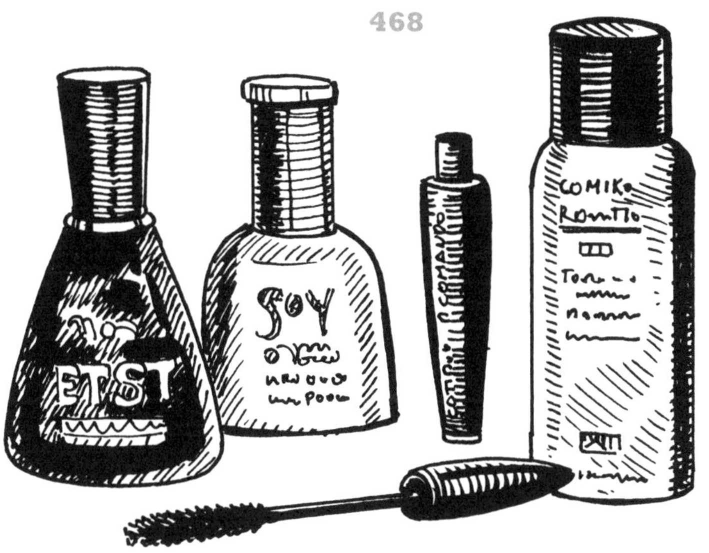

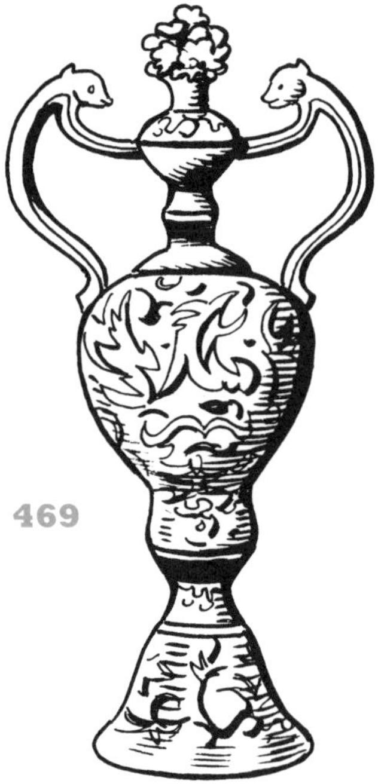

469   470   471 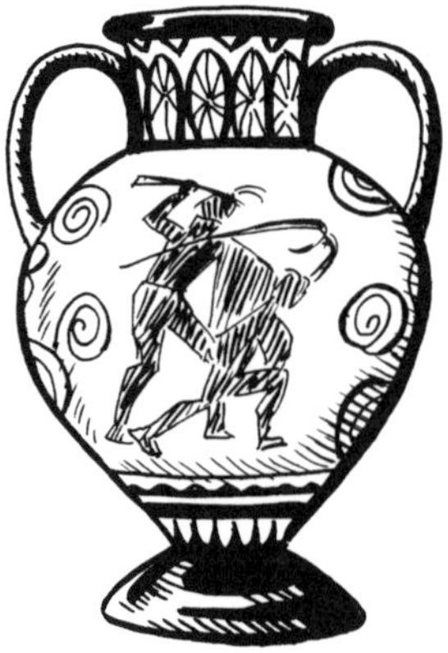 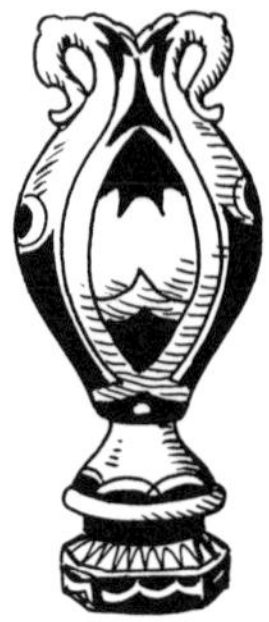   472   473   474 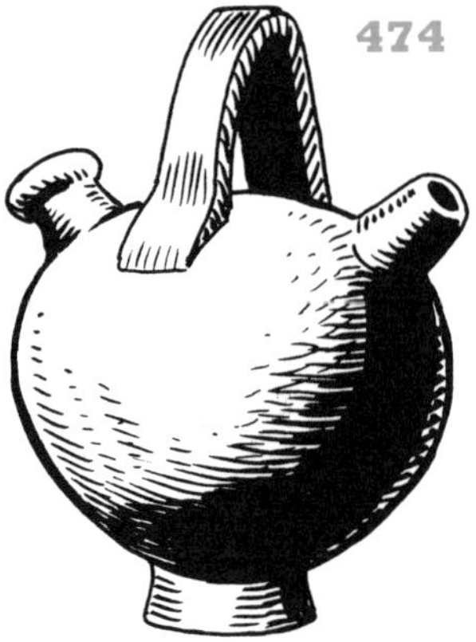   475 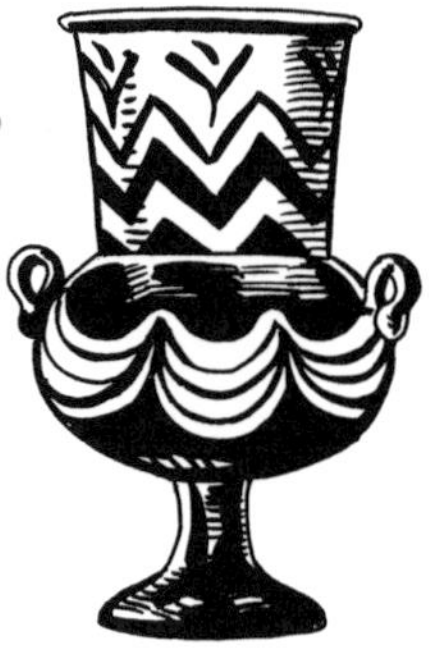 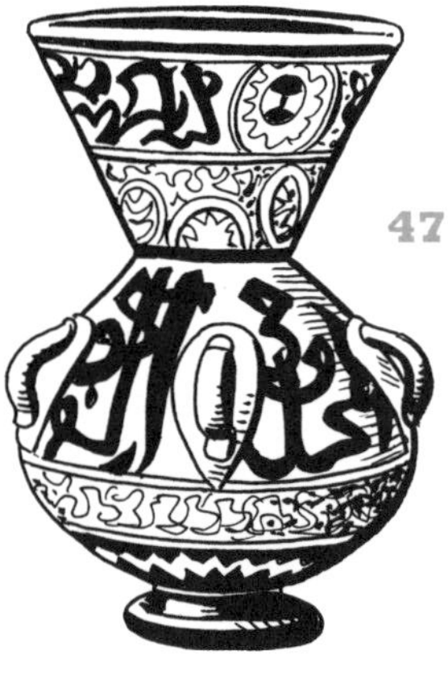   476 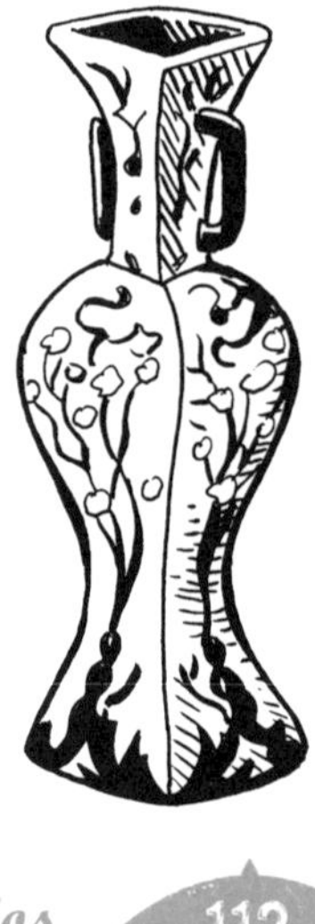   477 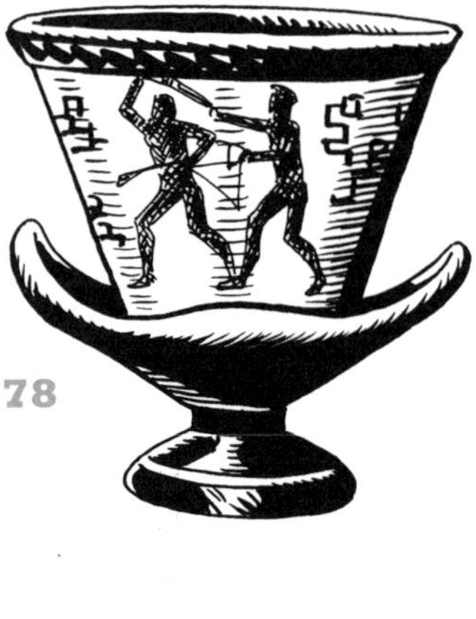   478

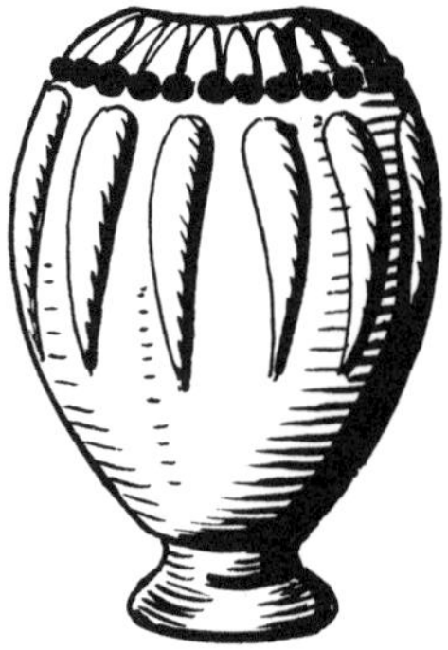

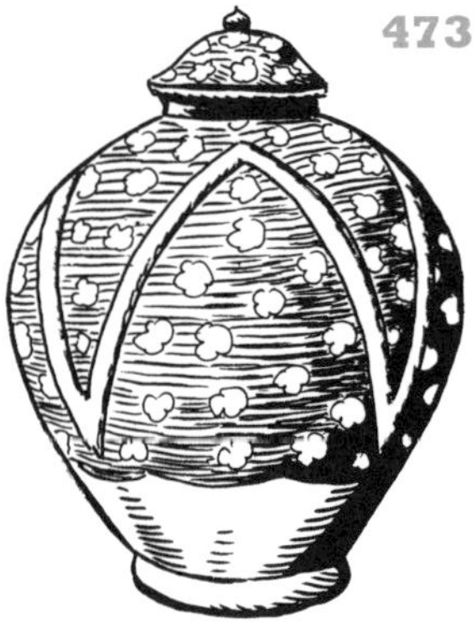

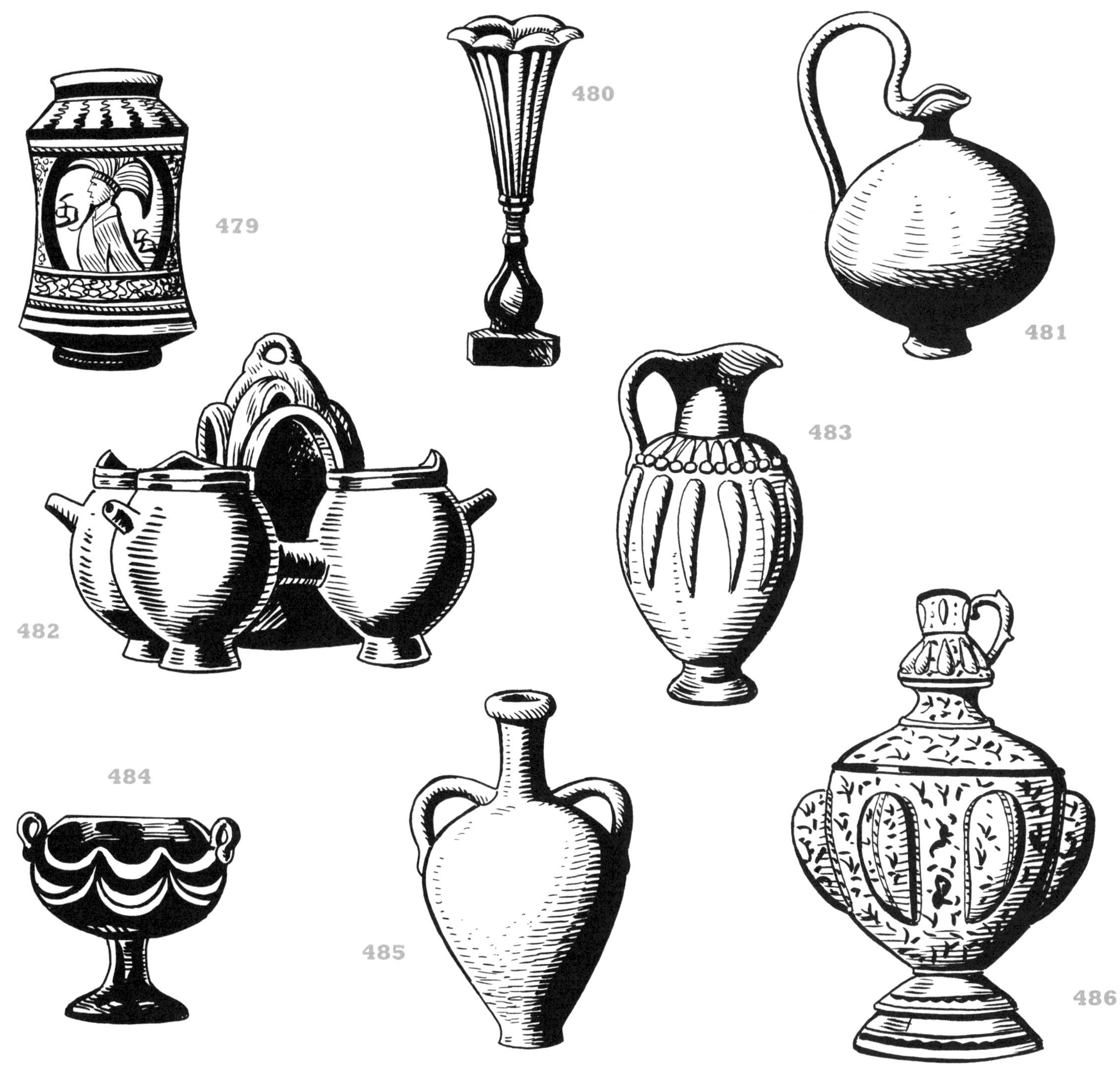

479
480
481
482
483
484
485
486

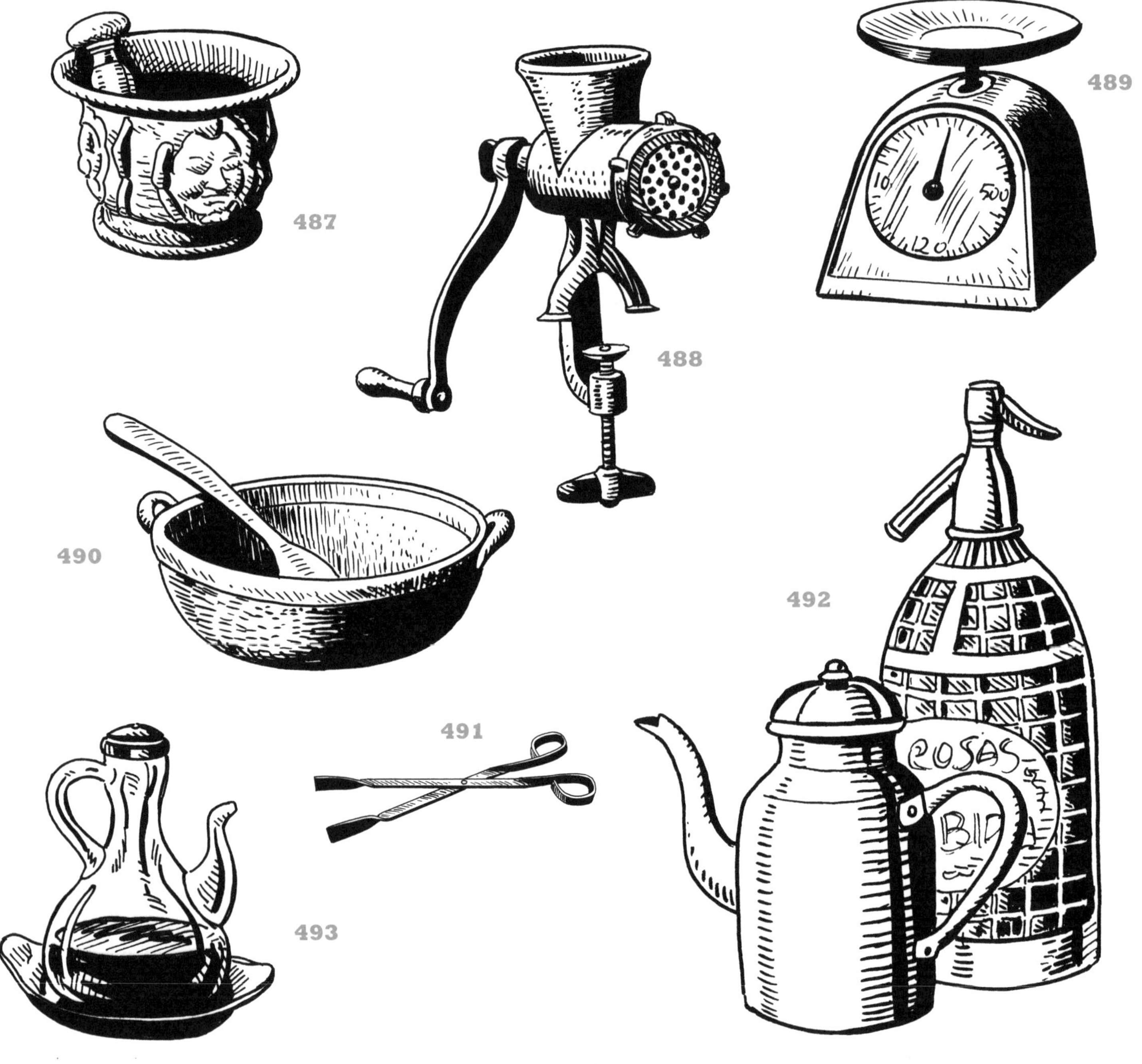

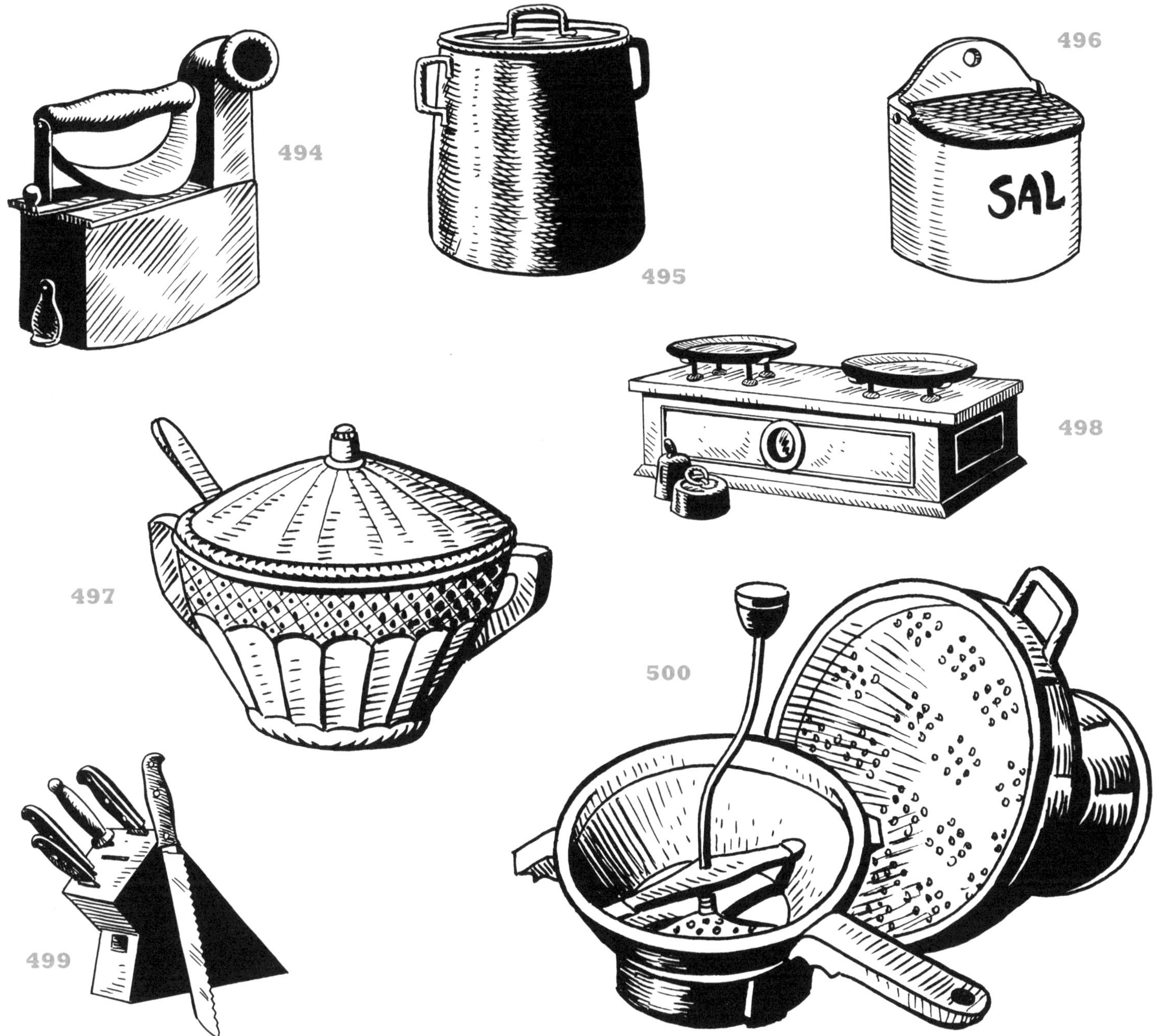

SAL

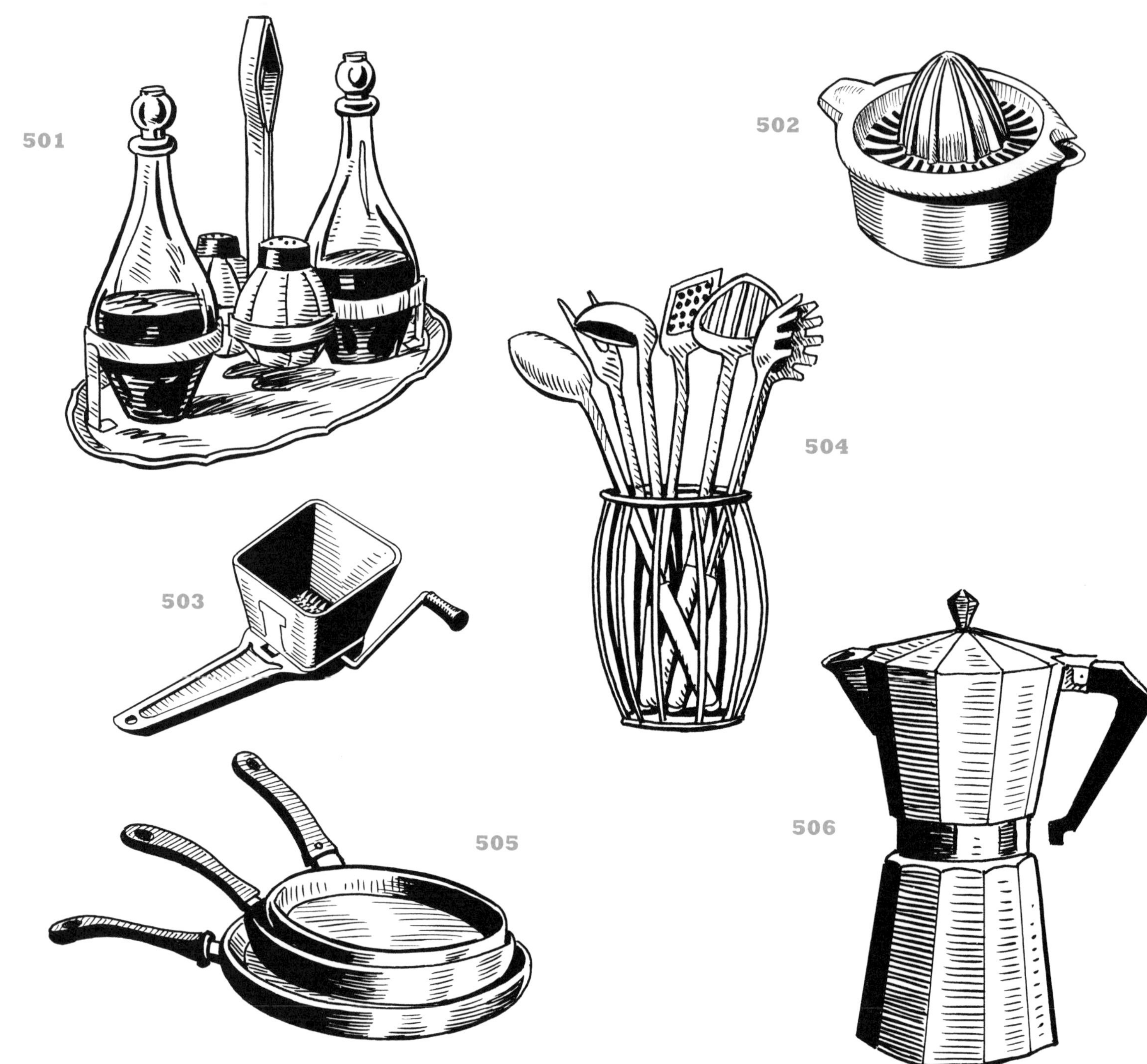

501
502
503
504
505
506

507

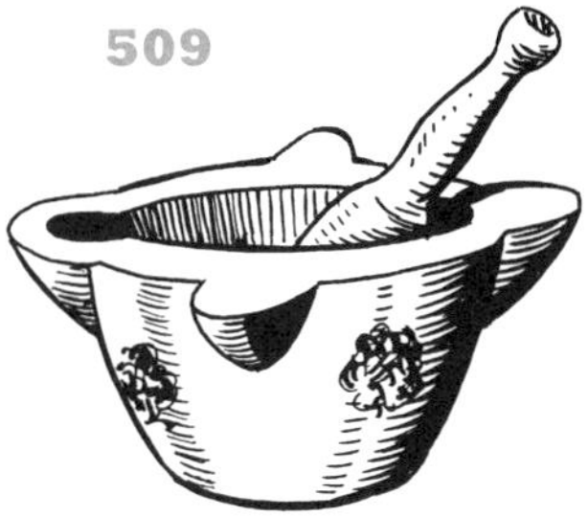

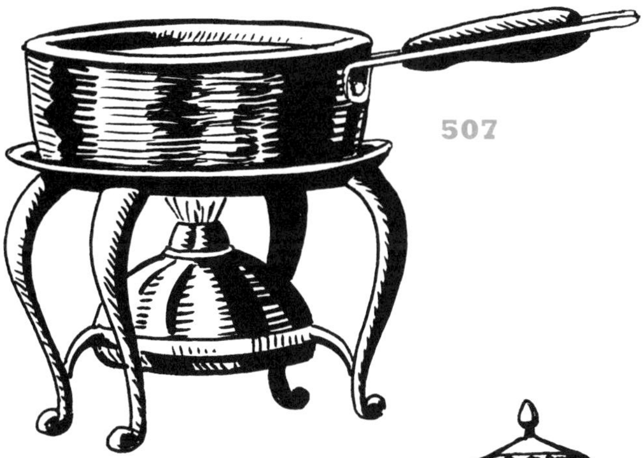

508

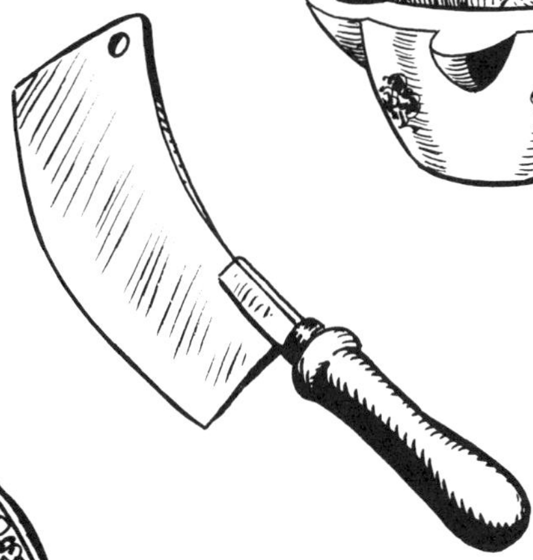

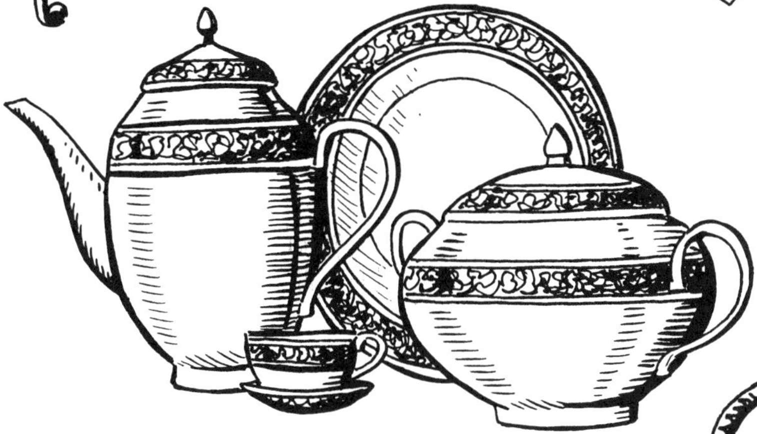

509

510

511

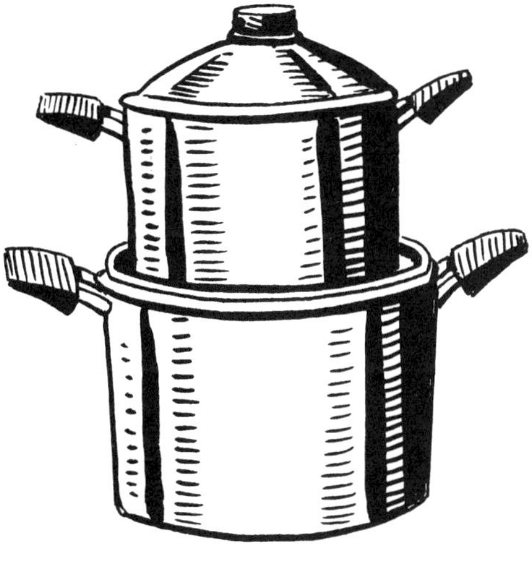

512

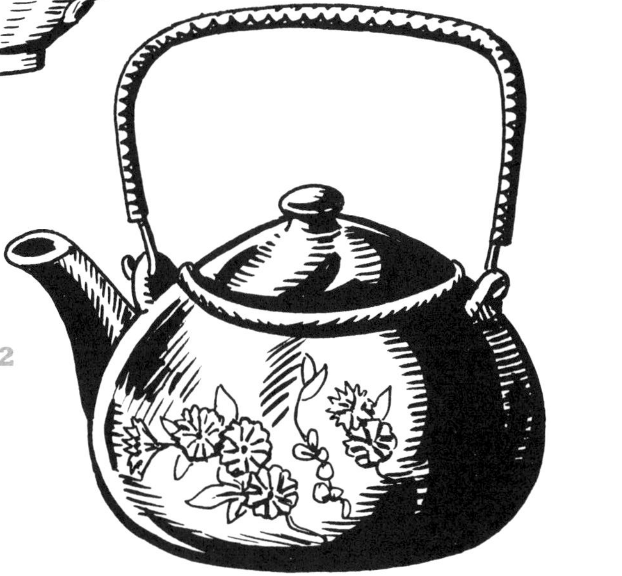

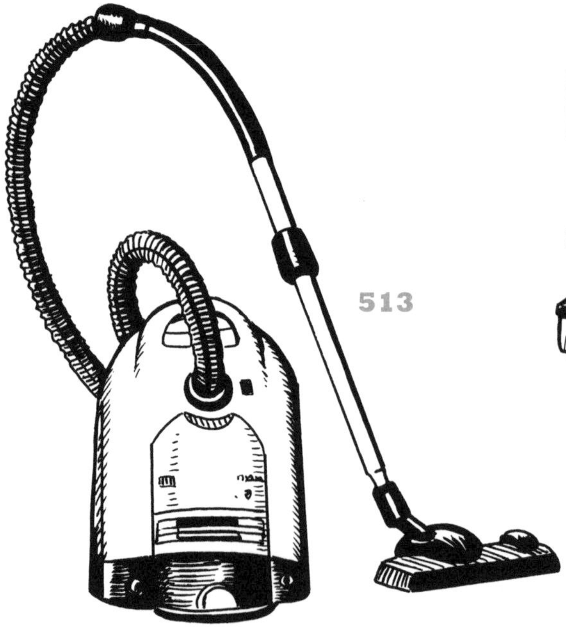

514

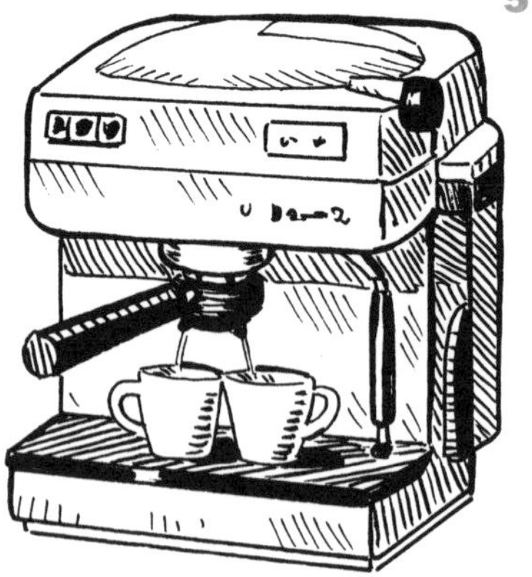

513

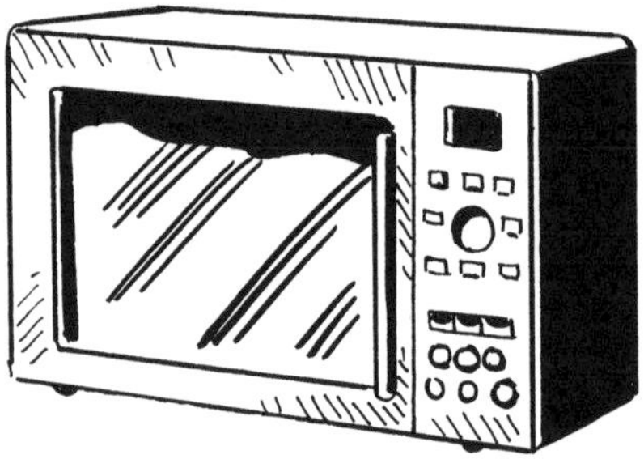

515

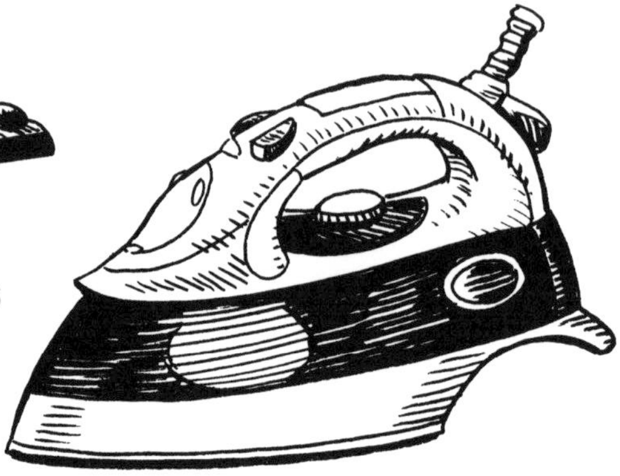

516

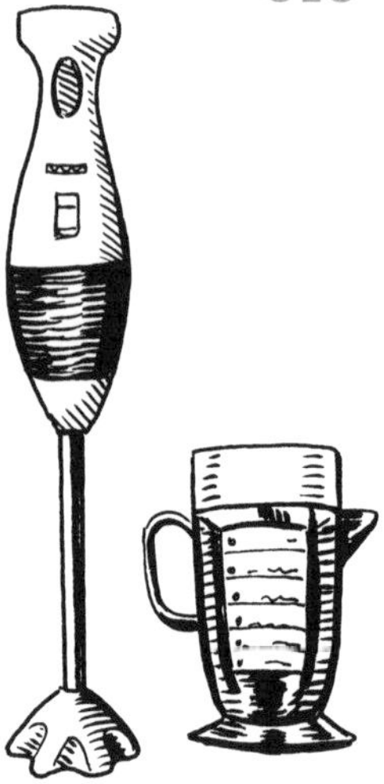

517

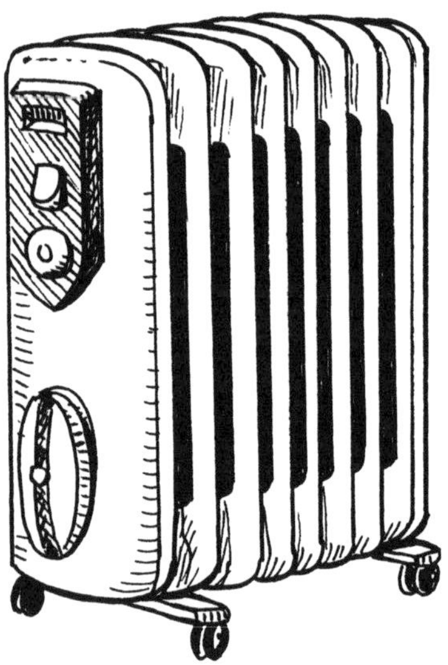

518

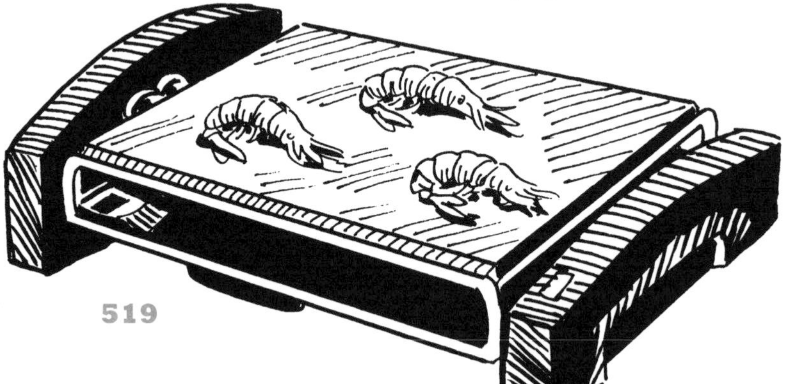

519

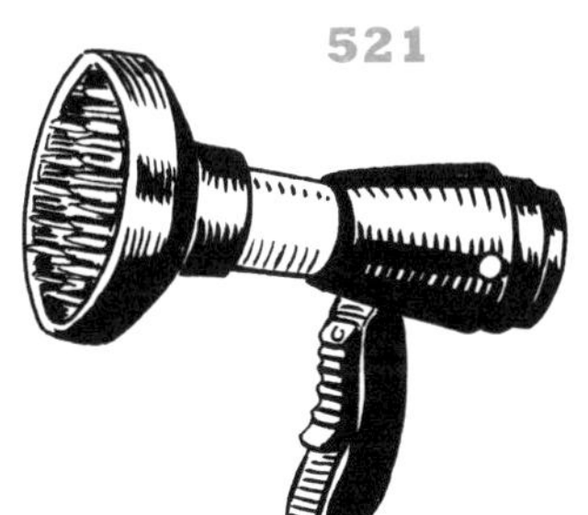

520

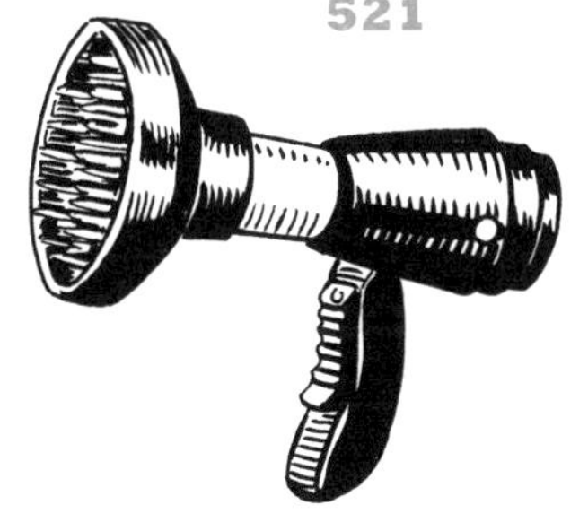

521

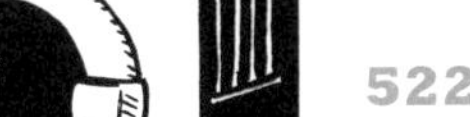

522

523

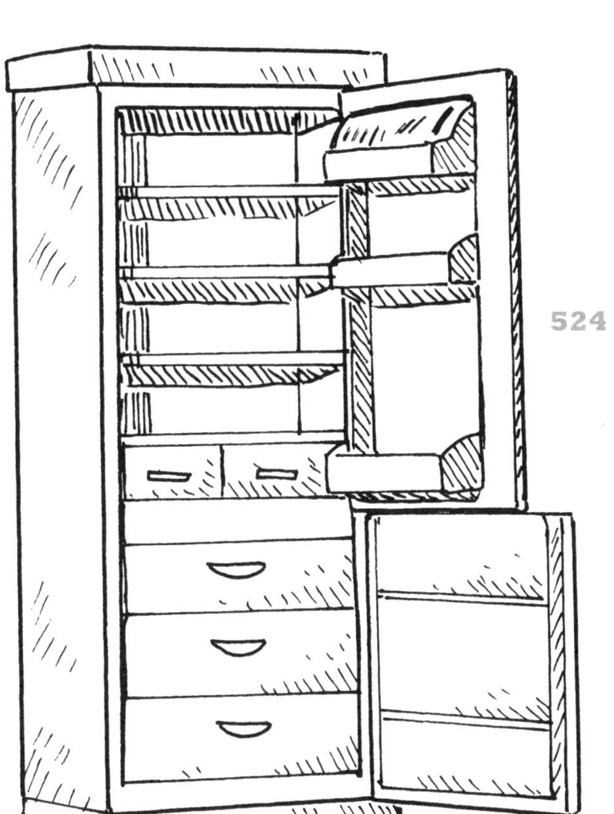

524

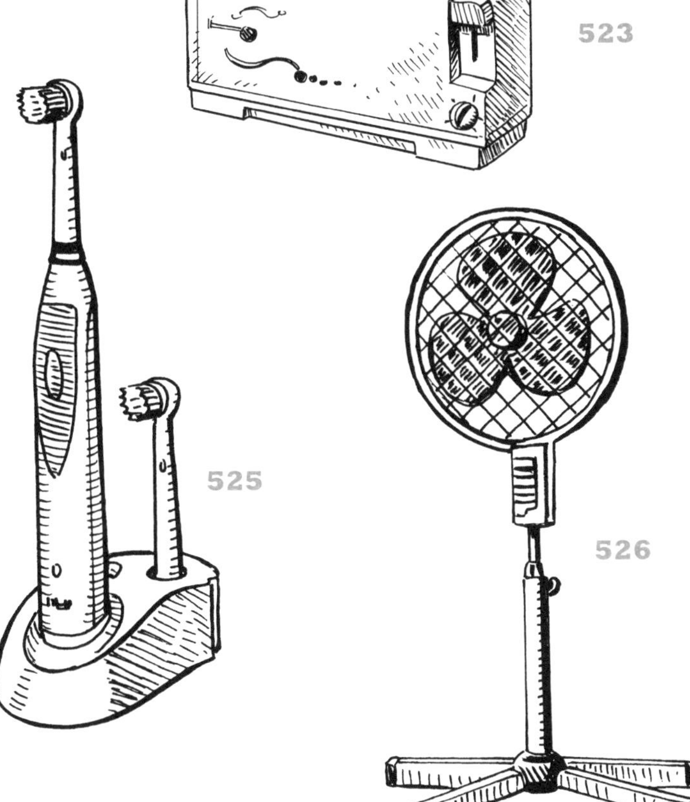

525

526

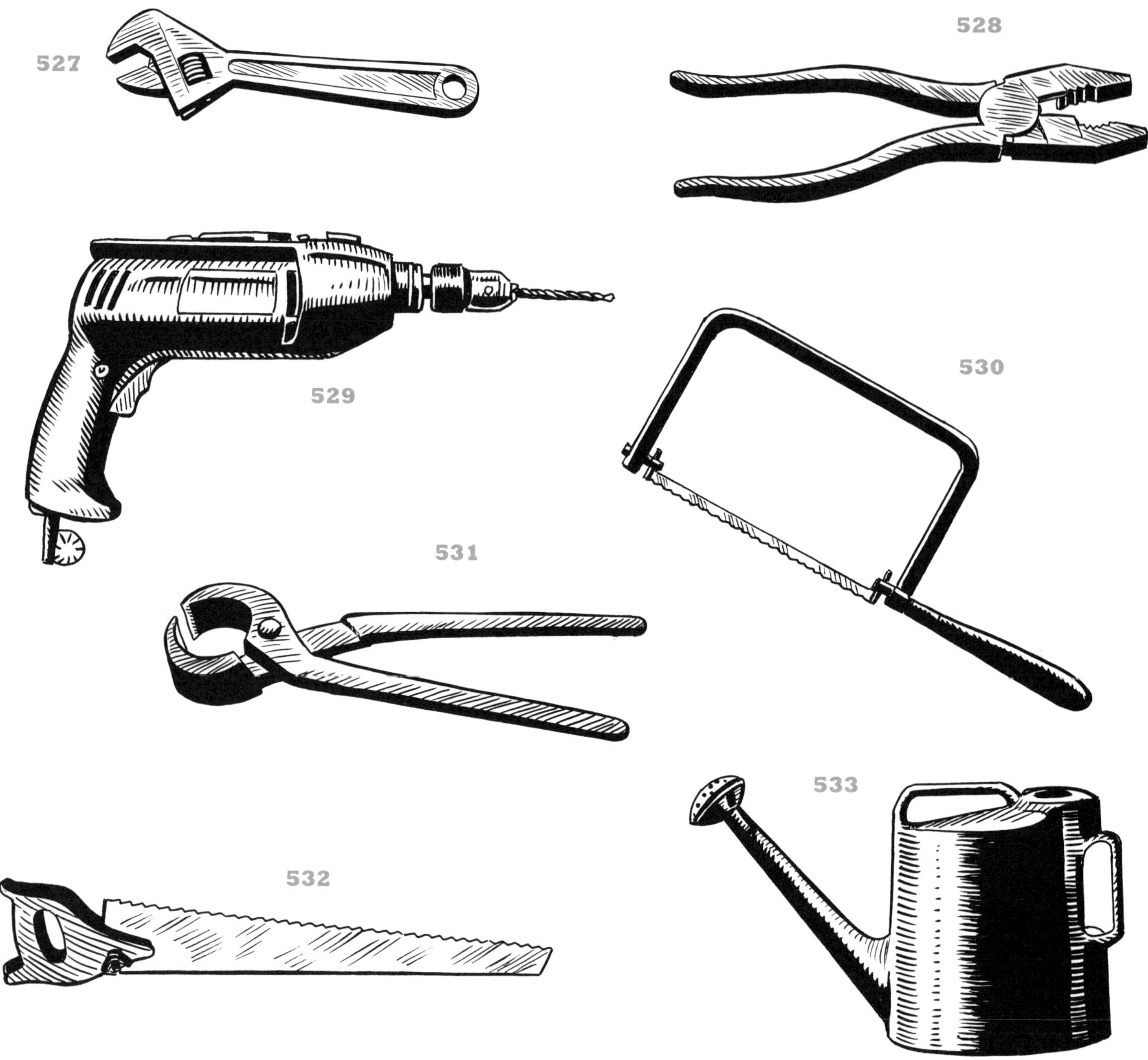

527
528
529
530
531
532
533

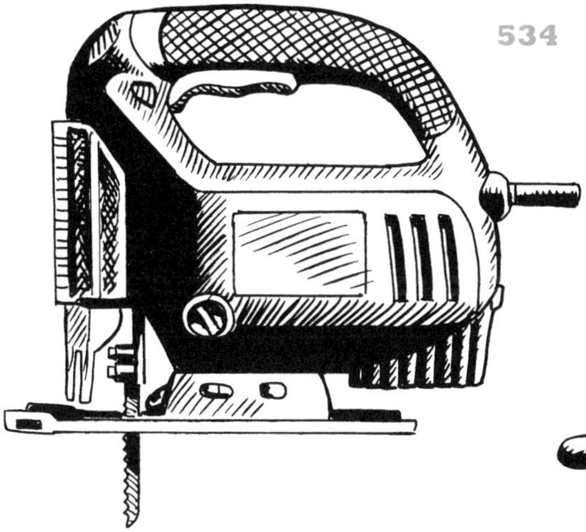

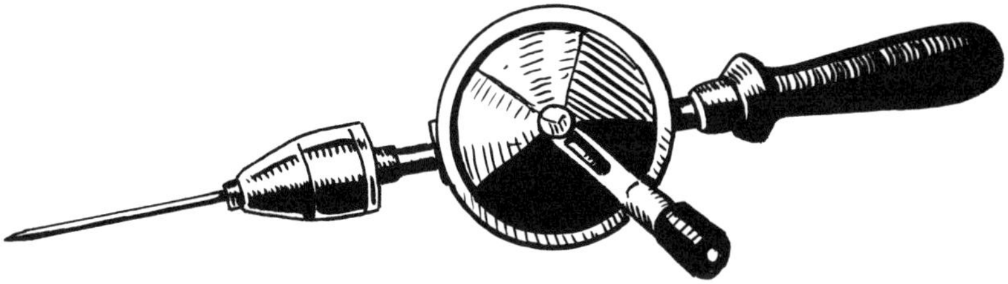

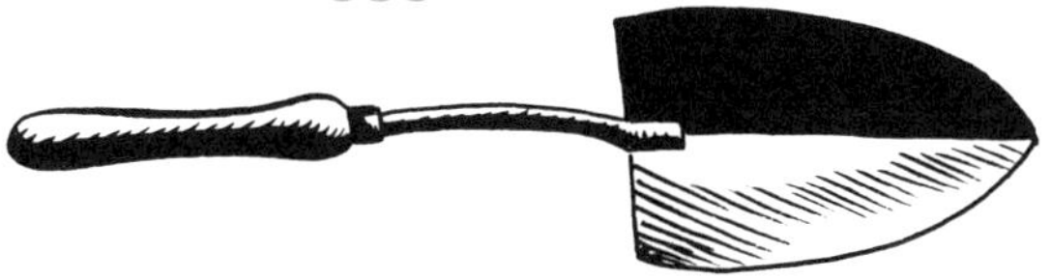

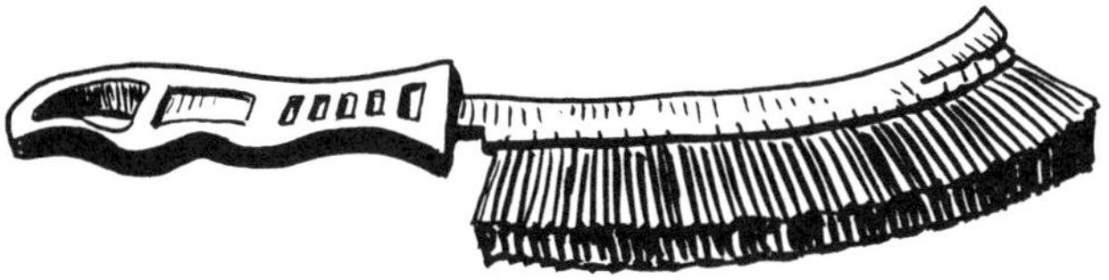

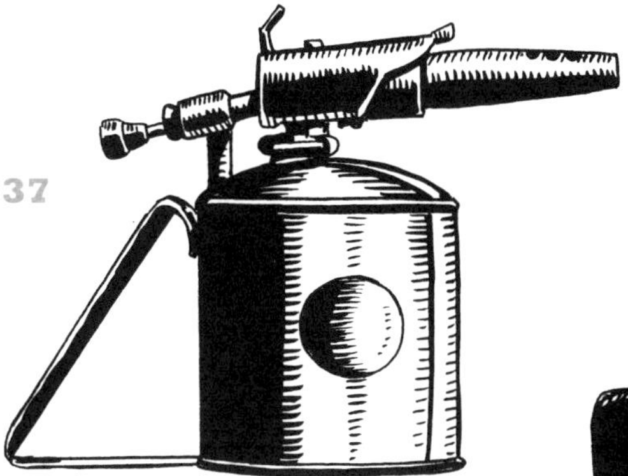

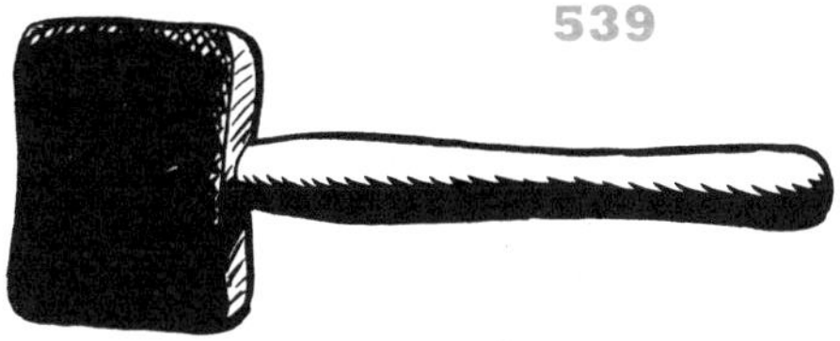

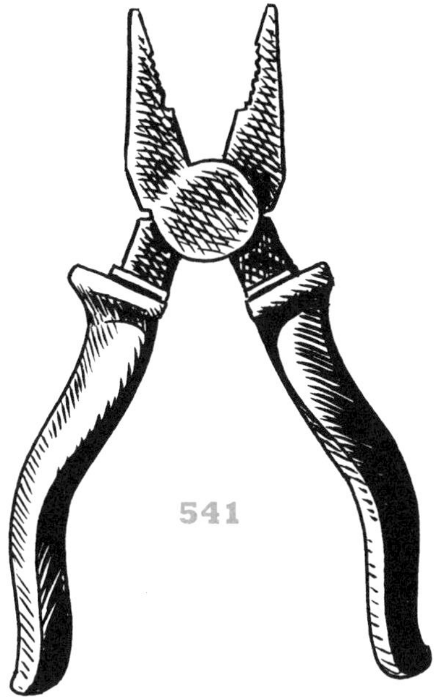

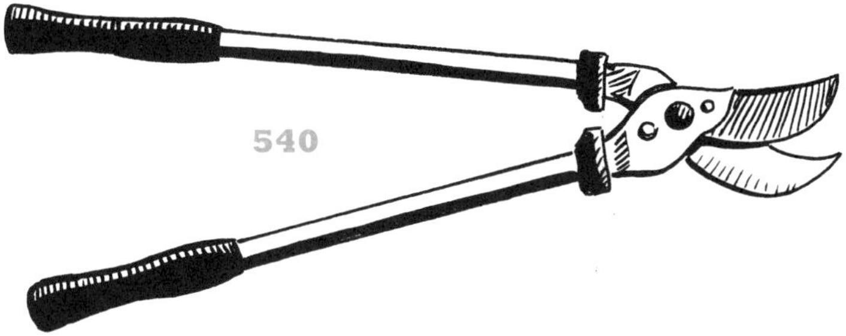

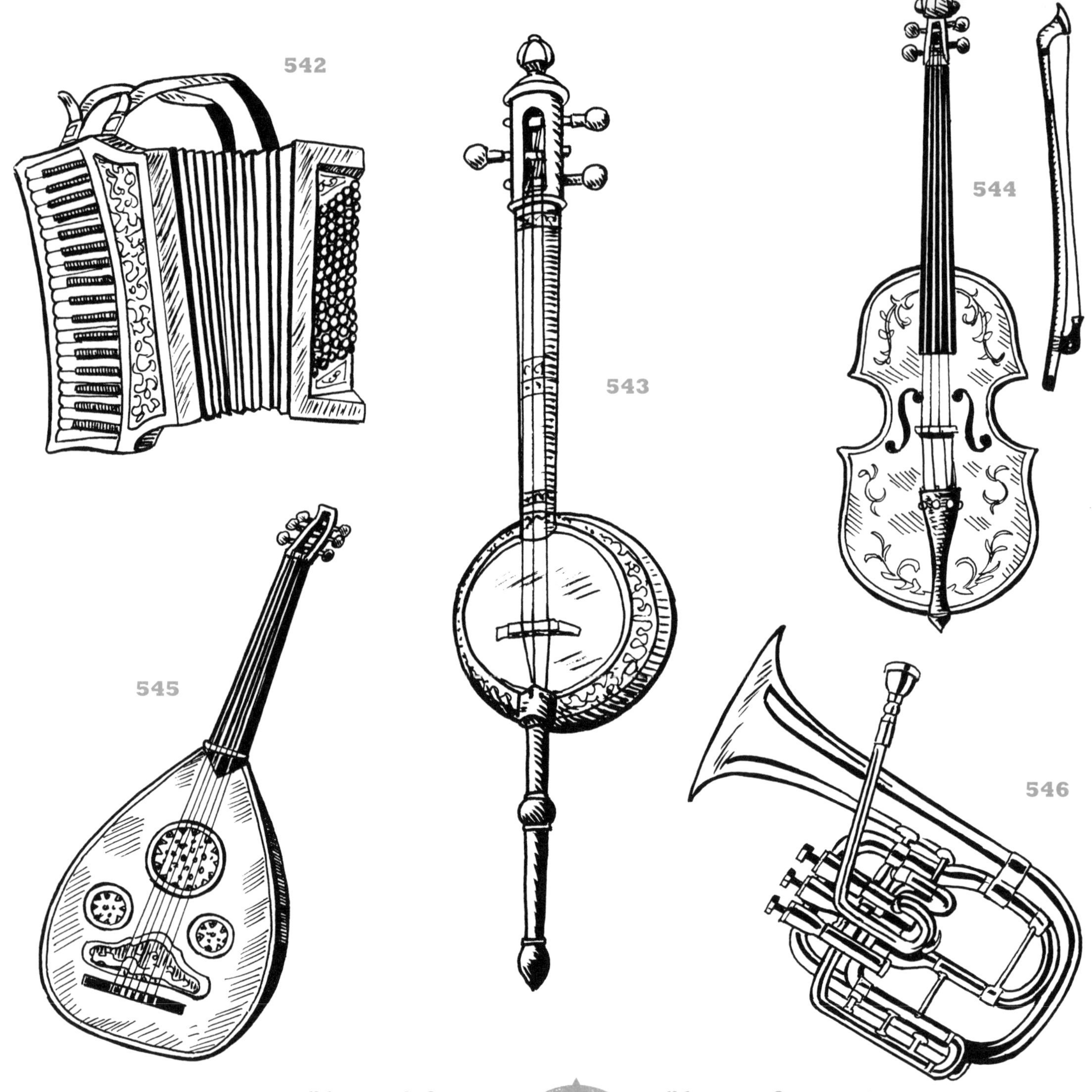
542
543
544
545
546

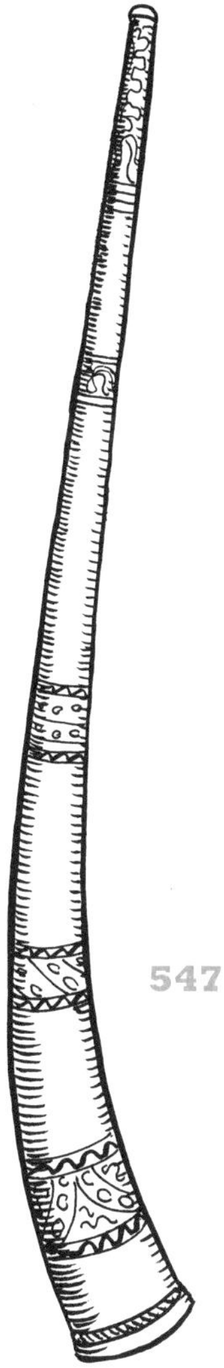

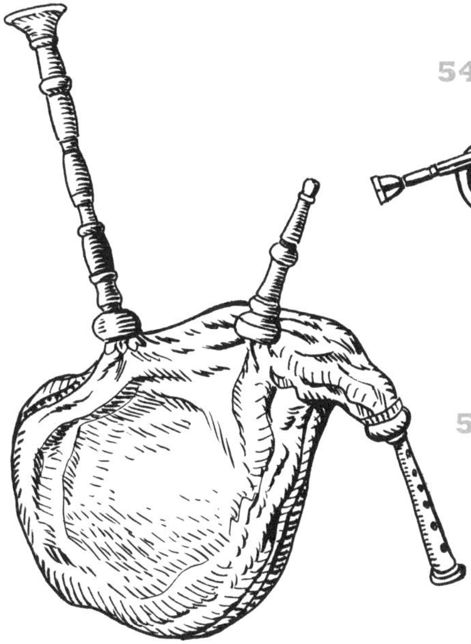

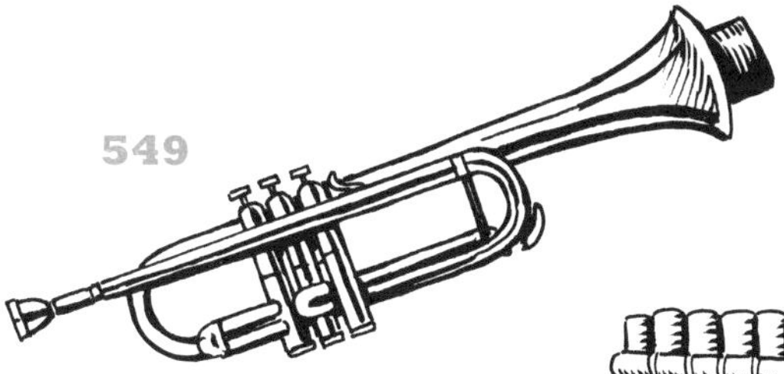

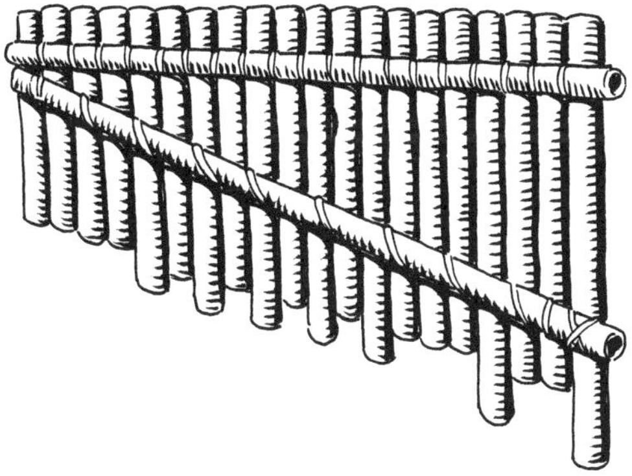

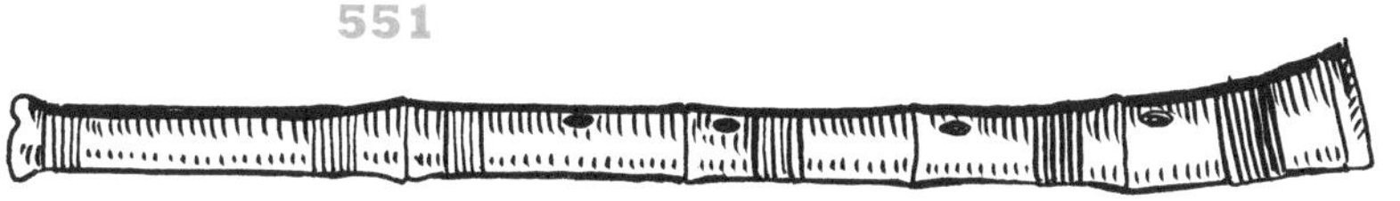

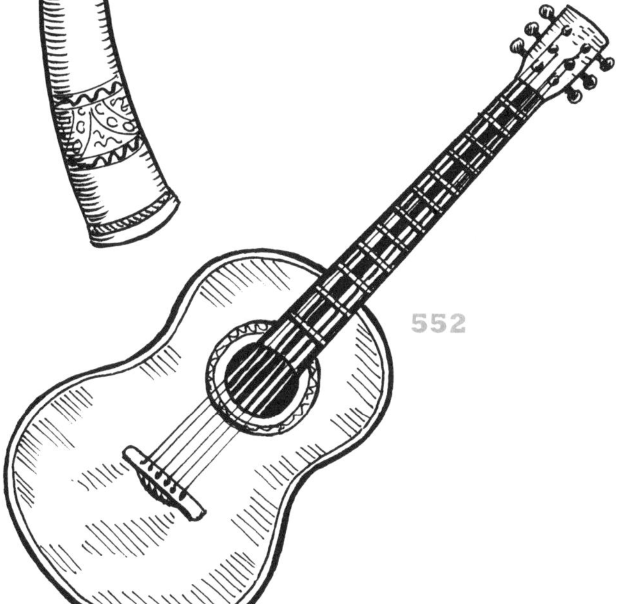

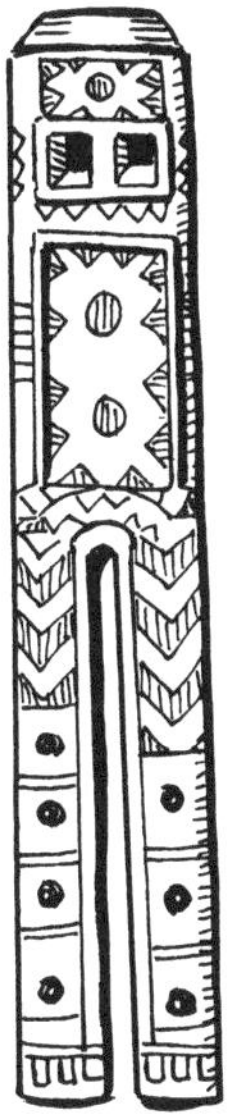

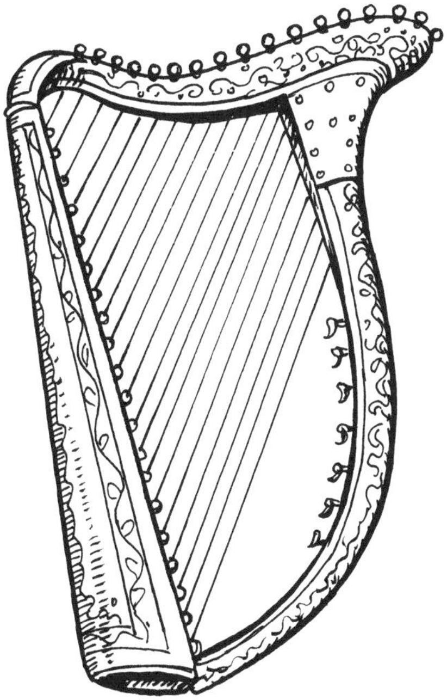

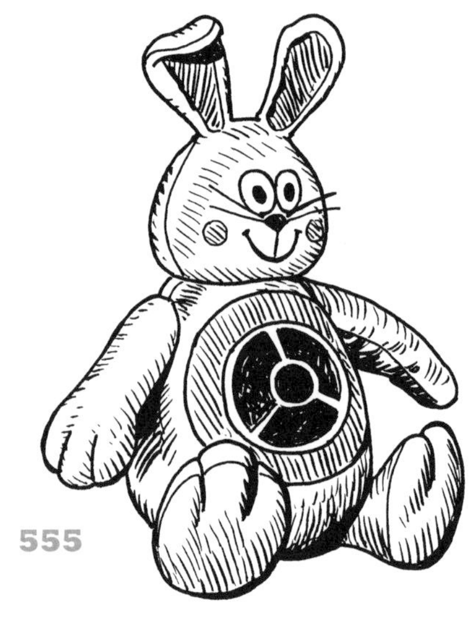

555

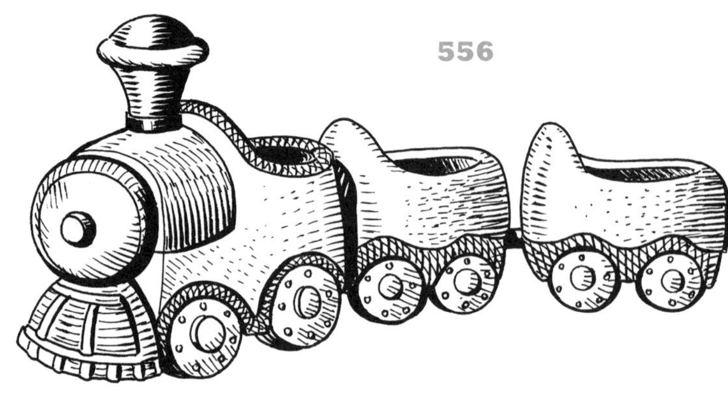

556

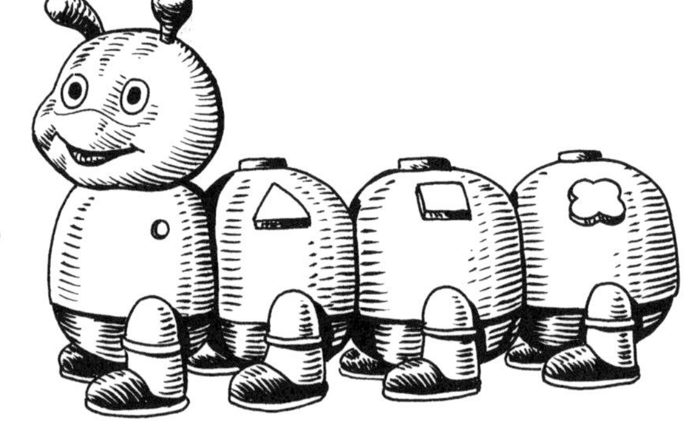

557

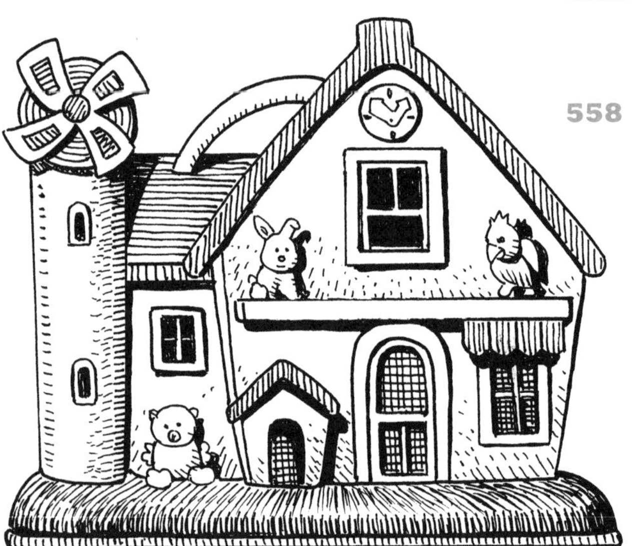

558

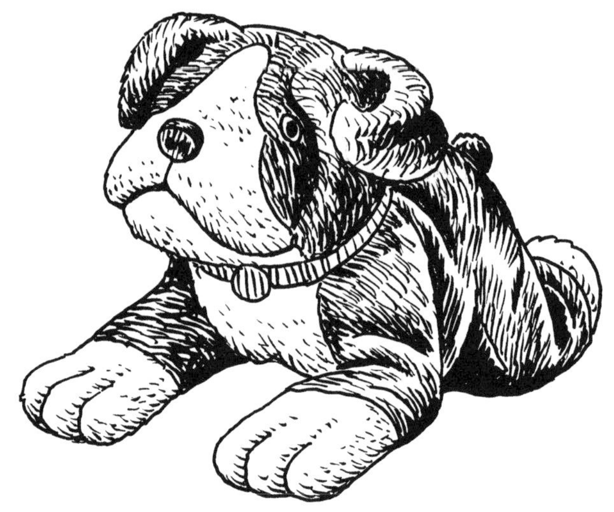

559

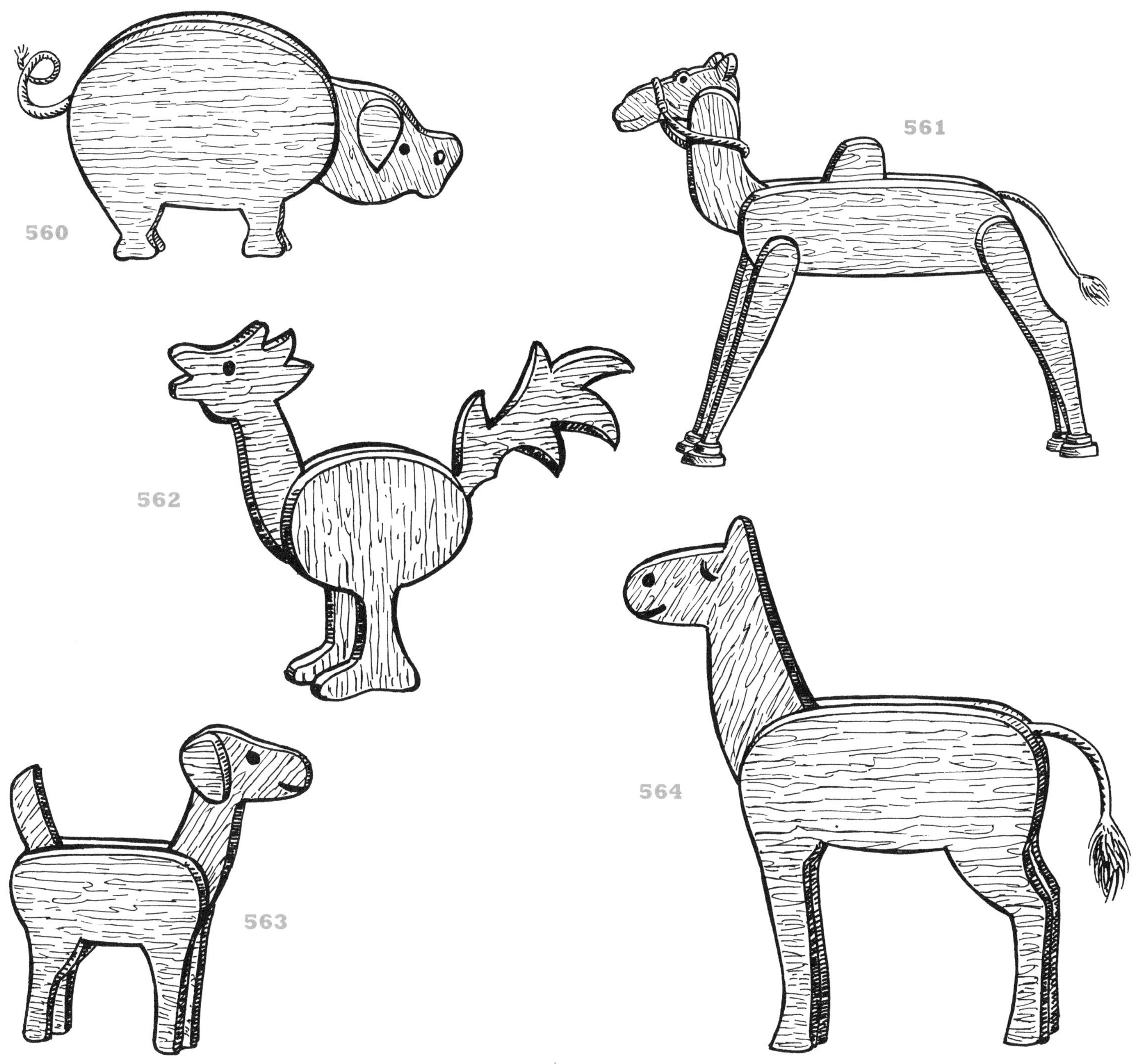

560
561
562
563
564

565

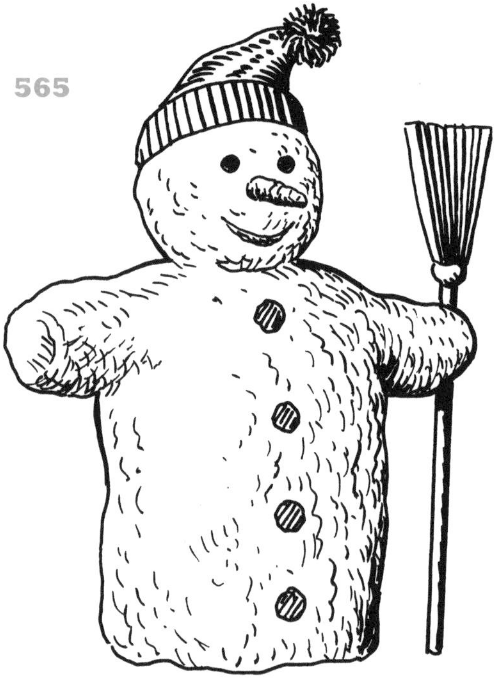

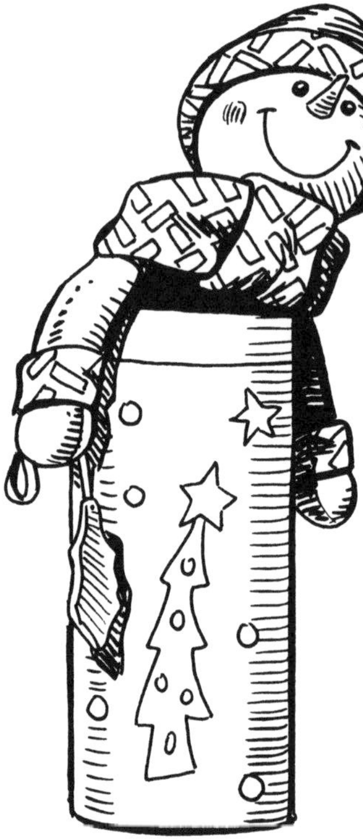

566

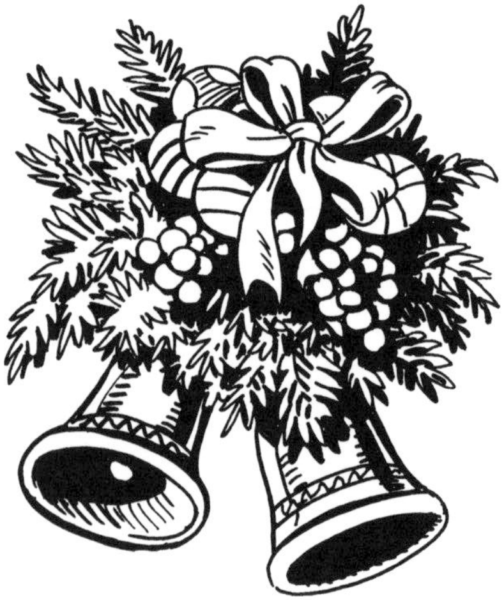

567

568

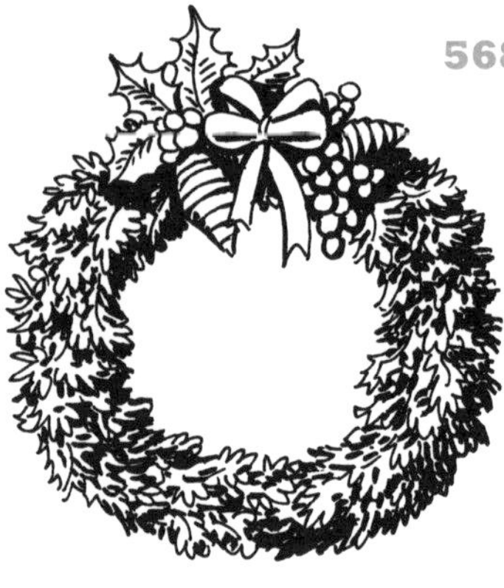

569

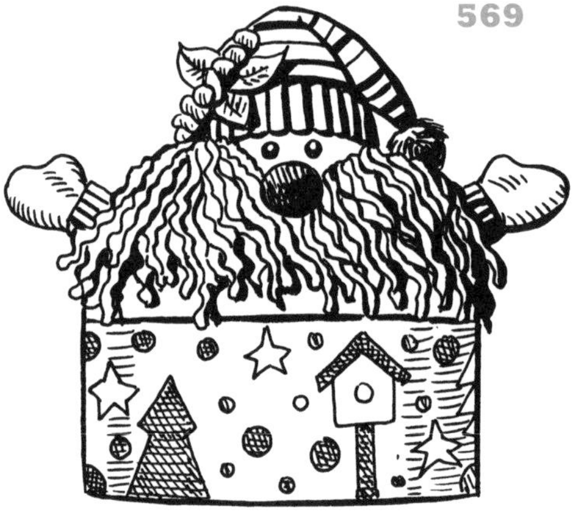

570

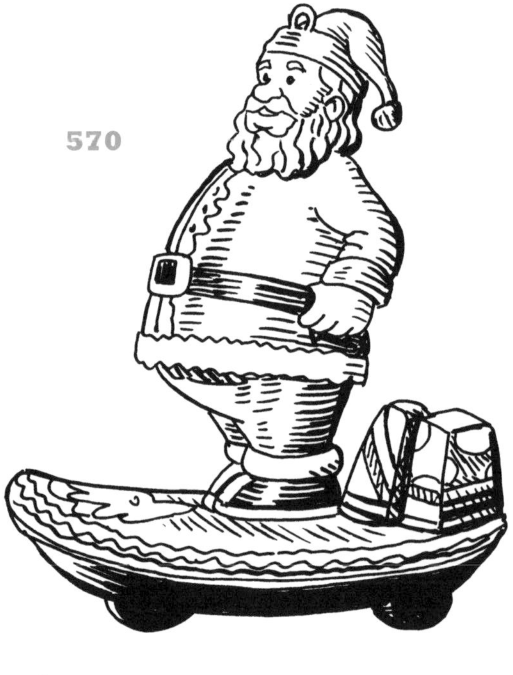

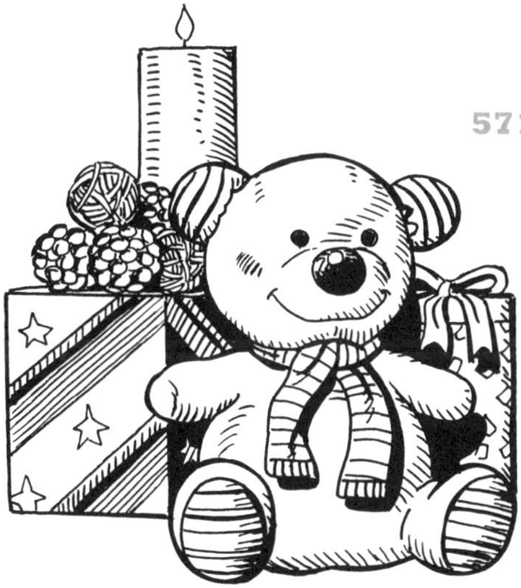

571

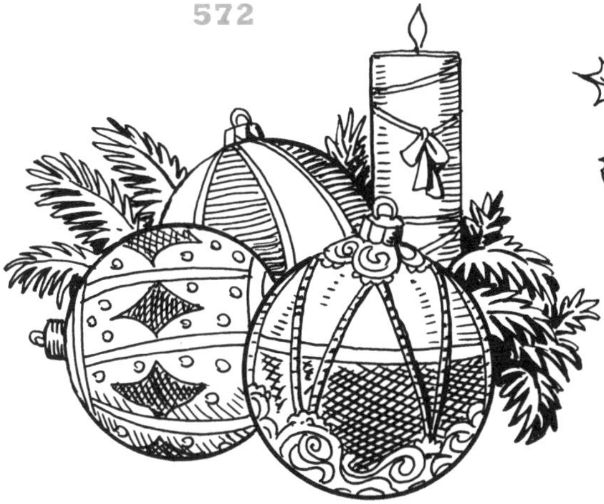

572

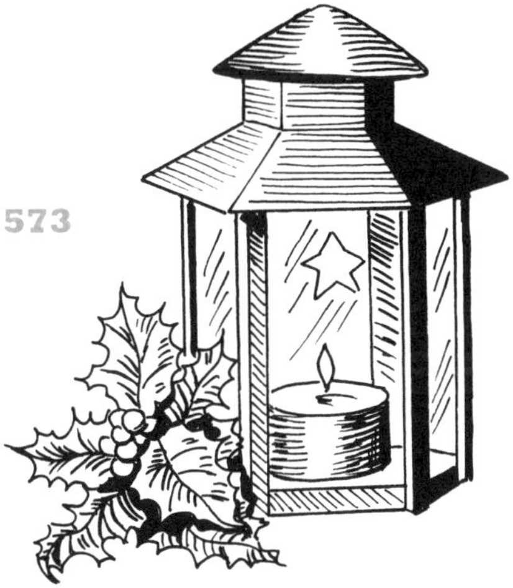

573

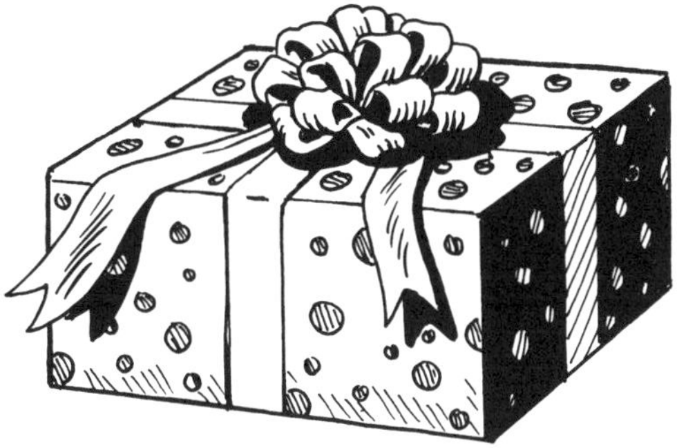

574

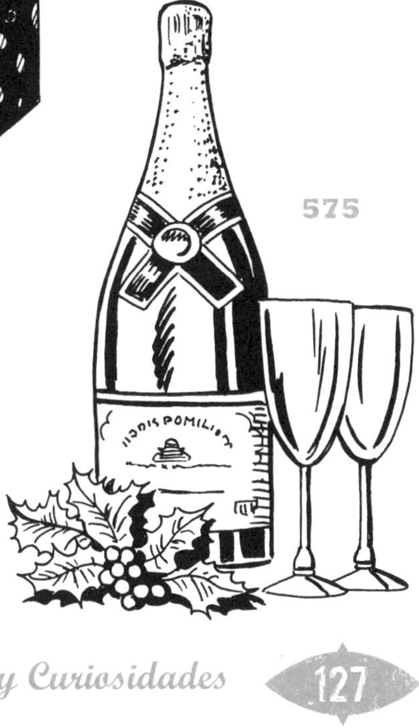

575

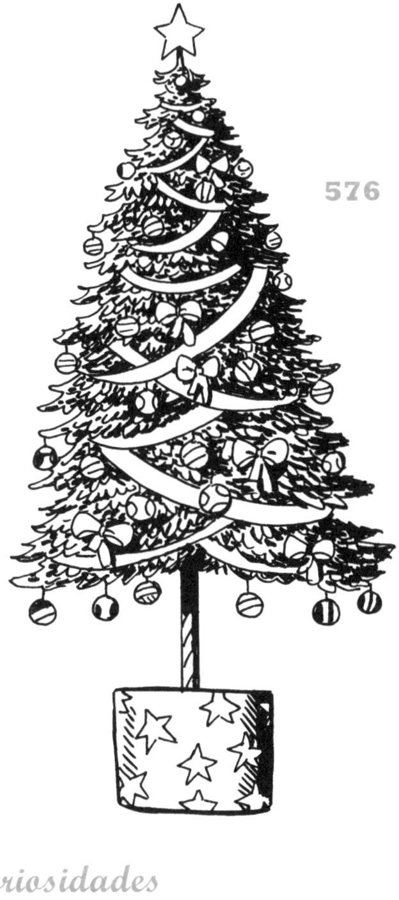

576

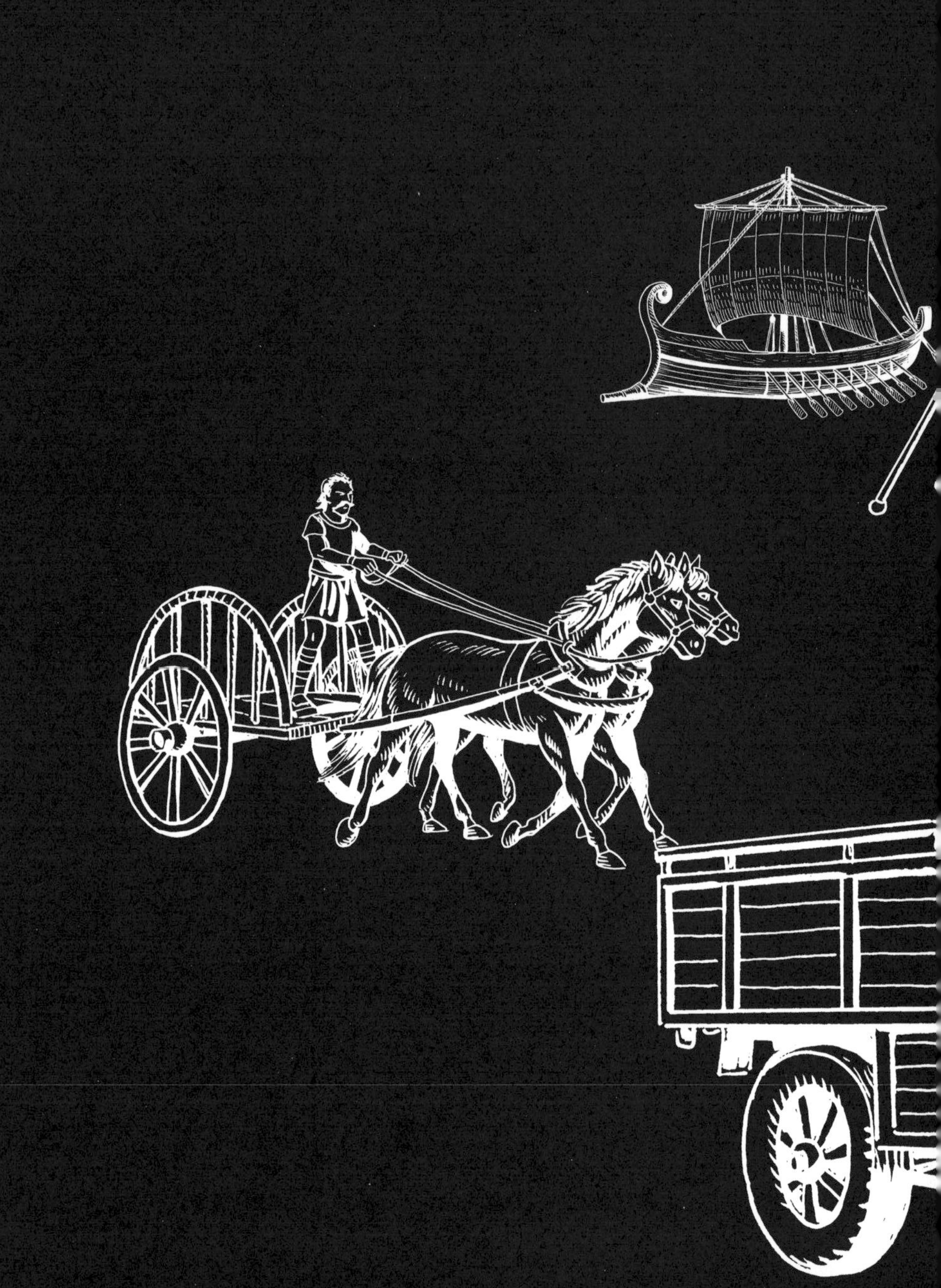

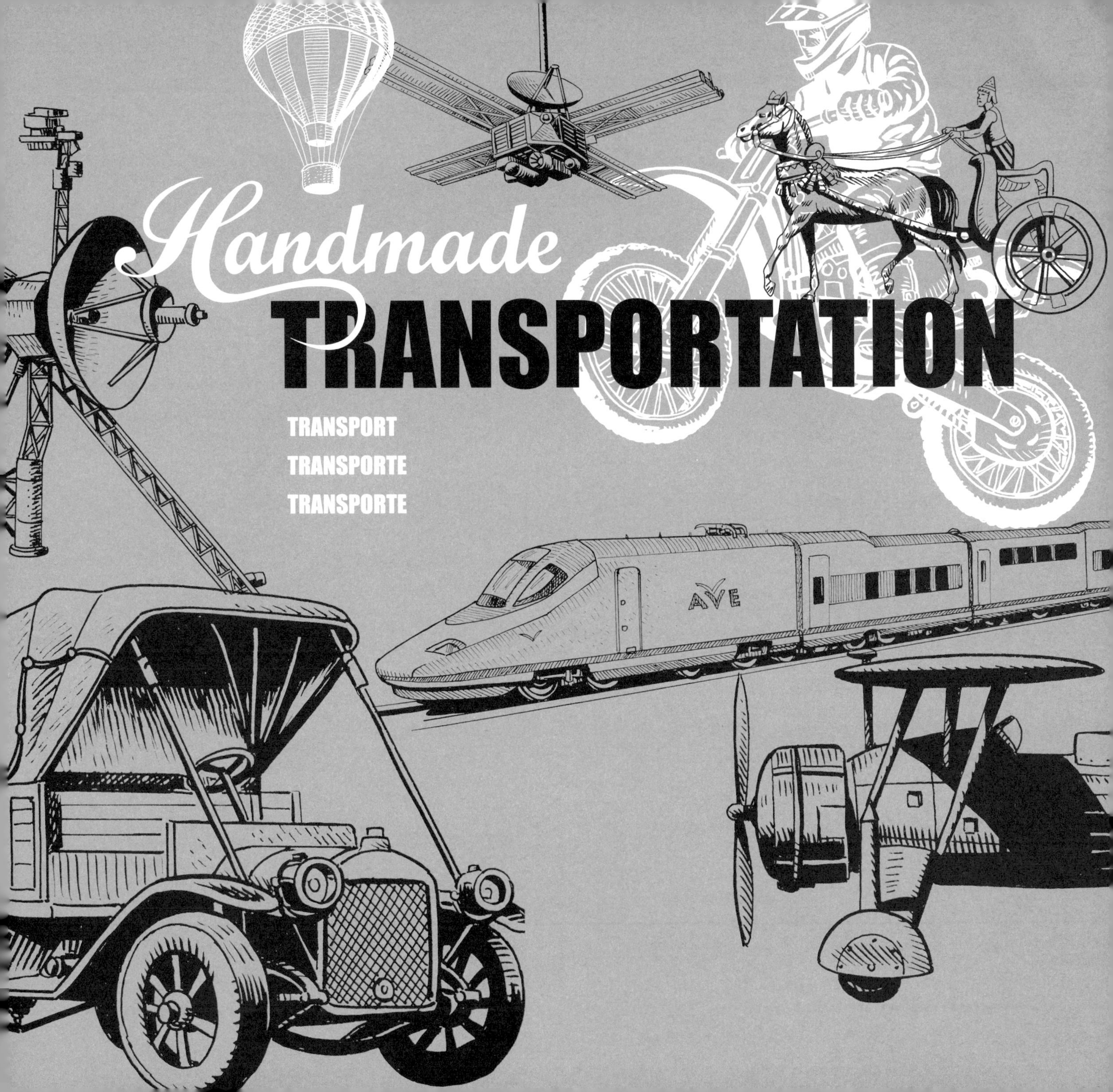

Handmade
TRANSPORTATION
TRANSPORT
TRANSPORTE
TRANSPORTE
AVE

577

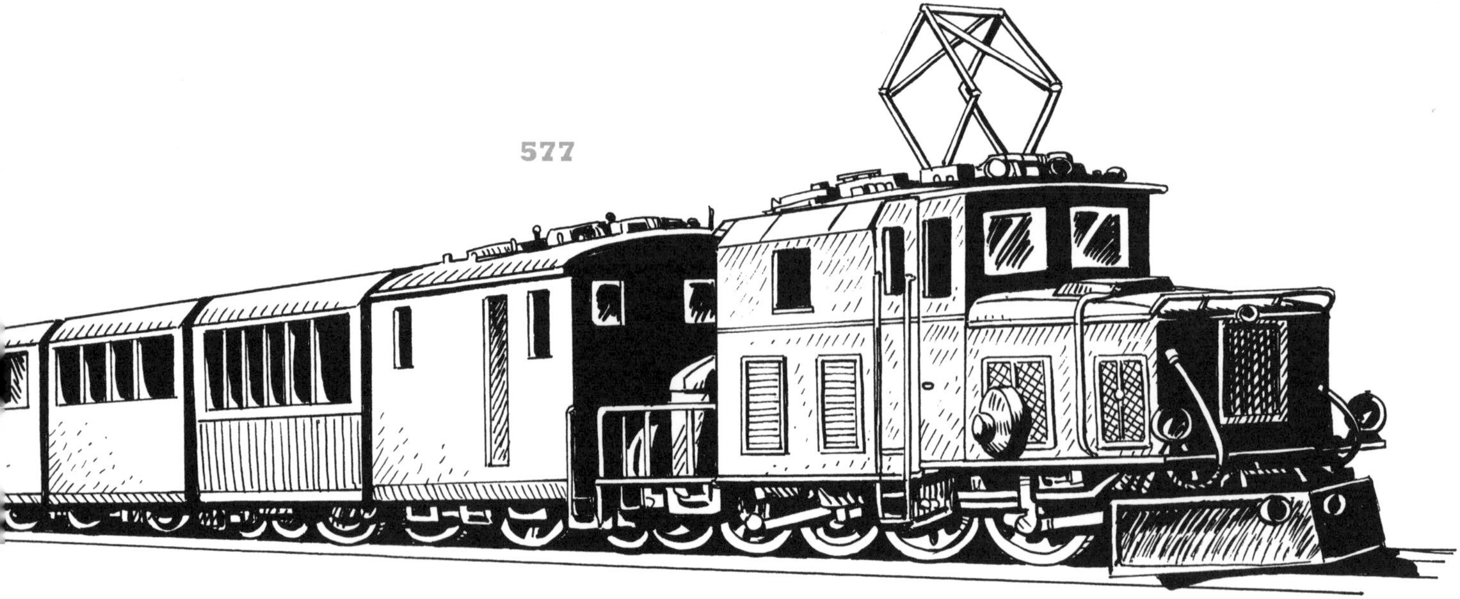

578

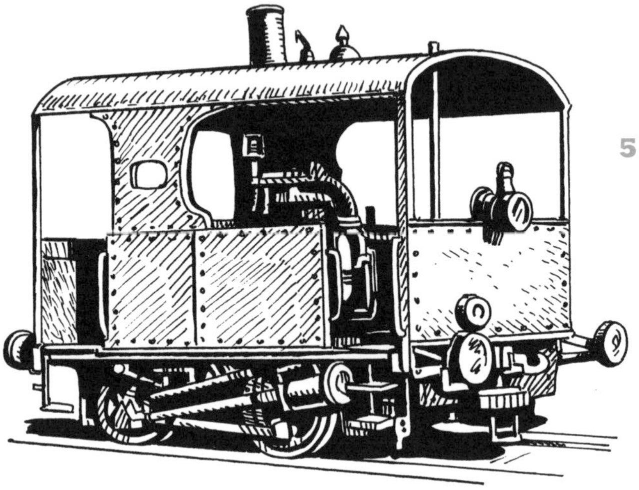

579

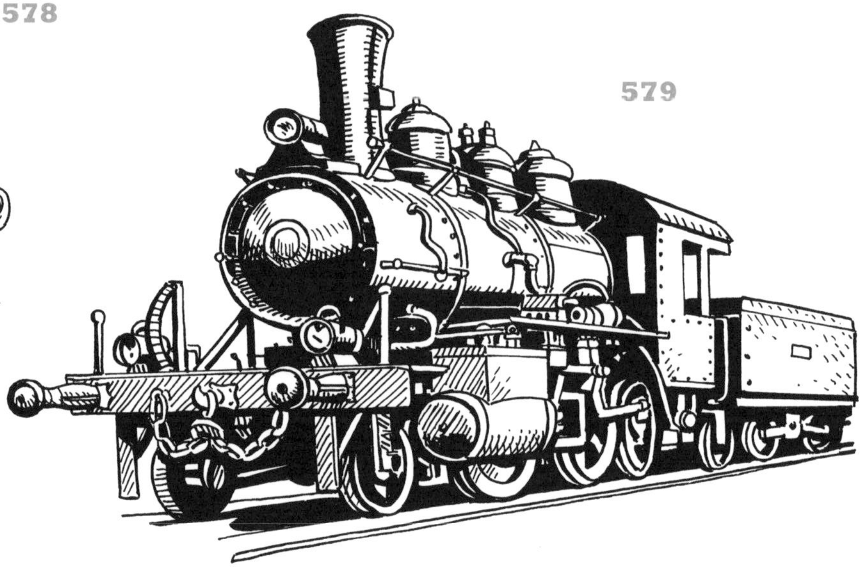

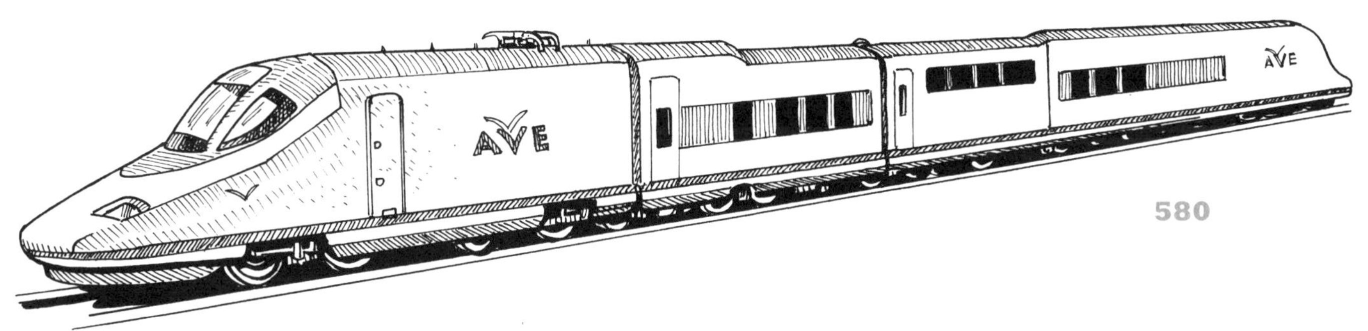

580

581

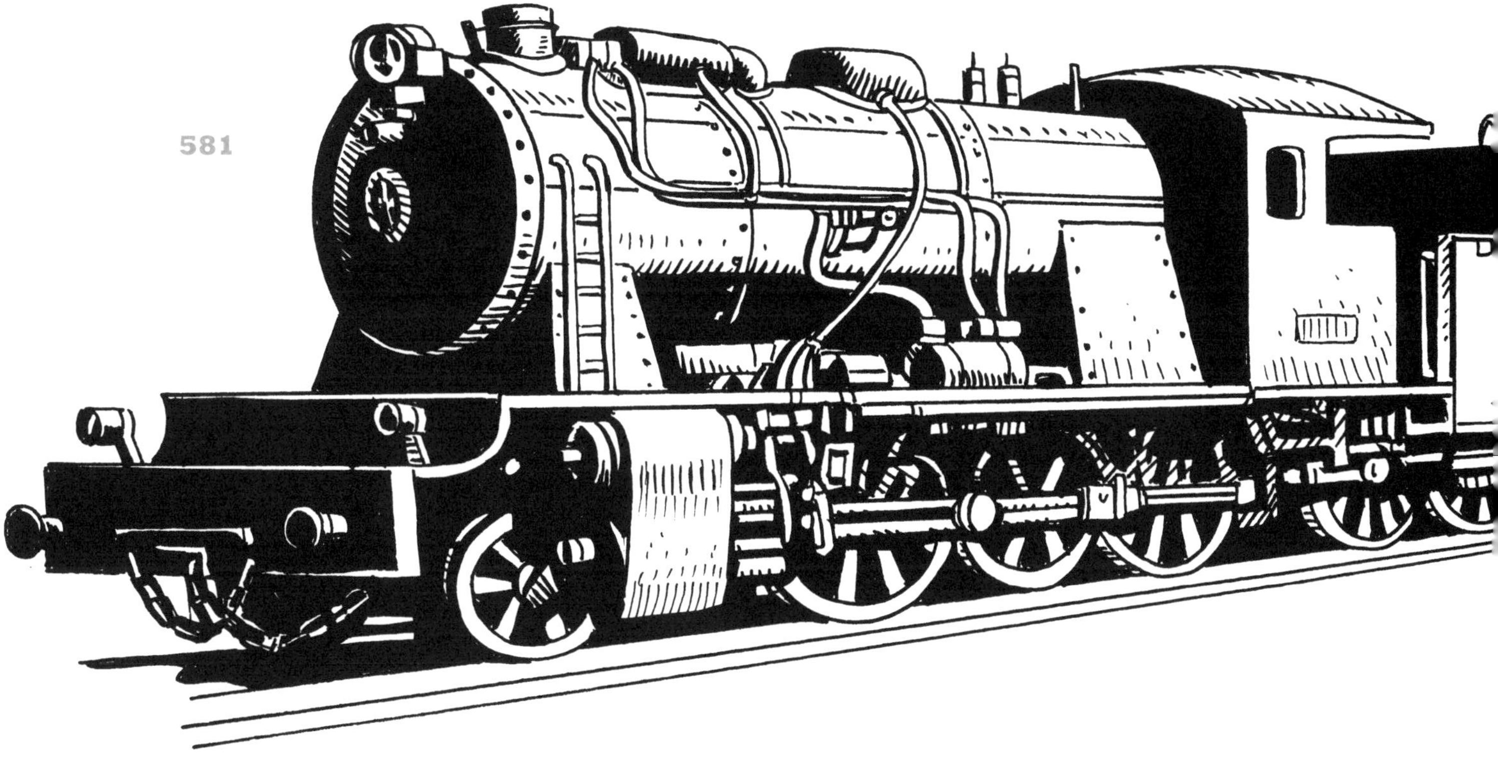

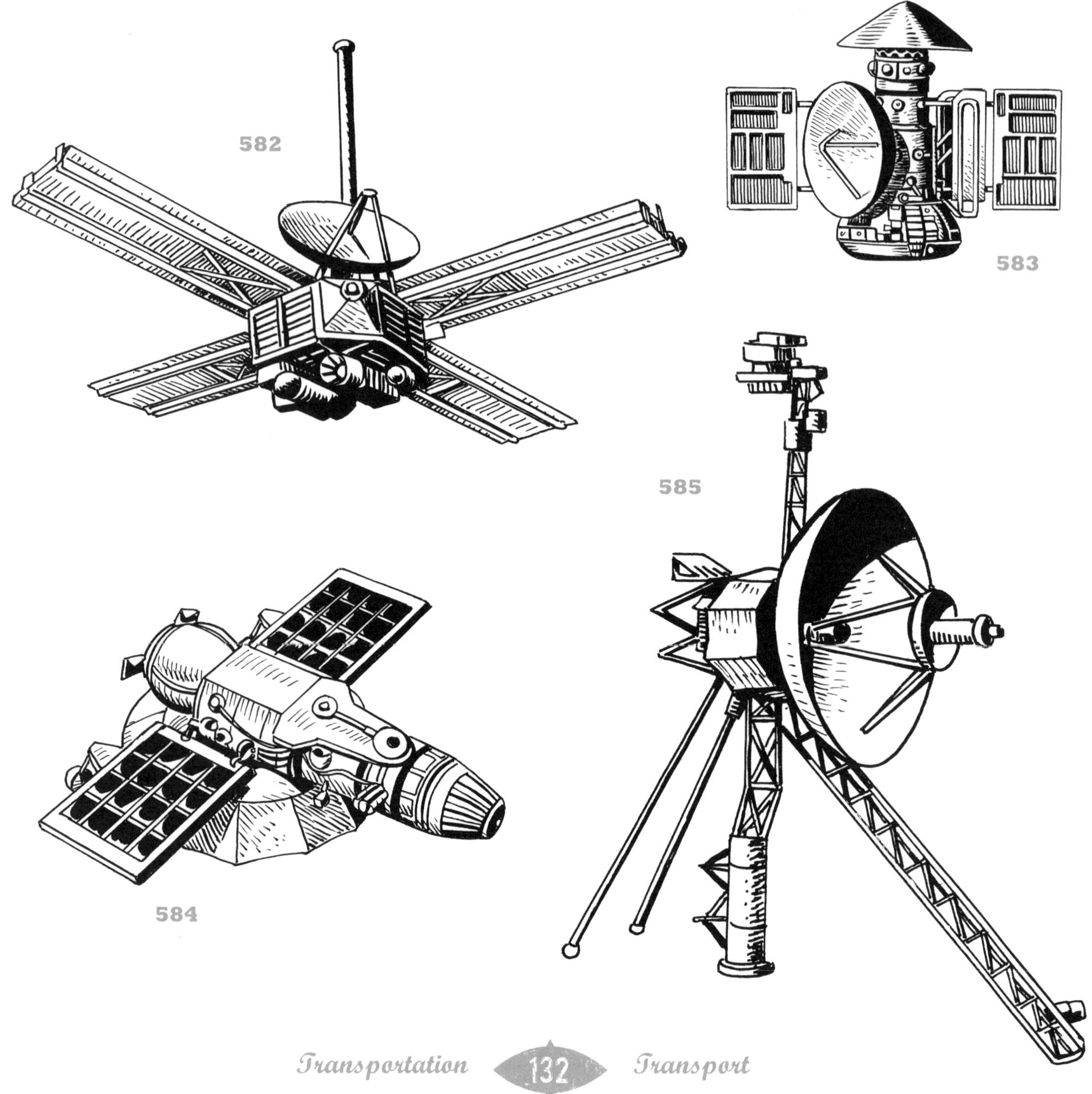

582
583
584
585

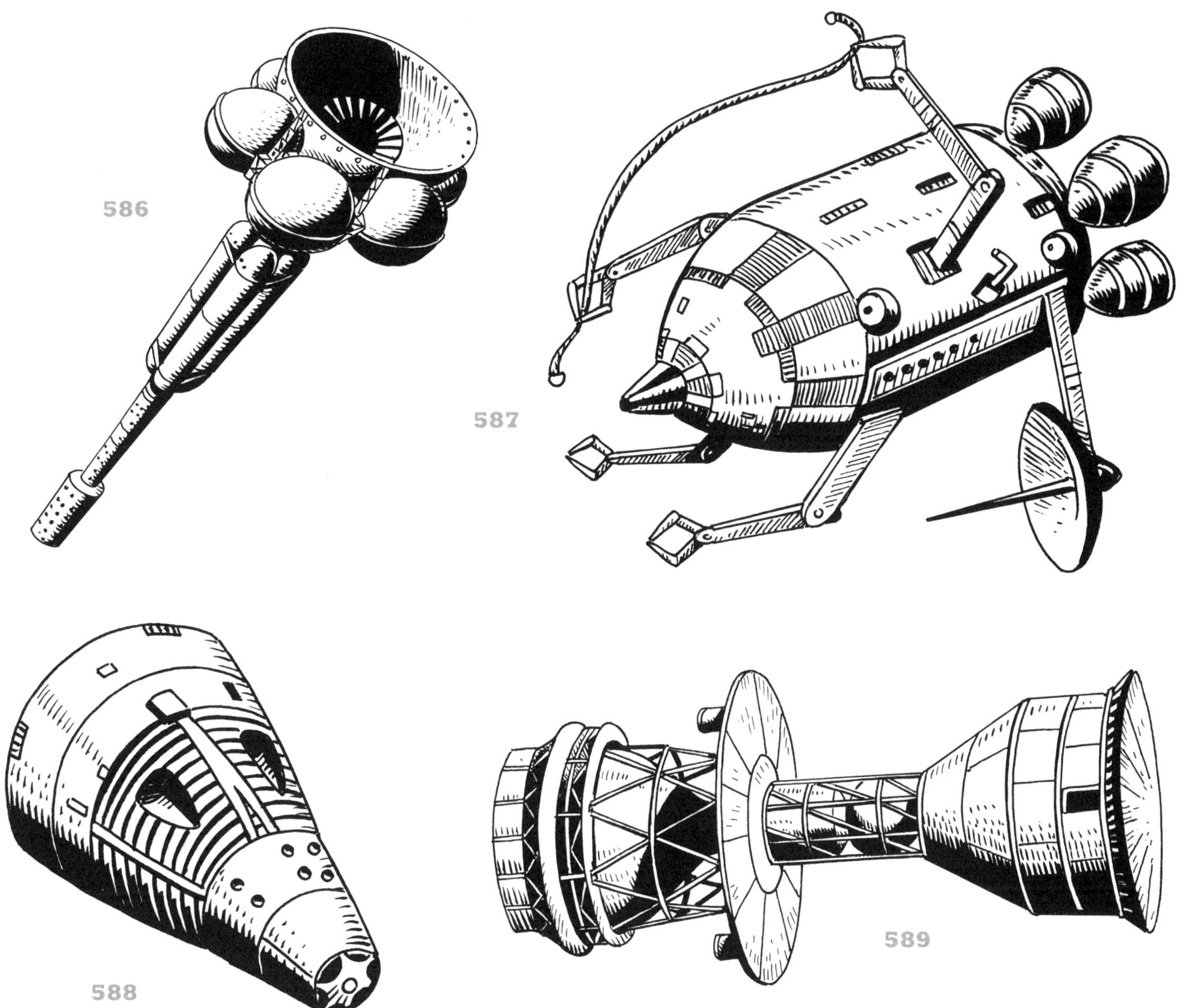

586
587
588
589

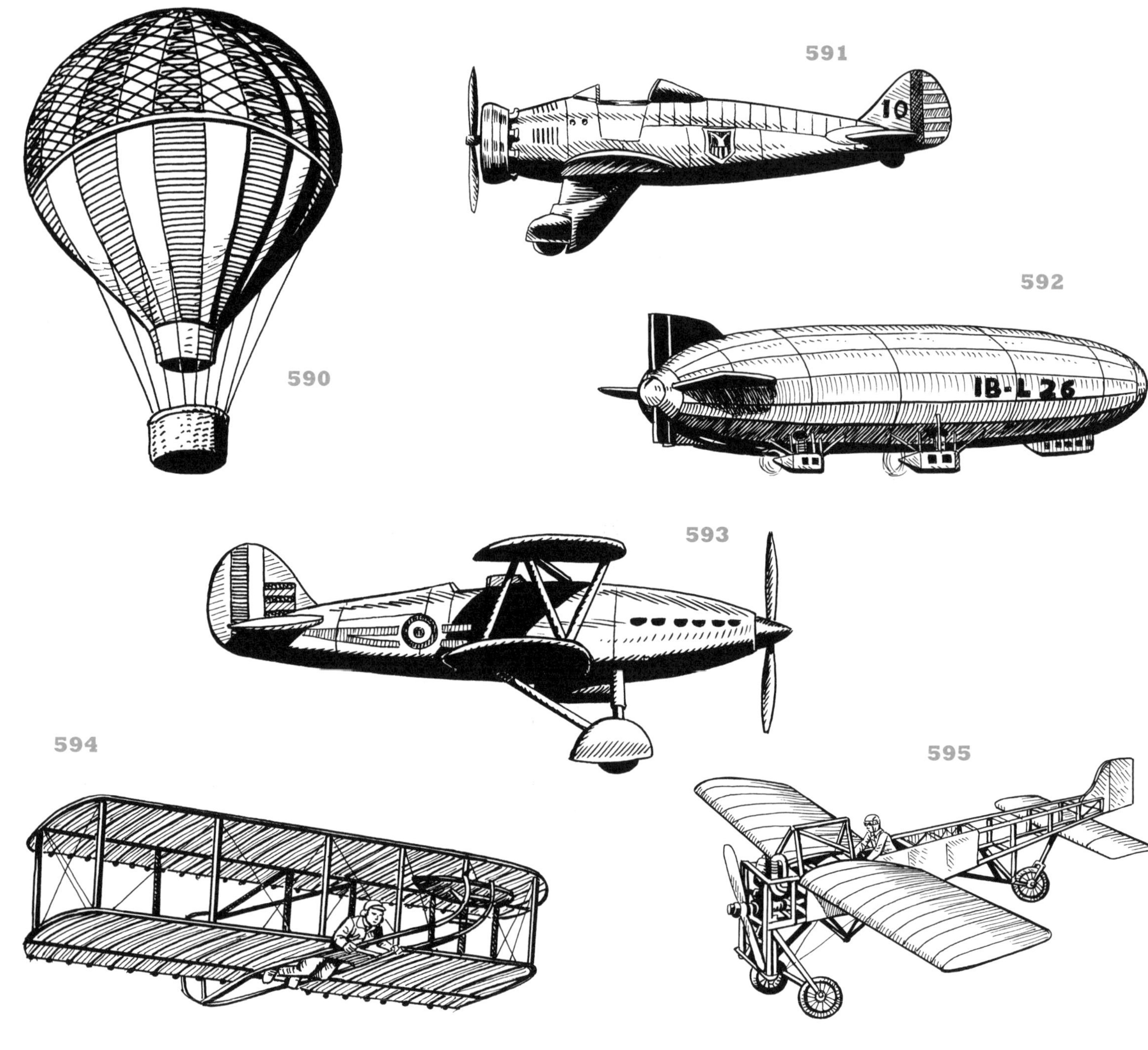
590
591
592
IB-L 26
593
594
595

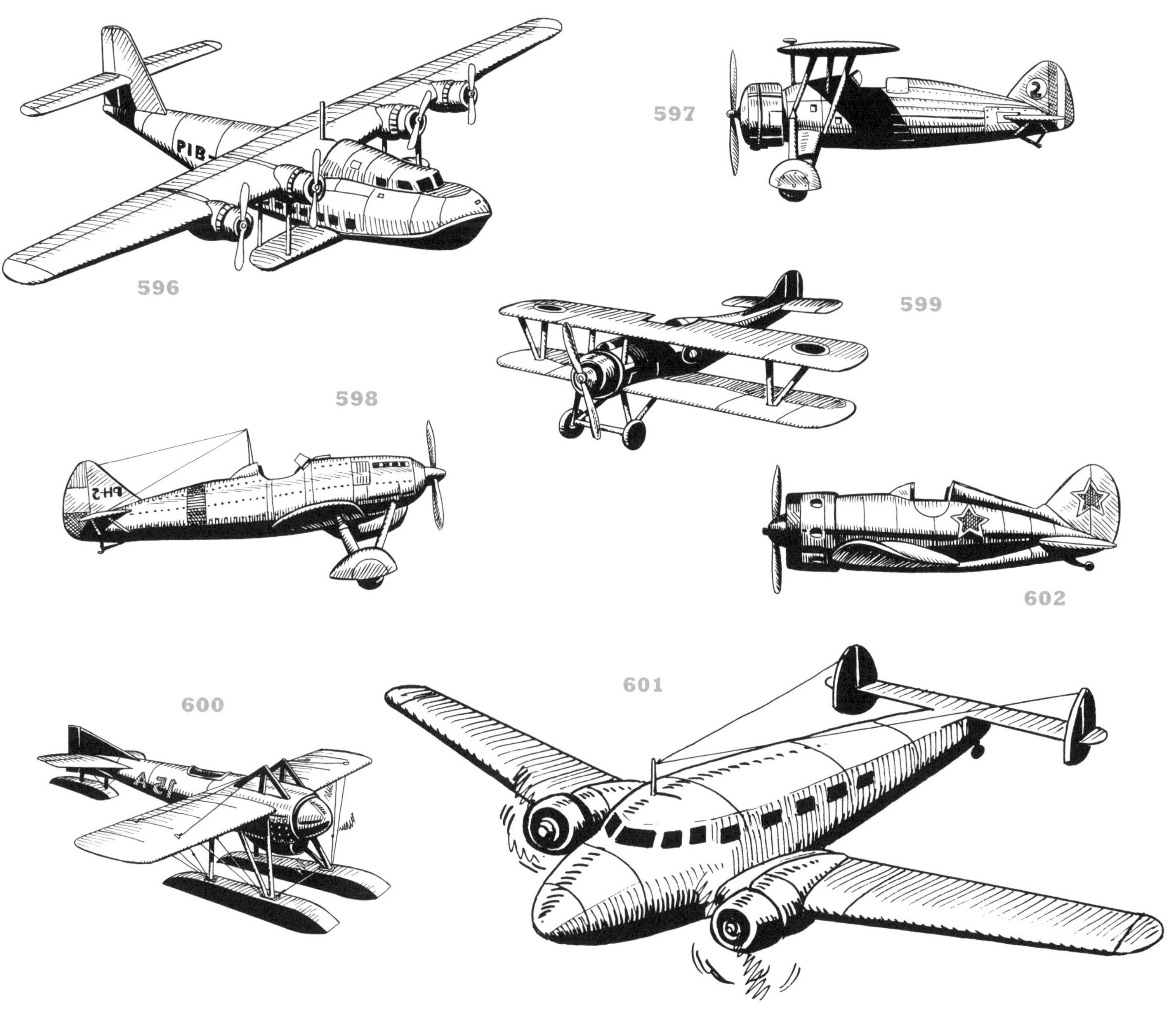

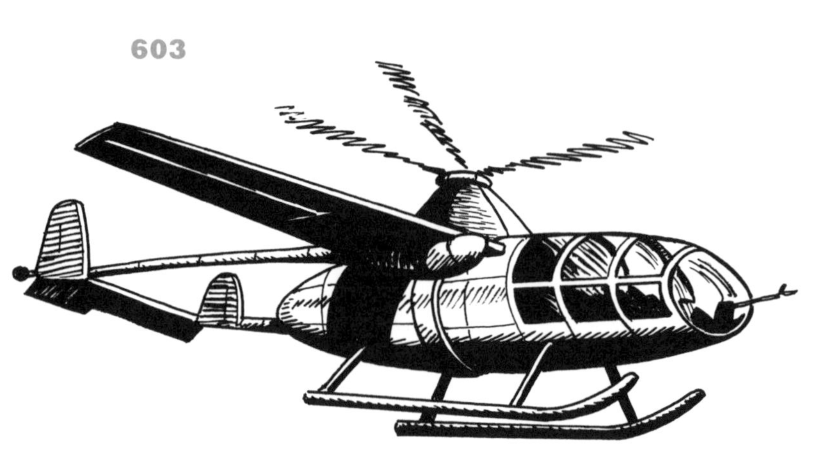

603

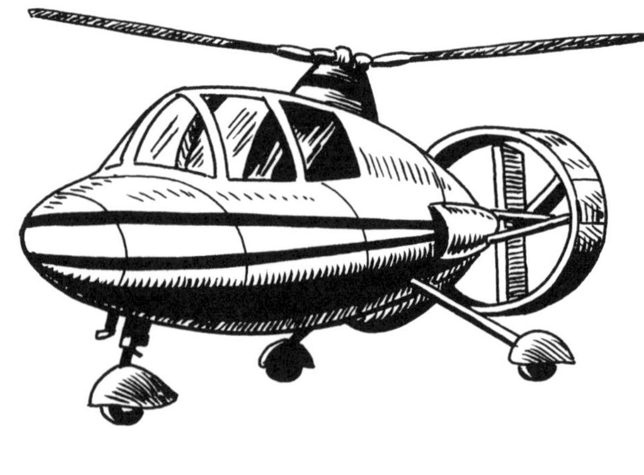

604

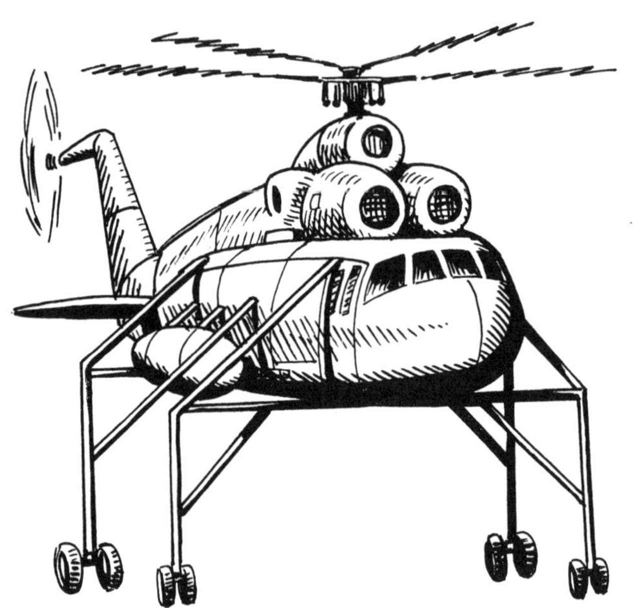

605

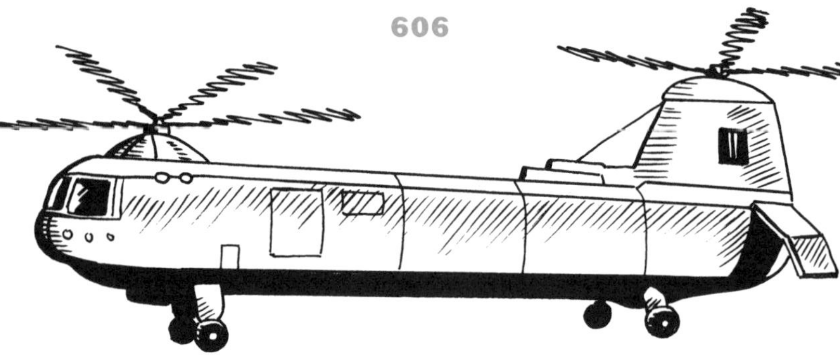

606

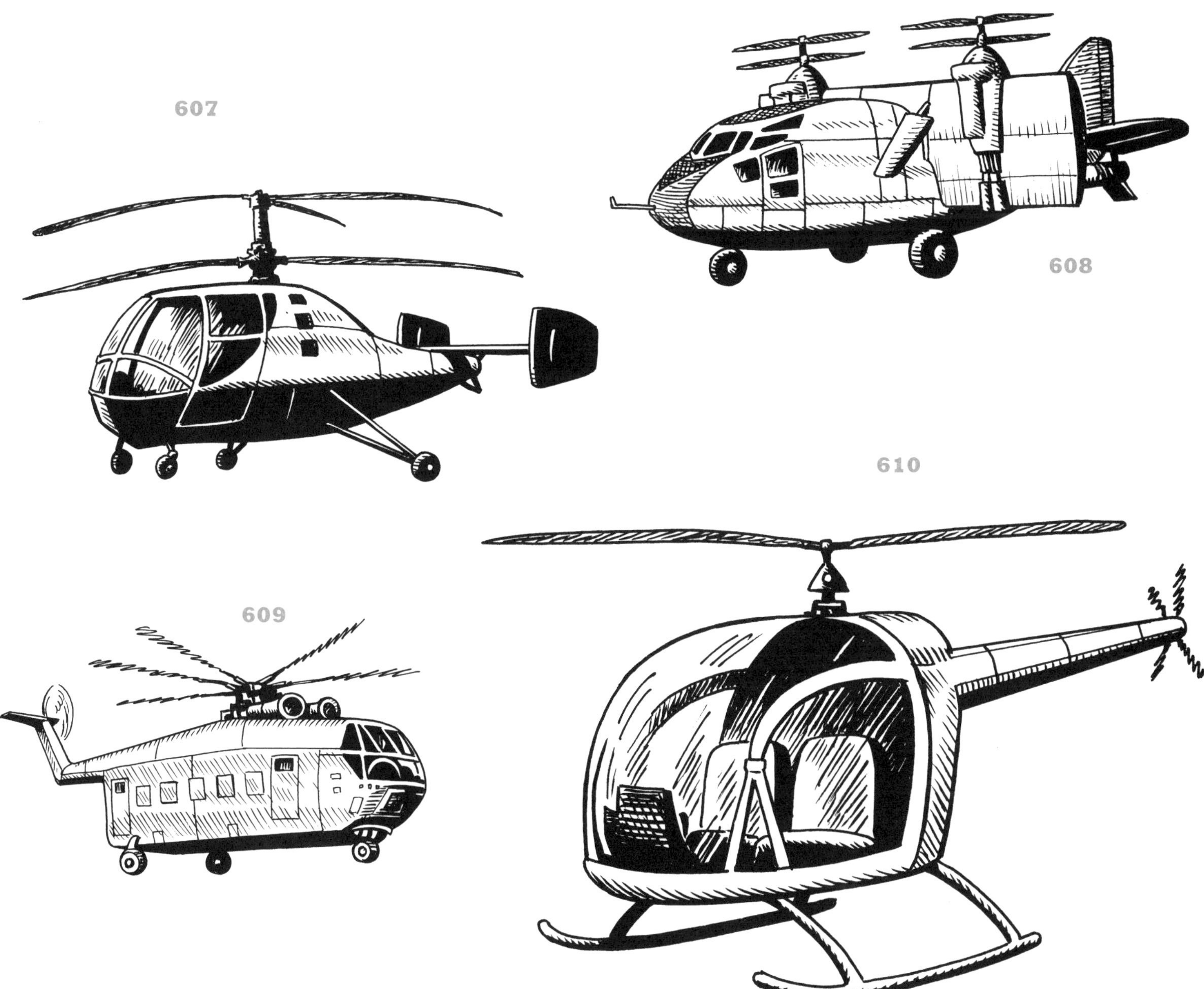

607
608
609
610

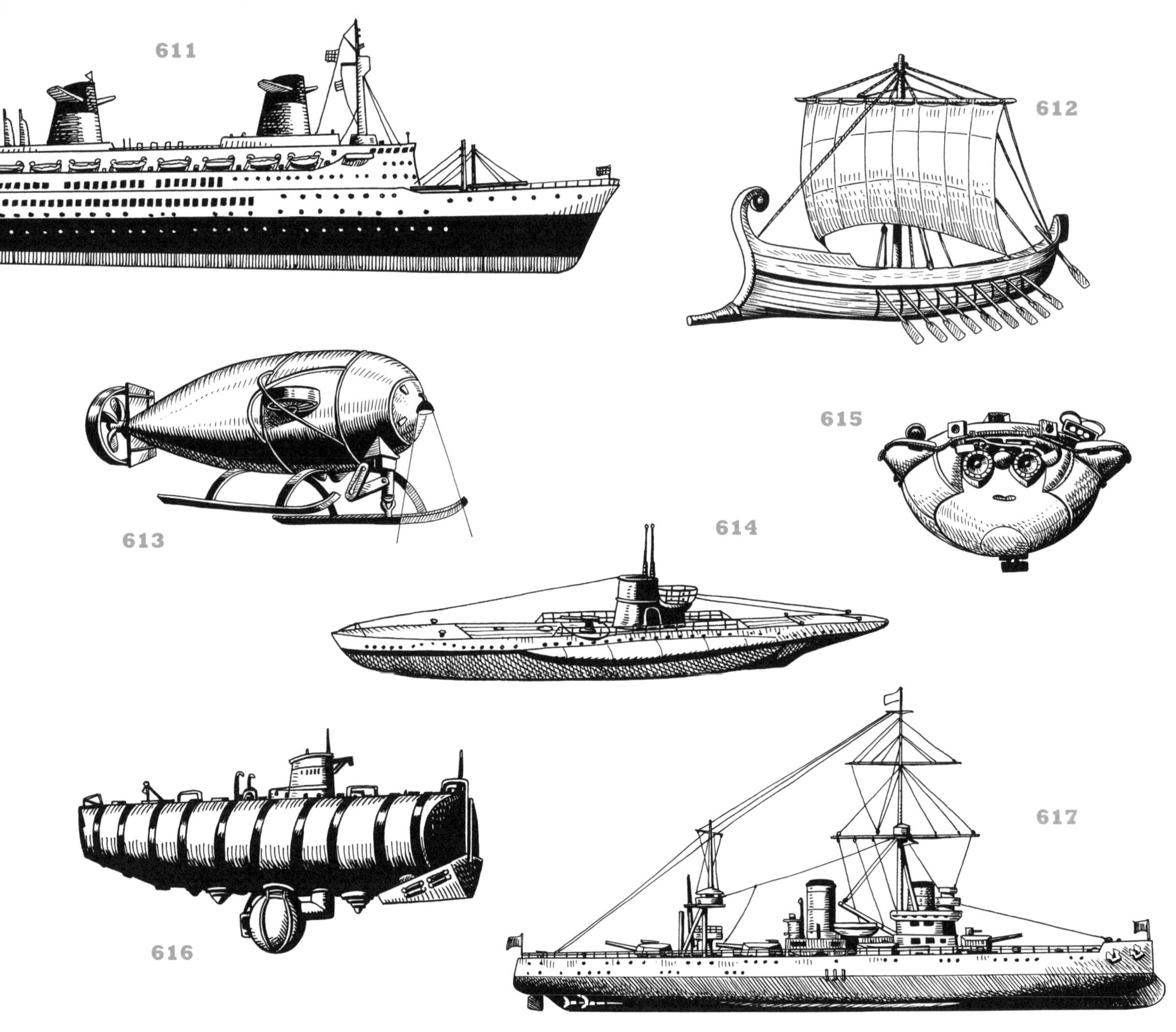

611
612
613
614
615
616
617

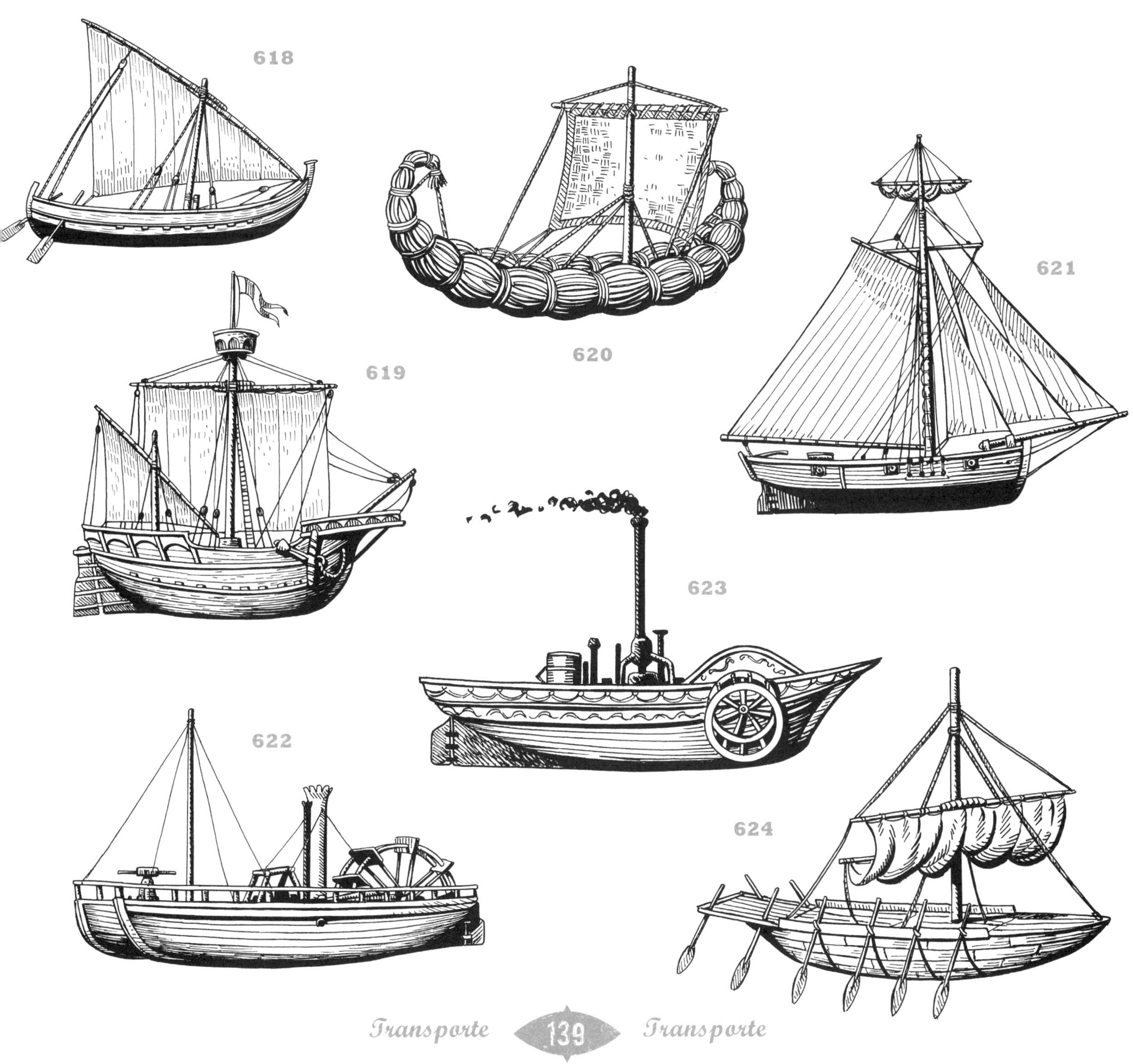

618
619
620
621
622
623
624

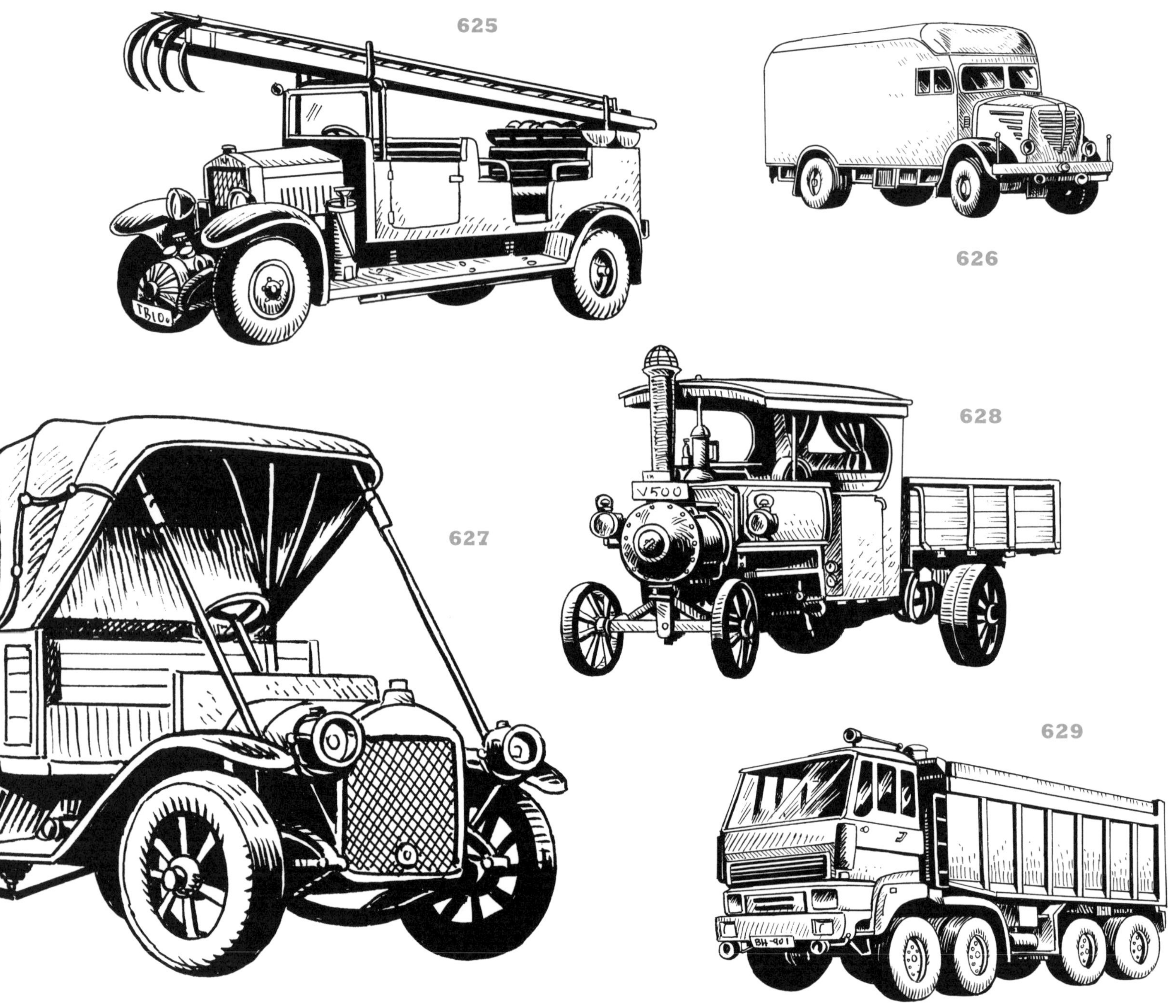

625
626
627
628
V500
629
BH-901

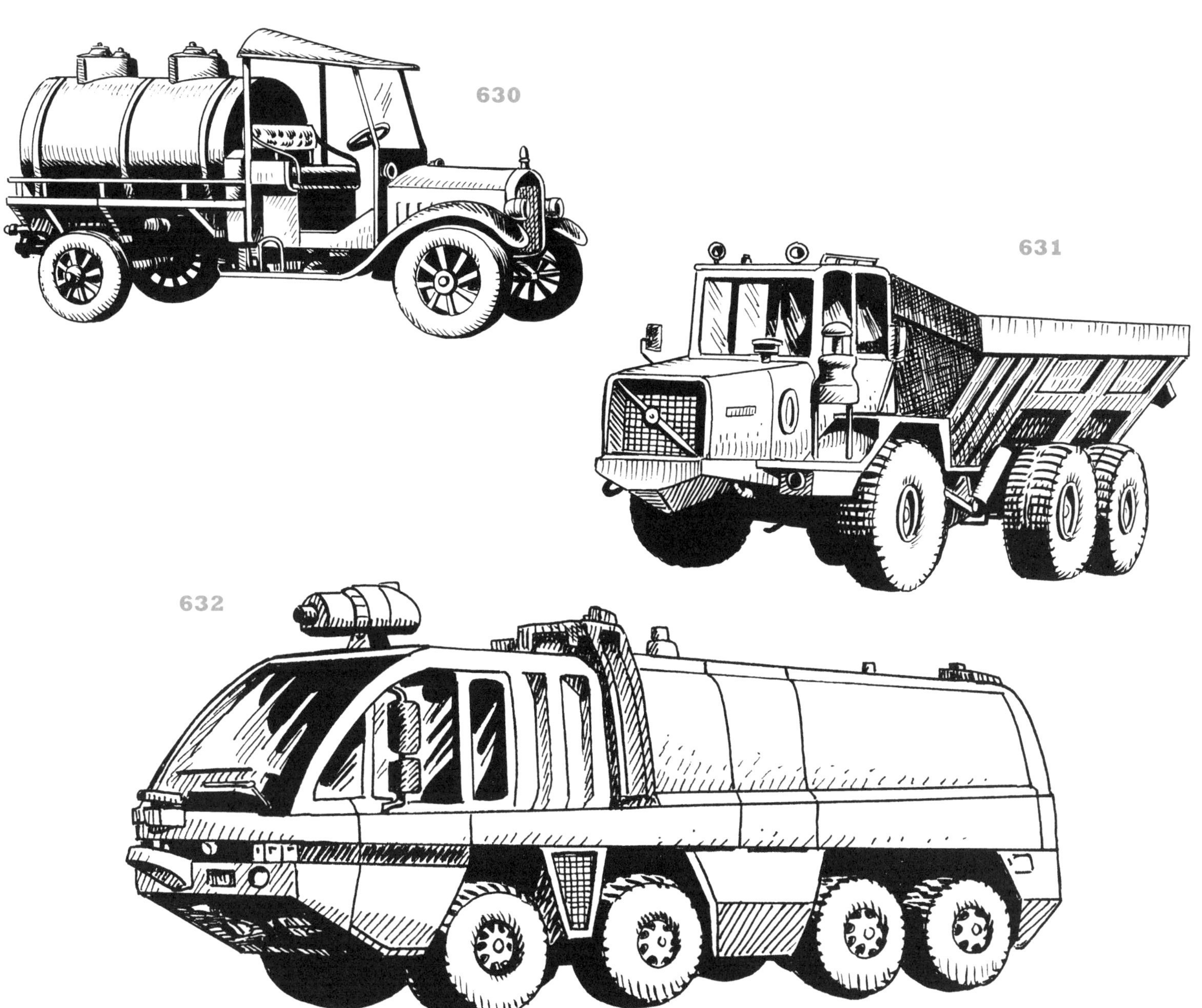

630
631
632

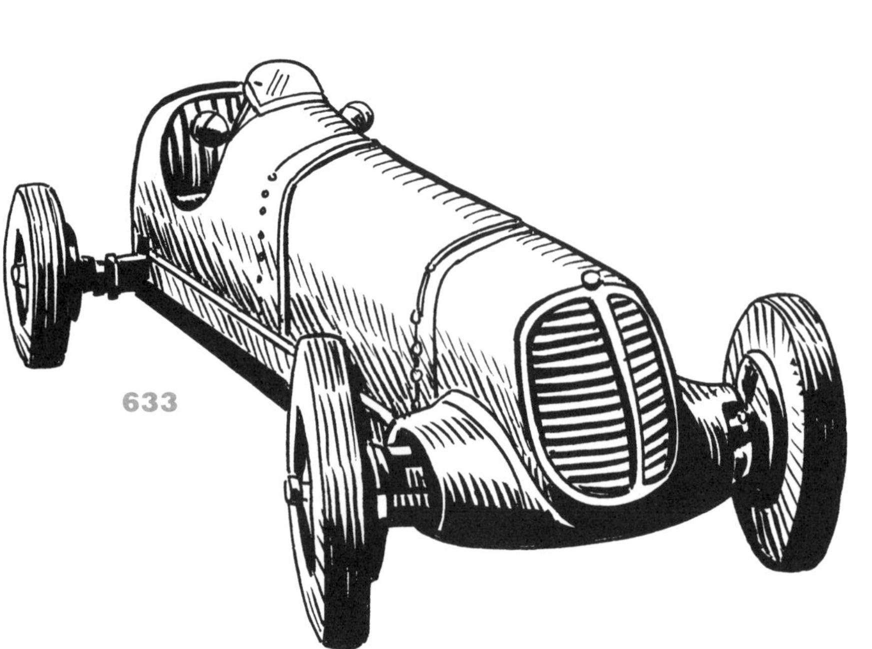

633

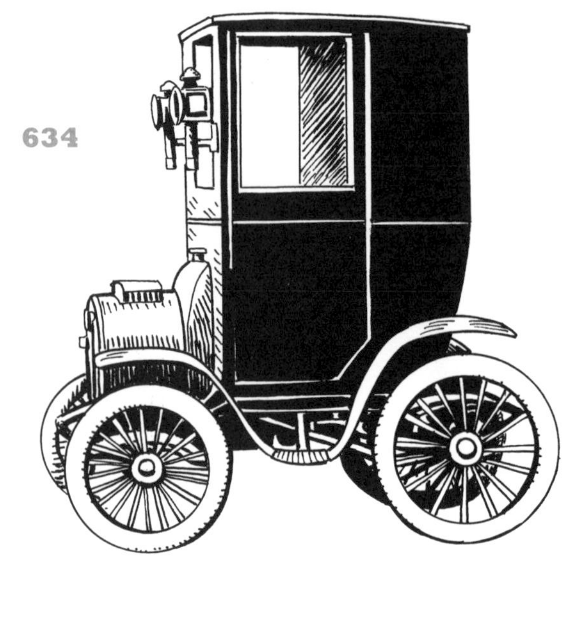

634

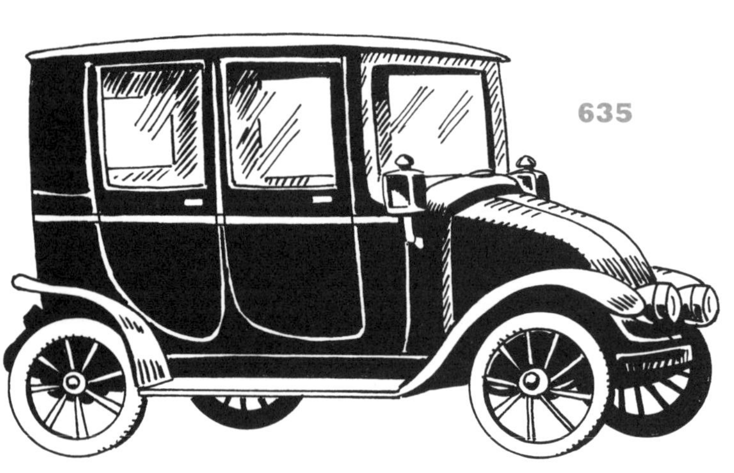

635

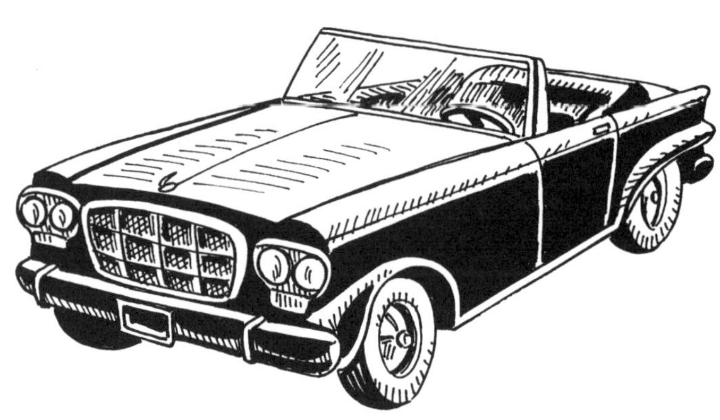

636

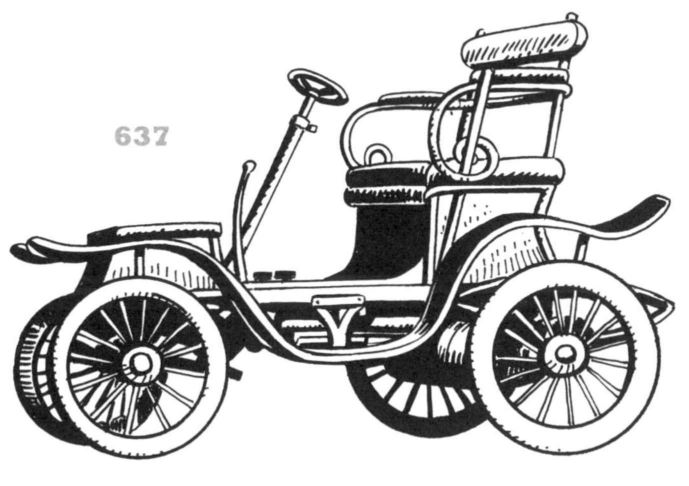

637

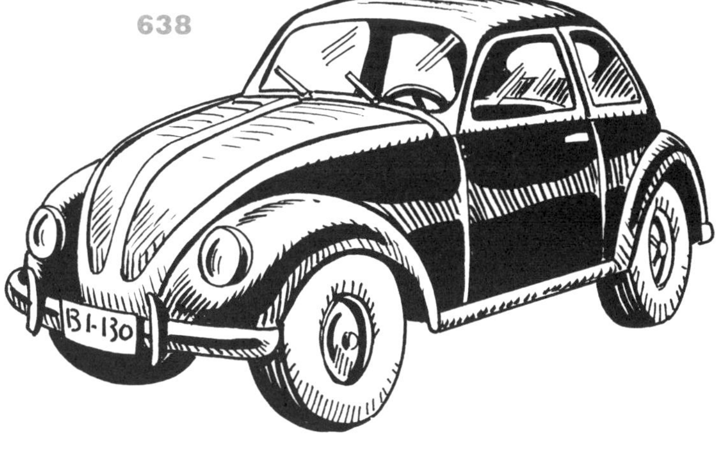

638

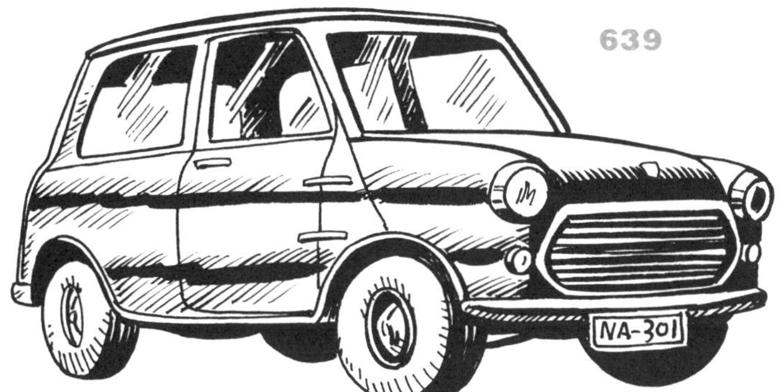

639

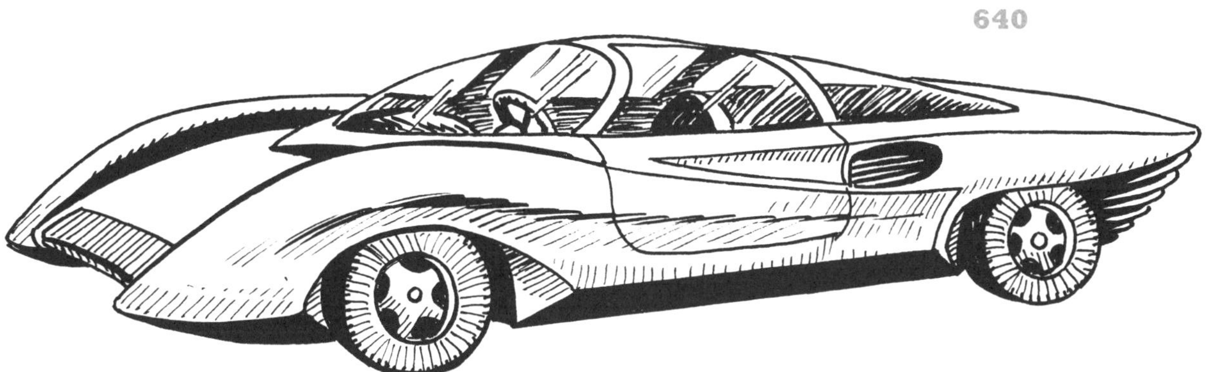

640

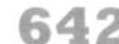
641
642 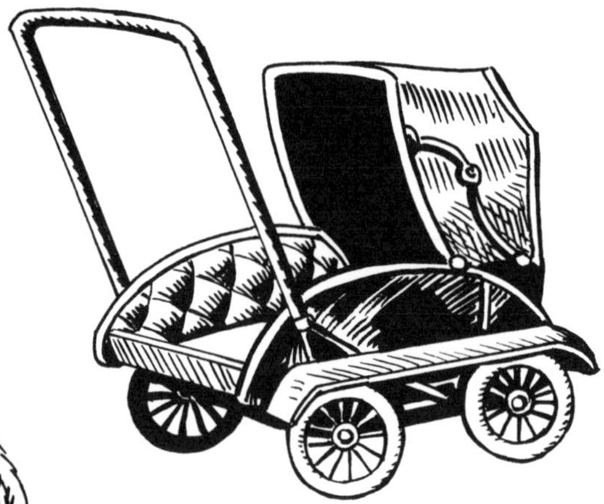 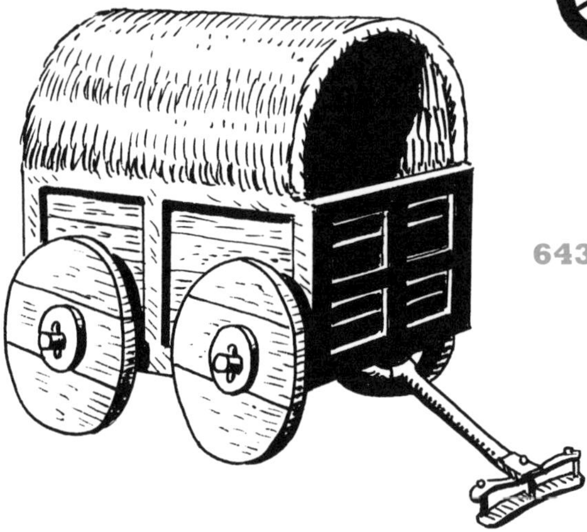
643
644 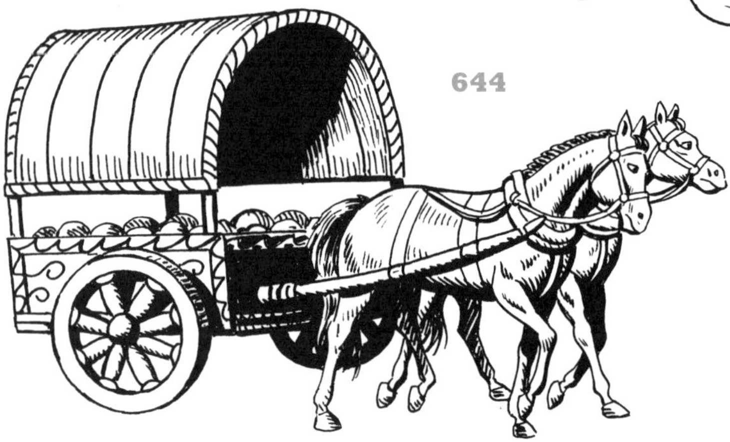
645

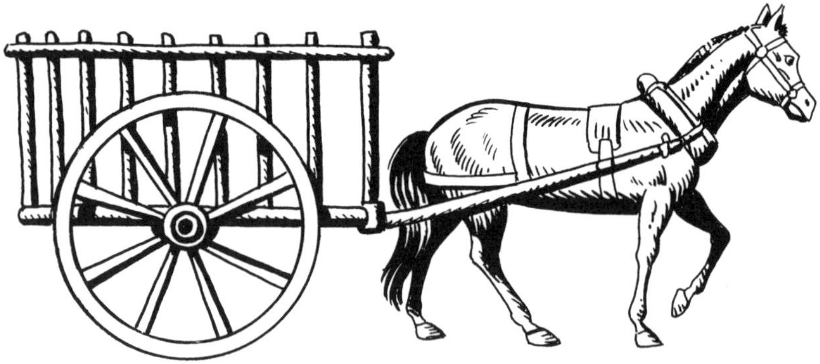

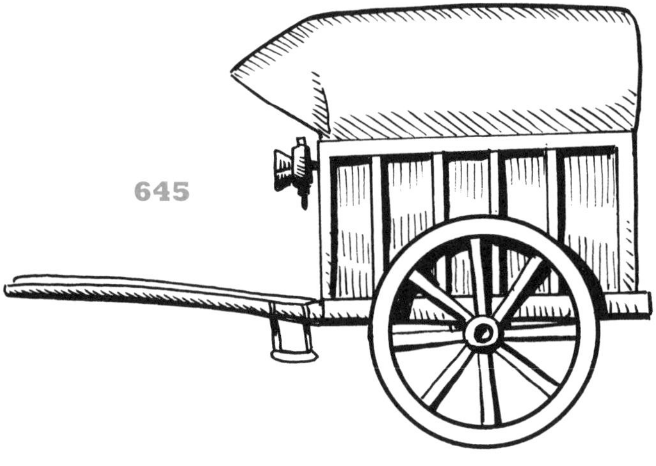

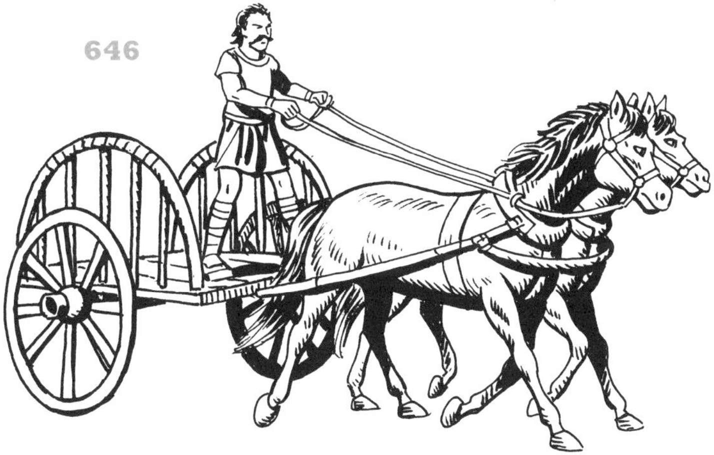

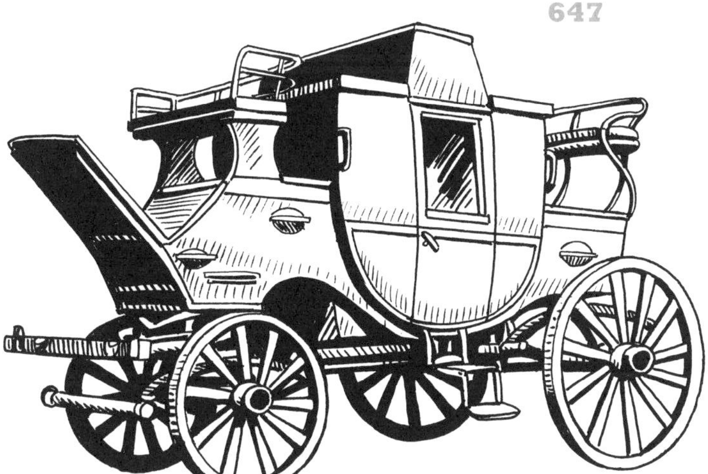

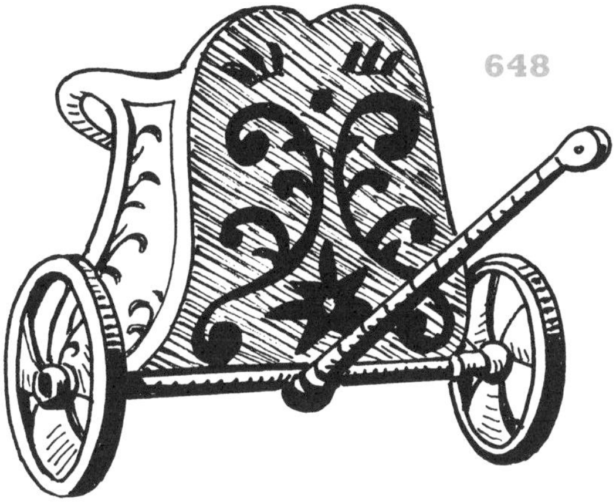

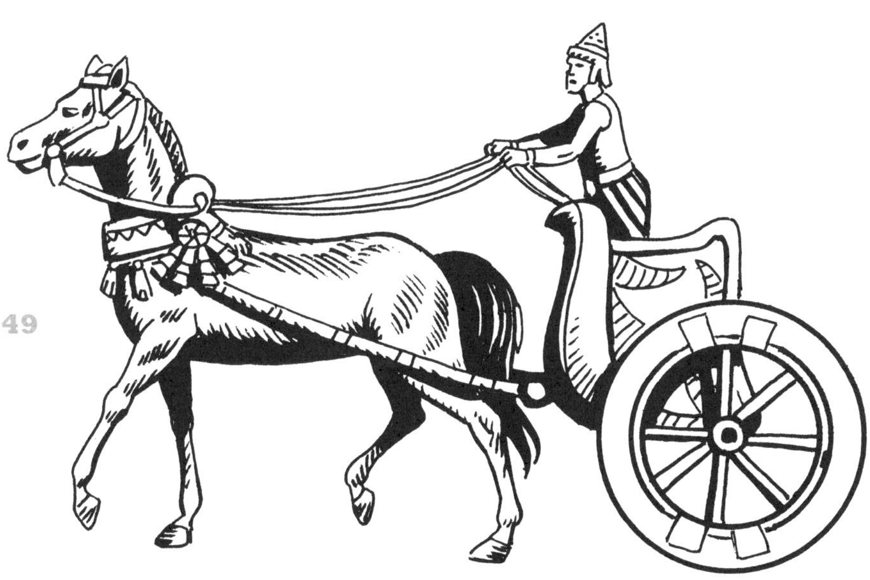

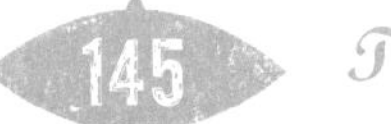

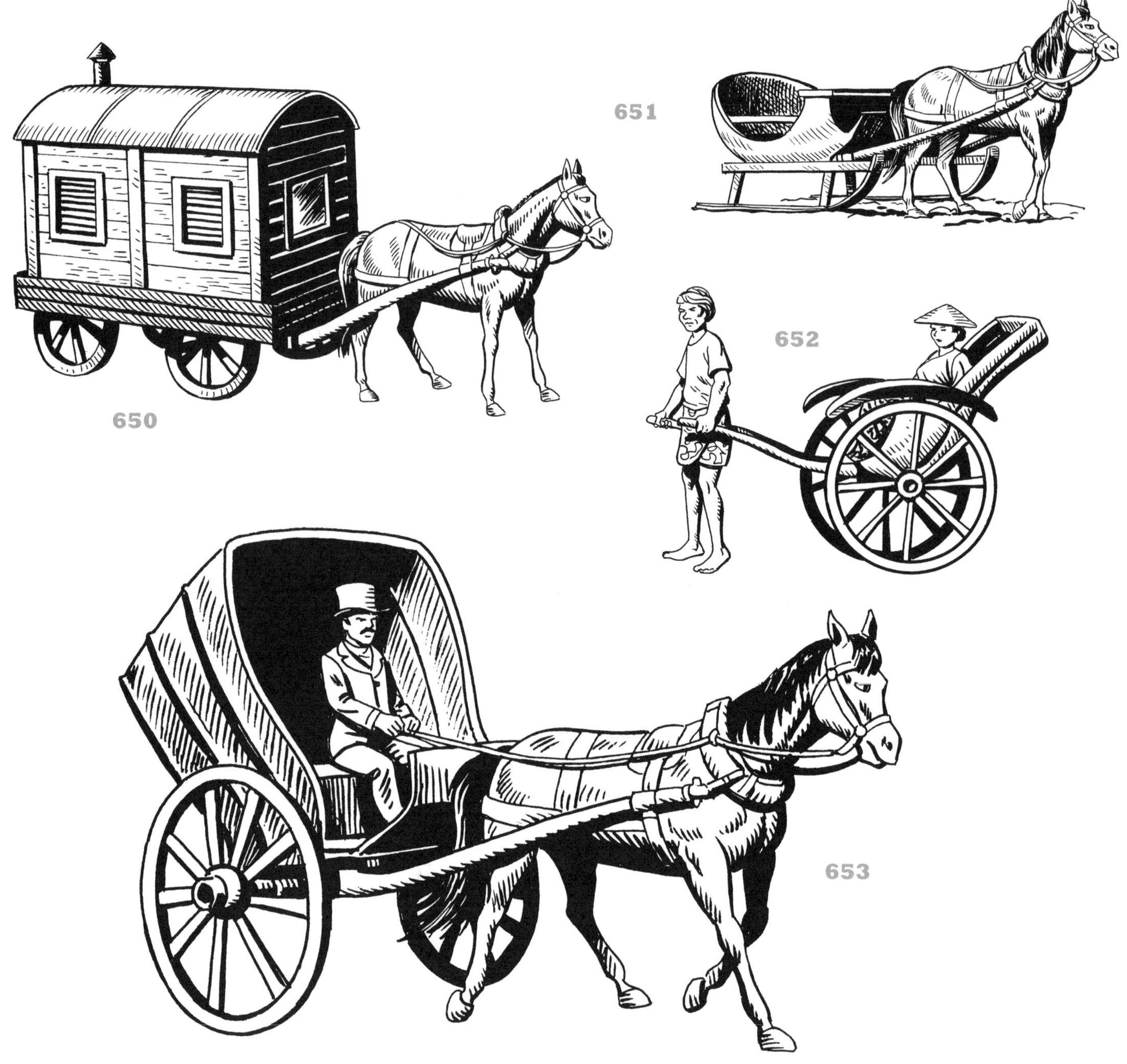

650
651
652
653

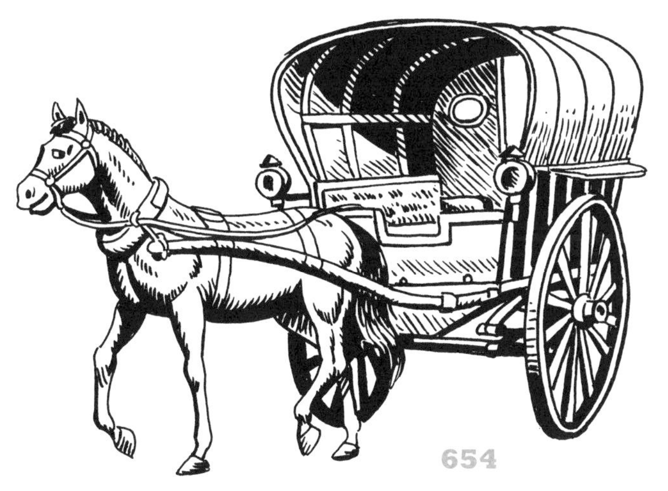

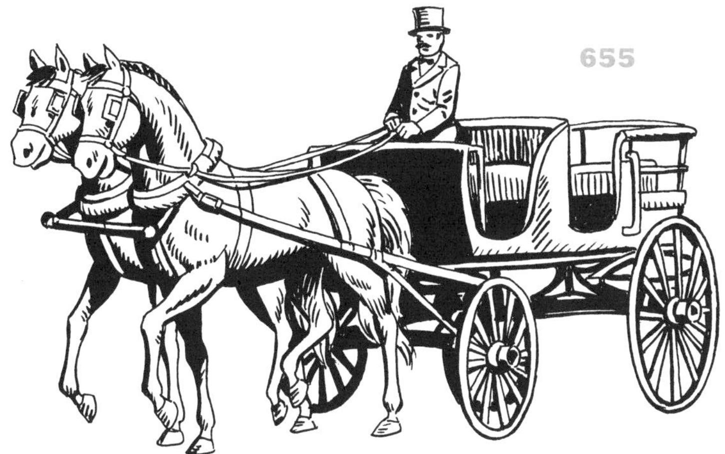

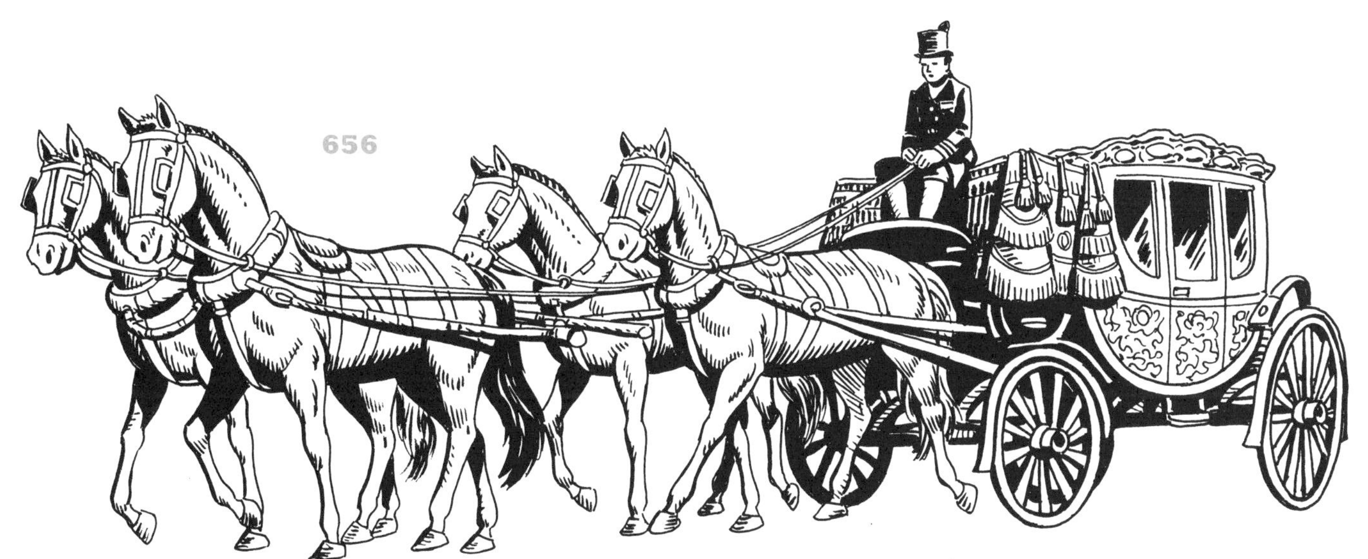

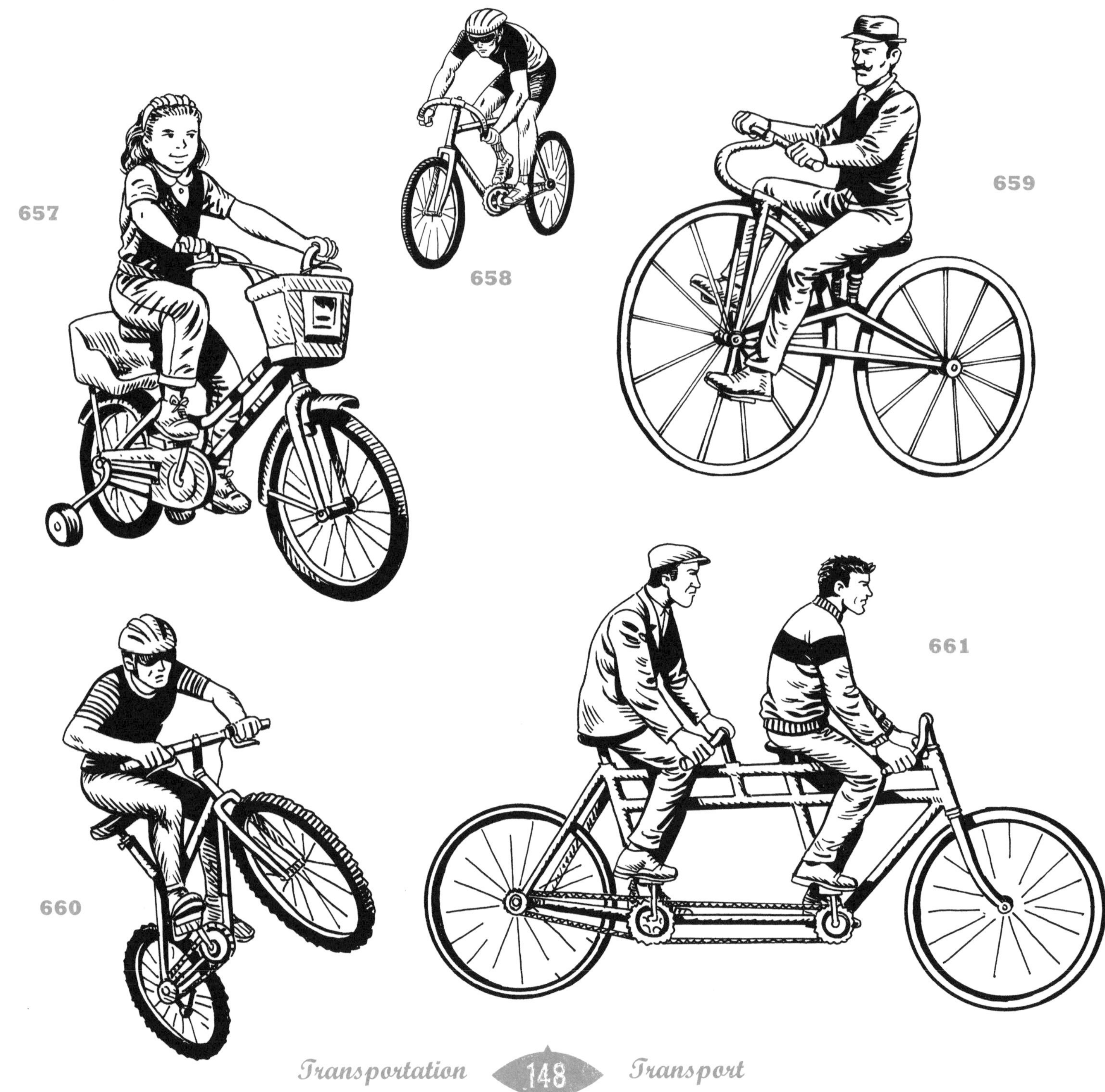
657
658
659
660
661

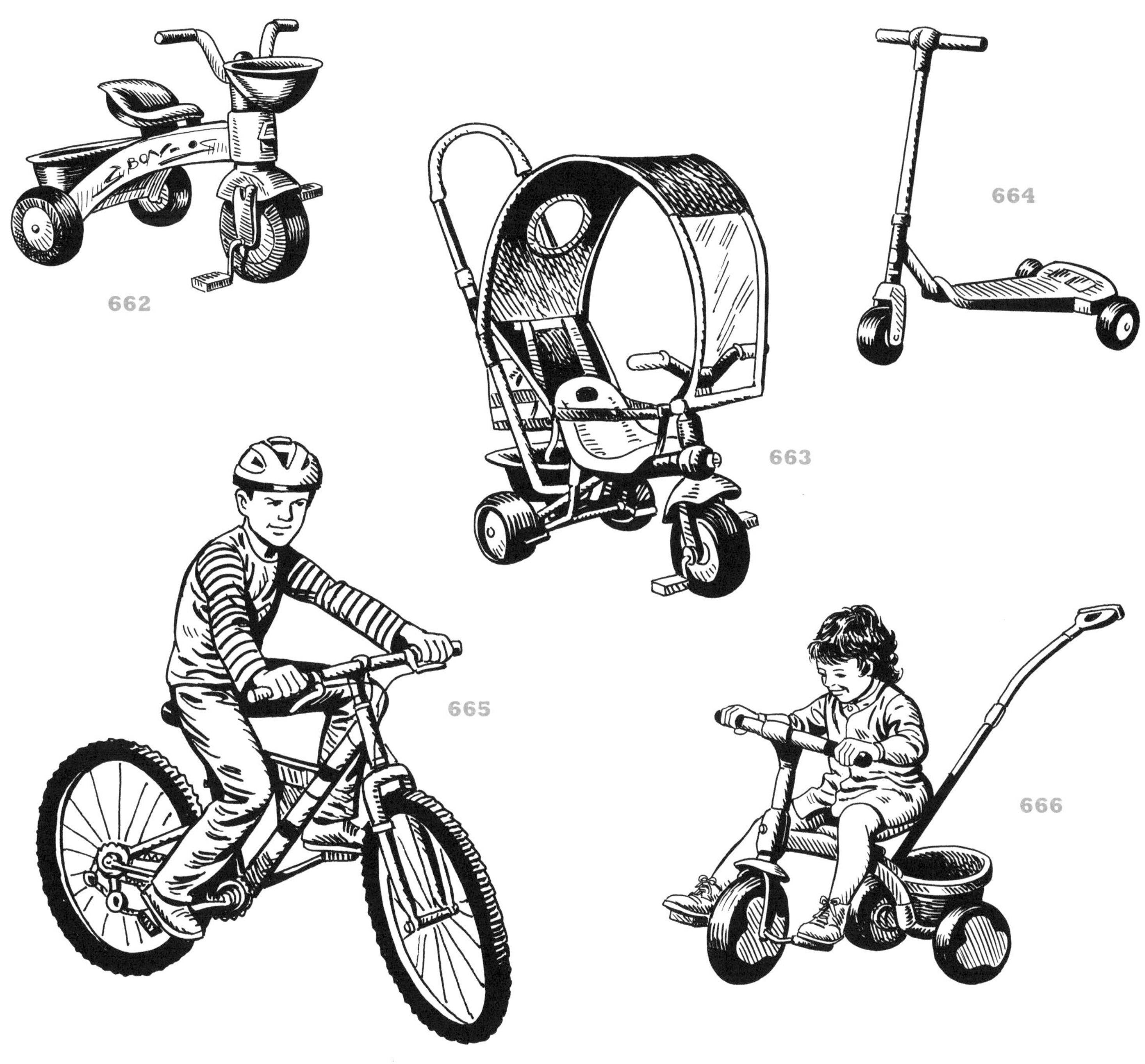
662
663
664
665
666

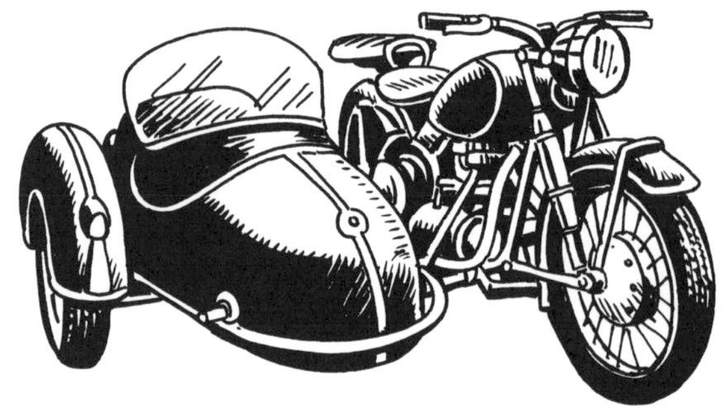

667

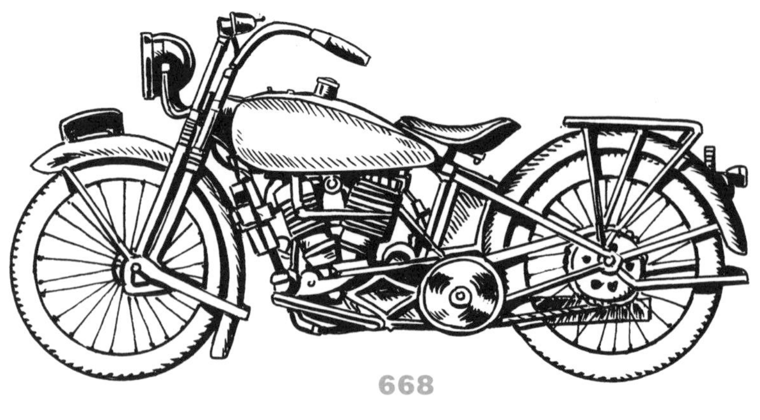

668

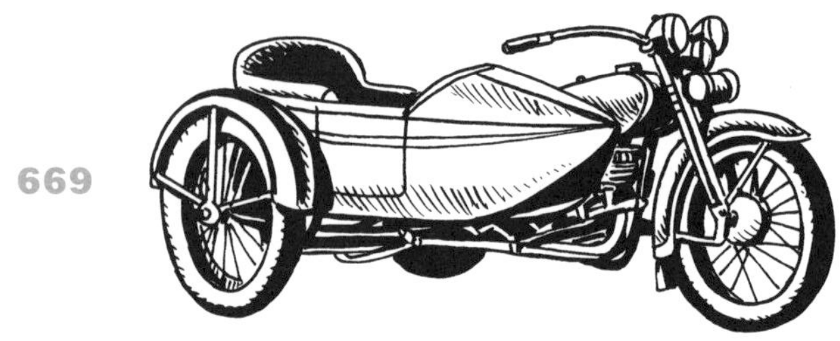

669

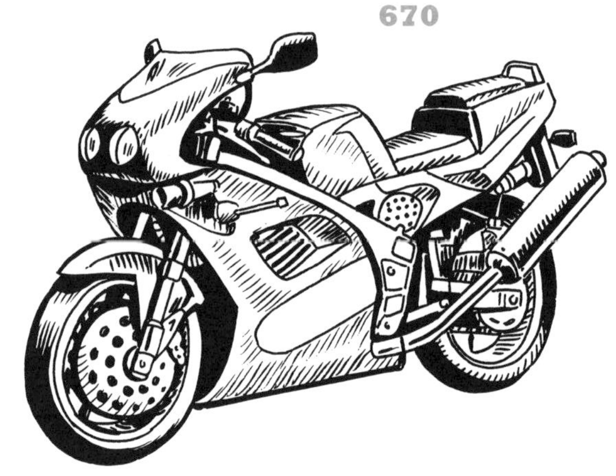

670

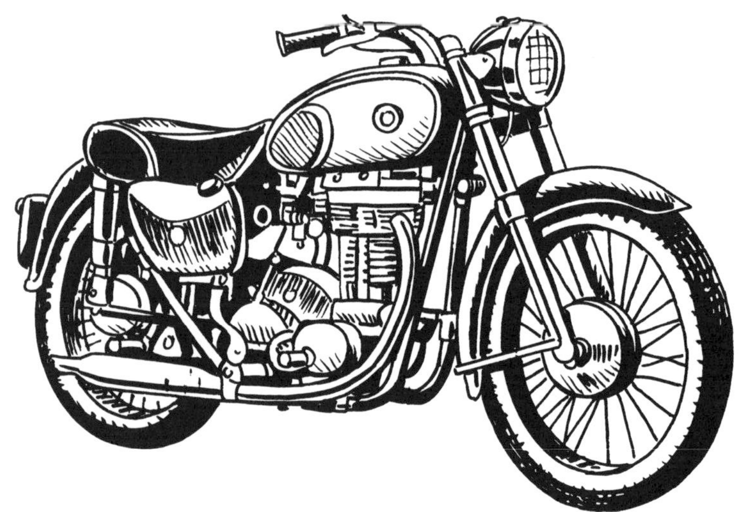

671

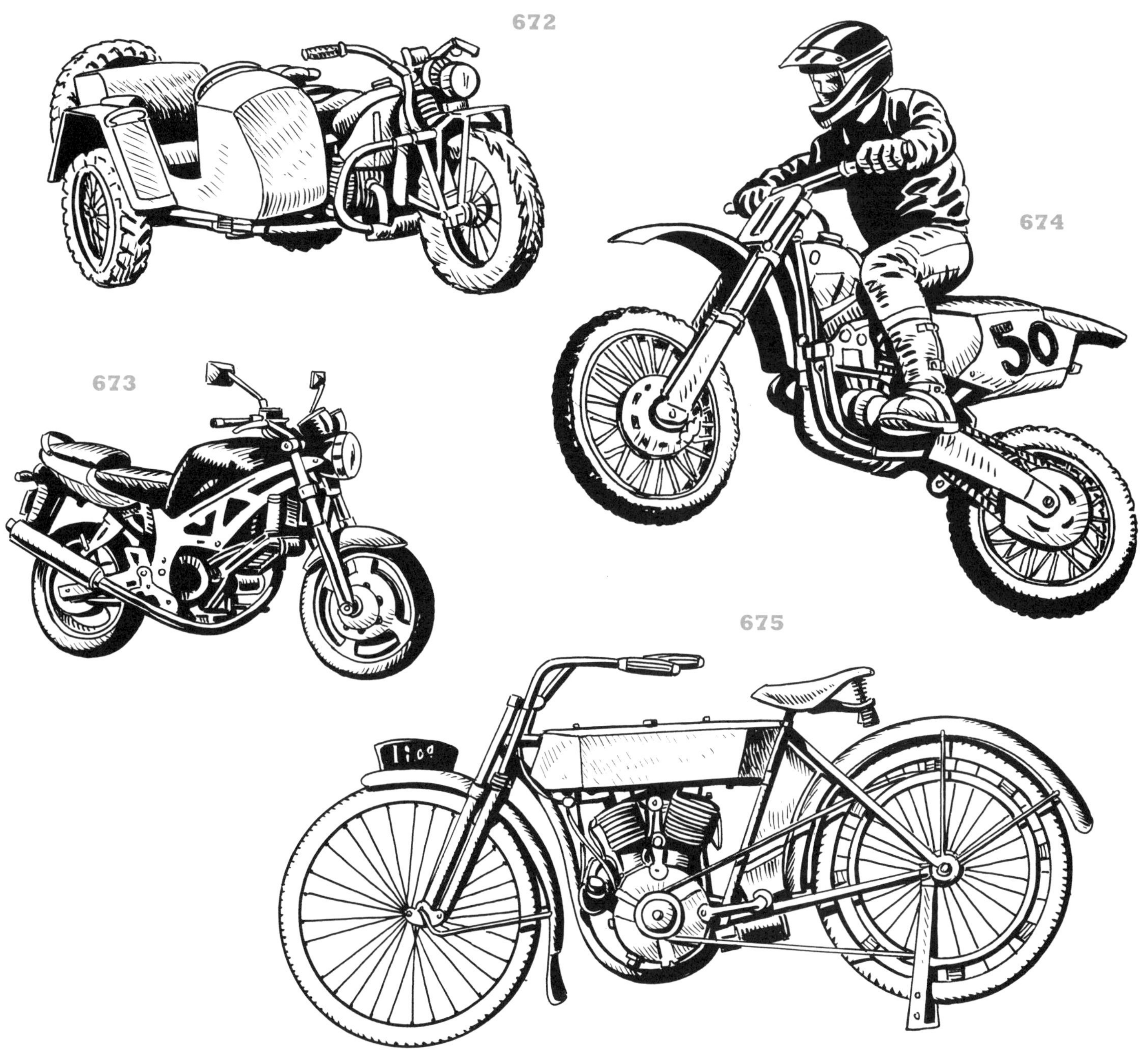

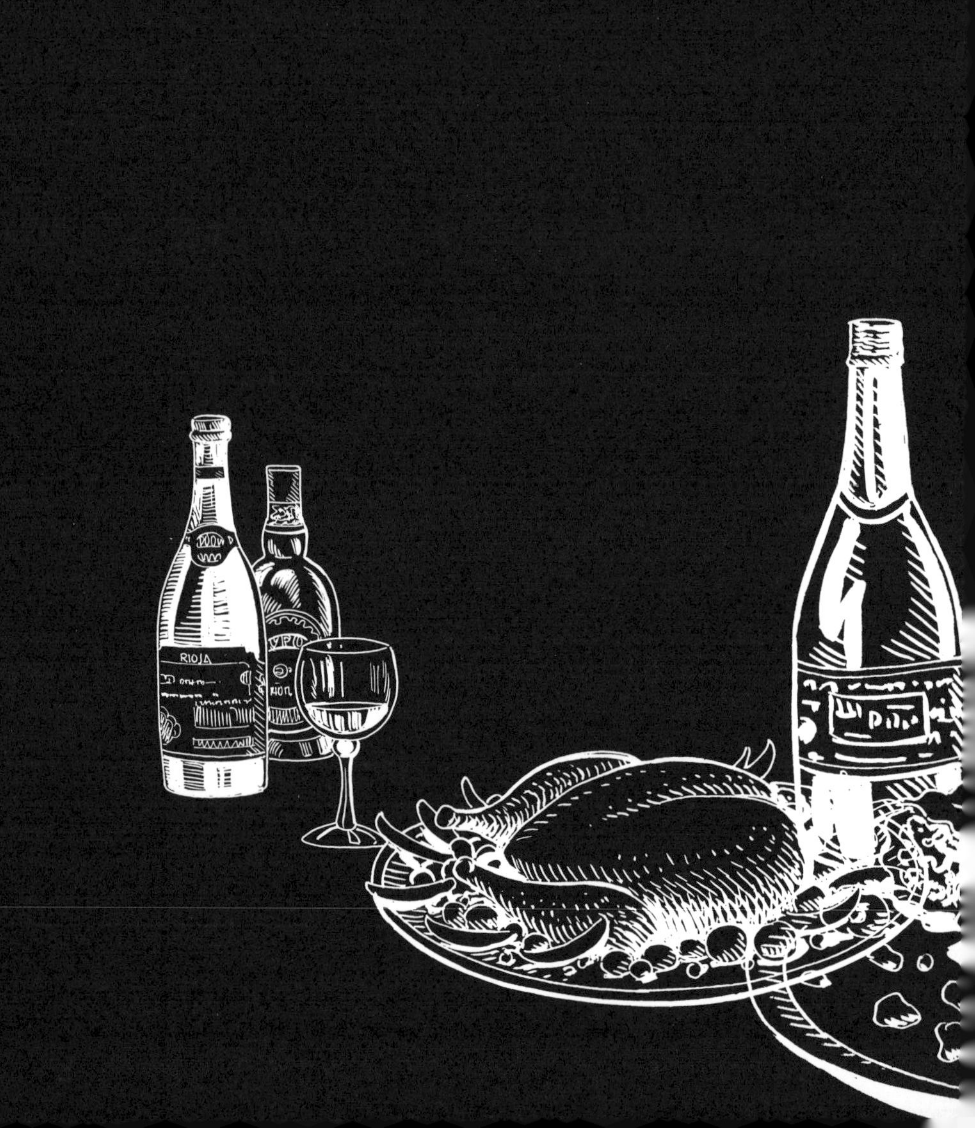

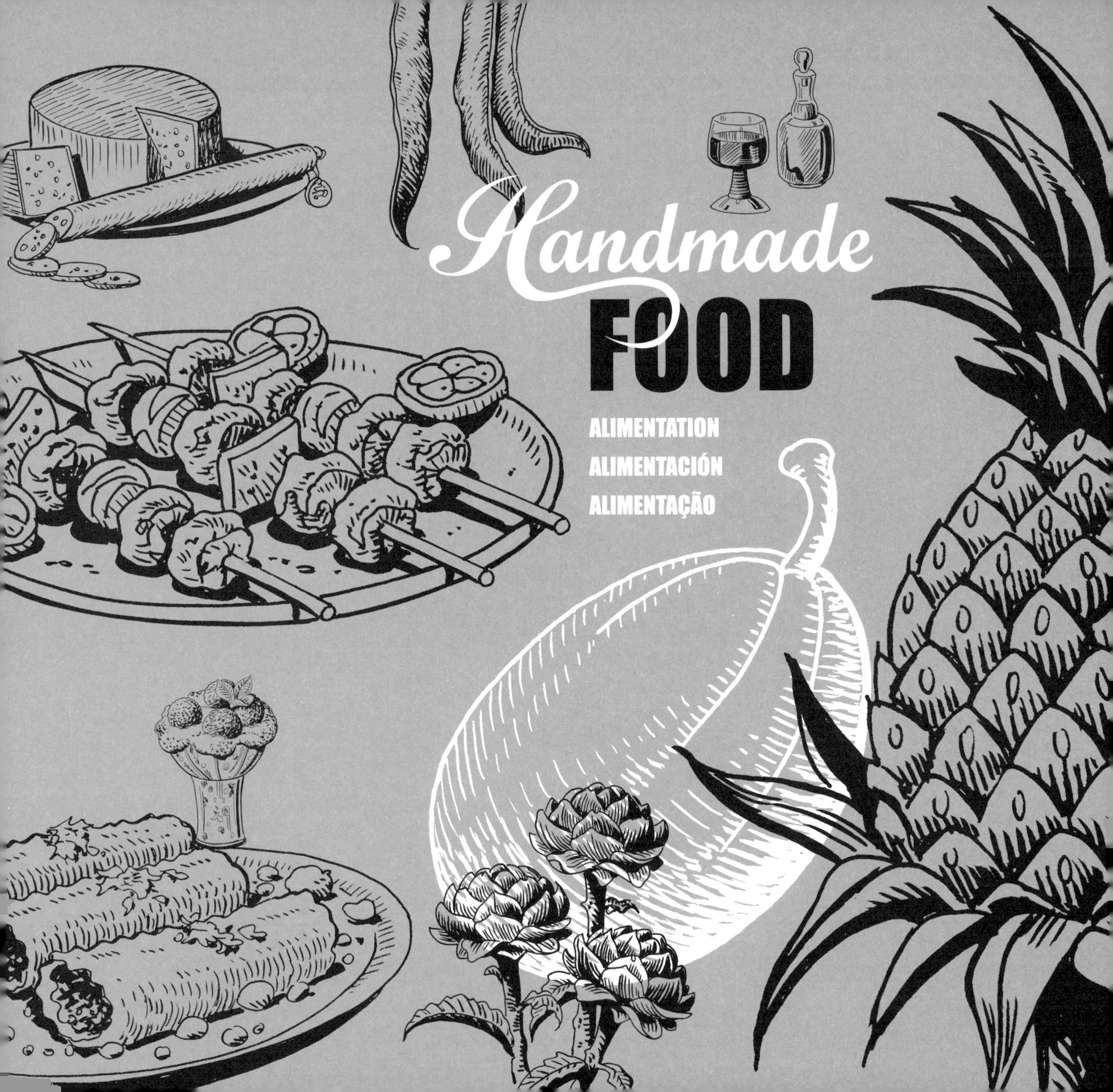

Handmade
FOOD
ALIMENTATION
ALIMENTACIÓN
ALIMENTAÇÃO

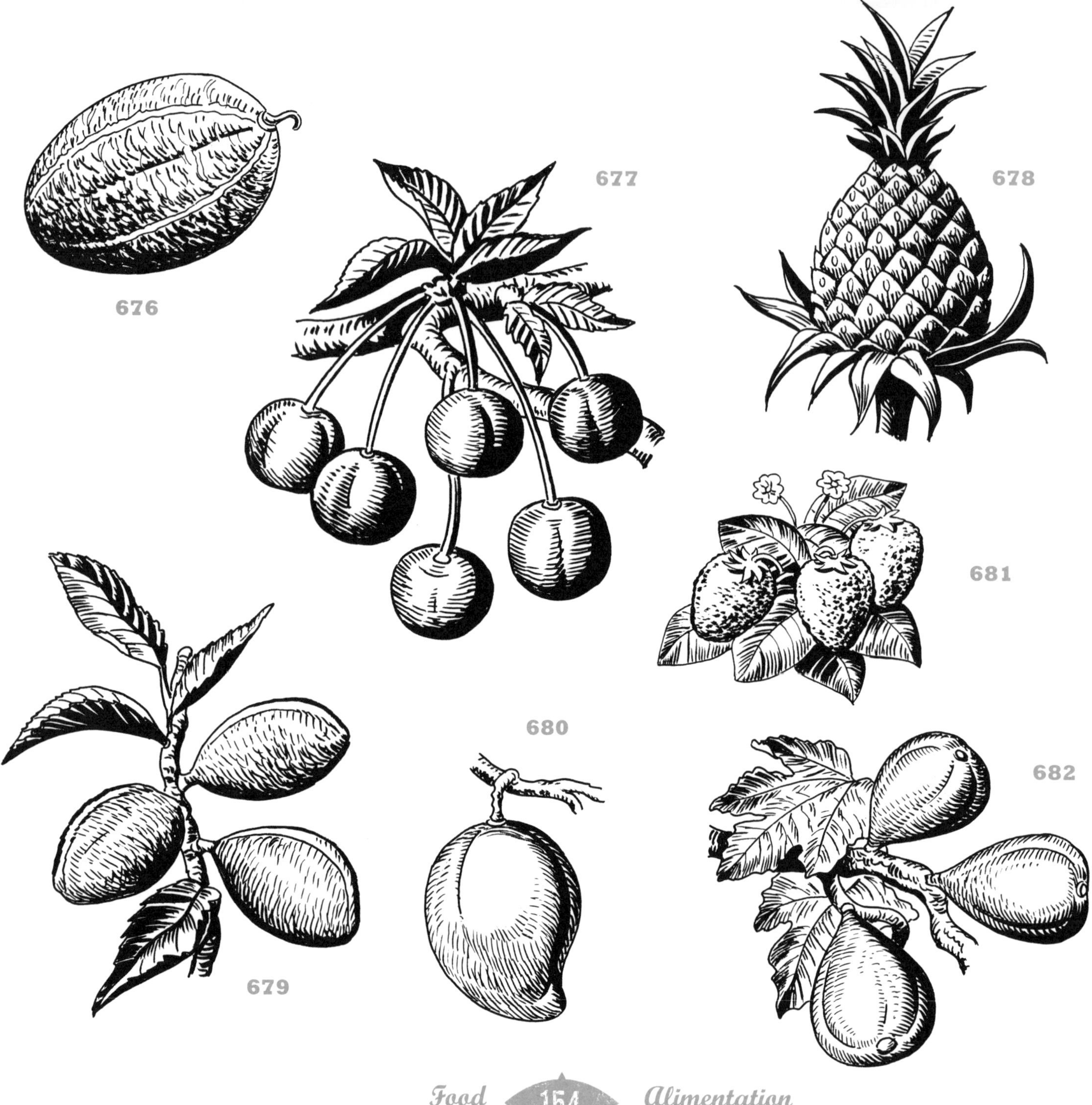

676
677
678
679
680
681
682

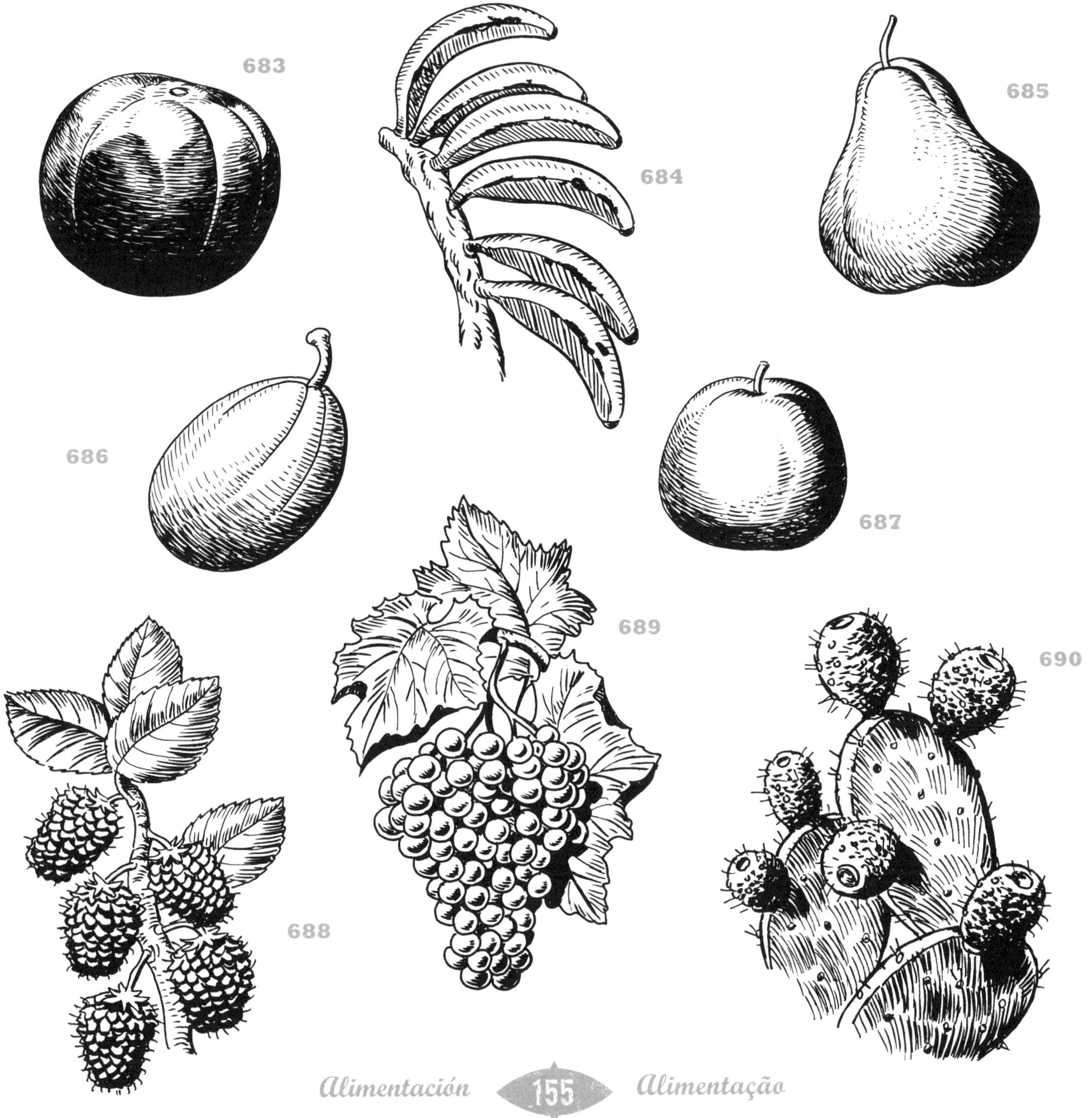

683
684
685
686
687
688
689
690

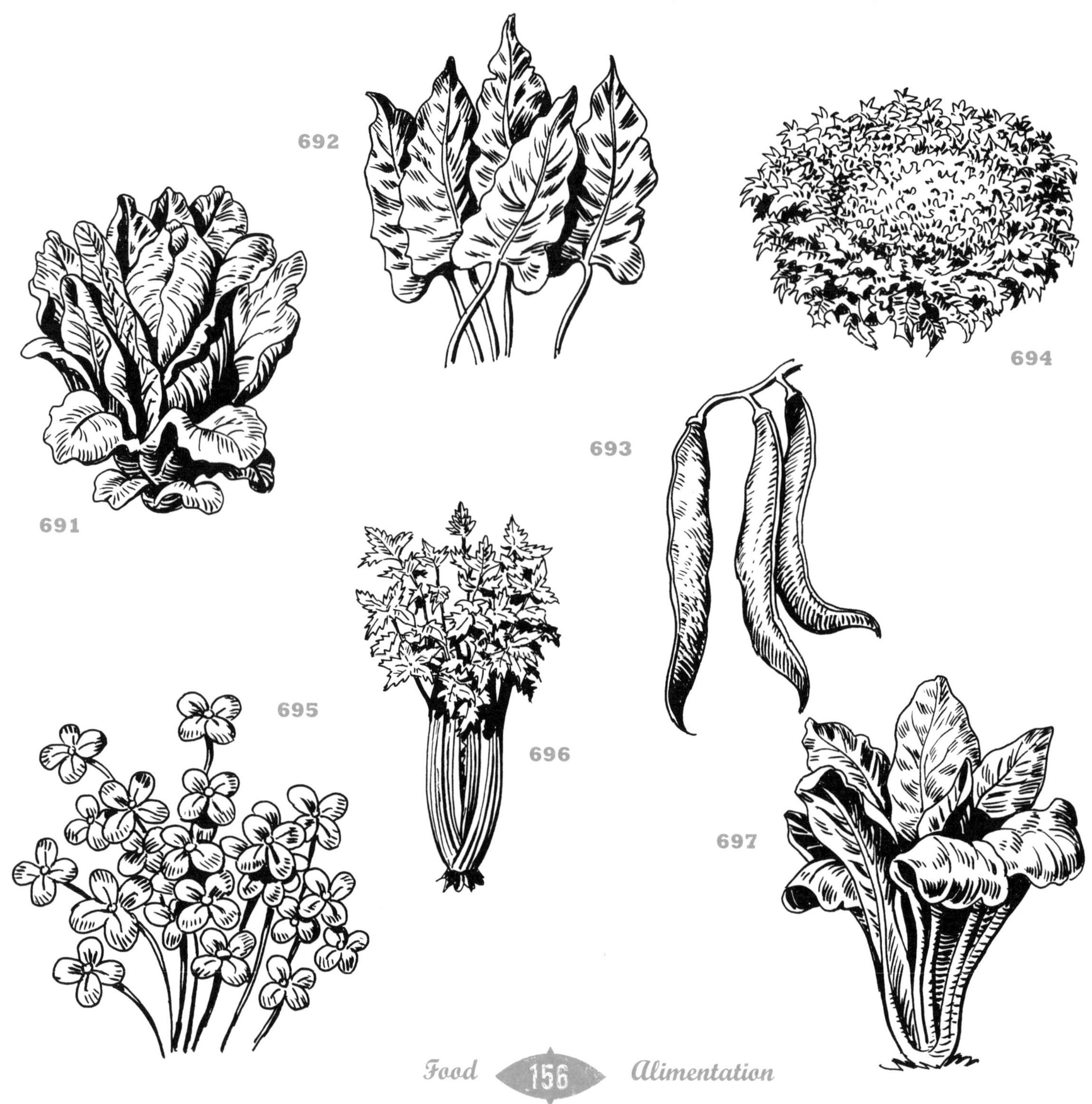

692
694
691
693
695
696
697

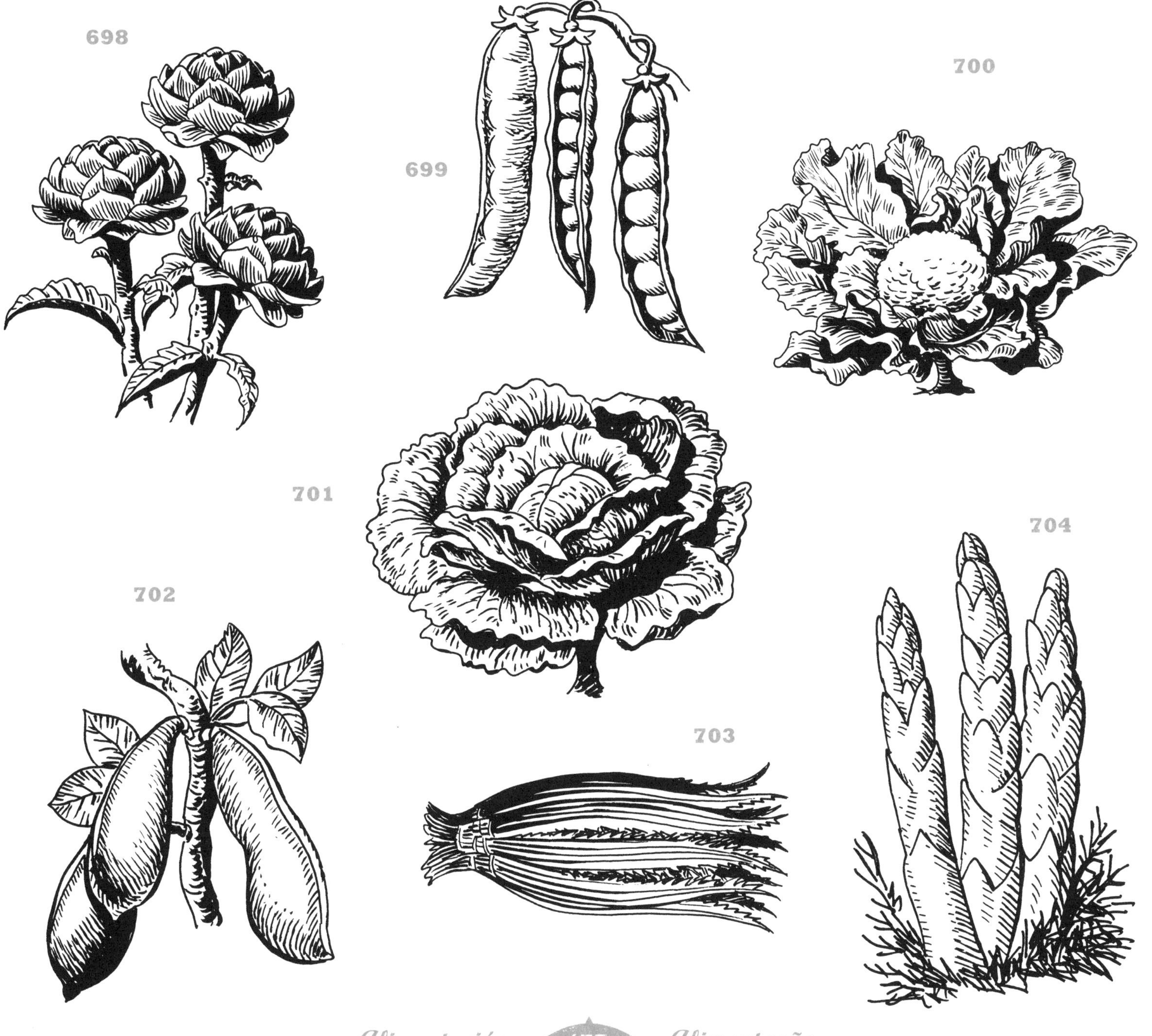

698
699
700
701
702
703
704

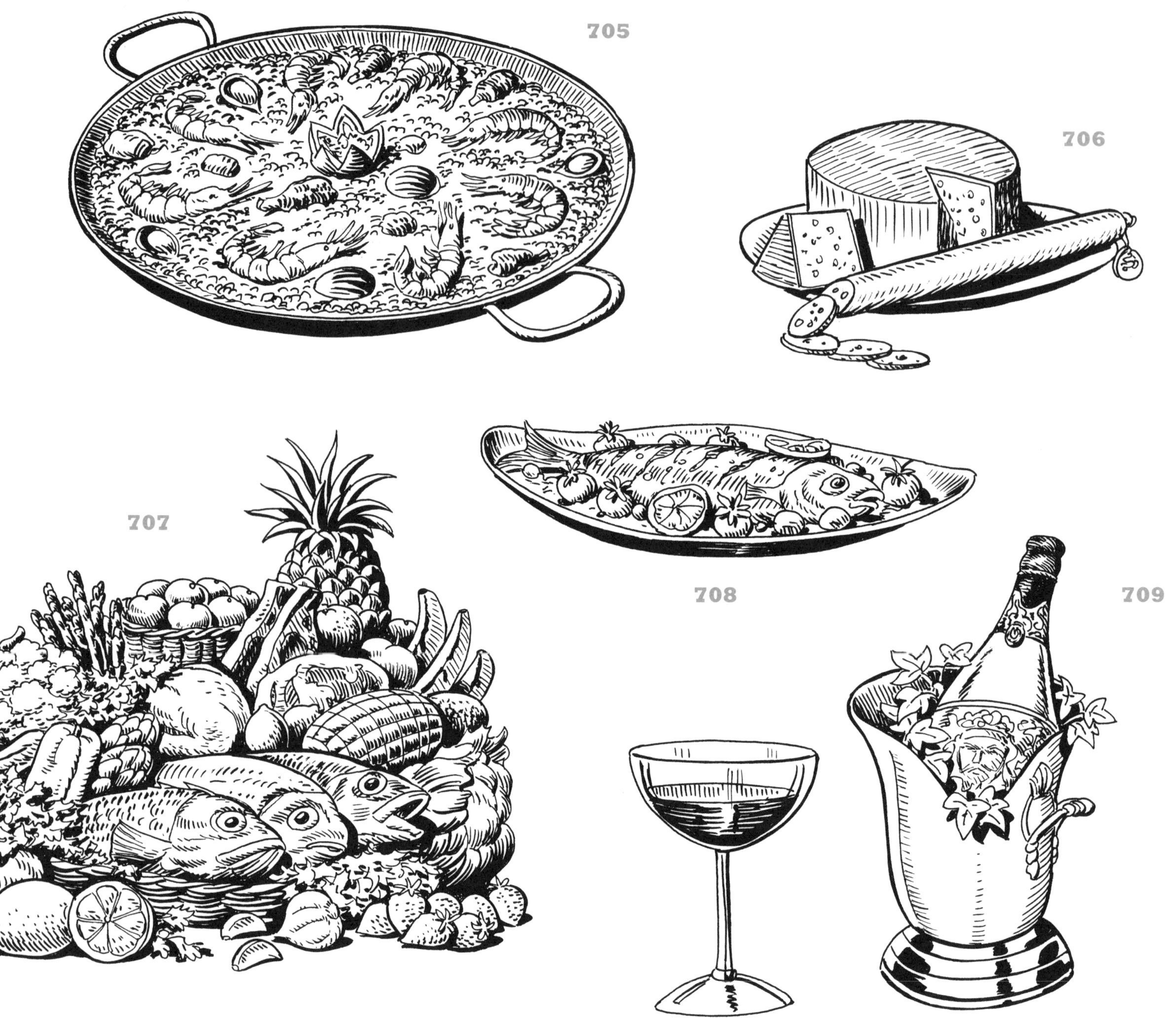

705
706
707
708
709

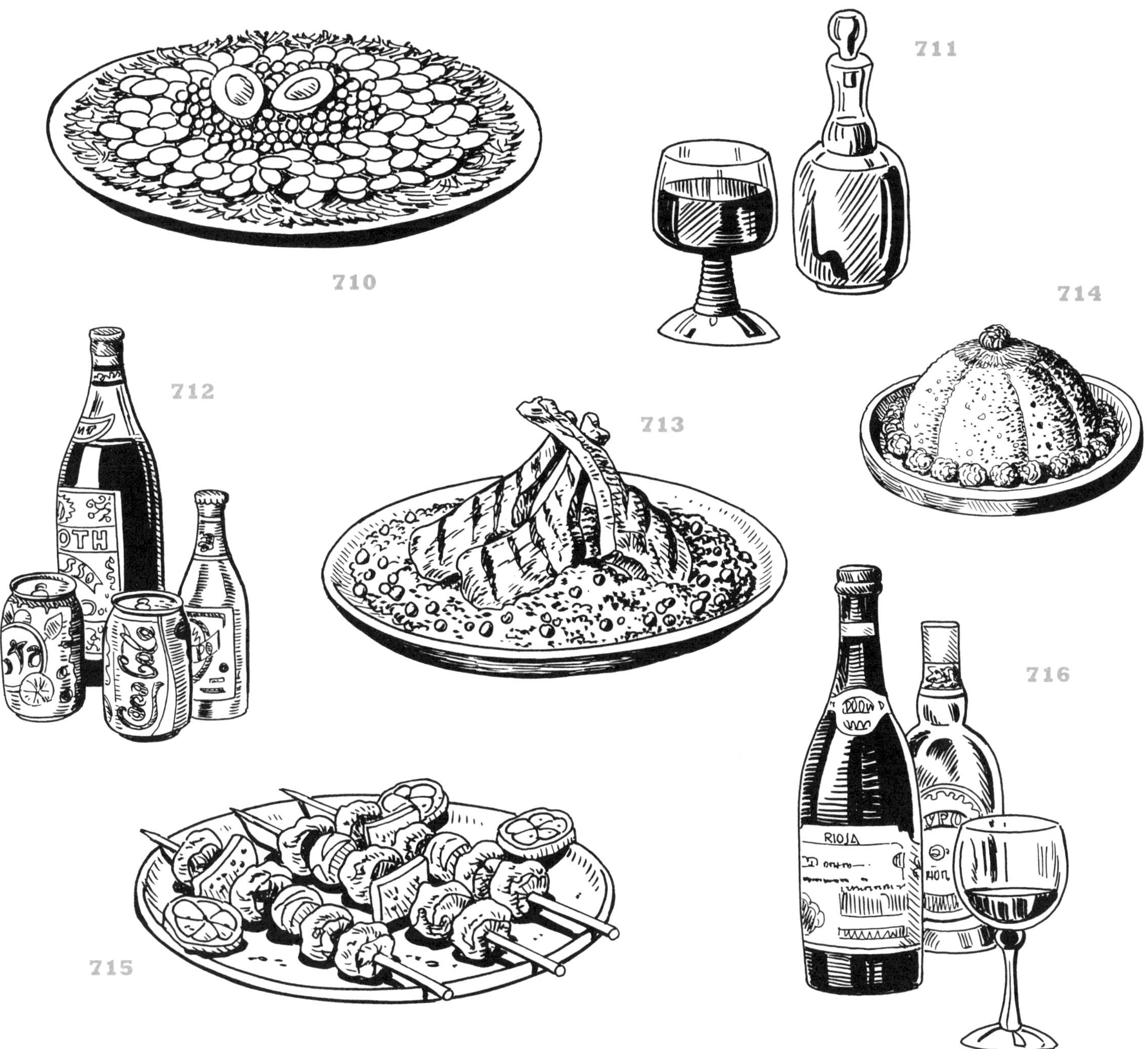

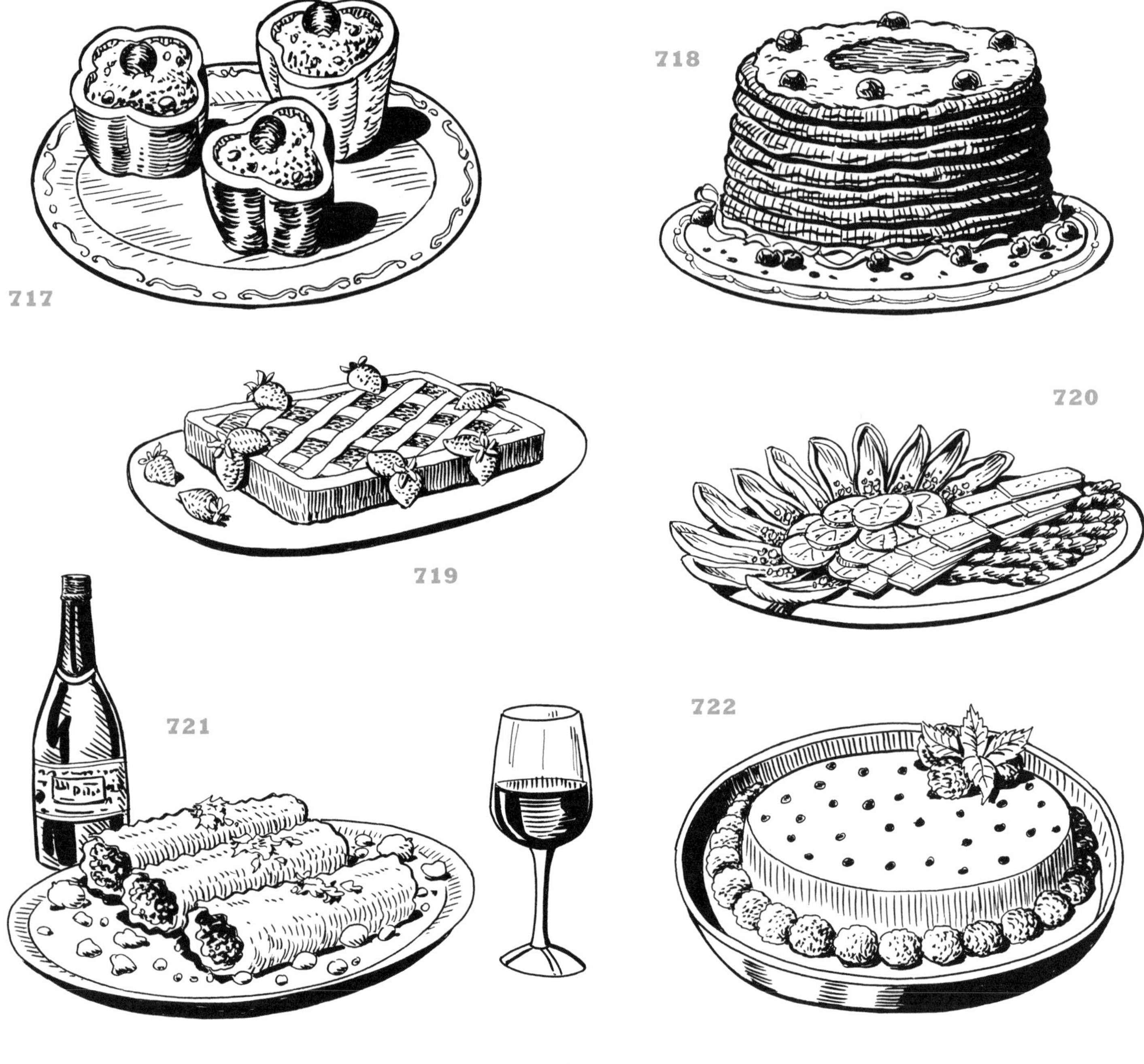

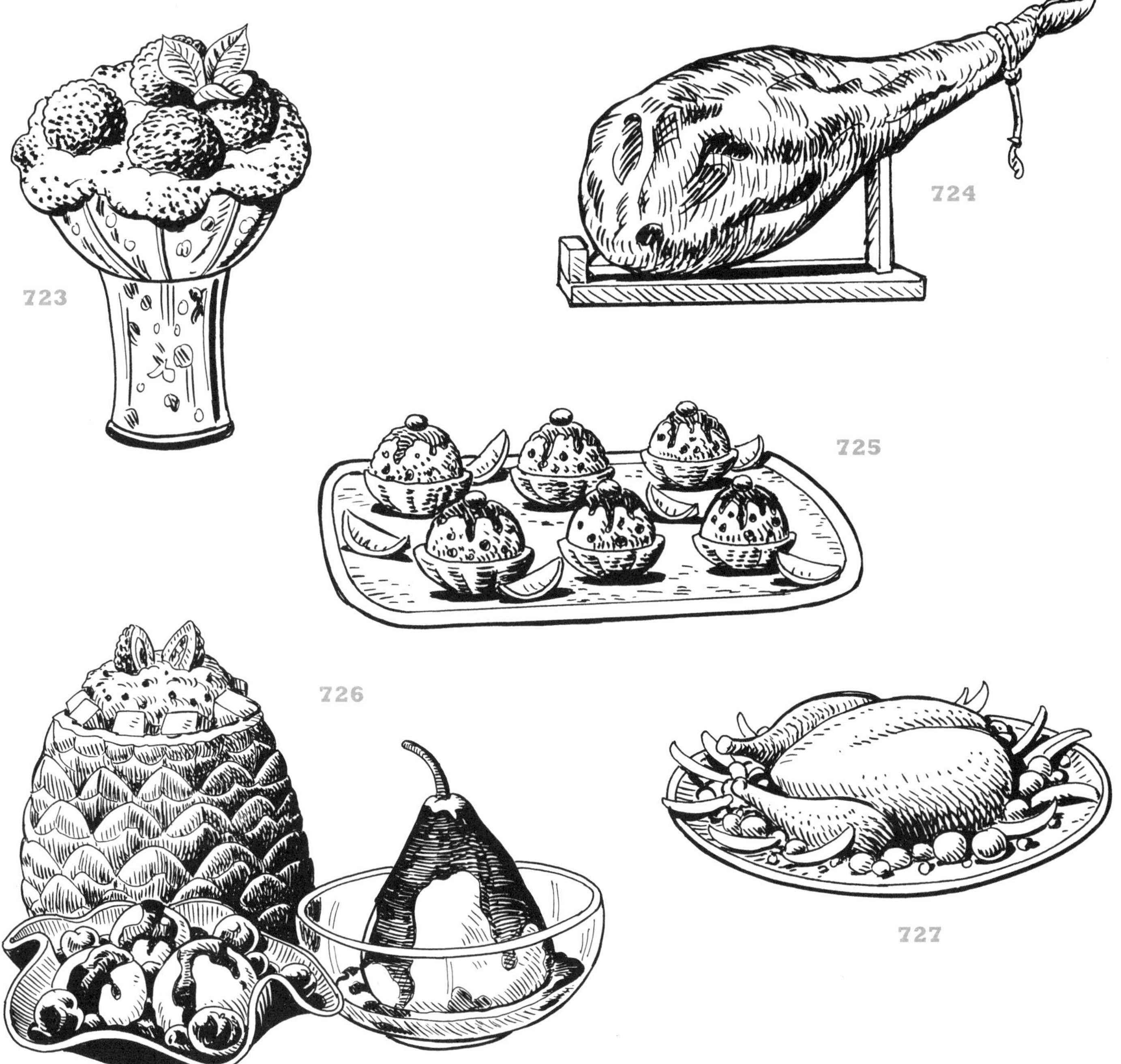

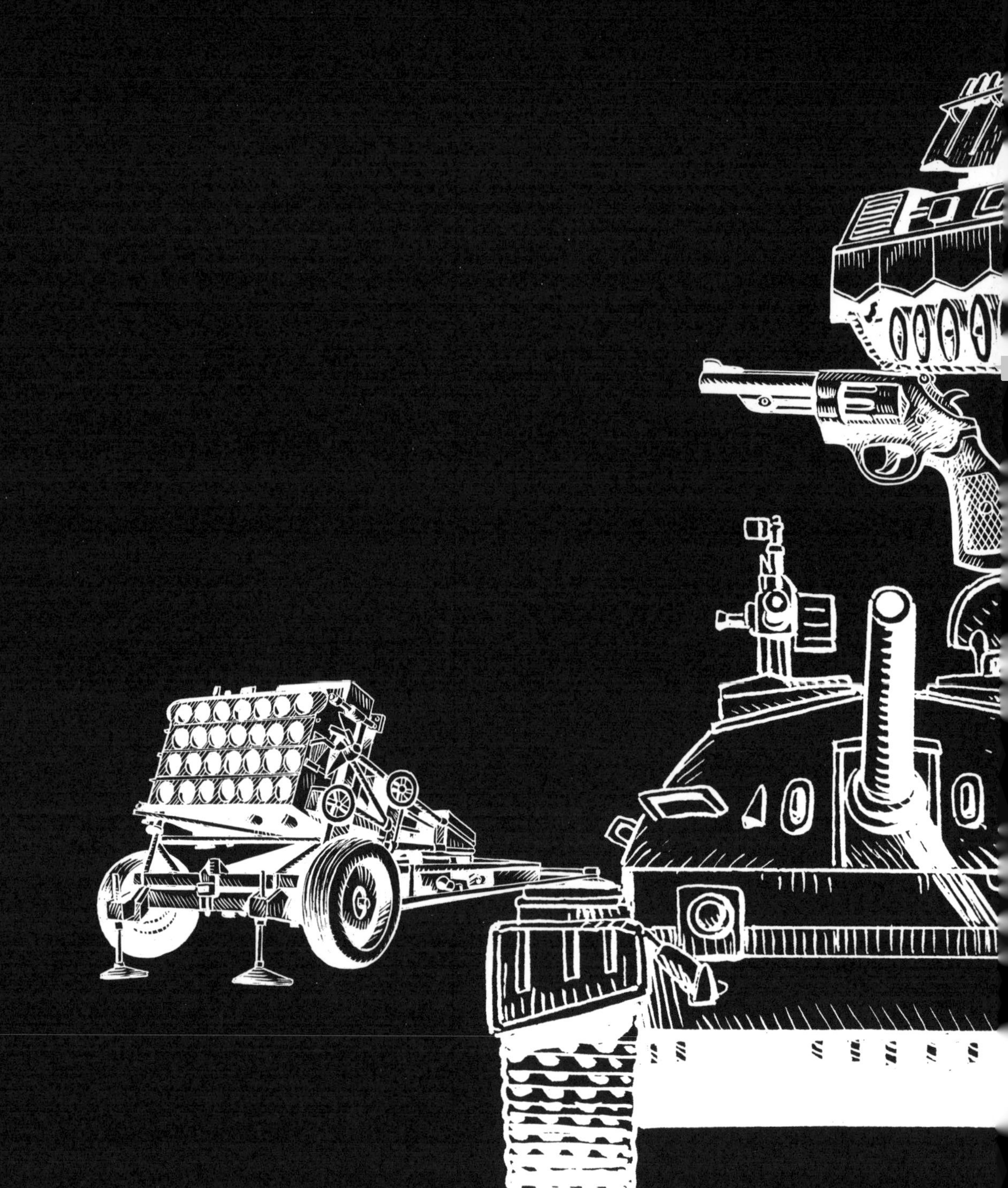

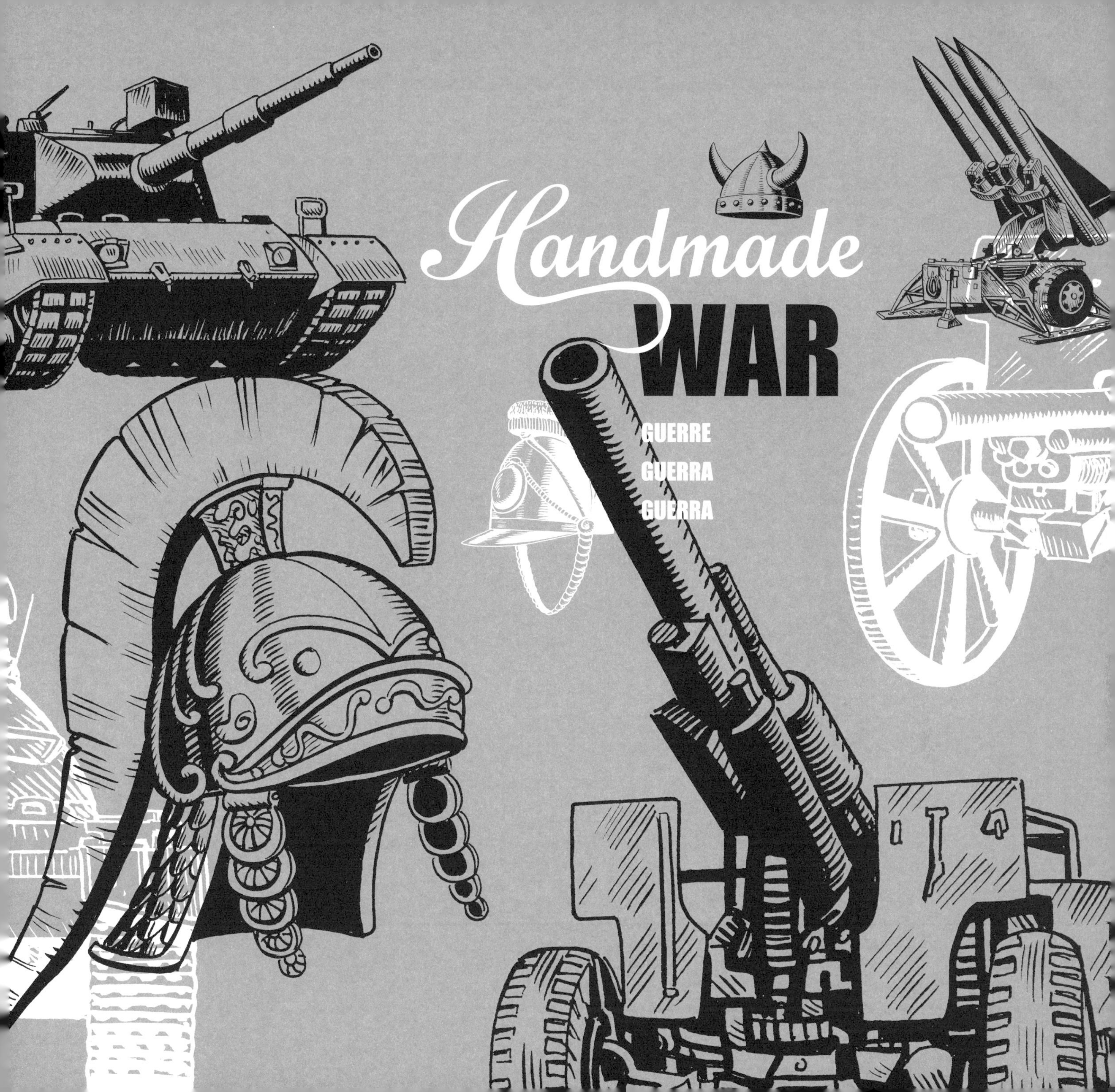
Handmade
WAR
GUERRE
GUERRA
GUERRA

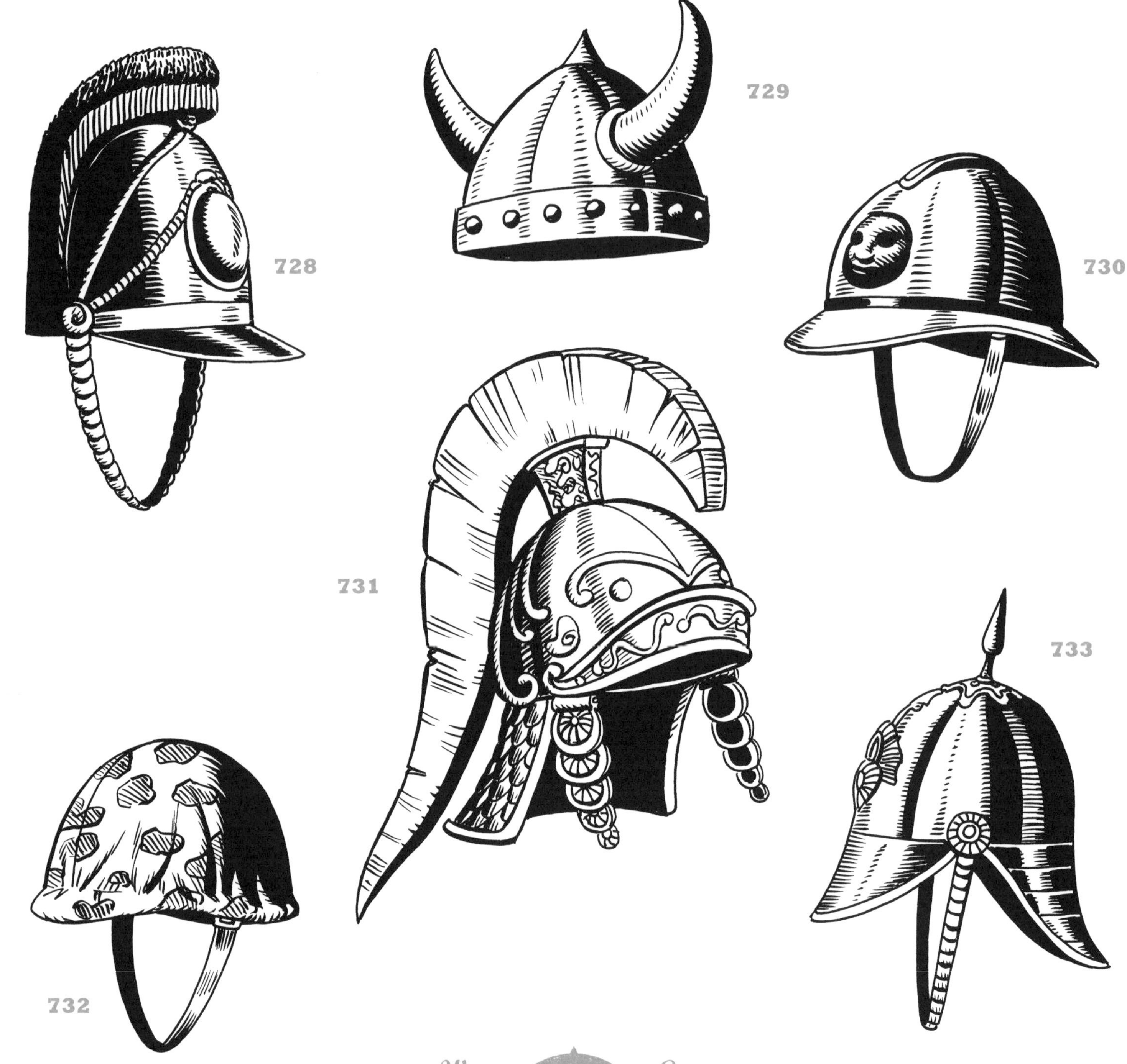

728
729
730
731
732
733

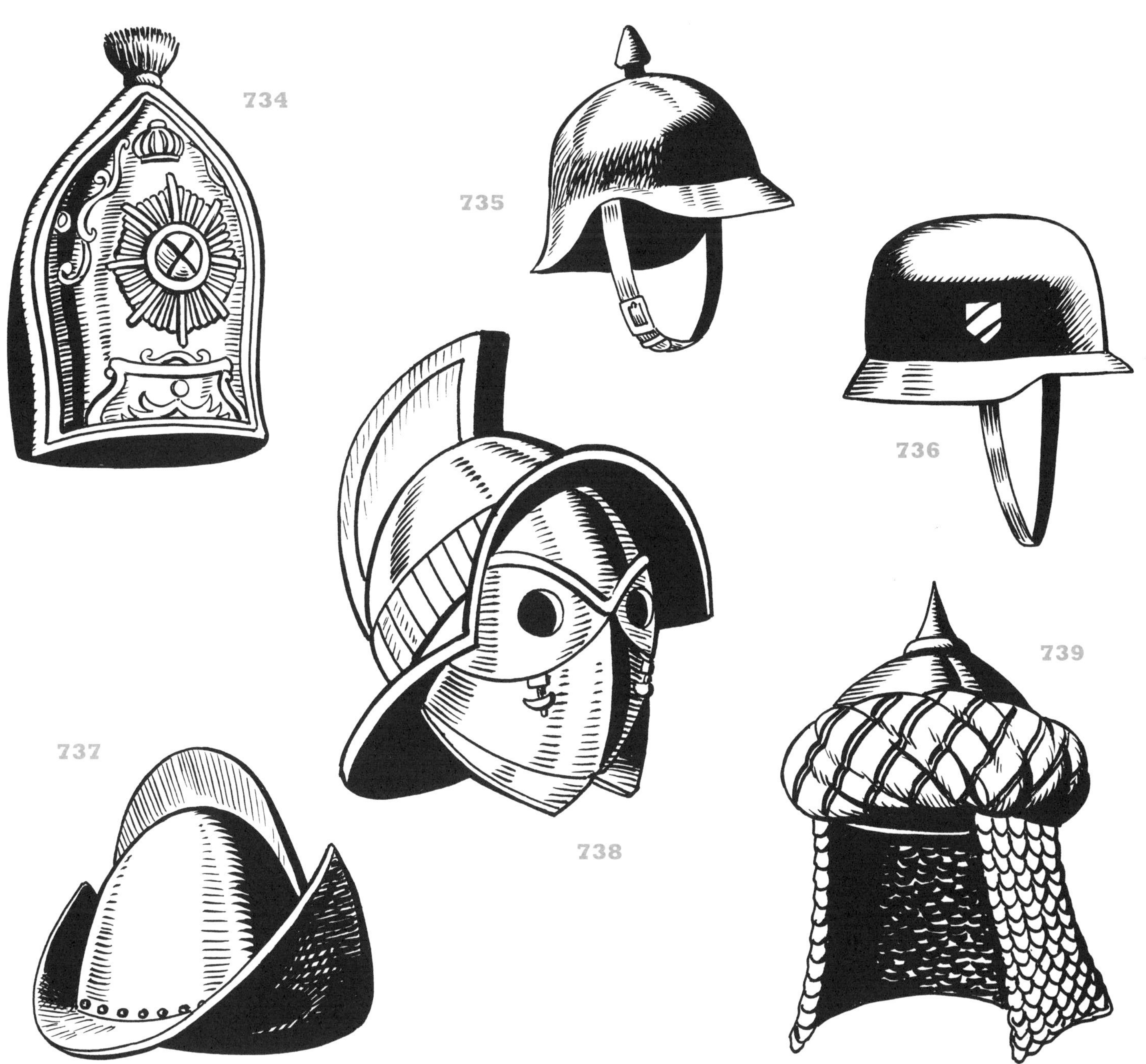
734
735
736
737
738
739

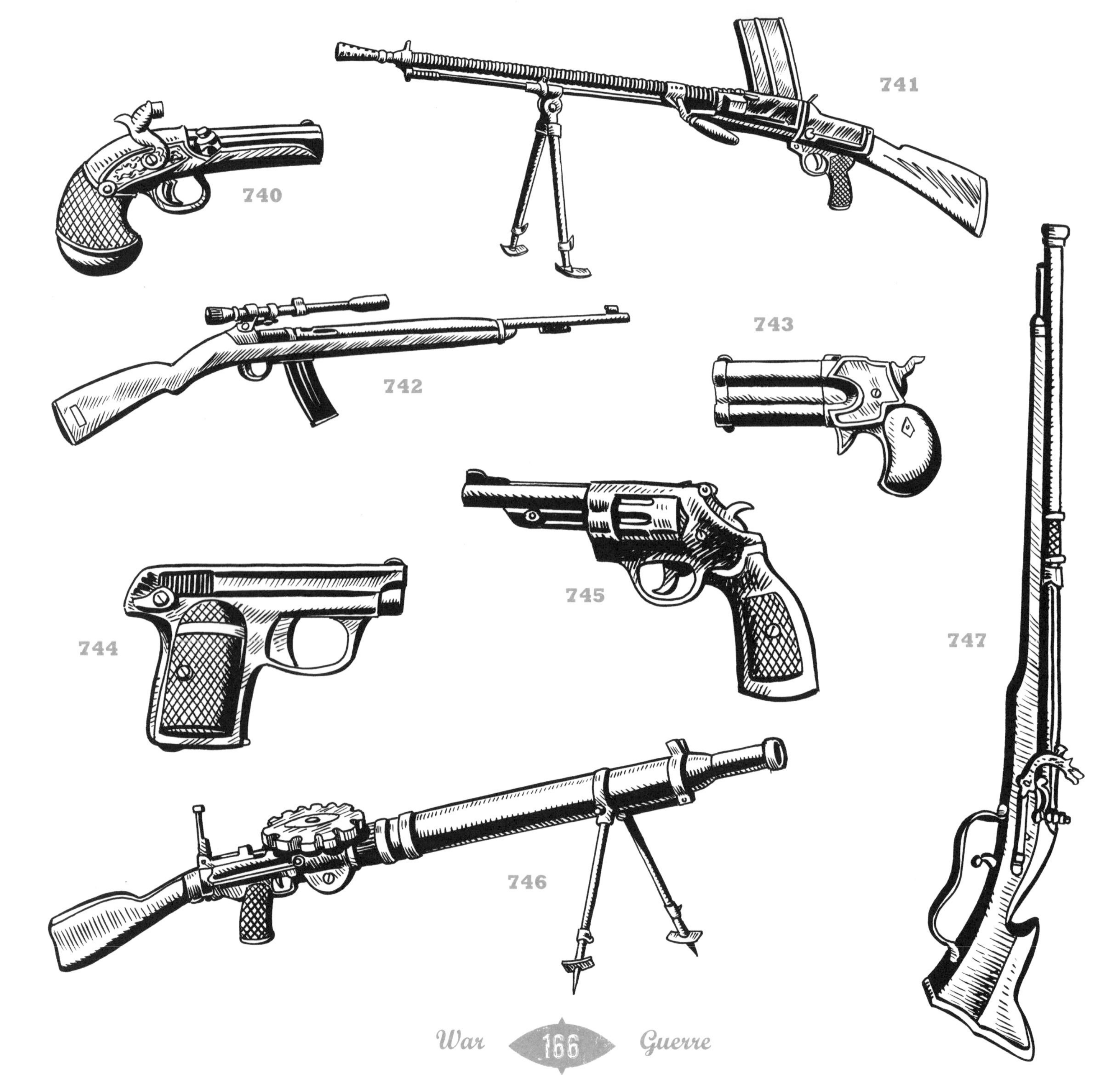
740
741
742
743
744
745
746
747

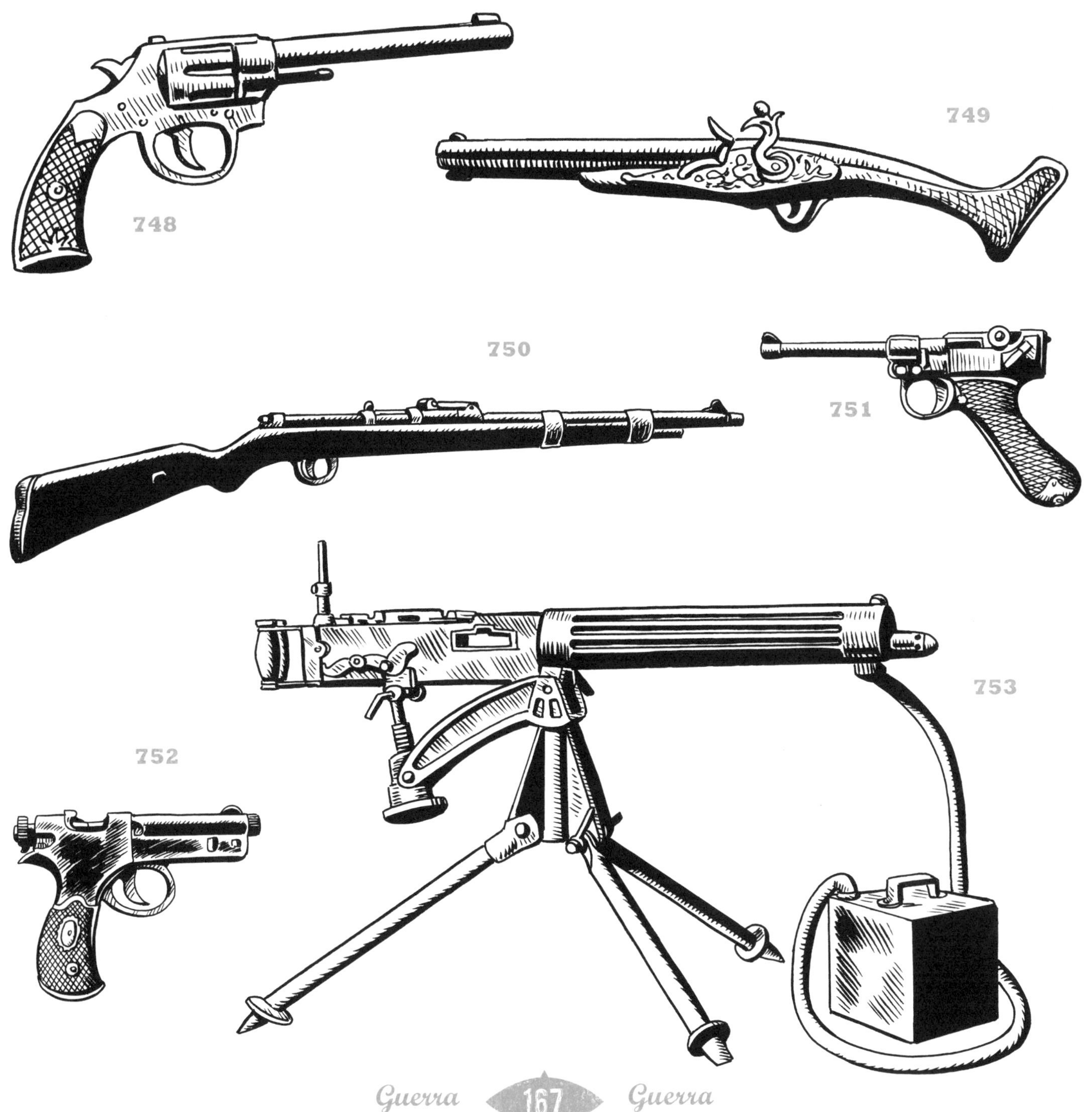
748
749
750
751
752
753

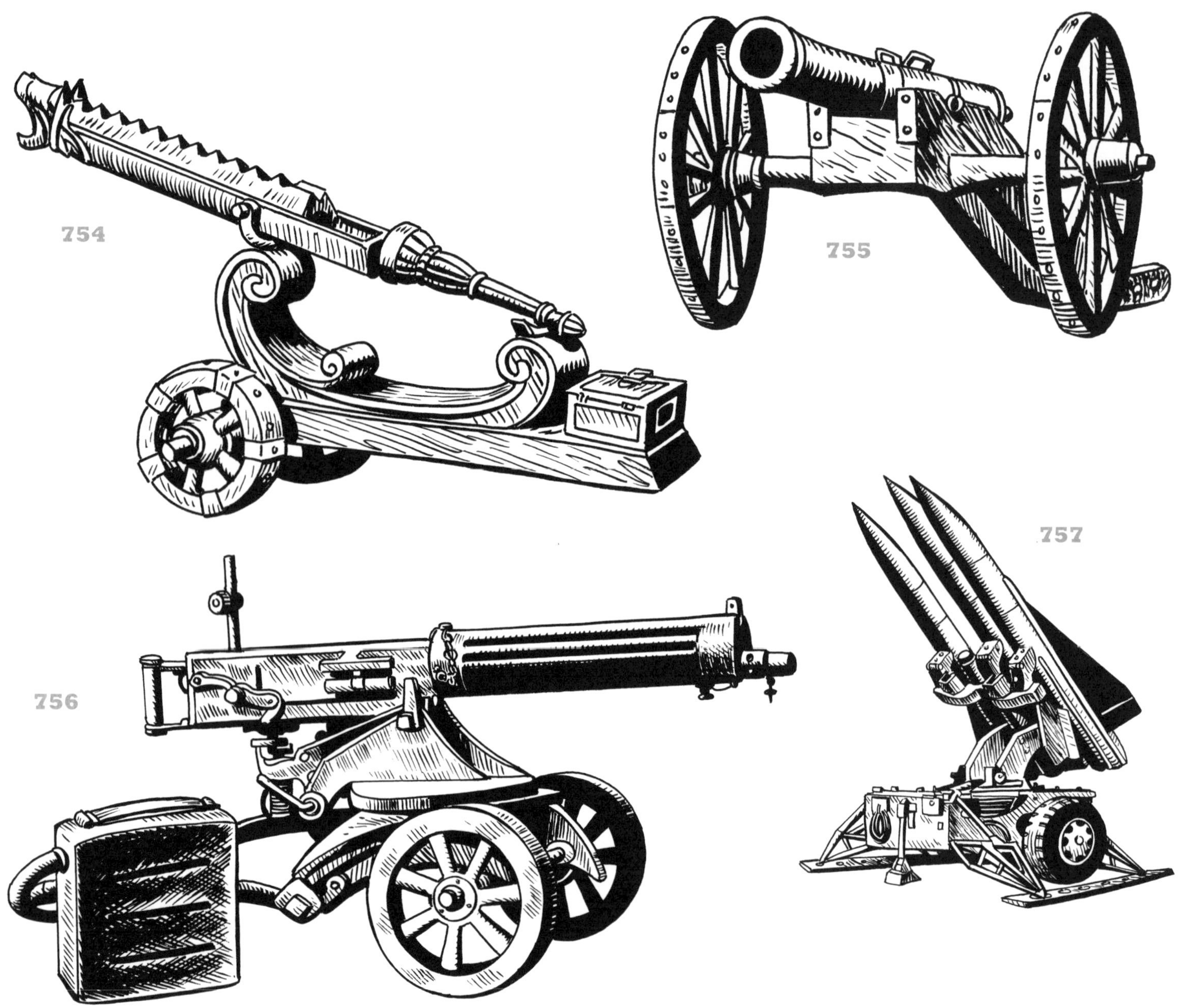
754
755
756
757

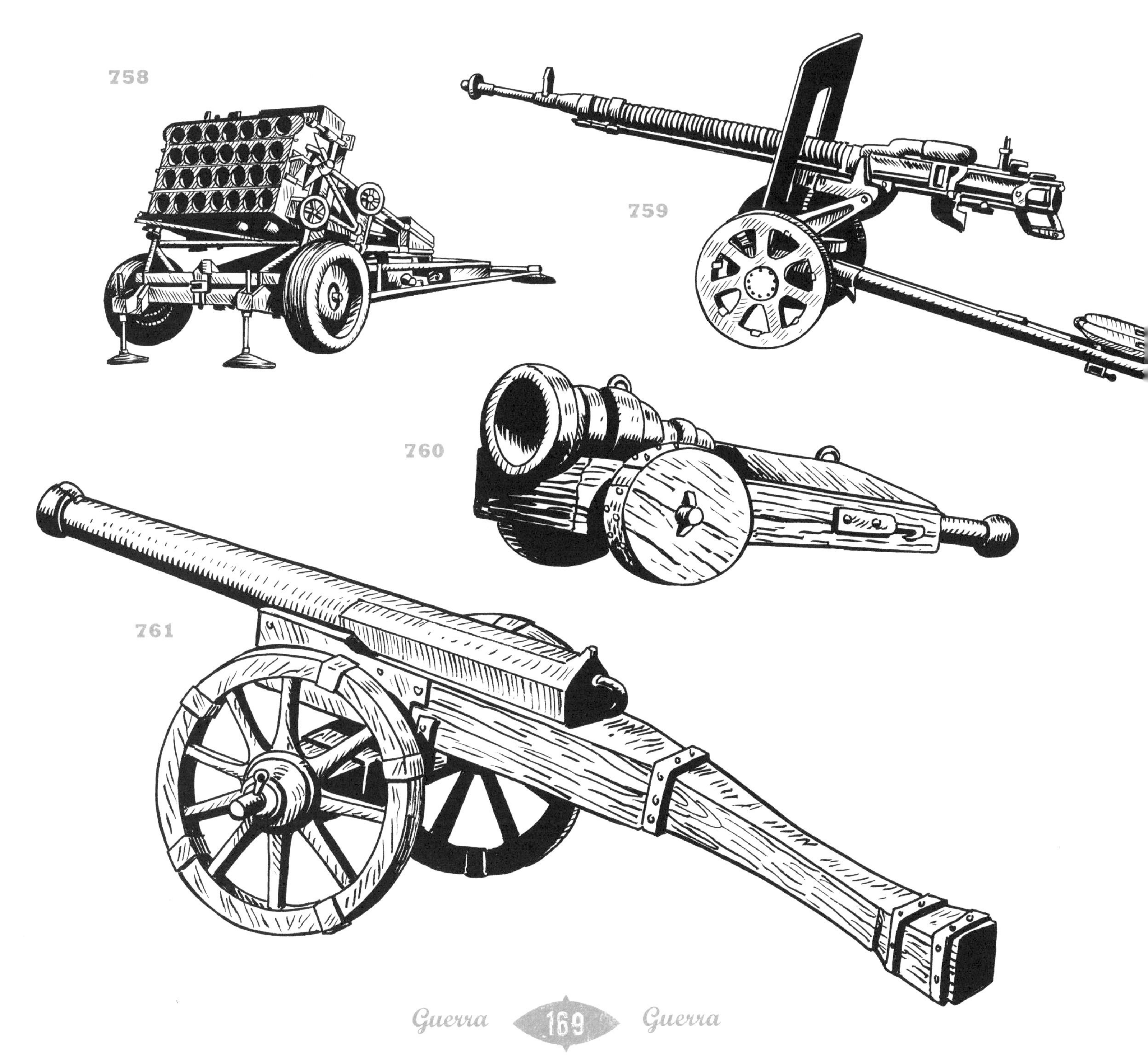

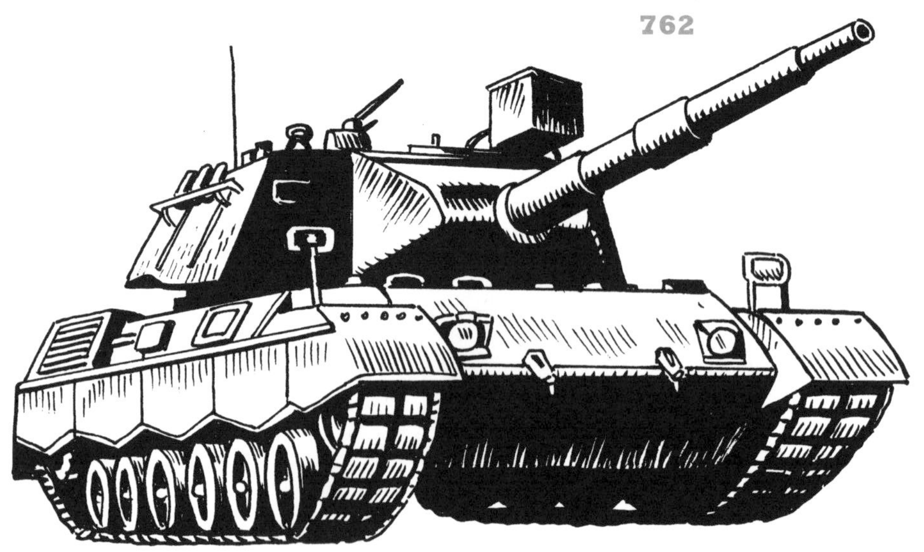

762

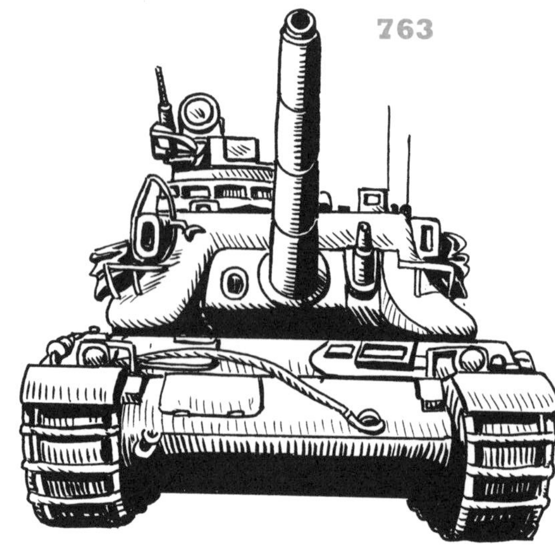

763

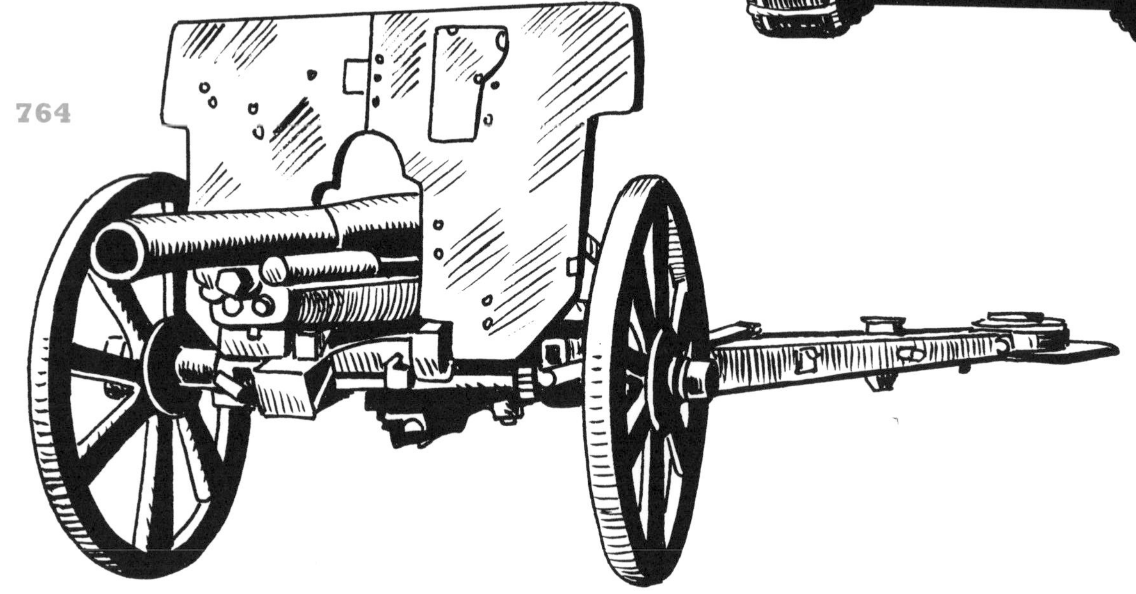

764

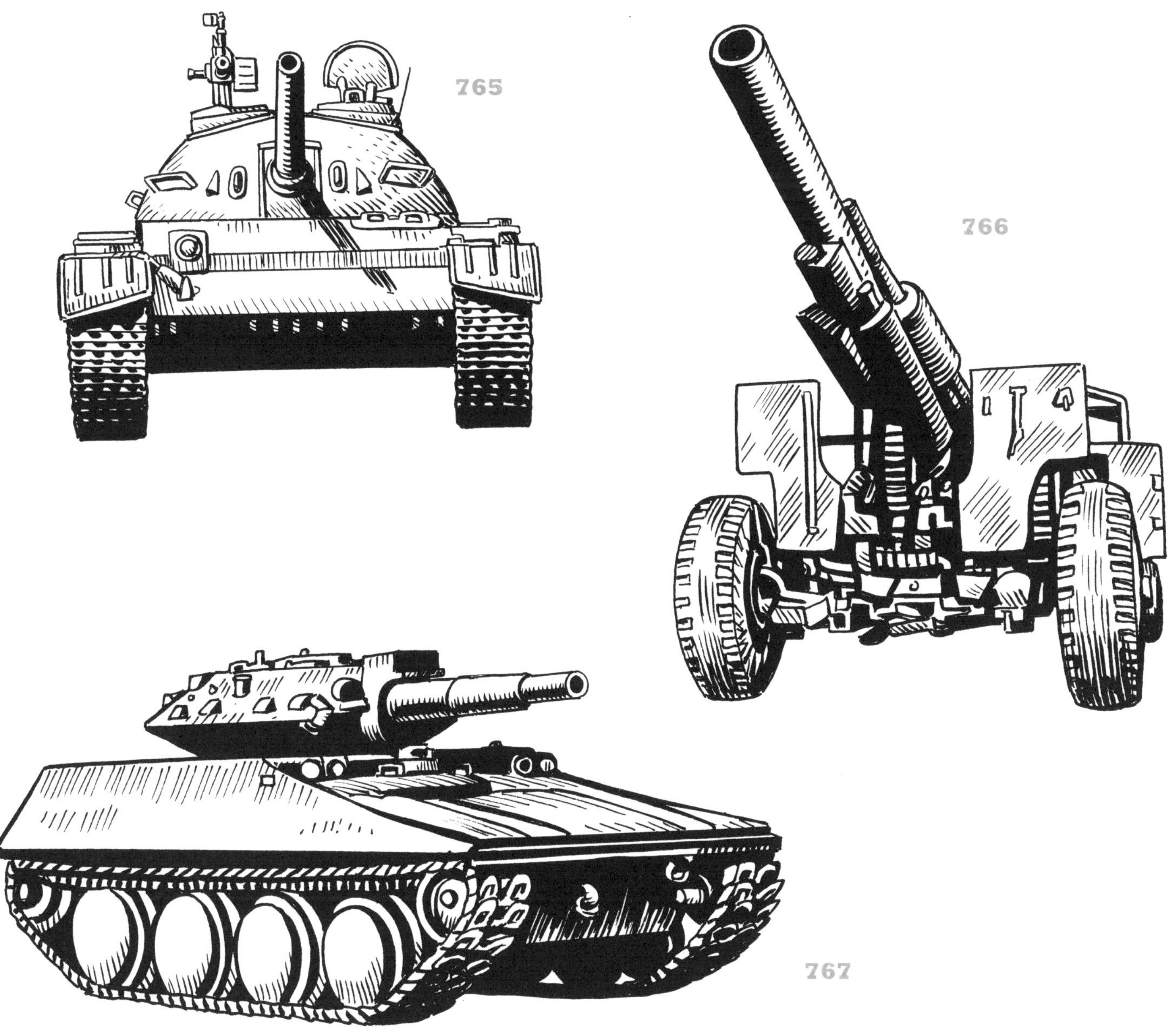

765
766
767